CHURCHILL, HITLER,

AND

"THE UNNECESSARY WAR"

CHURCHILL, HITLER,

AND

"THE UNNECESSARY WAR"

HOW BRITAIN LOST ITS EMPIRE AND THE WEST LOST THE WORLD

PATRICK J. BUCHANAN

CROWN PUBLISHERS
NEW YORK

Published in the United States by Crown Publishers, an imprint of
the Crown Publishing Group, a division of
Random House, Inc., New York.

www.crownpublishing.com

Crown is a trademark and the Crown colophon is a registered
trademark of Random House, Inc.

Library of Congress Cataloging-in-Publication Data

Buchanan, Patrick J. (Patrick Joseph), 1938–
Churchill, Hitler, and "the unnecessary war": how Britain lost its
empire and the West lost the world / Patrick J. Buchanan.—1st ed.
Includes bibliographical references and index.
1. World War, 1939–1945—Causes.   2. Great Britain—Foreign
relations—1936–1945.   3. Churchill, Winston, Sir, 1874–1965.
4. Hitler, Adolf, 1889–1945.   I. Title.
D742.G7B83 2008
940.53'11—dc22
2007048445

ISBN 978-0-307-40515-9

Printed in the United States of America

DESIGN BY LEONARD W. HENDERSON
MAPS BY JEFFREY L. WARD

1 3 5 7 9 10 8 6 4 2

First Edition

To Regis, William, James, and Arthur Crum
My Mother's Brothers
and Veterans of World War II

I HAVE A STRONG belief that there is a danger of the public opinion of this country . . . believing that it is our duty to take everything we can, to fight everybody, and to make a quarrel of every dispute. That seems to me a very dangerous doctrine, not merely because it might incite other nations against us . . . but there is a more serious danger, that is lest we overtax our strength. However strong you may be, whether you are a man or a nation, there is a point beyond which your strength will not go. It is madness; it ends in ruin if you allow yourself to pass beyond it.[1]

—LORD SALISBURY, 1897
The Queen's Speech

[A] EUROPEAN WAR can only end in the ruin of the vanquished and the scarcely less fatal commercial dislocation and exhaustion of the conquerors. Democracy is more vindictive than Cabinets. The wars of peoples are more terrible than those of kings.[2]

—WINSTON CHURCHILL, 1901
Speech to Parliament

CONTENTS

PREFACE

What Happened to Us?

AND IT CAME to pass, when they were in the field, that
Cain rose up against his brother Abel and slew him.
— GENESIS, 4:8

A LL ABOUT US we can see clearly now that the West is passing away.

In a single century, all the great houses of continental Europe fell.
All the empires that ruled the world have vanished. Not one European nation, save Muslim Albania, has a birthrate that will enable it
to survive through the century. As a share of world population, peoples of European ancestry have been shrinking for three generations.
The character of every Western nation is being irremediably altered
as each undergoes an unresisted invasion from the Third World. We
are slowly disappearing from the Earth.

Having lost the will to rule, Western man seems to be losing the
will to live as a unique civilization as he feverishly indulges in
La Dolce Vita, with a yawning indifference as to who might inherit
the Earth he once ruled.

What happened to us? What happened to our world?

When the twentieth century opened, the West was everywhere
supreme. For four hundred years, explorers, missionaries, conquerors,

and colonizers departed Europe for the four corners of the Earth to erect empires that were to bring the blessings and benefits of Western civilization to all mankind. In Rudyard Kipling's lines, it was the special duty of Anglo-Saxon peoples to fight "The savage wars of peace / Fill full the mouth of Famine / And bid the sickness cease." These empires were the creations of a self-confident race of men.

Whatever became of those men?

Somewhere in the last century, Western man suffered a catastrophic loss of faith—in himself, in his civilization, and in the faith that gave it birth.

That Christianity is dying in the West, being displaced by a militant secularism, seems undeniable, though the reasons remain in dispute. But there is no dispute about the physical wounds that may yet prove mortal. These were World Wars I and II, two phases of a Thirty Years' War future historians will call the Great Civil War of the West. Not only did these two wars carry off scores of millions of the best and bravest of the West, they gave birth to the fanatic ideologies of Leninism, Stalinism, Nazism, and Fascism, whose massacres of the people they misruled accounted for more victims than all of the battlefield deaths in ten years of fighting.

A quarter century ago, Charles L. Mee, Jr., began his *End of Order: Versailles 1919* by describing the magnitude of what was first called the Great War: "World War I had been a tragedy on a dreadful scale. Sixty-five million men were mobilized—more by many millions than had ever been brought to war before—to fight a war, they had been told, of justice and honor, of national pride and of great ideals, to wage a war that would end all war, to establish an entirely new order of peace and equity in the world."[1]

Mee then detailed the butcher's bill.

> By November 11, 1918, when the armistice that marked the end of the war was signed, eight million soldiers lay dead, twenty million more were wounded, diseased, mutilated, or

spitting blood from gas attacks. Twenty-two million civilians had been killed or wounded, and the survivors were living in villages blasted to splinters and rubble, on farms churned in mud, their cattle dead.

In Belgrade, Berlin and Petrograd, the survivors fought among themselves—fourteen wars, great or small, civil or revolutionary, flickered or raged about the world.[2]

The casualty rate in the Great War was ten times what it had been in America's Civil War, the bloodiest war of Western man in the nineteenth century. And at the end of the Great War an influenza epidemic, spread by returning soldiers, carried off fourteen million more Europeans and Americans.[3] In one month of 1914—"the most terrible August in the history of the world," said Sir Arthur Conan Doyle—"French casualties . . . are believed to have totaled two hundred sixty thousand of whom seventy-five thousand were killed (twenty-seven thousand on August 22 alone)."[4] France would fight on and in the fifty-one months the war would last would lose 1.3 million sons, with twice that number wounded, maimed, crippled. The quadrant of the country northeast of Paris resembled a moonscape.

Equivalent losses in America today would be eight million dead, sixteen million wounded, and all the land east of the Ohio and north of the Potomac unrecognizable. Yet the death and destruction of the Great War would be dwarfed by the genocides of Lenin, Stalin, Hitler, and what the war of 1939–1945 would do to Italy, Germany, Poland, Ukraine, the Baltic and Balkan nations, Russia, and all of Europe from the Pyrenees to the Urals.

The questions this book addresses are huge but simple: Were these two world wars, the mortal wounds we inflicted upon ourselves, necessary wars? Or were they wars of choice? And if they were wars of choice, who plunged us into these hideous and suicidal world wars that advanced the death of our civilization? Who are the statesmen responsible for the death of the West?

INTRODUCTION

The Great Civil War of the West

[W]AR IS THE creation of individuals not of nations.[1]
— SIR PATRICK HASTINGS, 1948
British barrister and writer

O F ALL THE EMPIRES of modernity, the British was the greatest—indeed, the greatest since Rome—encompassing a fourth of the Earth's surface and people. Out of her womb came America, Canada, Australia, New Zealand, and Ireland, five of the finest, freest lands on Earth. Out of her came Hong Kong and Singapore, where the Chinese first came to know freedom. Were it not for Britain, India would not be the world's largest democracy, or South Africa that continent's most advanced nation. When the British arrived in Africa, they found primitive tribal societies. When they departed, they left behind roads, railways, telephone and telegraph systems, farms, factories, fisheries, mines, trained police, and a civil service.

No European people fondly remembers the Soviet Empire. Few Asians recall the Empire of Japan except with hatred. But all over the world, as their traditions, customs, and uniforms testify, men manifest their pride that they once belonged to the empire upon whose flag the sun never set. America owes a special debt to Britain, for our laws, language and literature, and the idea of representative government.

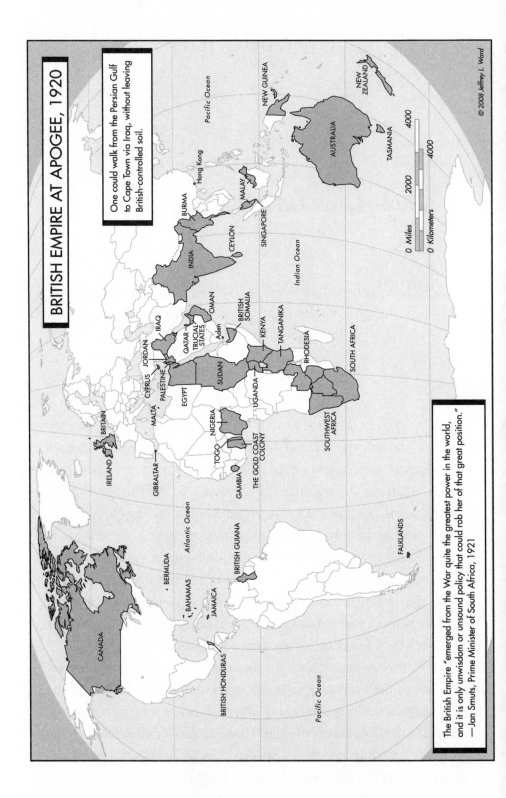

BRITISH EMPIRE AT APOGEE, 1920

One could walk from the Persian Gulf to Cape Town via Iraq, without leaving British-controlled soil.

The British Empire "emerged from the War quite the greatest power in the world, and it is only unwisdom or unsound policy that could rob her of that great position."
— Jan Smuts, Prime Minister of South Africa, 1921

© 2008 Jeffrey L. Ward

"[T]he transplanted culture of Britain in America," wrote Dr. Russell Kirk, "has been one of humankind's more successful experiments."[2]

As with most empires, the sins of the British are scarlet—the opium wars in China, the cold indifference to Irish suffering in the Potato Famine. But Britain's sins must be weighed in the balance. It was the British who were first to take up arms against slavery, who, at Trafalgar and Waterloo, were decisive in defeating the Napoleonic dictatorship and empire, who, in their finest hour, held on until Hitler was brought down.

Like all empires, the British Empire was one day fated to fall. Once Jefferson's idea, "All men are created equal," was wedded to President Wilson's idea, that all peoples are entitled to "self-determination," the fate of the Western empires was sealed. Wilson's secretary of state, Robert Lansing, saw it coming: "The phrase [self-determination] is simply loaded with dynamite. It will raise hopes which can never be realized. . . . What a calamity that the phrase was ever uttered! What misery it will cause!"[3]

Twenty-five years after Versailles, Walter Lippmann would denounce Wilson's doctrine of self-determination as "barbarous and reactionary."

> Self-determination, which has nothing to do with self-government but has become confused with it, is barbarous and reactionary: by sanctioning secession, it invites majorities and minorities to be intransigent and irreconcilable. It is stipulated in the principle of self-determination that they need not be compatriots because they will soon be aliens. There is no end to this atomization of human society. Within the minorities who have seceded there will tend to appear other minorities who in their turn will wish to secede.[4]

WILSON'S DOCTRINE OF SELF-DETERMINATION destroyed the Western empires.

But while the fall of the British Empire was inevitable, the suddenness and sweep of the collapse were not. There is a world of difference between watching a great lady grandly descend a staircase and seeing a slattern being kicked down a flight of stairs.

Consider: When Winston Churchill entered the inner cabinet as First Lord of the Admiralty in 1911, every nation recognized Britain's primacy. None could match her in the strategic weapons of the new century: the great battle fleets and dreadnoughts of the Royal Navy. Mark Twain jested that the English were the only modern race mentioned in the Bible, when the Lord said, "Blessed are the meek, for they shall inherit the earth."[5]

Yet by Churchill's death in 1965, little remained. "Of that colossal wreck, boundless and bare / The lone and level sands stretch far away."[6] At century's end, Labour Party elder statesman Sir Roy Denman looked back at the decline and fall of the nation and empire into which he had been born:

> At the beginning [of the twentieth century], Britain, as the centre of the biggest empire in the world, was at the zenith of her power and glory; Britain approaches the end as a minor power, bereft of her empire. . . . [O]n the world stage, Britain will end the century little more important than Switzerland. It will have been the biggest secular decline in power and influence since seventeenth-century Spain.[7]

WHAT HAPPENED TO GREAT BRITAIN? What happened to the Empire? What happened to the West and our world—is what this book is about.

For it was the war begun in 1914 and the Paris peace conference of 1919 that destroyed the German, Austro-Hungarian, and Russian empires and ushered onto the world stage Lenin, Stalin, Mussolini, and Hitler. And it was the war begun in September 1939 that led to the slaughter of the Jews and tens of millions of Christians, the devastation of Europe, Stalinization of half the continent, the fall of China to Maoist madness, and half a century of Cold War.

Every European war is a civil war, said Napoleon. Historians will look back on 1914–1918 and 1939–1945 as two phases of the Great Civil War of the West, where the once-Christian nations of Europe fell upon one another with such savage abandon they brought down all their empires, brought an end to centuries of Western rule, and advanced the death of their civilization.

In deciphering what happened to the West, George F. Kennan, the geostrategist of the Cold War, wrote, "All lines of inquiry lead back to World War I."[8] Kennan's belief that World War I was "the original catastrophe" was seconded by historian Jacques Barzun, who called the war begun in August 1914 "the blow that hurled the modern world on its course of self-destruction."[9]

These two world wars were fratricidal, self-inflicted wounds of a civilization seemingly hell-bent on suicide. Eight million soldiers perished in World War I, "twenty million more were wounded, diseased, mutilated, or spitting blood from gas attacks. Twenty-two million civilians had been killed or wounded. . . ."[10] That war would give birth to the fanatic and murderous ideologies of Leninism, Stalinism, Nazism, and Fascism, and usher in the Second World War that would bring death to tens of millions more.

And it was Britain that turned both European wars into world wars. Had Britain not declared war on Germany in 1914, Canada, Australia, South Africa, New Zealand, and India would not have followed the Mother Country in. Nor would Britain's ally Japan. Nor would Italy, which London lured in with secret bribes of territory from the Habsburg and Ottoman empires. Nor would America have gone to war had Britain stayed out. Germany would have been victorious, perhaps in months. There would have been no Lenin, no Stalin, no Versailles, no Hitler, no Holocaust.

Had Britain not given a war guarantee to Poland in March 1939, then declared war on September 3, bringing in South Africa, Canada,

Australia, India, New Zealand, and the United States, a German-Polish war might never have become a six-year world war in which fifty million would perish.

Why did Britain declare war on Germany, twice? As we shall see, neither the Kaiser nor Hitler sought to destroy Britain or her empire. Both admired what Britain had built. Both sought an alliance with England. The Kaiser was the eldest grandson of Queen Victoria. Thus the crucial question: Were these two devastating wars Britain declared on Germany wars of necessity, or wars of choice?

Critics will instantly respond that Britain fought the First World War to bring down a Prussian militarism that threatened to dominate Europe and the world, that Britain declared war in 1939 to stop a fanatic Nazi dictator who would otherwise have conquered Europe and the world, enslaved mankind, massacred minorities on a mammoth scale, and brought on a new Dark Age. And thank God Britain did declare war. Were it not for Britain, we would all be speaking German now.

Yet, in his memoir, David Lloyd George, who led Britain to victory in World War I, wrote, "We all blundered into the war."[11] In his memoirs, Churchill, who led Britain to victory in World War II, wrote:

> One day President Roosevelt told me that he was asking publicly for suggestions about what the war should be called. I said at once, "The Unnecessary War." There never was a war more easy to stop than that which has just wrecked what was left of the world from the previous struggle.[12]

WAS LLOYD GEORGE RIGHT? Was World War I the result of blunders by British statesmen? Was Churchill right? Was the Second World War that "wrecked what was left of the world" an "unnecessary war"? If so, who blundered? For these were the costliest and bloodiest wars in the history of mankind and they may have brought on the end of Western civilization.

About the justice of the causes for which Britain fought, few quarrel. And those years from 1914 to 1918 and 1939 to 1945 produced days of glory that will forever inspire men and reflect greatly upon the British people. Generations may pass away, but men will yet talk of Passchendaele and the Somme, of Dunkirk and El Alamein. Two-thirds of a century later, men's eyes yet mist over at the words "Fighter Command," the men and boys in their Hurricanes and Spitfires who rose day after day as the knights of old in the Battle of Britain to defend their "island home." And in their "finest hour" the British had as the king's first minister a statesman who personified the bulldog defiance of his people and who was privileged by history to give the British lion its roar. In the victory over Nazi Germany, the place of moral honor goes to Britain and Churchill. He "mobilized the English language and sent it into battle," said President Kennedy, when Churchill, like Lafayette, was made an honorary citizen of the United States.

Thus the question this book addresses is not whether the British were heroic. That is settled for all time. But were their statesmen wise? For if they were wise, how did Britain pass in one generation from being mistress of the most awesome of empires into a nation whose only hope for avoiding defeat and ruin was an America that bore no love for the empire? By 1942, Britain relied on the United States for all the necessities of national survival: the munitions to keep fighting, the ships to bring her supplies, the troops to rescue a continent from which Britain had been expelled in three weeks by the Panzers of Rommel and Guderian. Who blundered? Who failed Britain? Who lost the empire? Was it only the appeasers, the Guilty Men?

There is another reason I have written this book.

There has arisen among America's elite a Churchill cult. Its acolytes hold that Churchill was not only a peerless war leader but a statesman of unparalleled vision whose life and legend should be the model for every statesman. To this cult, defiance anywhere of U.S.

hegemony, resistance anywhere to U.S. power becomes another 1938. Every adversary is "a new Hitler," every proposal to avert war "another Munich." Slobodan Milosevic, a party apparatchik who had presided over the disintegration of Yugoslavia—losing Slovenia, Croatia, Macedonia, and Bosnia—becomes "the Hitler of the Balkans" for holding Serbia's cradle province of Kosovo. Saddam Hussein, whose army was routed in one hundred hours in 1991 and who had not shot down a U.S. plane in forty thousand sorties, becomes "an Arab Hitler" about to roll up the Persian Gulf and threaten mankind with weapons of mass destruction.

This mind-set led us to launch a seventy-eight-day bombing campaign on Serbia, a nation that never attacked us, never threatened us, never wanted war with us, whose people had always befriended us. After 9/11, the Churchill cult helped to persuade an untutored president that the liberation of Iraq from Saddam would be like the liberation of Europe from Hitler. We would be greeted in Baghdad as our fathers and grandfathers had been in Paris. In the triumphant aftermath of a "cakewalk" war, democracy would put down roots in the Middle East as it had in Europe after the fall of Hitler, and George W. Bush would enter history as the Churchill of his generation, while the timid souls who opposed his war of liberation would be exposed as craven appeasers.

This Churchill cult gave us our present calamity. If not exposed, it will produce more wars and more disasters, and, one day, a war of the magnitude of Churchill's wars that brought Britain and his beloved empire to ruin. For it was Winston S. Churchill who was the most bellicose champion of British entry into the European war of 1914 and the German-Polish war of 1939. There are two great myths about these wars. The first is that World War I was fought "to make the world safe for democracy." The second is that World War II was the "Good War," a glorious crusade to rid the world of Fascism that turned out wonderfully well.

Not for everyone. When President Bush flew to Moscow to celebrate the sixtieth anniversary of V-E Day, he stopped in one of the nations that was not celebrating, Latvia, and dispelled one of these myths. He told the world that while "V-E Day marked the end of Fascism . . . it did not end oppression," that what FDR and Churchill did to Eastern and Central Europe in collusion with Stalin "will be remembered as one of the greatest wrongs of history."[13] Bush called Yalta a sellout of free nations as shameful as Munich.

This book will argue that President Bush understated his case.

For their crimes, Hitler and his collaborators, today's metaphors for absolute evil, received the ruthless justice they deserved. But we cannot ignore the costs of Churchill's wars, or the question: Was it truly necessary that fifty million die to bring Hitler down? For World War II was the worst evil ever to befall Christians and Jews and may prove the mortal blow that brings down our common civilization. Was it "The Unnecessary War"?

CHURCHILL, HITLER,

AND

"THE UNNECESSARY WAR"

CHAPTER 1

The End of "Splendid Isolation"

[T]HE QUEEN CANNOT help feeling that our isolation is dangerous.[1]

— QUEEN VICTORIA,
January 14, 1896

Isolation is much less dangerous than the danger of being dragged into wars which do not concern us.[2]

— LORD SALISBURY, 1896

FOR AS LONG AS he had served the queen, Lord Salisbury had sought to keep Britain free of power blocs. "His policy was not one of isolation from Europe . . . but isolation from the Europe of alliances."[3] Britannia would rule the waves but stay out of Europe's quarrels. Said Salisbury, "We are fish."[4]

When the queen called him to form a new government for the third time in 1895, Lord Salisbury pursued his old policy of "splendid isolation." But in the years since he and Disraeli had traveled to the Congress of Berlin in 1878, to create with Bismarck a new balance of power in Europe, their world had vanished.

In the Sino-Japanese war of 1894–95, Japan defeated China, seized Taiwan, and occupied the Liaotung Peninsula. Britain's preeminent position in China was now history.

In the summer of 1895, London received a virtual ultimatum

from secretary of state Richard Olney, demanding that Great Britain accept U.S. arbitration in a border dispute between British Guiana and Venezuela. Lord Salisbury shredded Olney's note like an impatient tenured professor cutting up a freshman term paper. But President Cleveland demanded that Britain accept arbitration—or face the prospect of war with the United States.

The British were stunned by American enthusiasm for a war over a patch of South American jungle, and incredulous. America deployed two battleships to Britain's forty-four.[5] Yet Salisbury took the threat seriously: "A war with America . . . in the not distant future has become something more than a possibility."[6]

London was jolted anew in January 1896 when the Kaiser sent a telegram of congratulations to Boer leader Paul Kruger on his capture of the Jameson raiders, who had invaded the Transvaal in a land grab concocted by Cecil Rhodes, with the connivance of Colonial Secretary Joseph Chamberlain.

These two challenges, from a jingoistic America that was now the first economic power on earth, and from his bellicose nephew in Berlin, Wilhelm II, revealed to the future Edward VII that "his country was without a friend in the world" and "steps to end British isolation were required. . . ."[7]

On December 18, 1897, a Russian fleet steamed into the Chinese harbor of Port Arthur, "obliging British warships to vacate the area."[8] British jingoes "became apoplectic."[9] Lord Salisbury stood down: "I don't think we carry enough guns to fight them and the French together."[10]

In 1898, a crisis erupted in northeast Africa. Captain Jean-Baptiste Marchand, who had set off from Gabon in 1897 on a safari across the Sahara with six officers and 120 Senegalese, appeared at Fashoda in the southern Sudan, where he laid claim to the headwaters of the Nile. Sir Herbert Kitchener cruised upriver to instruct Marchand he was on imperial land. Faced with superior firepower, Marchand withdrew. Fashoda brought Britain and

France to the brink of war. Paris backed down, but bitterness ran deep. Caught up in the Anglophobia was eight-year-old Charles de Gaulle.[11]

In 1900, the Russian challenge reappeared. After American, British, French, German, and Japanese troops had marched to the rescue of the diplomatic legation in Peking, besieged for fifty-five days by Chinese rebels called "Boxers," Russia exploited the chaos to send a 200,000-man army into Manchuria and the Czar shifted a squadron of his Baltic fleet to Port Arthur. The British position in China was now threatened by Russia and Japan.

But what awakened Lord Salisbury to the depth of British isolation was the Boer War. When it broke out in 1899, Europeans and Americans cheered British defeats. While Joe Chamberlain might "speak of the British enjoying a 'splendid isolation, surrounded and supported by our kinsfolk,' the Boer War brought home the reality that, fully extended in their imperial role, the British needed to avoid conflict with the other great powers."[12]

Only among America's Anglophile elite could Victoria's nation or Salisbury's government find support. When Bourke Cockran, a Tammany Hall Democrat, wrote President McKinley, urging him to mediate and keep America's distance from Great Britain's "wanton acts of aggression," the letter went to Secretary of State John Hay.[13]

Hay bridled at this Celtic insolence. "Mr. Cockran's logic is especially Irish," he wrote to a friend. "As long as I stay here no action shall be taken contrary to my conviction that the one indispensable feature of our foreign policy should be a friendly understanding with England." Hay refused even to answer "Bourke Cockran's fool letter to the president."[14]

Hay spoke of an alliance with Britain as an "unattainable dream" and hoped for a smashing imperial victory in South Africa. "I hope if it comes to blows that England will make quick work of Uncle Paul [Kruger]."[15]

ENTENTE CORDIALE

SO IT WAS THAT as the nineteenth century came to an end Britain set out to court old rivals. The British first reached out to the Americans. Alone among Europe's great powers, Britain sided with the United States in its 1898 war with Spain. London then settled the Alaska boundary dispute in America's favor, renegotiated the fifty-year-old Clayton-Bulwer Treaty, and ceded to America the exclusive rights to build, operate, and fortify a canal across Panama. Then Britain withdrew her fleet from the Caribbean.

Writes British historian Correlli Barnett: "The passage of the British battlefleet from the Atlantic to the Pacific would now be by courtesy of the United States," and, with America's defeat of Spain, "The Philippines, Cuba and Puerto Rico, now American colonies, were gradually closed to British merchants by protective tariffs, for the benefit of their American rivals."[16]

Other historians, however, hail the British initiative to terminate a century of U.S.-British enmity as "The Great Rapprochement," and Berlin-born Yale historian Hajo Holborn regards the establishment of close Anglo-American relations as probably "by far the greatest achievement of British diplomacy in terms of world history."[17]

With America appeased, Britain turned to Asia.

With a Russian army in Manchuria menacing Korea and the Czar's warships at Port Arthur and Vladivostok, Japan needed an ally to balance off Russia's ally, France. Germany would not do, as Kaiser Wilhelm disliked Orientals and was endlessly warning about the "Yellow Peril." As for the Americans, their Open Door policy had proven to be bluster and bluff when Russia moved into Manchuria. That left the British, whom the Japanese admired as an island people and warrior race that had created the world's greatest empire.

On January 30, 1902, an Anglo-Japanese treaty was signed. Each nation agreed to remain neutral should the other become embroiled in an Asian war with a single power. However, should either become involved in war with two powers, each would come to the aid of the other. Confident its treaty with Britain would checkmate Russia's ally France, Japan in 1904 launched a surprise attack on the Russian naval squadron at Port Arthur. An enraged Czar sent his Baltic fleet to exact retribution. After a voyage of six months from the Baltic to the North Sea, down the Atlantic and around the Cape of Good Hope to the Indian Ocean, the great Russian fleet was ambushed and annihilated by Admiral Heihachiro Togo in Tshushima Strait between Korea and Japan. Only one small Russian cruiser and two destroyers made it to Vladivostok. Japan lost two torpedo boats. It was a victory for Japan to rival the sinking of the Spanish Armada and the worst defeat ever inflicted on a Western power by an Asian people.

Britain had chosen well. In 1905, the Anglo-Japanese treaty was elevated into a full alliance. Britain now turned to patching up quarrels with her European rivals. Her natural allies were Germany and the Habsburg Empire, neither of whom had designs on the British Empire. Imperial Russia, Britain's great nineteenth-century rival, was pressing down on China, India, Afghanistan, the Turkish Straits, and the Middle East. France was Britain's ancient enemy and imperial rival in Africa and Egypt. The nightmare of the British was a second Tilsit, where Napoleon and Czar Alexander I, meeting on a barge in the Neiman in 1807, had divided a prostrate Europe and Middle East between them. Germany was the sole European bulwark against a French-Russian dominance of Europe and drive for hegemony in Africa, the Middle East, and Asia—at the expense of the British Empire.

With Lord Salisbury's blessing, Joe Chamberlain began to court Berlin. "England, Germany and America should collaborate: by so doing they could check Russian expansionism, calm turbulent France and guarantee world peace," Chamberlain told future German chancellor Bernhard von Bulow.[18] The Kaiser put him off. Neither he nor his advisers believed Britain could reconcile with her old nemesis France, or Russia, and must eventually come to Berlin hat-in-hand. Joe warned the Germans: Spurn Britain, and we go else-where.

The Kaiser let the opportunity slip and, in April 1904, learned to his astonishment that Britain and France had negotiated an entente cordiale, a cordial understanding. France yielded all claims in Egypt, and Britain agreed to support France's preeminence in Morocco. Centuries of hostility came to an end. The quarrel over Suez was over. Fashoda was history.

The entente quickly proved its worth. After the Kaiser was per-suaded to make a provocative visit to Tangier in 1905, Britain backed France at the Algeciras conference called to resolve the crisis. Ger-many won economic concessions in Morocco, but Berlin had solidi-fied the Anglo-French entente. More ominous, the Tangier crisis had propelled secret talks already under way between French and British staff officers over how a British army might be ferried across the Channel to France in the event of a war with Germany.

Unknown to the Cabinet and Parliament, a tiny cabal had made a decision fateful for Britain, the empire, and the world. Under the guidance of Edward Grey, the foreign secretary from 1905 to 1916, British and French officers plotted Britain's entry into a Franco-German war from the first shot. And these secret war plans were being formulated by Liberals voted into power in public revulsion against the Boer War on a platform of "Peace, Retrenchment, and Reform." Writes historian Robert Massie,

> [O]n January 16 [1906], without the approval of either the Prime Minister or Cabinet, secret talks between British and French staff officers began. They focussed on plans to send 100,000 British soldiers to the Continent within two weeks of an outbreak of hostilities. On January 26, when Campbell-Bannerman returned to London and was in-formed, he approved.[19]

As CHURCHILL WROTE decades later, only Lord Rosebery read the real meaning of the Anglo-French entente. "Only one voice—Rosebery's—was raised in discord: in public 'Far more likely to lead to War than Peace'; in private 'Straight to War.' "[20] While praising Rosebery's foresight, Churchill never repudiated his own support of the entente or secret understandings: "It must not be thought that I regret the decisions which were in fact taken."[21]

In August 1907, Britain entered into an Anglo-Russian convention, ending their eighty-year conflict. Czar Nicholas II accepted Britain's dominance in southern Persia. Britain accepted Russia's dominance in the north. Both agreed to stay out of central Persia, Afghanistan, and Tibet. The Great Game was over and the lineups completed for the great European war. In the Triple Alliance were Germany, Austria-Hungary, and Italy. Opposite was the Franco-Russian alliance backed by Great Britain, which was allied to Japan. Only America among the great powers remained free of entangling alliances.

"YOU HAVE A NEW WORLD"

BRITAIN HAD APPEASED AMERICA, allied with Japan, and entered an entente with France and Russia, yet its German problem remained. It had arisen in the aftermath of the Franco-Prussian war. After the French defeat at Sedan and the abdication of Napoleon III, a united Germany stretching from France to Russia and from the Baltic to the Alps had emerged as the first power in Europe. Disraeli recognized the earthshaking importance of the unification of the German states under a Prussian king.

The war represents the German revolution, a greater political event than the French revolution of the last century. . . . There is not a diplomatic tradition, which has not been swept away. You have a new world. . . . The balance of power has been entirely destroyed.[22]

BISMARCK HAD ENGINEERED the wars on Denmark, Austria, and France, but he now believed his nation had nothing to gain from war. She had "hay enough for her fork."[23] Germany should not behave "like a nouveau riche who has just come into money and then offended everyone by pointing to the coins in his pocket."[24] He crafted a series of treaties to maintain a European balance of power favorable to Germany—by keeping the Austro-Hungarian Empire allied, Russia friendly, Britain neutral, and France isolated. Bismarck opposed the building of a fleet that might alarm the British. As for an overseas empire, let Britain, France, and Russia quarrel over colonies. When a colonial adventurer pressed upon him Germany's need to enter the scramble for Africa, Bismarck replied, "Your map of Africa is very nice. But there is France, and here is Russia, and we are in the middle, and that is my map of Africa."[25]

As the clamor for colonies grew, however, the Iron Chancellor would succumb and Germany would join the scramble. By 1914, Berlin boasted the world's third largest overseas empire, encompassing German East Africa (Tanganyika), South-West Africa (Namibia), Kamerun (Cameroon), and Togoland. On the China coast, the Kaiser held Shantung Peninsula. In the western Pacific, the House of Hohenzollern held German New Guinea, German Samoa, the Bismarck Archipelago, the Marshall, Mariana, and Caroline islands, and the Northern Solomons, of which Bougainville was the largest. However, writes Holborn,

> Not for a moment were Bismarck's colonial projects intended to constitute a revision of the fundamentals of his continental policy. Least of all were they designs to undermine British naval or colonial supremacy overseas. Bismarck was frank when he told British statesmen that Germany, by

the acquisition of colonies, was giving Britain new hostages, since she could not hope to defend them in an emergency.[26]

By 1890, Bismarck had been dismissed by the new young Kaiser, who began to make a series of blunders, the first of which was to let Bismarck's treaty with Russia lapse. This left Russia nowhere to turn but France. By 1894, St. Petersburg had become the ally of a Paris still seething over the loss of Alsace-Lorraine. France had broken free of the isolation imposed upon her by Bismarck. The Kaiser's folly in letting the Reinsurance Treaty with Russia lapse can hardly be overstated.

While Germany was a "satiated power, so far as Europe itself was concerned, and stood to gain little from a major war on the European continent," France and Russia were expansionist.[27] Paris hungered for the return of Alsace. Russia sought hegemony over Bulgaria, domination of the Turkish Straits to keep foreign warships out of the Black Sea, and to pry away the Austrian share of a partitioned Poland.

More ominous, the Franco-Russian Alliance of 1894 stipulated that a partial mobilization by any member of the Triple Alliance—Austria, Italy, or Germany—would trigger hostilities against all three.[28] As George Kennan writes in *The Fateful Alliance*,

A partial Austrian mobilization against Serbia, for example (and one has only to recall the events of 1914 to understand the potential significance of this circumstance) could alone become the occasion for the launching of a general European war.[29]

PUTTING THE KAISER DOWN

THOUGH BOASTFUL AND BELLIGERENT, the Kaiser had never plotted to bring down the British Empire. The eldest grandson of

Queen Victoria, proud of his British blood, he had rushed to her bed-
side as she sank toward death and "softly passed away in my arms."[30]
He had marched in the queen's funeral procession. The new king,
Edward VII, was deeply moved. As he wrote his sister, Empress Frederick, the Kaiser's mother who had been too ill to travel to the funeral, "William's touching and simple demeanour, up to the last, will
never be forgotten by me or anyone. It was indeed a sincere pleasure
for me to confer upon him the rank of Field Marshal in my Army."[31]
At the luncheon for Edward, the Kaiser rose to declare:

> I believe that the two Teutonic nations will, bit by bit, learn
> to know each other better, and that they will stand together
> to help in keeping the peace of the world. We ought to form
> an Anglo-Germanic alliance, you to keep the seas, while we
> would be responsible for the land; with such an alliance not
> a mouse could stir in Europe without our permission.[32]

"[B]y dint of his mother's teaching and admiration for her family,
[the Kaiser] wanted only good relations with Britain," writes Giles
MacDonogh, biographer of Wilhelm II.[33] It was a "British alliance
for which [the Kaiser] strove all his professional life. . . ."[34]

Why did the Kaiser fail? Certainly, his ministers who goaded him
into collisions with England with the Kruger telegram and in the
Moroccan crises of 1905 and 1911 bear much of the blame. But Mac-
Donogh lays most of it on British statesmen and their haughty contempt of the Kaiser and Germany:

> Faced by his Uncle Bertie [Edward VII], or high-handed
> ministers such as Lord Salisbury or Sir Edward Grey, he felt
> the British put him down; they treated him as a grandson or
> nephew and not as the German emperor. Germany was
> never admitted to full membership of that board of great
> powers. He and his country were patronised, and he took it
> very personally.[35]

When the Kaiser once inquired of Lord Salisbury where he might have a colony that would not be in the way of the British Empire, the great peer replied, "We don't want you anywhere."[36]

When Edward VII paid a visit to Kiel during the Russo-Japanese war, and the Kaiser suggested "that Russia's cause was that of Europe, and that a Japanese victory over Russia would bring the world face to face with 'the Yellow Peril,'" Edward had laughed in his face, "and for eighteen months thereafter the personal relations between uncle and nephew sank to the lowest point which they ever reached."[37]

Yet on the death in 1910 of Edward VII, who detested the nephew he called "Willy," the Kaiser again sought reconciliation with a grand gesture. He sailed to England and marched in Edward's funeral—in the uniform of a British field marshal. As he strode behind Edward's casket, the Kaiser's feelings, Barbara Tuchman writes, were mixed. There was nostalgia for the great royal family to which he, too, belonged, but also

> a fierce relish in the disappearance of his uncle from the European scene. He had come to bury Edward his bane; Edward the arch plotter, as William conceived it, of Germany's encirclement. Edward, his mother's brother whom he could neither bully nor impress, whose fat figure cast a shadow between Germany and the sun. "He is Satan. You cannot imagine what a Satan he is."[38]

As his clumsy courtship failed, the Kaiser tried to force Britain to pay heed to him and to Germany with bellicose intrusions in African affairs. But where the British chose to appease the Americans, with the Kaiser they took a different course. And beyond the enmity between Wilhelm II and Edward VII, the Kaiser had, even while Queen Victoria was alive, committed one of the great blunders in German history. He decided to challenge Britannia's rule of the waves with a High Seas Fleet. "The building of the German Fleet," writes Massie, "ended the century of Splendid Isolation."[39]

THE HIGH SEAS FLEET

SEVERAL FACTORS LED to the fateful decision. Soon after he ascended the throne, the Kaiser was mesmerized by an 1890 book by U.S. naval captain A. T. Mahan, "a tall beanpole of a man, with a great bald dome rising above calm hooded eyes."[40] Mahan was more scholar than sea dog. His thesis in *The Influence of Sea Power Upon History* was that it had been the Royal Navy, controlling the oceanic crossroads of the world, that had ensured the defeat of Napoleon and made Great Britain the world's preeminent power. Navalists everywhere swore by Captain Mahan. It was at Mahan's recommendation that Assistant Secretary of the Navy Theodore Roosevelt had put Admiral George Dewey in command of the Pacific Squadron of six battleships and three cruisers that steamed into Manila harbor in 1898 to sink the Spanish fleet before breakfast.

The Japanese had made *The Influence of Sea Power* a textbook in their naval and war colleges. But nowhere was Mahan more a "prophet with honor" than in Imperial Germany.[41] " 'I am just now not reading but devouring Captain Mahan's book and am trying to learn it by heart,' the Kaiser wrote in 1894. 'It is on board all my ships and constantly quoted by all my captains and officers.' "[42] When France was forced to back down at Fashoda, the Kaiser commiserated, "The poor French. They have not read their Mahan!"[43]

It was in 1896 that the Kaiser came to appreciate what it meant to be without a navy. After he had sent his provocative telegram to the Boer leader Kruger, congratulating him on his capture of the Jameson raiders, which had enraged the British, the Kaiser discovered he was impotent to intervene to help the Boers. Any German convoy ordered to East Africa must traverse the North Sea, the East Atlantic, and the Cape of Good Hope, or the Mediterranean and the Suez Canal. Its sinking would be child's play for the Royal Navy. Rudely awakened to German vulnerability at sea, the Kaiser wrote bitterly to Chancellor Hohenlohe,

Once again it becomes obvious how foolish it was to begin our colonial policy a decade ago without having a fleet. Our trade is locked in a life-and-death struggle with the English, and our press boasts loudly of this every day, but the great merchant marine which plies the oceans of the world under our flag must renounce itself to complete impotence before their 130 cruisers, which we can proudly counter with four.[44]

Thus, on the strong recommendation of his new naval minister, the Anglophobic Prussian admiral Alfred von Tirpitz, the Kaiser decided to build a world-class navy. Purpose: Defend the North Sea and Baltic coasts, break any blockade, protect the trade on which Germany depended for a fourth of her food. The Kaiser saw his navy both as an instrument of his world policy and a force to counter the Russian and French fleets. But Admiral Tirpitz left no doubt as to its principal purpose. "This intention was conveyed," writes British historian Lawrence James, "in the belligerent preamble to the 1900 Navy Law which insisted that 'Germany must have a Fleet of such strength that a war, even against the mightiest naval Power, would involve such risks as to threaten the supremacy of that Power.' "[45]

This was the "risk theory" of Tirpitz. While the German fleet might be defeated in war, it would be strong enough to inflict such damage on the Royal Navy, shield of the empire, that Britain would seek to avoid any war with Germany rather than imperil the empire. Thus, as the German fleet became stronger, Britain would appease Germany and not interfere as she grew as a world power. A great fleet would also enable the Kaiser to play the role of world statesman commensurate with his nation's stature. Tirpitz believed the more powerful the fleet, the greater the certainty Britain would stay neutral in a Franco-German war. Of Britain's haughty attitude toward him and his country, the Kaiser said, "Nothing will change until we are so strong on the seas that we become valuable allies."[46] Tirpitz and the Kaiser were mistaken.

Oddly, it was a British blunder that convinced many Germans that the Kaiser and Tirpitz were right: Germany needed a High Seas Fleet.

In December 1899, in the first weeks of the Boer War, the Cabinet authorized the Royal Navy to intercept and inspect foreign ships to prevent war matériel from reaching the Boers in the Transvaal and Free State. Three German passenger ships, the *Bundesrath*, the *Herzog*, and the *General*, were stopped and forced into port, where they "suffered the humiliation of being searched."[47] As Thomas Pakenham, the historian of the Boer War, writes,

> The search was negative in all three cases, and this only fed the flames of anglophobia in Germany. How dare the British Navy stop our mail steamers, cried the German Press. And how convenient it all was for the German government, whose great Navy Bill steamed majestically through the Reichstag. . . . Who could have guessed that these earth tremors of 1900 were to lead to the earthquake of 1914?[48]

Understandably, Britain only seemed to see the High Seas Fleet from her own point of view, never from the vantage point of Berlin. To the Germans, it was not Britain that threatened them, but giant Russia and revanchist France. In the last decade of the nineteenth century, both powers had spent far more on warships than Germany. By 1901, the combined naval armaments expenditures of Paris and St. Petersburg were three times that of Berlin.[49] And if Britain could claim the right to a Royal Navy greater than the combined fleets of the next two naval powers—"The Two-Power Standard" written into British law by Lord Salisbury in 1889—was not Germany entitled to naval supremacy in her home waters, the Baltic Sea? As Tirpitz told the Reichstag, "We should be in a position to blockade the Russian fleet in the Baltic ports, and to prevent at the same time the entrance to that sea of a French fleet. We must also protect our ports in the North Sea from blockade."[50]

Was this so unreasonable? By the twentieth century, Germany's trade and merchant marine rivaled Britain's, and Germany was under a far greater potential naval threat.

Still, writes Roy Denman, "The balance of power in Europe was under threat. The High Seas Fleet based on the Channel ports would have been for Britain an unacceptable danger."[51] But had not Britain survived secure for centuries with its greatest rival, France, having warships in the Channel ports? One British critic of his nation's anti-German policy argues that the Kaiser's Germany could make a far more compelling case for a world-class navy than the Britain of Victoria and Edward.

> And why should Germany not have a fleet to protect her commerce? Surely, she had more reason to build one than Great Britain. The island power had no Russia at the mouth of the Humber, nor had she a France impinging on the beach of Cardigan Bay. All the avenues to the Atlantic were open for England. It was very different for German maritime service.
>
> No one knew this better than the chiefs of the British admiralty.[52]

NOR WERE GERMAN fears of the Royal Navy misplaced. British war plans called for a blockade of Germany. Some at the Admiralty were avidly seeking an opportunity to stalk and sink the German fleet before it could grow to a size and strength to challenge the Royal Navy.

In 1905, a European crisis was precipitated by a provocative stunt by the Kaiser. Goaded by his foreign office, he interrupted a Mediterranean cruise to appear suddenly in Tangier, riding a white charger, to support the independence of Morocco, an open-door policy in that North African nation, and Germany's right to equal treatment in commercial affairs. This was a direct challenge to French hegemony in Morocco, agreed to in the British-French entente. It was during this crisis that the First Sea Lord, Admiral Sir John Fisher, wrote to Lord Lansdowne, the foreign secretary, urging him to exploit the situation to foment war with Germany:

> This seems a golden opportunity for fighting the Germans in alliance with the French, so I earnestly hope you may be able to bring this about. . . . All I hope is that you will send a telegram to Paris that the English and French Fleets are one. We could have the German Fleet, the Kiel Canal, and Schleswig-Holstein within a fortnight.[53]

In his *Memoirs*, Fisher, a confidant of the king, confessed "that in 1908 he had a secret conversation with his Majesty [Edward VII] . . . 'in which I urged that we should Copenhagen the German fleet at Kiel a la Nelson, and I lamented that we possessed neither a Pitt nor a Bismarck to give the order.' "[54] "Copenhagen" was a reference to Nelson's charge into the Danish harbor in 1801, where, in a surprise attack, the intrepid British admiral sank every Danish ship in sight.

"My God, Fisher, you must be mad!" said the King.[55]

German admirals feared "Jackie" Fisher was neither mad nor joking. The idea of a British fleet steaming into Wilhelmshaven and Kiel and sending the High Seas Fleet to Davy Jones's locker—in a surprise attack without a declaration of war, as Japan had done at Port Arthur—had been raised by other Admiralty officials and a Germanophobic British press.

Indeed, in November 1906, an "invasion scare . . . convulsed Germany" and "was followed, in January, 1907, by a fantastic rumour that Fisher was coming, which caused panic in Kiel for two days."[56] The Kaiser, "beside himself over the English threat," ordered his naval expansion accelerated.[57]

What the Kaiser and Tirpitz failed to appreciate, however, was that the High Seas Fleet threatened the indispensable pillar of the

British Empire. That empire's dependence on seaborne commerce, a result of Britain's half-century commitment to free trade, made the supremacy of the Royal Navy on the high seas a matter of national and imperial survival. For generations Britain had lived by an iron rule: The Royal Navy must be 10 percent stronger in capital ships than the combined fleets of the next two strongest sea powers.

Moreover, the Kaiser failed to see the strategic crisis he had created. To reach the Atlantic, German warships would have to traverse the North Sea and pass through the Channel within sight of Dover, or sail around the Scottish coast near the naval base of the Grand Fleet at Scapa Flow.

> It was an irrevocable fact of geography that the British Isles cut athwart all German overseas routes. . . . Mahan in 1902 described the situation very clearly. "The dilemma of Great Britain is that she cannot help commanding the approaches to Germany by the very means essential to her own existence as a state of the first order." Obviously Britain was not going to surrender the keys to her islands and empire.[58]

The Kaiser's decision to build a great navy represented a threat to Britain in her home waters. Should Germany achieve naval superiority in the North Sea, it was not only the empire that was imperiled but also England and Scotland. British statesmen found this intolerable.

"Germany's naval policy was suicidal," writes Holborn.[59]

> By forcing Britain to take sides in the alignment of the European powers, German naval policy completed the division of Europe into two political camps armed to the teeth and ready to take up open hostilities; for any misunderstanding could seriously affect the precarious balance of power on which the European nations had staked their security.[60]

As Germany began building dreadnoughts every year, the young new First Lord of the Admiralty spoke in Scotland in 1912, in pointed words of warning to the Kaiser and Admiral Tirpitz. Said Winston Churchill:

> There is . . . this difference between the British naval power and the naval power of the great and friendly empire—and I trust it may long remain the great and friendly empire—of Germany. The British Navy is to us a necessity and, from some points of view, the German Navy is to them more in the nature of a luxury. Our naval power involves British existence. . . . It is the British Navy which makes Great Britain a great power. But Germany was a great power, respected and honored, all over the world before she had a single ship.[61]

IN GERMANY, the deliberate mistranslation of Churchill's word "luxury" as " 'Luxusflotte,' suggesting that Tirpitz's fleet was a sensual indulgence, stoked the fires of public outrage."[62]

The German Naval Laws of 1898 and 1900 that laid the foundation of the High Seas Fleet had historic consequences. By constructing a great navy, four hundred nautical miles from the English coast, the Kaiser forced the Royal Navy to bring its most powerful warships home from distant waters to build up the Home and Channel Fleets. "[I]n 1896 there had been 74 ships stationed in home waters and 140 overseas," writes James, "fourteen years later these totals were 480 and 83 respectively."[63] With the British Empire stripped of its shield, Britain was forced to resolve conflicts with imperial rivals Russia and France—the two powers that most threatened Germany.

Rather than enhance German security, the High Seas Fleet sank all hope of detente with Britain and pushed her into de facto alliances with France and Russia. The Kaiser's decision to challenge the Royal Navy would prove a principal factor in Germany's defeat and his own dethronement. For it was the arrival of a British Expeditionary Force in France in August 1914 that blunted the German drive into France, leading to four years of stalemate war that ended with Wilhelm's abdication and flight to Holland.

"German foreign policy ought to have been mainly concerned with keeping England preoccupied by her overseas interests in Africa and the Near and Far East," writes German historian Andreas Hillgruber.[64] By building a great fleet to challenge the Royal Navy, Germany "tied England to Europe."[65]

But the fault lies not with the Germans alone. The British were never willing to pay the Kaiser's price for calling off Tirpitz's challenge. During the 1912 Haldane mission to Germany, Britain could have gotten limits on the High Seas Fleet in return for a British pledge of neutrality in a Franco-German war. "The Germans were willing to make a naval deal in return for a neutrality statement," writes British historian Niall Ferguson, "[I]t was on the neutrality issue that the talks really foundered. And arguably it was the British position which was the more intransigent."[66]

BALANCE-OF-POWER POLITICS

BRITAIN'S REFUSAL TO GIVE a neutrality pledge in return for limits on the High Seas Fleet demonstrates that beneath the Anglo-German friction lay clashing concepts of security. To Britain, security rested on a balance of power—a divided Europe with British power backing the weaker coalition.

To Germany, bordered east and west by nations fearful of her power, security lay in unifying Europe under her leadership, as Bismarck had done. British and German concepts of security were irreconcilable. Under Britain's balance-of-power doctrine, the Kaiser could become an ally only if Germany were displaced as first power in Europe. Historian John Laughland describes the Kaiser's rage and frustration:

When the British Lord Chancellor, Lord Haldane, tried to make it clear to the German ambassador in London on 3 December 1912 that Britain would not tolerate "a unified Continental Group under the leadership of one single power," the Kaiser, on reading the report of the conversation, covered it with the most violent marginal comments. In a characteristic attack of anger, he declared the English principle of the "balance of power" to be an "idiocy," which would turn England "eternally into our enemy."[67]

THE KAISER WAS CORRECT. As long as Germany remained the greatest power in Europe, Britain would line up against her. Britain's balance-of-power policy commanded it. Britain thus left a powerful Germany that had sought an alliance or entente, or even British neutrality, forever frustrated.

The Kaiser roared that Haldane had revealed British policy " 'in all its naked shamelessness' as the 'playing off of the Great Powers against each other to England's advantage.' "[68] British doctrine meant England "could not tolerate our becoming the strongest power on the continent and that the latter should be united under our leadership!!!"[69] To the Kaiser, the British policy amounted to a moral declaration of war on Germany, not because of what she had done, but because of who she was: the first power in Europe.[70]

To British statesmen, maintaining a balance of power was dogma. In 1938, Lord Londonderry, back from a meeting with Hitler, wrote Churchill, "I should like to get out of your mind what appears to be a strong anti-German obsession."[71] Churchill replied that Londonderry was "mistaken in supposing that I have an anti-German obsession," and went on to explain:

> British policy for four hundred years has been to oppose the strongest power in Europe by weaving together a combination of other countries strong enough to face the bully.

Sometimes it is Spain, sometimes the French monarchy, sometimes the French Empire, sometimes Germany. I have no doubt about who it is now. But if France set up to claim the over-lordship of Europe, I should equally endeavour to oppose them. It is thus through the centuries we have kept our liberties and maintained our life and power.[72]

TWICE THIS POLICY would bring Britain into war with Germany until, by 1945, Britain was too weak to play the role any longer. She would lose her empire because of what Lord Salisbury had said in 1877 was "the commonest error in politics . . . sticking to the carcass of dead policies."[73]

THE SECRETS OF SIR EDWARD GREY

THE STATESMAN MOST RESPONSIBLE for the abandonment of splendid isolation for a secret alliance with France was Edward Grey. When the Liberals took power in 1905, he became foreign secretary, would serve a decade, and would become the leading statesman behind Britain's decision to plunge into the Great War. But this was not what the Liberal Party had promised, and this was not what the British people had wanted. "Grey's Germanophobia and his zeal for the Entente with France were from the outset at odds with the majority of the Liberal Cabinet," writes Ferguson:

[W]ithin half a year of coming into office, Grey had presided over a transformation of the Entente with France, which had begun life as an attempt to settle extra-European quarrels, into a de facto defensive alliance. [Grey] had conveyed to the French that Britain would be prepared to fight with them against Germany in the event of a war.[74]

Prime Minister Campbell-Bannerman and his successor, Herbert Henry Asquith, had approved of the military staff talks, but neither the Cabinet nor Parliament was aware that Sir Edward had committed Britain to war if France were invaded. In 1911, two new ministers were brought in on the secret: Chancellor of the Exchequer David Lloyd George and the thirty-seven-year-old Home Secretary, who soon moved over to the Admiralty: Winston Churchill.

In 1912, Churchill and Grey persuaded France to shift the bulk of her fleet to the Mediterranean to counter the Austro-Hungarian and Italian fleets. While the 1912 exchange of letters on the redeployment of the French fleet stated that Britain was not committed to defend France, Grey and Churchill knew this was exactly what France expected. Should war break out, the Royal Navy was to keep the High Seas Fleet out of the Channel and away from the coast of France. Lord Esher, adviser to George V, told Asquith that the plans worked out between the general staffs of Britain and France "certainly committed us to fight, whether the Cabinet likes it or not."[75]

"FRIENDS FOREVER"

BY 1914 THERE WAS a war party in every country. In May of that year, Col. Edward Mandell House, the eminence grise of the White House, whom Wilson once described as "my second personality . . . my independent self," visited the great capitals of Europe to take the temperature of the continent.[76] House came home with a chilling assessment:

> The situation is extraordinary. It is jingoism run stark mad. Unless someone acting for you [Wilson] can bring about a different understanding, there is some day to be an awful cataclysm. No one in Europe can do it. There is too much hatred, too many jealousies. Whenever England consents, France and Russia will close in on Germany and Austria.[77]

Germany saw her situation exactly as did Colonel House.

British hawks looked to a European war to enhance national prestige and expand the empire. A war in which French and Russian armies tore at Germany from east and west, as the Royal Navy sent the High Seas Fleet to the bottom, rolled up the Kaiser's colonies, and drove German trade from the high seas seemed a glorious opportunity to smash the greatest rival to British power since Napoleon. And the cost of the victory, the dispatch of a British Expeditionary Force to fight beside the mighty French army that would bear the brunt of battle, seemed reasonable.

Yet, as the summer of 1914 began, no one expected war. The naval arms race had ended in 1913 when Tirpitz conceded British superiority by telling the Reichstag Budget Committee he was ready to accept a 60 percent rule, a sixteen-to-ten ratio in favor of the Royal Navy. Germany could not sustain a buildup of both her army and the Kaiser's fleet. In the end, the High Seas Fleet had nothing to do with Britain's decision to go to war, but everything to do with converting Britain from a friendly power aloof from the alliances of Europe into a probable enemy should war come.

On June 23, 1914, the Second Battle Squadron of the Royal Navy, including four of its newest dreadnoughts, *Audacious, Courageous, Ajax,* and *King George V,* sailed into Kiel. And this time, unlike 1906, there was no "invasion scare," no panic in Kiel. A large and excited crowd awaited. The British officers were received at the Royal Castle by Crown Prince Henry and Princess Irene. Admiral Tirpitz arrived the following day from Berlin, boarded his flagship *Friedrich Karl,* and invited all senior British officers to his cabin for a briefing on the High Seas Fleet. That afternoon, every British and German warship in Kiel fired a twenty-one-gun salute as the royal yacht *Hohenzollern* entered the harbor. The British admiral and his captains were invited aboard by the Kaiser, who donned the uniform of a British Admiral of the Fleet and inspected *King George V.*

That day, the Kaiser's yacht regatta began. British and German naval officers visited one another's warships and attended parties together. Tensions between the two nations had eased. On June 28, the Kaiser was aboard his racing yacht *Meteor* when an urgent telegram was brought out. Archduke Franz Ferdinand, the heir to the Austrian throne of the octogenarian Emperor Franz Josef, whose only son had committed suicide, and his wife Sophie had been assassinated in Sarajevo.

"The character of Kiel Week changed," writes Massie. "Flags were lowered to half-mast, and receptions, dinners and a ball at the Royal Castle were canceled. Early the next morning, the Kaiser departed, intending to go to Vienna and the Archduke's funeral."[78] As the British warships sailed out of Kiel, the masts of the German warships flew the signal "Pleasant Journey." *King George V* responded with a wireless message,

> Friends Today
> Friends in Future
> Friends Forever[79]

CHAPTER 2

Last Summer of Yesterday

THE NATIONS SLITHERED over the brink into the
boiling cauldron of war.[1]
— DAVID LLOYD GEORGE,
War Memoirs

This war is really the greatest lunacy ever committed by
the white races.[2]
—ADMIRAL TIRPITZ, 1915

NOT UNTIL FOUR weeks after the assassination of the archduke was the Balkan crisis brought up in the British Cabinet.

On July 17, 1914, the Chancellor of the Exchequer, Lloyd
George, was telling a Guildhall audience the assassination in Sarajevo
was "no more than a very small cloud on the horizon . . . and you
never get a perfectly blue sky in foreign affairs."[3] On July 23, Lloyd
George spoke of how Anglo-German relations "were very much better than they were a few years ago."[4]

But on July 24, after yet another desultory Cabinet debate on
the perennial crisis of Home Rule for Ireland, the ministers were
asked to remain for a few minutes. Sir Edward Grey began to read
the ultimatum Austria had just delivered to Serbia, and the gravity
of it all began to sink in on the thirty-nine-year-old First Lord of
the Admiralty:

> [Grey] had been reading . . . or . . . speaking for several min-
> utes before I could disengage my mind from the tedious and
> bewildering debate which had just closed. . . . [G]radually as
> the phrases and sentences followed one another, impressions
> of a wholly different character began to form in my
> mind. . . . The parishes of Fermanagh and Tyrone faded
> back into the mists and squalls of Ireland and a strange light
> began immediately, but by imperceptible gradations, to fall
> and grow upon the map of Europe.[5]

So recalled Winston Churchill.

In his report to the king that evening, H. H. Asquith, prime minister since 1908, described Austria's ultimatum as "the gravest event
for many years past in European politics as it may be the prelude to a
war in which at least four of the Great Powers may be involved."[6]
Asquith meant Austria, Germany, Russia, and France. As he wrote
Venetia Stanley, the young woman of whom he was deeply enam-
ored, "We are within measurable, or imaginable, distance of a real
Armageddon. Happily, there seems to be no reason why we should be
anything more than spectators."[7]

"GEARED UP AND HAPPY"

THE AUSTRIANS DID NOT want a European war. Vienna wanted
a short, sharp war to punish Serbia for murdering the heir to the
throne and to put an end to Serb plotting to pull apart their empire.
For they suspected that Belgrade's ambition was to gather the
South Slavs into a united nation where Serbia would sit at the head
of the table.

The Austrian ultimatum had been drafted in anticipation of certain rejection, to justify an Austrian declaration of war. But on July 26,
Serbia accepted nine of Austria's ten demands, balking only at Vi-

Last Summer of Yesterday

enna's demand to send a delegation to Belgrade to oversee the investigation and prosecution of the conspirators who had murdered the archduke. Yet, even on this point, the Serbs agreed to refer the matter to the International Court of Justice.

The Kaiser was relieved and elated. Austria had scored a brilliant diplomatic coup and he could not see what more she wanted. "It was a capitulation of the most humiliating sort," exclaimed the Kaiser. "With it disappears every reason for war."[8]

But when the Austrian ambassador in Belgrade received the Serb reply, he picked up his packed bags, boarded the first train out, and, once over the frontier, telephoned Vienna. When news hit that Serbia had failed to submit to all ten Austrian demands, crowds were in the streets clamoring for war. On July 27, the Austro-Hungarian empire declared war. On the twenty-eighth, Belgrade was shelled from across the Danube. But in London, writes the historian Robert Massie, "even after Austria declared war and bombarded Belgrade, few in Britain had an inkling that within seven days, England would enter a world war. The man in the street, the majority in the Cabinet and House of Commons still saw the crisis as a distant furor over 'Serbian murderers.' "[9]

"The Cabinet was overwhelmingly pacific," says Churchill. "At least three-quarters of its members were determined not to be drawn into a European quarrel, unless Great Britain were herself attacked, which was not likely."[10] Asquith's Cabinet was split between Liberal Imperialists and Little Englanders. Barbara Tuchman describes the latter:

> Heirs of Gladstone, they, like their late leader, harbored a deep suspicion of foreign entanglements and considered the aiding of oppressed peoples to be the only proper concern of foreign affairs, which were otherwise regarded as a tiresome interference with Reform, Free Trade, Home Rule, and the Lords' Veto.[11]

Grey and Churchill believed that if France was attacked, Britain must fight. But Britain had no treaty alliance with France. Indeed, why had Britain remained outside the Franco-Russian alliance if not to retain her freedom of action? Gladstone had stayed out of the Franco-Prussian war, and the Liberals wanted Asquith to stay out of this war. Of eighteen ministers who had participated in the Cabinet meeting on Saturday, August 1, twelve opposed war. A Liberal caucus in the House had voted 4–1 for neutrality.[12] The *Manchester Guardian* spoke of "an organised conspiracy to drag us into war."[13]

The editor of the *Times*, however, could not disguise his disgust:

> Saturday was a black day for everyone who knew what was going on—more than half the Cabinet rotten and every prospect of a complete schism or a disastrous or dishonouring refusal to help France. . . . Winston has really done more than anyone else to save the situation.[14]

Seven Cabinet members were ready to resign rather than go to war. "The Cabinet was absolutely against war and would never have agreed to being committed to war at this moment," wrote Churchill.[15] Those favoring Britain's going to war, should it come, were Grey and Churchill, who had made commitments to France. But only the First Lord relished the prospect. On July 25, when it appeared that Grey's call for a conference of ambassadors to halt the slide to war might succeed, Churchill "exclaimed moodily that it looked after all as if we were in for a 'bloody peace.' "[16]

"Churchill was the only Minister to feel any sense of exultation at the course of events," writes biographer John Charmley.[17] On July 28, he had written his wife Clementine: "My darling one & beautiful: Everything tends toward catastrophe & collapse. I am interested, geared up and happy. Is it not horrible to be built like that?"[18]

That same day, the Kaiser was desperately trying to avert the war to which Churchill looked forward with anticipation. "William was 'feverishly active' on the 28th, casting this way and that to keep the peace. He had no idea what the Austrians wanted."[19] By July 30, the German chancellor Bethmann-Hollweg, who had worked with Sir Edward Grey to prevent the spread of the Balkan wars of 1912–1913, had resignedly told the Prussian Ministry of State, "we have lost control and the stone has begun to roll."[20]

THE FIRST LORD

AND WHO WAS THIS First Lord whose lust for war caused senior Cabinet colleagues to recoil? Born at Blenheim, ancestral home of the Duke of Marlborough, on November 30, 1874, to twenty-year-old American heiress Jennie Jerome and Randolph Churchill, a rising star in the Tory Party, Winston Churchill had been a poor student, except for a love of history and mastery of the English language. After five years at Harrow, and three tries, he had been accepted at the Royal Military Academy at Sandhurst. There he excelled, departing in December 1894 eighth in his class.

In October 1896, the young cavalry officer of the 4th Hussars arrived in Bombay. In four years, he would be elected to Parliament. Those years were full of the "crowded hours" of which Theodore Roosevelt had written.

During his first leave from India, Churchill sailed to Cuba to observe the Spanish in action against the rebels. On return, he learned of a punitive expedition to be led by Sir Bindon Blood to the Northwest Frontier to put down a Pashtun uprising on the Afghan border. A year earlier, Churchill had extracted from Sir Bindon a promise to take him along if there was to be fighting. Winston returned from the expedition after six weeks to write *The Story of the Malakind Field Force*, dedicating the book to Sir Bindon. The Prince of Wales sent a note to the young author praising his work.

Churchill then had his mother, a famous beauty, intercede with

Prime Minister Salisbury to have him assigned to the army of General Kitchener, who was starting upriver to the Sudan to avenge the death of General "Chinese" Gordon by the Mahdi's army at Khartoum. At Omdurman, Churchill rode in the last cavalry charge of the empire. He would claim to have slain up to half a dozen enemy and came home to write *The River War*, which charged Kitchener with dishonorable treatment of wounded Dervishes.

But it was the Boer War that made Churchill famous. Traveling to South Africa as a correspondent, he was riding an armored train to the front when it was derailed by Boer commandos under Louis Botha, who took him prisoner. Held with captured British officers in Pretoria—the Boers rejected his protest that he was a journalist and a noncombatant—Churchill escaped. When news, as told by he himself, reached London, he became an international figure. He returned to South Africa, saw action at the humiliating British defeat at Spion Kop, marched to the relief of Ladysmith, and came home one of the most famous young men in the world. Weeks before his twenty-sixth birthday, he was elected to Parliament. There he would remain, with two brief interludes, for sixty-four years.

Like his father, a Chancellor of the Exchequer, Winston entered politics as a Conservative. But by 1904 he was in rebellion against the campaign by Joe Chamberlain for Tory abandonment of a free-trade policy that had been British tradition since the repeal of the Corn Laws in 1846. Chamberlain was proposing tariffs to protect British markets against the flood of imports from across the Atlantic as a protectionist America was leaving Britain in the dust, and Germany was approaching industrial parity. In February, Churchill wrote to Prime Minister Arthur Balfour, Salisbury's nephew and successor, and declared himself "a Unionist Free Trader . . . opposed to what is generally known as Home Rule [for Ireland] and Protection in any form," and "a wholehearted opponent of Mr. Chamberlain."[21]

Meanwhile, the Tory Party in Churchill's Oldham District was fed up with him. So it was that Churchill crossed over to the Liberal

Party. His timing proved perfect as he rode into power and into the Cabinet in the Liberal landslide of 1906. By 1911, he was First Lord and the most forceful advocate in the Cabinet for Britain's immediate entry into any Franco-German war.

THE SCHLIEFFEN PLAN

IN PRODDING THE CABINET into war, the ace of trumps for Grey and Churchill was Belgium. Seventy-five years earlier, France, Prussia, and Great Britain had signed a treaty guaranteeing Belgium's neutrality. The 1839 pact was grounded in British history. Believing that control of the Channel coast opposite Dover by a great hostile power was a threat to her vital interests, England had gone to war with Philip II of Spain, Louis XIV, and Napoleon. After Belgium had been torn from the carcass of Napoleon's empire, Britain had extracted a guarantee of Belgium's neutrality. The European powers respected this as a vital British interest. When France was maneuvered into war by Bismarck in 1870, the Iron Chancellor had given assurances to Gladstone that when von Moltke's army marched into France, it would not tread on Belgian soil. With Belgium unmolested, Gladstone saw no vital interest in who prevailed in the Franco-Prussian war.

The 1839 treaty, however, had an exit clause: It authorized, but did not require, Britain to go to war should any nation violate the neutrality of Belgium:

> The language of the 1839 treaty was unusual on one point: It gave the the signatories the right, but not the duty, of intervention in case of violation. In 1914, as the possibility of German violation loomed, the noninterventionists in the Cabinet clung to this point. Britain, they said, had no obligation to defend Belgium, especially if Belgium itself chose not to fight.[22]

And the world had changed since 1839. Napoleon had said of Prussia that it "was hatched from a cannon ball." By 1914, the cannonball was the heart of a nation of seventy million, stretching from France to Russia and the Baltic to the Alps, that produced 15 percent of the world's goods to Britain's 14 percent—and twice as much steel. Germany was the most powerful nation in Europe and, after Russia, the most populous. In 1870, Germany had crushed France in six weeks. Her army was the greatest fighting force on earth. But Germany was virtually friendless, and the arrogance and bellicosity of the Kaiser and his haughty countrymen were among the causes. In his travel notes Crown Prince Henry wrote, "Our country is not much loved anywhere and indeed frequently hated."[23] Writes German historian Andreas Hillgruber:

> Public opinion in other European nations slowly came to sense a threat, less because of the goals of German policy per se than the crude, overbearing style that Germany projected on the international stage. Without this background, one cannot understand the truly radical hate for Germany and all things German that broke out in the Entente countries with the war of 1914.[24]

In France she was especially hated. The Kaiser's grandfather, against the advice of Bismarck, had amputated Alsace and Lorraine after the 1870 war. The Prussian General Staff had persuaded the emperor that the provinces must be annexed to keep France permanently on the defensive. But their loss had made of France a mortal enemy resolute upon revenge. Of Alsace-Lorraine, the French had a saying, first attributed to Gambetta: "Speak of it never, think of it always!"

Russia was now France's ally. And given her size, resources, and population, Germans feared, Russia must soon assume leadership of all the Slavic peoples. The German General Staff, with an unreliable ally in Italy, a crumbling ally in Austria, and an immense Russian Empire growing in power as she laid down railroad tracks into Poland, preferred that if war must come, it come sooner rather than later. Time was not on Germany's side. "The future [belongs] to Russia, which grows and grows, and which hangs over us like an increasingly horrible incubus," said Bethmann-Hollweg. "In a few years there will be no defense against it."[25]

Germany's war plans were dictated by geography. Wedged between a hostile France and a rising Russia, Germany had to prepare for a two-front war, with the French attacking in Alsace and Russia marching into Prussia. The elder Moltke, the field marshal who had led Prussia to her victories over Austria and France, had adopted a defensive strategy against France, with a limited offensive in the east to drive Russia out of Poland, then to allow "its enemies to wreck their armies by hurling them against walls of [German] fire and steel."[26]

"We should exploit in the West the great advantages which the Rhine and our powerful fortifications offer to the defensive," Moltke had said as early as 1879, and "apply all the fighting forces which are not absolutely indispensable for an imposing offensive against the east."[27]

This remained strategic doctrine until a new figure arrived in Berlin: the legendary Count Alfred von Schlieffen, Chief of the General Staff from 1891 to 1906, a "man without hobbies [who] often worked until midnight, then relaxed by reading military history to his daughters."[28]

The Schlieffen Plan, laid down in virtual tablets of stone, called for the German army, no matter where war erupted, to strike first and hardest to crush Germany's strongest enemy, France, then to shift her armies by rail to meet the Russian steamroller before it rumbled into East Prussia. When the great war comes, Count Schlieffen instructed his generals, "the whole of Germany must throw itself upon one enemy, the strongest, most powerful, most dangerous enemy, and that can only be France."[29] In the Prussian-led German

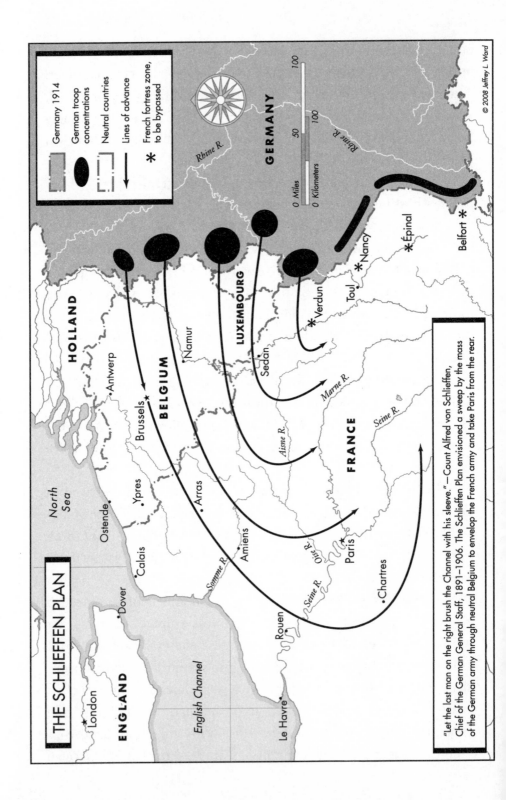

THE SCHLIEFFEN PLAN

ENGLAND

London

Dover

English Channel

North Sea

Calais

Ostende

Ypres

Arras

Amiens

Somme R.

Rouen

Le Havre

Seine R.

Oise R.

Paris

Chartres

Seine R.

HOLLAND

Antwerp

BELGIUM

Brussels

Namur

Ypres

LUXEMBOURG

Sedan

Aisne R.

Marne R.

FRANCE

Verdun ✴

Toul

Nancy ✴

✴ Épinal

Belfort ✴

GERMANY

Rhine R.

Rhine R.

Legend

- Germany 1914
- ⬤ German troop concentrations
- ⌐ Neutral countries
- → Lines of advance
- ✴ French fortress zone, to be bypassed

0 Miles 50 100

0 Kilometers 100

© 2008 Jeffrey L. Ward

"Let the last man on the right brush the Channel with his sleeve." —Count Alfred von Schlieffen, Chief of the German General Staff, 1891–1906. The Schlieffen Plan envisioned a sweep by the mass of the German army through neutral Belgium to envelop the French army and take Paris from the rear.

army, the Schlieffen Plan was sacred text. "It was often said in 1914, and has often been repeated since [that] 'mobilization means war,' " writes historian A.J.P. Taylor: "This was not true."[30]

> All the Powers except one could mobilize and yet go on with diplomacy, keeping their armies within their frontiers. Mobilization was a threat of a high order, but still a threat. The Germans, however, had run mobilization and war into one. In this sense, Schlieffen . . . though dead, was the real maker of the First World War. "Mobilization means war" was his idea. In 1914, his dead hand automatically pulled the trigger.[31]

However, a rapid defeat of France required not only that the German army mobilize and move swiftly on unalterable timetables, but also that it not be halted, pinioned, and bled on the great French fortresses of Belfort-Epinal and Toul-Verdun. The solution was Belgium. Under the Schlieffen Plan, weak German forces in Alsace and Lorraine were to hold out against an anticipated French invasion, while the German right wing, seven-eighths of the army in the west, smashed into Belgium, far to the north of the French forts. After storming through Belgium, which would hopefully yield without a fight, the army would break out into the undefended north of France and execute a giant wheeling movement, enveloping Paris and the French army from the rear. "When you march into France," Count Schlieffen admonished his generals, "let the last man on the right brush the Channel with his sleeve."[32]

Schlieffen had died at eighty in 1913. On his deathbed, he was heard to mutter, "It must come to a fight. Only make the right wing strong."[33]

From the marshaling of men and munitions, trains and horses, to the designated stepping-off points on the frontier, every detail of Schlieffen's plan had been engraved on the minds of the General

Staff. The plan could not be altered. Its core principle was that France must be defeated first and swiftly, and the only avenue to certain victory passed through Belgium. If Belgium resisted, she must be mercilessly crushed. German survival commanded it. Dismissing quibbles over Belgian neutrality, Moltke's nephew, who now headed the General Staff, declared, "We must put aside all commonplaces as to the responsibility of the aggressor. Success alone justifies war."[34]

The British were largely unaware of the Schlieffen Plan, and few had any idea that a seventy-five-year-old treaty to defend Belgian neutrality might drag them into a great European war most had no desire to fight. But the supremely confident German General Staff was unconcerned. Warned that violating Belgium's neutrality could bring a British army across the Channel, Moltke told Tirpitz, "The more English the better."[35] A few British divisions would not stop the German juggernaut, and any British soldiers in France would be caught in the net along with the French, and be unavailable for fighting elsewhere.

The Germans had forgotten Bismarck, who warned that preventive war is "like committing suicide out of fear of death."[36] It would be the arrival of a British Expeditionary Force of 120,000 men that crossed the Channel in the first two weeks without hindrance from the High Seas Fleet that would blunt the German advance and defeat the Schlieffen Plan.

"WINSTON ALONE WAS BUOYANT"

BY SATURDAY, AUGUST 1, Russia had begun to mobilize and Germany and France were on the brink. Yet Asquith's Cabinet remained divided. Most of his ministers were willing to consider war if Belgium was invaded. But some opposed war, no matter the provocation. Grey sought to move the Cabinet toward war without forcing resignations. Privately, Asquith supported him. Publicly, he temporized to hold the government together.

Of Asquith, Churchill would write, "When the need required it, his mind opened and shut smoothly and exactly, like the breach of a gun."[37] But Asquith had not yet decided to force the issue.

The First Lord took the lead. "Winston very bellicose and demanding immediate mobilization," wrote Asquith, "occupied at least half the time."[38]

By that evening, Germany had declared war on Russia, which had refused to halt its mobilization, and on France, which had refused to declare neutrality. Sunday morning, Grey convinced a Cabinet majority to agree that the Royal Navy would block any move by the High Seas Fleet into the Channel to attack French shipping or bombard the coast. Saturday night, exceeding his authority, Grey had already given that assurance to Cambon, the French ambassador. Cabinet Minister John Burns immediately resigned.

"The Cabinet sat almost continuously throughout Sunday [August 2]," wrote Asquith's daughter Violet. "When they broke up for an interval at luncheon time all those I saw looked racked with anxiety and some stricken with grief. Winston alone was buoyant."[39]

By the end of the second Cabinet meeting on Sunday, a majority had agreed: If Germany invaded Belgium, and the Belgians fought and called on Britain for aid, British honor and the 1839 treaty meant she must fight. Five Cabinet members were about to join Burns and resign. Seeing no cause to justify a vast expenditure of British blood and treasure in a Franco-German war, they pleaded with Lloyd George to lead them out. Had Lloyd George agreed, and had all six ministers resigned Monday, Asquith's Cabinet would have broken up, his government might have fallen, and history would have taken another course.

"The key figure was Lloyd George, and Churchill played a major role in winning his support for a declaration of war," writes Charmley.[40] As Lloyd George vacillated, Churchill pressed him to take his stand on the issue of Belgium's neutrality. Churchill knew public opinion would swing around to war when the Germans invaded

Belgium, as they must. He believed that Lloyd George would swing with it. Churchill knew his man.

As late as July 27, Lloyd George had volunteered that he "knew of no Minister who would be in favour of it [war]," adding, "[T]here could be no question of our taking part in any war."[41] But the Chancellor could see the Unionists uniting behind Grey and Churchill. Having opposed the Boer War, Lloyd George did not want to repeat the painful experience "of standing out against a war-inflamed populace."[42] If the nation was going to fight, he would stand with the nation. For Lloyd George knew that if he did not, his position as heir apparent to leadership of the Liberal Party, a position he had spent twenty-five years building, would be lost, probably to his young rival, the First Lord. Lloyd George might then end his brilliant career as a backbencher in a Liberal Party led by Winston Churchill.

"It was an historic disaster—though not for his own career—that Lloyd George did not support the opponents of intervention at this crucial juncture," writes Ferguson.[43] That there was opportunism in Lloyd George's refusal to lead the antiwar ministers out of the Cabinet, and in his quiet campaign to persuade them to hold off resigning until they learned whether the German Army would violate the neutrality of Belgium, seems undeniable. Biographer Peter Rowland writes, "The truth of the matter was, quite simply, he did not want to resign. . . . [H]e was looking around, during those last days of July, for a face-saving formula which would enable him to stay put as Asquith's second-in-command."[44]

Lloyd George's secretary and mistress, later his wife, confirms it. Wrote Frances Stevenson Lloyd George, forty years later: "My own opinion is that L.G.'s mind was really made up from the first, that he knew we would have to go in, and that the invasion of Belgium was, to be cynical, a heaven-sent excuse for supporting a declaration of war."[45]

After Churchill wrote a note to Lloyd George in Cabinet to "bring your mighty aid to the discharge of our duty," the Chancellor, at the August 1 Cabinet meeting, shoved a note back across the table to the First Lord: "If you do not press us too hard tonight, we might come together."[46]

Yet there was cynicism and opportunism also in Churchill's clucking concern for Belgium. As Manchester writes, Churchill "didn't care for the Belgians; he thought their behavior in the Congo disgraceful."[47] Of all the colonial powers in Africa, none had acted with greater barbarity than the Belgium of King Leopold.

> Such was the rapacity of his regime that the cost in human life due to murder, starvation, disease and reduced fertility has been estimated at ten million: half the existing population. There was nothing hyperbolic about Joseph Conrad's portrayal of "the horror" of this in *The Heart of Darkness*.[48]

Churchill also "suspected the existence of a secret agreement between Brussels and Berlin which would permit the Germans to cross Belgium on their way to France."[49] There was another reason the First Lord did not consider a violation of Belgium's neutrality to be a casus belli. If war came, Churchill was determined to violate Belgian neutrality himself by ordering the Royal Navy to blockade Antwerp to prevent its becoming a port of entry for goods destined for Germany.

"[I]f Germany had not violated Belgian neutrality in 1914, Britain would have," writes Niall Ferguson. "This puts the British government's much-vaunted moral superiority in fighting 'for Belgian neutrality' in another light."[50] The German invasion of Belgium enabled the British war party to put a high moral gloss on a war they had already decided to fight for reasons of realpolitik. As early as 1911, during the second Moroccan crisis, Churchill had confided to Lloyd George his real reason for committing himself morally and secretly to bringing Britain into any Franco-German war.

It is not for Morocco, nor indeed for Belgium, that I would take part in this terrible business. One cause alone should justify our participation—to prevent France from being trampled down & looted by the Prussian junkers—a disaster ruinous to the world, & swiftly fatal to our country.[51]

Late Sunday, word came of Berlin's ultimatum to Brussels. Asquith ordered mobilization. By Monday morning, Lloyd George had deserted the anti-interventionists and enlisted in the war party. Two years later, he would replace Asquith and lead Britain to victory.

Over that weekend the mood of the British people underwent a sea change. A peace demonstration scheduled for Sunday in Trafalgar Square dissolved. Millions who did not want to go to war for France were suddenly wildly enthusiastic about war for Belgium. As Lloyd George observed, a poll on August 1 "would have shown 95 per cent against . . . hostilities. . . . A poll on the following Tuesday (4 August) would have resulted in a vote of 99 percent in favor."[52]

Said Churchill, "[E]very British heart burned for little Belgium."[53]

By Monday morning's Cabinet meeting, King George had a request from King Albert, calling on Britain to fulfill its obligation under the 1839 treaty. Belgium would fight rather than let the Kaiser make her a doormat on which German soldiers wiped their boots as they marched into France. That afternoon, Sir Edward Grey called on the House to defend "British interests, British honour, and British obligations." The invasion of Belgium, said Grey, was "the direst crime that ever stained the pages of history."[54]

The British interests were to prevent Germany from crushing France as a Great Power and occupying the Channel coast. British obligations, said Grey, had been written into the 1839 treaty. British honor had been placed on the line when Britain had persuaded France to transfer the French fleet to the Mediterranean. Said Sir Edward,

[I]f the German fleet came down the English Channel and bombarded and battered the undefended coasts of France, we could not stand aside [cheers broke out in the House] and see the thing going on practically in sight of our eyes, with our arms folded, looking on dispassionately, doing nothing![55]

Grey's address carried the House and prepared the nation for the ultimatum that would bring a declaration of war on August 4. When he returned to his office, Grey received U.S. ambassador Walter Hines Page. Tears in his eyes, he told Page, "Thus, the efforts of a lifetime go for nothing. I feel like a man who wasted his life."[56]

That evening Grey stood with a friend looking out at St. James Park as the lamps were being lit. "The lamps are going out all over Europe," said Grey. "We shall not see them lit again in our lifetime."[57]

On August 4, after von Kluck's divisions crossed the Belgian frontier, the prime minister's wife came to see him in his office.

"So it is all up?" said Margot Asquith.

Without looking up, tears in his eyes, Asquith replied, "Yes, it is all up."[58]

It was with heavy hearts that Grey and Asquith led their country into war. Lloyd George was of a similar cast of mind. On the eve of a war he now supported, but with a troubled conscience, he wrote,

I am moving through a nightmare world these days. . . . I have fought hard for peace & succeeded so far in keeping the Cabinet out of it, but I am driven to the conclusion that if the small nationality of Belgium is attacked by Germany all my traditions & even prejudices will be engaged on the side of war. I am filled with horror at the prospect. I am even more horrified that I should ever appear to have a share in it but I must bear my share of the ghastly burden though it scorches my flesh to do so.[59]

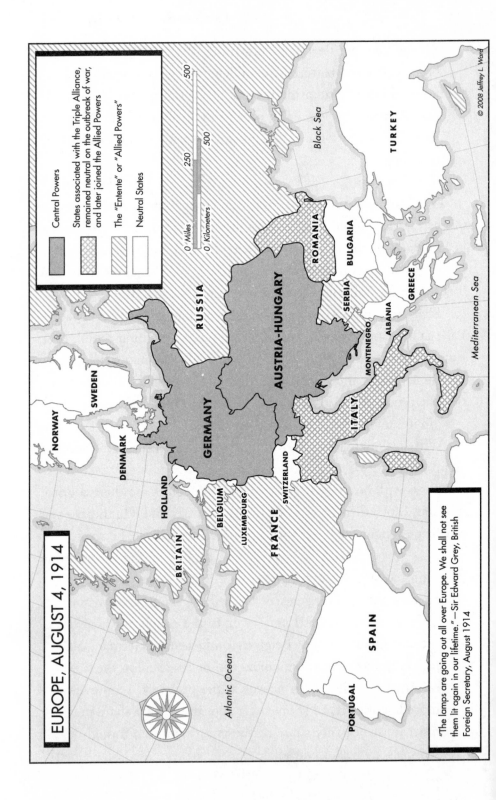

EUROPE, AUGUST 4, 1914

Central Powers

States associated with the Triple Alliance, remained neutral on the outbreak of war, and later joined the Allied Powers

The "Entente" or "Allied Powers"

Neutral States

0 Miles   250   500

0 Kilometers   500

NORWAY

SWEDEN

DENMARK

BRITAIN

HOLLAND

BELGIUM

LUXEMBOURG

GERMANY

FRANCE

SWITZERLAND

RUSSIA

AUSTRIA-HUNGARY

ROMANIA

ITALY

SERBIA

MONTENEGRO

BULGARIA

ALBANIA

GREECE

TURKEY

Black Sea

Mediterranean Sea

Atlantic Ocean

PORTUGAL

SPAIN

"The lamps are going out all over Europe. We shall not see them lit again in our lifetime." — Sir Edward Grey, British Foreign Secretary, August 1914

© 2008 Jeffrey L. Ward

"[Lloyd George] was sickened by the huge crowds jubilantly thronging Whitehall and Parliament Square and his face was white as he sat slumped in his seat in the Commons," listening to Grey make the case for war.[60] Cheered on his way to Parliament, Lloyd George muttered: "This is not my crowd. . . . I never want to be cheered by a war crowd."[61]

The prime minister felt equal revulsion. Making his way through the cheering throngs, Asquith "expressed his loathing for the levity and quoted Robert Walpole, 'Now they ring the bells but soon they will wring their hands.' "[62] "It is curious," Asquith would later write,

> how, going to and from the House, we are now always surrounded and escorted by cheering crowds of loafers and holiday makers. I have never before been a popular character with "the man in the street," and in all this dark and dangerous business it gives me scant pleasure. How one loathes such levity.[63]

At 11 P.M., August 4, as the ultimatum expired and the moment came when Britain was at war, a tearful Margot Asquith left her husband to go to bed, and as she began to ascend the stairs, "I saw Winston Churchill with a happy face striding towards the double doors of the Cabinet room."[64]

Lloyd George was sitting within with his disconsolate prime minister when, as he later told a friend:

> Winston dashed into the room, radiant, his face bright, his manner keen, one word pouring out after another how he was going to send telegrams to the Mediterranean, the North Sea, and God knows where. You could see he was a really happy man.[65]

Churchill was exhilarated. Six months later, after the first Battle of Ypres, with tens of thousands of British soldiers in their graves, he would say to Violet Asquith, "I think a curse should rest on me—because I am so happy. I know this war is smashing and shattering the lives of thousands every moment and yet—I cannot help it—I enjoy every second."[66]

Said Sir Maurice Hankey, "Churchill was a man of a totally different type from all his colleagues. He had a real zest for war. If war there must needs be, he at least could enjoy it."[67]

A year earlier, in his book *Pillars of Society*, A. G. Gardiner had written prophetically of the young First Lord:

> He sees himself moving through the smoke of battle—triumphant, terrible, his brow clothed with thunder, his legions looking to him for victory, and not looking in vain. He thinks of Napoleon; he thinks of his great ancestor. Thus did they bear themselves; thus, in this rugged and most awful crisis, will he bear himself. It is not make-believe, it is not insincerity; it is that in that fervid and picturesque imagination there are always great deeds afoot with himself cast by destiny in the Agamemnon role. . . . He will write his name big in the future. Let us take care he does not write it in blood.[68]

WHY BRITAIN FOUGHT

WAS WORLD WAR I a necessary war?

Writes British historian John Keegan, "The First World War was . . . an unnecessary conflict. Unnecessary because the train of events that led to its outbreak might have been broken at any point during the five weeks that preceded the first clash of arms, had prudence or common goodwill found a voice."[69]

Had the Austrians not sought to exploit the assassination of Ferdinand to crush Serbia, they would have taken Serbia's acceptance of nine of their ten demands as vindication. Had Czar Nicholas II been more forceful in rescinding his order for full mobilization, Germany would not have mobilized, and the Schlieffen Plan would not have begun automatically to unfold. Had the Kaiser and Bethmann realized the gravity of the crisis, just days earlier, they might have seized on Grey's proposal to reconvene the six-power conference that resolved the 1913 Balkan crisis. The same six ambassadors were all in London, including Germany's Prince Lichnowsky, an Anglophile desperate to avoid war with Britain.

Had Grey himself conveyed to Lichnowsky, more forcefully and "just a few days earlier," that Britain would likely be drawn into a European war, writes one historian, "Berlin almost certainly would have changed its position more quickly and firmly. Austria might then have deferred its declaration of war, and Russia would have had little reason to mobilize."[70] The Great War might have been averted.

And it is in Britain's decisions and actions that we are most interested. For it was the British decision to send an army across the Channel to fight in Western Europe, for the first time in exactly one hundred years, that led to the defeat of the Schlieffen Plan, four years of trench warfare, America's entry, Germany's collapse in the autumn of 1918, the abdication of the Kaiser, the dismemberment of Germany at Versailles, and the rise to power of a veteran of the Western Front who, four years after the war's end, was unreconciled to his nation's defeat. "It cannot be that two million Germans should have fallen in vain," cried Adolf Hitler in 1922. "No, we do not pardon, we demand—vengeance."[71]

Britain turned the European war of August 1 into a world war. For, while the wave of public sentiment against the invasion of "brave little Belgium" swept Parliament over the brink and into war, Grey, Haldane, Churchill, and Asquith had steered her toward the falls for other reasons:

1. Preserve France as a Great Power. In his speech to the Commons on August 3, Grey declared: "If France is beaten in a struggle of life and death . . . I do not believe that . . . we should be in a position to use our force decisively . . . to prevent the whole of the West of Europe opposite to us . . . falling under the domination of a single Power."[72]

Grey believed in a domino theory. The day after his address, he told a colleague, "It will not end with Belgium. Next will come Holland, and after Holland, Denmark . . . England['s] position would be gone if Germany were thus permitted to dominate Europe."[73] To Grey, the Kaiser was Napoleon and the risks of neutrality—a German-dominated Europe—outweighed the risks of war. "If we are engaged in war, we shall suffer but little more than we shall suffer if we stand aside."[74]

Sir Edward was tragically mistaken.

2. British Honor. What brought the Cabinet around behind Grey was not France or an abstraction like the balance of power. It was Belgium. Had the Germans not invaded Belgium, had the Belgians not fought, the Cabinet would not have supported the ultimatum. Grey would then have resigned; Asquith's government would have fallen; days would have passed before a new government was formed. New elections might have had to be called. There would have been no ultimatum of August 3, no declaration of war of August 4. In his speech of August 6, "What are we fighting for?," Asquith gave this answer: Britain had a duty "to uphold Belgian neutrality in the name of law and honour" and "to vindicate the principle . . . that small nations are not to be crushed."[75]

In justifying the decision for war, Asquith, writes Ferguson, adopted "the idiom of the public-school playground: 'It is impossible for people of our blood and history to stand by . . . while a big bully sets to work to thrash and trample to the ground a victim who has given him no provocation.' "[76] In his memoirs, Grey, too, does not give as a casus belli any imperiled vital British interest, but regards it as a matter of national honor:

[Had we not come in] we should have been isolated; we should have had no friend in the world; no one would have hoped or feared anything from us, or thought our friendship worth having. We should have been discredited . . . held to have played an inglorious and ignoble part . . . We should have been hated.[77]

Lord Grey is saying here that Britain had to enter the war because the character and credibility of the British nation were at issue. Allies of the empire all over the world, who relied on British commitments, were watching. Had Britain not gone to war, had she stood aside as France was crushed, who would then trust Britain to stand by them?

What Grey was saying is that the empire was held together by a belief that, in any crisis, the British army and Royal Navy would be there. That belief, critical to maintaining the empire, could not survive a British neutrality as Belgium and France were being assaulted, invaded, and overrun.

3. Retention of Power. Why did the antiwar Liberals in the Cabinet not resign? Because Lloyd George begged them to wait. Because they feared a breakup of the Cabinet would bring about the fall of Asquith's government, and new elections that might bring to power the Unionists who backed Grey, Churchill, and war. Already, Churchill had sounded out the Conservative leader Bonar Law on a national unity government.

Indeed, on Sunday, August 2, Law had written Asquith offering the Tories' "unhesitating support in any measures they may consider necessary," adding, "[i]t would be fatal to the honour and security of the United Kingdom to hesitate in supporting France and Russia."[78]

Bonar Law's letter did not mention Belgium.

If Britain must go to war, Liberals believed, better that they lead her and conclude the peace. The Liberal Imperialists steered their country to war, and, rather than risk the loss of power, the Little Englanders went along.

> Since their triumph in 1906, the Liberals had seen their electoral support wither away. By 1914, Herbert Asquith's government was on the verge of collapse. Given the failure of their foreign policy to avert a European war, he and his Cabinet colleagues ought to have resigned. But they dreaded the return to Opposition. More, they dreaded the return of the Conservatives to power. They went to war partly to keep the Tories out.[79]

And the German General Staff accommodated them. "By requiring a German advance through the whole of Belgium," writes Ferguson, "the Schlieffen Plan helped save the Liberal government."[80]

4. Germanophobia. Britain resented the rise of Germany and feared that a defeat of France would mean German preeminence in Europe and the eclipse of Britain as an economic and world power. During his tour in the late summer of 1919 to sell America on his Versailles Treaty, a tour that ended when he was felled by a stroke, Wilson said in St. Louis and St. Paul: "This war, in its inception, was a commercial and industrial war. . . . The German bankers and the German merchants and the German manufacturers did not want this war. They were making conquest of the world without it, and they knew it would spoil their plans."[81]

Churchill himself had imbibed deeply of Grey's Germanophobia. As he said in 1912: "I could never learn their beastly language, nor will I till the Emperor William comes over here with his army."[82]

In 1907, preparing for the Hague Conference on disarmament, U.S. secretary of state Elihu Root sent Ambassador Henry White to London to ascertain British views. According to Allan Nevins, Root's biographer, White was "startled" by what he heard into the stark realization that a European war involving Britain was a possibility. White had several conversations with Balfour, one of which was overheard by White's daughter, who took notes:

> *Balfour (somewhat lightly):* "We are probably fools not to find a reason for declaring war on Germany before she builds too many ships and takes away our trade."
>
> *White:* "You are a very high-minded man in private life. How can you possibly contemplate anything so politically immoral as provoking a war against a harmless nation which has as good a right to a navy as you have? If you wish to compete with German trade, work harder."
>
> *Balfour:* "That would mean lowering our standard of living. Perhaps it would be simpler for us to have a war."
>
> *White:* "I am shocked that you of all men should enunciate such principles."
>
> *Balfour (again lightly):* "Is it a question of right or wrong? Maybe it is just a question of keeping our supremacy."[83]

5. Imperial Ambition and Opportunism. The British war party saw France and Russia as bearing the cost in blood of land battle in Europe while the Royal Navy, supreme at sea, ravaged Germany's trade, seized her markets, and sank the High Seas Fleet, as the empire gobbled up every German colony from Togoland to the Bismarck Archipelago. A war where France and Russia fought the German army, while Britain did most of her fighting outside Europe, or at sea, matched perfectly the ambitions and strengths of the British Empire.

Thus, in early August 1914, a Cabinet that had come to power in public revulsion against an imperial war in South Africa was happily poring over maps, plotting the plunder of Germany's colonies, as Asquith mused to his colleagues, "We look more like a gang of

Elizabethan buccaneers than a meek collection of black-coated Liberal Ministers."[84]

For Britain, World War I was not a war of necessity but a war of choice. The Germans did not want war with Britain, nor did they seek to destroy the British Empire. They feared a two-front war against a rising Russian Empire and a France resolute upon revenge for 1870 and the loss of Alsace-Lorraine. Berlin would have paid a high price for British neutrality.

WHY THE LIBERALS WENT ALONG

IDEOLOGY AND EMOTION HELPED to sweep the Liberal Party along to war. Once Belgium was attacked, everything changed. Writes British historian Peter Clarke,

> Serbia was belatedly seized upon as a small nation struggling to be free—Lloyd George was to make a speech about how much the world owed the "little 5-foot-5 nations"—but it was Belgium which immediately fitted this particular paradigm. . . . [A] war on behalf of Belgium was not seen as an assertion of realpolitik in the national interest . . . but a struggle of right and wrong in the Gladstonian tradition.[85]

Once Belgium became Britain's cause, Liberals who had opposed war only hours before enthusiastically joined the crusade. Three days after war was declared, H. G. Wells wrote in the Liberal *Daily News*, "Every sword drawn against Germany is a sword drawn for peace. . . . The defeat of Germany may open the way to disarmament and peace throughout the earth. . . ."[86] The *Daily News* echoed Wells, "We have no quarrel with the German people . . . no, it is not the people with whom we are at war, it is the tyranny which has held them in its vice."[87] To the *News*, the Germans were a good people; it was the "despots and diplomatists" who had brought on the war.[88] Writes historian Correlli Barnett:

> The shameful war out of which Britain must at all costs keep had thus swiftly changed its nature to a war of Good against Evil. Spiritual exaltation was now manifested at a temperature not seen since the religious transports of the original evangelical movement of the early nineteenth century. As a writer in the *Daily News* put it in September 1914, "Humanity is going to pay a great price, but not in vain ... [T]he reward is its liberty and a larger, nobler life."[89]

When Wilson took America into the war, he, too, had his Damascene moment, awakening to the truth that a European war whose origins he could not discern in December 1916, a war in which he had said both sides were fighting for the same ends, was now a "war to end wars" and "to make the world safe for democracy," the latter "a phrase first coined by H. G. Wells in August, 1914."[90] Wilson became history's champion of moralistic intervention. In the 1930s, others would take up the great cause and make League of Nations moralism the polestar of British policy.

Despite their sudden enthusiasm for war when Belgium was invaded, the Liberal Party and the people had no vote in Britain's decision to enter the bloodiest conflict in Western history. Writes Taylor,

> [T]he war came as though King George V still possessed the undiminished prerogatives of Henry VIII. At 10:30 P.M. on 4 August 1914, the king held a privy council at Buckingham Palace which was attended by only one minister and two court officials. This council sanctioned the proclamation of a state of war from 11 P.M. That was all. The Cabinet played no part once it had resolved to defend the neutrality of

Belgium. It did not consider the ultimatum to Germany, which Sir Edward Grey . . . sent after consulting only the Prime Minister, Asquith, and perhaps not even him. Nor did the Cabinet authorize the declaration of war. . . . The parliament . . . did not give formal approval to the government's acts until it voted a credit of (100) million (pounds) . . . on 6 August.[91]

"More astonishing, when viewed though modern eyes," writes David Fromkin, were the reflexive decisions of the Dominions, thousands of miles from Europe, to send their sons to fight and die in a war against an enemy that had neither attacked nor threatened them or the British Empire.

"The governments and parliaments of the Dominions were not consulted." Instead, each "governor general issued the royal proclamation on his own authority, as did the viceroy of India." Canada, Australia, New Zealand, South Africa, India (which then included Pakistan and Bangladesh), and much of Africa were swept up in a war without first being asked.[92]

Thus did Britain, her empire trailing behind, enter upon a thirty years' war of Western civilization. From the killing fields of this mighty conflict, four European empires would never return. No European nation would emerge without wounds that would diminish it forever.

THE KAISER'S CULPABILITY

NEITHER THE KAISER NOR Chancellor Bethmann is blameless for what the Great War historian Jacques Barzun calls the "blow that hurled the modern world on its course of self-destruction."[93] But neither entered it with the "zest" of the First Lord. In early July, the Kaiser had acceded to Vienna's request to stand by Austria in the event of a war with Serbia, which might mean a collision with Russia. This was the famous "blank cheque." But as the Kaiser sailed off on his summer vacation to tour Norwegian fjords, Berlin implored the dithering Austrians to settle accounts with the Serbs quickly. Writes Keegan, "Austria had simply wanted to punish Serbia (though it had lacked the courage to act alone). Germany had wanted a diplomatic success that would leave its Austrian ally stronger in European eyes; it had not wanted war."[94]

But the Austrians waited four weeks to act, and when they did they set in train the events that led to the European war. Yet, in the last hours before August 1, the Kaiser and Bethmann tried to pull back from a war that neither wanted. When the Kaiser returned to Berlin in late July, Bethmann, offering to resign, told him that things had gotten out of hand and an Austrian war on Serbia might now ignite a European conflagration. The Kaiser rebuked him, "You cooked this broth, and now you are going eat it."[95]

> Only at the eleventh hour did they begin to lose their nerve: the Kaiser first, on July 28, and then Bethmann who . . . frantically sought to apply the brakes . . . [B]ut it was the German military which ultimately secured, by a combination of persuasion and defiance, the mobilization orders, the ultimata and declarations of war which unleashed the conflict.[96]

After Serbia's reply to the Austrian note, a diplomatic surrender in the Kaiser's eyes, he wrote to Emperor Franz Josef, "[E]very cause for war [now] falls to the ground."[97] After the Austrian declaration of war and shelling of Belgrade, he wrote again, "Stop in Belgrade!"[98] His diplomats and generals held up the note.

A European war, the Kaiser believed and hoped, could still be avoided. He implored his cousin, the Czar, to rescind his order for full mobilization, as Russian mobilization meant German mobilization, and under the Schlieffen Plan, that meant immediate war on France if she did not declare neutrality. And that meant marching through Belgium, which risked war with Britain and her worldwide empire.

The Kaiser wrote George V to accept his proposal that Germany not attack France if she remained neutral in a war with Russia. But when he called in Moltke and ordered him to halt the army's advance to the frontier, a "crushed" Moltke said, "Your Majesty, it cannot be done."[99]

Invoking the great field marshal who had led Prussia to its victories over Austria in 1866 and France in 1870, the Kaiser gave Moltke a cutting reply: "Your uncle would have given me a different answer."[100]

"Wounded," Moltke returned to headquarters and "burst into tears of abject despair . . . I thought my heart would break."[101]

In casting the Kaiser as villain in the tragedy, historians use his crude and bellicose marginal notes on state documents. But these were like the notations Richard Nixon made on his news summaries and muttered in the confidentiality of the Oval Office as the voice-activated tapes were running—fulminations and threats never carried out.

None of the monarchs—Nicholas II, Wilhelm II, George V, or Franz Josef—wanted war. All sensed that the great war, when it came, would imperil the institution of monarchy and prepare the ground for revolution. In the final hours, all four weighed in on the side of peace. But more resolute and harder men had taken charge of affairs.

To those who say the Kaiser's High Seas Fleet was a provocation to Great Britain, were not the Royal Navy's dreadnoughts a provocation? And if France, with a population of 39 million, was maintaining an army the size of Germany's, which had seventy million people, which of the two nations was the more militaristic?[102]

GERMAN WAR AIMS

COULD BRITAIN HAVE DEFENDED her honor and secured her vital interests had she not gone to war when Germany invaded Belgium? In *The Pity of War*, Ferguson argues "yes."

> That Britain could have limited its involvement in a continental war is a possibility which has been all but ignored by historians. . . . Yet it should now be clear that the possibility was a very real one. Asquith and Grey acknowledged this in their memoirs. Both men emphasized that Britain had not been obliged to intervene by any kind of contractual obligation to France. In Asquith's words, "We kept ourselves free to decide, when the occasion arose, whether we should or should not go to war."[103]

If Britain would have been judged dishonorable by not coming to the aid of France, it was only because Grey and Churchill, without the approval of Parliament, had committed her to go to war for France. Grey's reason for tying Britain's destiny to France was fear that a German victory would make Belgium, Holland, and Denmark vassals, give the High Seas Fleet a berth on the Channel coast, and make the Kaiser "supreme over all the Continent of Europe and Asia Minor."[104] "[But] was that really the German objective? Was the Kaiser really Napoleon?" asks Ferguson.[105]

Tuchman portrays the Kaiser on the eve of war as a ruler trapped, searching for a way out of the conflagration he sees coming. When Russia mobilized, the Kaiser went into a tirade against the nation that had conspired against Germany—and against the arch-conspirator, his dead uncle:

> The world will be engulfed in the most terrible of wars, the ultimate aim of which is the ruin of Germany. England, France and Russia have conspired for our annihilation . . . that is the naked truth of the situation which was slowly but surely created by Edward VII. . . . The encirclement of Germany is at last an accomplished fact. We have run our heads into the noose. . . . The dead Edward is stronger than the living I.[106]

On July 31, in the last hours before war, the Kaiser wired his cousins, Czar Nicholas II and King George V, in desperation and near despair:

> It is not I who bears the responsibility for the disaster which now threatens the entire civilized world. Even at this moment the decision to stave it off lies with you. No one threatens the honour and power of Russia. The friendship for you and your empire which I have borne from the deathbed of my grandfather has always been totally sacred to me . . . [T]he peace of Europe can still be maintained by you, if Russia decides to halt the military measures which threaten Germany and Austro-Hungary.[107]

Is this the mind-set of a Bonaparte launching a war of conquest in Europe or a war for world domination? Contrast, if you will, the Kaiser's anguish on the eve of the greatest war in history with the exhilaration of the First Lord of the Admiralty.

The British inner Cabinet, however, had persuaded itself that the Kaiser was a Prussian warmonger out to conquer not only Europe but the world. Here is Cabinet Minister Haldane: "I thought, from my study of the German General Staff, that once the German war party had got into the saddle, it would be war not merely for the overthrow of France or Russia, but for domination of the world."[108] Churchill echoed Haldane, calling the Kaiser a "continental tyrant" whose goal was nothing less than "the dominion of the world."[109]

A quarter of a century later, in *Great Contemporaries*, Churchill would exonerate the Kaiser of plotting a war for European or world hegemony: "[H]istory should incline to the more charitable view and acquit William II of having planned and plotted the World War."[110]

Indeed, how could a country with but a narrow outlet to the North Sea, in the heart of the smallest continent, dominate a world that included France and her overseas territories, the Russian empire, the Ottoman Empire, the United States, Latin America, Japan, China, and a British Empire that encompassed a fourth of the Earth's surface and people?

"Conscious of the shadow of the dead Edward, the Kaiser would have welcomed any way out of the commitment to fight both Russia and France and, behind France, the looming figure of a still-undeclared England," writes Tuchman.[111] On the cusp of war, the Kaiser was in near despair and the German General Staff in near panic to get its armies marching before the nation was crushed between France and Russia. When, a day after Britain declared war, Austria had not yet declared war on France or Russia, "Moltke told Tirpitz . . . that, if Austria continued to shy away, Germany—only days after declaring war—would have to sue for peace on the best terms it could get."[112] On August 6, Vienna finally declared war on Russia.

In his 2007 *History of the English-Speaking Peoples Since 1900*, historian Andrew Roberts, contradicting Churchill, who had concluded the Kaiser blundered into war, insists Wilhelm II had "gargantuan ambitions" and that his High Seas Fleet fleet was "an invasion fleet."[113] Quoting Fromkin on what was at stake in 1914, Roberts writes, "It was about the most important issue in politics: who should rule the world?"[114]

But was it? Was the Kaiser out to "rule the world"?

THE BUTCHER-BIRD OF EUROPE?

IN DEFENSE OF THE declaration of war on Germany, it is yet said that Britain had to save the world from "Prussian militarism"—the relentless drive for world domination of the Teutonic warrior race. Yet, in retrospect, this appears a modern myth not unlike the infamous Black Legend, in which the English once held that only evil emanated from Catholic Spain. Looking back on the century 1815–1914, from Waterloo to the Great War, Germany appears to have been among the least militaristic of European powers.[115]

Nation	Number of Wars
Britain	10
Russia	7
France	5
Austria	3
Germany	3

From 1871 to 1914, the Germans under Bismarck and the Kaiser did not fight a single war. While Britain, Russia, Italy, Turkey, Japan, Spain, and the United States were all involved in wars, Germany and Austria had clean records. And if Germany had not gone to war in forty-three years, and the Kaiser had never gone to war in his twenty-five years on the throne, how can one call Germany—as British statesmen did and British historians still do—the "butcher-bird of Europe"?

In the Seven Years' War, Frederick the Great had been an ally of Pitt. During his reign, 1740–1786, "Prussia spent fewer years at war . . . than any other major European power."[116] In the Napoleonic wars, Prussia had been overrun and almost vanished from the map and Prussians under Field Marshal Gebhard von Blücher had come to Wellington's rescue at Waterloo. In the three wars Prussia fought between 1815 and 1914, the first was provoked by Denmark in 1864 and involved disputed duchies. The second, in 1866 with Austria, over the same duchies, was a "Teutonic" civil war of seven weeks, and a far less bloody affair than our own Civil War. On Bismarck's advice, the King of Prussia left the Habsburg empire intact and denied himself a triumphal parade through Vienna. The third was the Franco-Prussian War of 1870, declared by Napoleon III, who thought he could emulate his great ancestor and march to Berlin.

What were Prussia's territorial gains from the only wars she fought in the century after Waterloo? Two duchies, Schleswig and Holstein, and two provinces, Alsace and Lorraine. Is this the record of a butcher-bird nation hell-bent on world domination?

In 1914, Churchill denounced Wilhelm II as a Prussian warlord out to take over the world. Yet the Kaiser had never fought a war in his twenty-five years in power and he had never seen a battle. In the two Moroccan crises of 1905 and 1911, it was he who had backed down. The German army had never fought the English and indeed had not fought a battle in nearly half a century. Churchill, however, was already a veteran of wars. He had seen action with Sir Bindon Blood on the Northwest Frontier. He had ridden with Kitchener's cavalry in the massacre of the Dervishes at Omdurman in the Sudan. He had been captured riding in an armored train in the first days of the Boer War, been held as a POW, escaped, and then marched with the British army to the relief of Ladysmith. Britain had engaged in many more wars than Germany in the century before Sarajevo, and Churchill had himself seen more war than almost any soldier in the German army.

THE "SEPTEMBER PROGRAMME"

TRUE, WHEN GERMANY APPEARED to be on the road to swift victory, Bethmann-Hollweg issued his September Programme, which called for the annexation of the northeast coast of France. But the Programme was put out only after Britain had declared war. No historian has found any German plan or official document dated prior to August 1, 1914, that called for the annexation of Belgian or French territory.

As for Sir Roy Denman's point—"The High Seas Fleet based on the Channel ports would have been for Britain an unacceptable danger"—had Britain demanded guarantees of no German naval bases on the Channel coast, Bethmann and Moltke would readily have given them.[117] The Royal Navy could have guaranteed it, as the war demonstrated, when the German fleet left Kiel only once, for the Battle of Jutland. Germany had nothing to gain from war with Britain and much to lose should Britain blockade her, sink her merchant fleet, seize her colonies, and bring the empire in against her. "Had Britain, in fact, stayed out, it would have been foolish [for Germany] to have reneged on such a bargain."[118]

In the hours before war, Bethmann secretly suggested to Grey that, in return for British neutrality, Germany would agree not to annex any French territory and respect Holland's neutrality. Grey, secretly committed to fight for France, dismissed the proposal as "impossible & disgraceful," so great an act of dishonor "the good name of this country would never recover."[119]

Yet Britain had stood aside in 1870 as Prussia invaded France.

What were the other war aims of the September Programme?

A) A war indemnity from France for fifteen or twenty years to prevent her rearmament and a commercial treaty giving German products equal access to French markets.

B) An economic association of France, Belgium, Holland, Denmark, Austria-Hungary, Poland, and perhaps Italy, Sweden, and

Norway, led by Germany; a customs union, not a political union.[120] Fifteen years earlier, the Kaiser had proposed a United States of Europe to challenge America for world economic supremacy.[121]

C) Cession to Germany of territories to enable her to unite her African colonies into a single bloc.

D) A Holland independent, but united economically with Germany, and perhaps a defensive alliance.

E) Poland and the Baltic states to be extracted from Russia with Poland becoming independent. The Baltic states would either be given independence or be annexed by Germany or Poland.

"[E]ven in anticipating a military victory," writes American historian David Calleo, "Germany's actual territorial expansion in Europe was to be relatively modest."[122] Would these war aims have posed a threat to Britain?

"Did they imply a Napoleonic strategy?" asks Ferguson.[123]

"Hardly. All the economic clauses of the September Programme implied was the creation—some eighty years early, it might be said—of a German-dominated European customs union. . . . Germany's European project was not one with which Britain, with her maritime empire intact, could not have lived."[124]

> German objectives, had Britain remained out, would not in fact have posed a direct threat to the Empire; the reduction of Russian power in Eastern Europe, the creation of a Central European Customs Union, and acquisition of French colonies—these were all goals that were complementary to British interests.[125]

Instead, Britain declared war, a war that would last fifty-one months and consume the lives of 702,000 British soldiers and 200,000 more from the Dominions, India, and Africa, with twice as many wounded or crippled.[126]

What would have happened if Britain had declared neutrality and stayed out? The Germans would have triumphed in France as in 1870 or there would have been a stalemate and armistice. The United States would not have come in. No American or British soldiers and many fewer French and Germans would have died. A victorious Kaiser would have taken some French colonies in Africa, which would have replaced one British colonial rival with another. The Germans would have gone home victorious, as they did in 1871.

Russia would still have been defeated, but the dismantling of Russia's empire was in Britain's national interest. Let the Germans pay the cost, take the casualties, and accept the eternal enmity for breaking it up. A triumphant Germany would have faced resentful enemies in both France and Russia and rebellious Slavs to the south. This would have presented no problem for the British Empire. The Germans would have become the dominant power in Europe, with the British dominant on the oceans, America dominant in the Western Hemisphere, and Britain's ally, Japan, dominant in Asia.

Before August 1914, Lenin had been living in a garret in Geneva. In 1917, as the Romanov dynasty was falling and Russia seemed on the verge of chaos, the German General Staff transported Lenin in a sealed train across Germany. Their hope was for revolutionary chaos in Russia that might force St. Petersburg to sue for peace. Had Britain not declared war, the war would not have lasted until 1917— and Lenin would likely have died unmourned in Geneva. And had the Bolsheviks still come to power in Russia, a victorious German army would have marched in and made short work of them.

Germany, as the most powerful nation in Europe, aligned with a free Poland that owed its existence to Germany, would have been the western bulwark against any Russian drive into Europe. There would have been no Hitler and no Stalin. Other evils would have arisen, but how could the first half of the twentieth century have produced more evil than it did?

Had Sir Edward revealed to the Cabinet his secret discussions with France and the moral commitments they implied—that Britain must go to war if France were invaded—his policy would have been rejected by the Cabinet and repudiated by Parliament. Churchill later admitted as much:

> [If in 1912] the Foreign Secretary had, in cold blood, proposed a formal alliance with France and Russia . . . the Cabinet of the day would never have agreed to it. I doubt if four ministers would have agreed to it. But if the Cabinet had been united upon it, the House of Commons would not have accepted their guidance. Therefore the Foreign Minister would have had to resign. The policy which he had advocated would have stood condemned and perhaps violently repudiated; and upon that repudiation would have come an absolute veto upon all those informal preparations and noncommittal discussions on which the defense power of the Triple Entente was erected.[127]

"No bargain had been entered into," wrote Churchill, but "We were morally committed to France."[128] Churchill concedes that he and Grey were morally committed to a war they knew the Cabinet and Parliament opposed. "In other words," concludes historian Jim Powell, "Churchill believed that if Grey had operated openly, Britain might not have been able to get into the war!"[129] As Francis Neilson, who had resigned from the House over the war, wrote, both "Bonar Law and Austen Chamberlain said after the First World War—that if Grey's commitments had been laid before the House, they doubted whether . . . [the war] would have taken place."[130]

The importance of Grey's secret collusion with France is difficult to overstate. Had he been open with the Cabinet and sought to persuade them of the necessity of committing Britain to France, they would have rejected his alliance. France and Russia, knowing that they could not rely on the British to fight beside them, would have been far more disposed to compromise in the Balkan crisis of July 1914. By secretly committing Britain to war for France, Grey, Churchill, and Asquith left the Kaiser and German Chancellor in the dark, unaware a war with France meant war with the British Empire. Had he known, the Kaiser would have made his belated effort to abort a war far sooner and more successfully. Churchill concedes it in *The World Crisis:* "[O]ur Entente with France and the [secret] military and naval conversations that had taken place since 1906 had led us into a position where we had all the obligations of an alliance without its advantages."[131]

Adds Neilson, "[I]f Balfour had been in power, they would have made no secret of the understanding with France and Russia and there would have been no war."[132] "We went to war," said Lord Loreburn, "because we were tied to France in the dark."[133]

An anecdote related by British naval historian Russell Grenfell in his *Unconditional Hatred* has about it the ring of historical truth:

> British embroilment in the war of 1914–18 may be said to date from January 1906, when Britain was in the throes of a General Election. Mr. Haldane, the Secretary of State for War, had gone to the constituency of Sir Edward Grey, the Foreign Secretary, to make an electioneering speech in his support. The two politicians went for a country drive together, during which Grey asked Haldane if he would initiate discussions between the British and French General staffs in preparation for the possibility of joint action in the event of a Continental war. Mr. Haldane agreed to do so. The million men who were later to be killed as a result of this rural conversation could not have been condemned to death in more haphazard a fashion. At this moment not even the Prime Minister, Sir Henry Campbell-Bannerman, let alone other members of the Cabinet, knew what was being arranged.[134]

"WINSTON IS BECOMING A REAL DANGER"

EVEN FRIENDLY BIOGRAPHERS AND memoirists seem astonished by Winston Churchill's lust for war in 1914. "Amid the gathering storm," writes Roy Jenkins, "Churchill was a consistent force for intervention and ultimately for war."[135] Lord Morley, Gladstone's biographer, spoke of the "daemonic energy" of "that splendid condottiere at the Admiralty."[136]

From the first inkling that war might come, Churchill acted like a war leader. He was decisive, unconflicted, resolute. Hearing a Turkish crew was about to take possession of two dreadnoughts ordered from British shipyards, he "requisitioned" the ships and ordered their Turkish crews repelled "by armed force if necessary," should they attempt to board.[137]

In 1911, the Turks had sounded out Great Britain on an alliance, but Churchill, "with the arrogance of his class in that time, had replied that they had ideas above their station."[138] He warned the Turks "not to alienate Britain which 'alone among European states . . . retains supremacy of the sea.' "[139] Churchill's insults would prove costly. On August 2, Germany and Turkey signed a secret alliance and in 1915 Turkish troops inflicted on British and Anzac troops at Gallipoli one of the greatest Allied defeats of the war. Churchill's affront to the Turks was "an almost unbelievable act," writes William Manchester, that tore down "a British bulwark and thereby set the stage for a disaster whose chief victim would be he himself."[140]

On August 1, Churchill had requested the Cabinet's authorization to mobilize the fleet. The Cabinet refused. Late that evening, learning of Germany's declaration of war on Russia, Churchill went to 10 Downing Street to tell Asquith he was calling up reservists and ordering the Royal Navy onto a war footing, unless ordered otherwise. Asquith, bound by the Cabinet decision, "simply looked at me and said no word. . . . I then walked back to the Admiralty across the Parade Ground and gave the order."[141]

On learning the 23,000-ton German battle cruiser *Goeben* was in the Mediterranean, Churchill ordered British warships to hunt her down and prepare to attack. "Winston, who has got on all his war paint, is longing for a sea fight in the early hours of tomorrow morning, resulting in the sinking of the *Goeben*," Asquith wrote on August 4, "the whole thing fills me with sadness."[142] When a British diplomat discovered *Goeben* in Taranto harbor, the First Lord was tempted to order her sunk before the 11 P.M. ultimatum expired. Churchill feared *Goeben* would slip away in the dark. She did. After war was declared, he would cross the Channel to discuss tactics and strategy with field commanders, prompting Lloyd George to remark, "Our greatest danger is incompetent English junkers. Winston is becoming a great danger."[143]

Churchill's Cabinet colleagues were both awed and repelled by his lust for war. On September 14, Asquith wrote to Venetia Stanley, "I am almost inclined to shiver, when I hear Winston say that the last thing he would pray for is Peace."[144] Yet, that same month, Grey wrote to Clementine, "I can't tell you how much I admire his courage & gallant spirit & genius for war."[145]

In January of 1915, half a year into the war, with tens of thousands of British soldiers already in their graves, including his own friends, Churchill, according to Margot Asquith's diary account, waxed ecstatic about the war and his historic role in it:

> My God! This is living History. Everything we are doing and saying is thrilling—it will be read by a thousand generations, think of that! Why I would not be out of this glorious delicious war for anything the world could give me (eyes glowing but with a slight anxiety lest the word "delicious" should jar on me).[146]

Consider the change that had taken place in the character of the First Lord, now relishing "this glorious delicious war," from the twenty-six-year-old MP who had stood with his late father against the folly of excessive armaments. Said young Churchill to the House of Commons in May 1901:

> A European war cannot be anything but a cruel, heart-rending struggle, which, if we are ever to enjoy the bitter fruits of victory, must demand, perhaps for several years, the whole manhood of the nation, the entire suspension of peaceful industries, and the concentration to one end of every vital energy of the community [and] can only end in the ruin of the vanquished and the scarcely less fatal commercial dislocation and exhaustion of the conquerors. Democracy is more vindictive than Cabinets. The wars of peoples will be more terrible than the wars of kings. . . .[147]

Churchill was unafraid to break the rules of war. As he had been prepared to blockade Antwerp before the Germans invaded, so he brushed aside international law, mined the North Sea, and imposed upon Germany a starvation blockade that violated all previous norms of civilized warfare. In the war's first week, Churchill had wanted to occupy Ameland, one of the Dutch Frisian Islands, though Holland was neutral. To Churchill, writes Martin Gilbert, "Dutch neutrality need be no obstacle."[148]

Churchill urged a blockade of the Dardanelles while Turkey was still neutral. In December 1914, he recommended that the Royal Navy seize the Danish island of Bornholm, though Denmark, too, was neutral. Yet it had been Berlin's violation of Belgium's neutrality that Churchill invoked as a moral outrage to convince Lloyd George to support war on Germany and that had brought the British people around to support war.

When the Germans accommodated Britain's war party by regarding the 1839 treaty as a "scrap of paper," the relief of Grey and Churchill must have been immense. The declaration of war was their triumph. And when British divisions crossed the Channel, the troops were sent, as the secret war plans dictated, not to brave little Belgium but straight to France.

How did the American people see the war in Europe?

"On August 5 the British Navy dredged up and cut the German cables, and on August 6 there was not a single Berlin or Vienna dateline from the American press."[149] The First Lord had made certain the British would decide how the Americans viewed their war.

CHAPTER 3

"A Poisonous Spirit of Revenge"

INJUSTICE, ARROGANCE, DISPLAYED in the hour of
triumph will never be forgotten or forgiven.[1]
— LLOYD GEORGE, 1919

Those three all-powerful, all-ignorant men . . . sitting
there carving continents with only a child to lead them.[2]
— ARTHUR BALFOUR

AS WELLINGTON SAID of Waterloo, it had been a "damn near-run thing." After the Italian rout at Caporetto and the defeat of Rumania and Russia, a million German soldiers had been released in 1918 to join their comrades on the Western Front for the last great German offensive of the war. By April, Ludendorff's armies were back on the Marne and Field Marshal Sir Douglas Haig was issuing his order recalling Nelson at Trafalgar: "With our backs to the wall, and believing in the justice of our cause, each of us must fight on to the end. . . . Every position must be held to the last man: there must be no retirement."[3]

In the end, the Americans proved decisive. By spring 1918, 300,000 doughboys were in France; by summer, 1,000,000. With Yanks moving into the front lines at 250,000 a month, German morale sank and the German lines buckled.

On October 5, 1918, Prince Max of Baden sounded out President Wilson on a peace based on the Fourteen Points he had laid out in January. Three days later, Wilson asked Prince Max if Germany would accept the points. On October 12, Prince Max gave assurances that his object in "entering into discussions would be only to agree upon practical details for the application" of the Fourteen Points to a treaty of peace.[4]

Wilson now began to add conditions. Safeguards must be provided to guarantee Allied "military supremacy" and a democratic and representative government must be established.[5] Prince Max agreed. The Kaiser had to go. On October 23, Wilson took the German offer to the Allies.

The British and French, after four years of bloodletting that had cost them together two million dead and six million wounded, balked at Wilson's mild terms. Under a threat from Colonel House of a separate peace, Prime Minister Lloyd George went along, with one reservation. Britain could not agree to the second of Wilson's points: freedom of the seas. The Royal Navy must be free to do whatever necessary to protect the empire. France succeeded in inserting a claim to full compensation "for all damage done to the civilian population of the Allies and their property by the aggression of Germany by land, by sea, and from the air."[6]

Matthias Erzberger, the leader of the Catholic Center Party who had urged fellow Germans to agree to an armistice, was given the thankless task of meeting Marshal Ferdinand Foch, the Allied Supreme Commander, and signing the armistice in a railway carriage in Compiègne Forest on November 11, 1918. Erzberger would be assassinated in the Black Forest in 1921 for the "crime of November 11."[7]

"HANG THE KAISER!"

IN GREAT BRITAIN, a "khaki election" was called by the government to exploit the triumph of British arms and war's end, as the Unionists had done in the first khaki election in 1900, when Joe Chamberlain had campaigned on the slogan "A seat lost to the Government is a seat won by the Boers."[8]

In echo of Wilson, Lloyd George began his campaign November 12, one day after the armistice, with a statesmanlike call for a magnanimous peace.

> We must not allow any sense of revenge, any spirit of greed, any grasping desire to over-rule the fundamental principles of righteousness. Vigorous demands will be made to hector and bully the Government in the endeavour to make them depart from the strict principles of right and to satisfy some base, sordid, squalid idea of vengeance and avarice. We must relentlessly set our faces against that.[9]

Lloyd George had misread the mood of his country and of press baron Alfred Lord Northcliffe, the Napoleon of Fleet Street whom he had denied a place on the delegation to the peace conference. Whipped up by Northcliffe's papers, the public rejected such noble sentiments and took up the cry "Hang the Kaiser!" Ever attentive to popular opinion, Lloyd George was soon pledging to bring home a peace in which Germany would be made to pay the "full cost of the war." They will pay to the utmost farthing, he roared to one crowd; "we will search their pockets for it."[10]

"Squeeze the lemon until the pips squeak!" was the theme of one Liberal candidate. The Parliament elected that December that gave Lloyd George a majority of 340, the greatest in British history, has been described as "one of the most insular, reactionary and benighted in the annals of Westminster," made up, said Stanley Baldwin, of "hard-faced men who look as if they had done well out of the war."[11]

From the House of Commons to Lloyd George came a "Round Robin" letter signed by 237 coalition members, a "vengeance telegram," demanding "the utmost severity for Germany."[12] The signers wanted every last pound of German flesh. Among its chief sponsors was the MP for the Ripon Division of Yorkshire, Edward Frederick Lindley Wood. A generation later, "Major Wood," now Lord Halifax, would be the foreign minister forced to deal with the consequences of the punitive peace he and his colleagues had demanded.

The khaki election of 1918 and the peace of vengeance British voters demanded that Lloyd George bring home validate the insight of George Kennan: "[S]uffering does not always make men better. . . . [P]eople are not always more reasonable than governments . . . [P]ublic opinion . . . is not invariably a moderating force in the jungle of politics."[13]

Arriving in Paris with a mandate for no mercy, Lloyd George found his resolve to impose a harsh peace more than matched by Georges Clemenceau, "the Tiger of France," whose ravaged nation had lost 1.3 million of its sons.

> The Tiger had one great love—France; and one great hate—Germany. As a young man of twenty-nine he had seen Paris under the heel of the German invader, and the smoke billowing up from the brutal burning of the palace at St. Cloud. As an old man of seventy-two, he had seen the gray German hosts pour into his beloved France. He was determined that it should not happen again. Motivated though he was by this great hate, he was not so vindictive as Marshal Foch or President Poincaré.[14]

Clemenceau was determined to impose on "le Boche" a treaty that would so cripple Germany she could never menace France again. His fear and hatred were caught in a remark attributed to him: "There are twenty million Germans too many."[15]

"HELL'S DIRTIEST WORK"

"DEMOCRACY IS MORE VINDICTIVE than Cabinets," Churchill had told the Parliament in 1901. "The wars of peoples will be more terrible than those of kings."[16] The twentieth century would make a prophet of the twenty-six-year-old MP. And the peace the peoples demanded and got in 1919 would prove more savage, for, wrote one historian, "it was easier for despotic monarchs to forget their hatreds than for democratic statesmen or peoples."[17]

At the Congress of Vienna in 1815, Napoleon's foreign minister Talleyrand had sat with Castlereagh of England, Metternich of Austria, Alexander I of Russia, and Frederick William III of Prussia, the coalition that had destroyed Napoleon's empire, to create a new structure of peace. At Brest-Litovsk in 1918, Germans and Russians had negotiated the terms. But though Germany's fate was to be decided, no German had been invited, for the Allies had come to Paris to punish them as the guilty nation responsible for destroying the peace.

"We have no quarrel with the German people. We have no feeling towards them but one of sympathy and friendship. It was not upon their impulse that their government acted in entering upon this war," Wilson had said on April 2, 1917, as America entered the war.[18] By 1919, Wilson had concluded that people were "responsible for the acts of their government."[19]

When German representatives were summoned to Paris to receive the terms of the Allies, they were stunned at the amputations to be forced upon them. Eupen and Malmédy were to be taken from Germany and given to Belgium. Alsace and Lorraine were to be reannexed by France.

Clemenceau wanted to annex the Saar but Wilson balked. The Saar was placed under the League of Nations—de facto French control—and its coal mines given to France. The 650,000 Germans of the Saar were granted the right, in fifteen years, to vote on whether they wished to return to Germany. Should they so decide, Germany must buy her mines back. In Schleswig, a plebiscite was to be held to divide the land with Denmark.

The East Prussian port of Memel was seized by Lithuania.

Only on the insistence of Lloyd George, who reportedly said he would no more transfer Upper Silesia to the Poles "than he would give a clock to a monkey," was a plebiscite held in those lands that had been under German sovereignty for centuries.[20] In the plebiscite, 60 percent of the people voted to stay with Germany, but five-sixths of the industrial area and almost all the mines were ceded to Warsaw. A disgusted British observer, Sir Robert Donald, called the plebiscite a "tragic farce" and the stripping of Upper Silesia from Germany "robbery under arms."[21]

The Hanseatic League port city of Danzig, German for centuries, was declared a Free City and placed under League of Nations administration and Polish control. East Prussia was separated from Germany by a "Polish Corridor" that put a million Germans under Warsaw's rule.

Versailles stripped from Germany one-tenth of her people and one-eighth of her territory. Germany's overseas empire, the third largest on Earth, was wholly confiscated. All private property of German citizens in German colonies was declared forfeit. Japan was awarded the German concession in Shantung and all German islands north of the Equator. The German islands south of the Equator went to New Zealand and Australia. Germany's African colonies were divided among South Africa, Britain, and France. Germany's rivers were internationalized and she was forced to open her home market to Allied imports, but denied equal access to Allied markets.

Territories cut away, colonies gone, Germany was to have her limbs broken so she could never fight again. Germany was forbidden ever again to build armored cars, tanks, heavy artillery, submarines, or an air force. The High Seas Fleet was seized as war booty, as was the German merchant fleet. Her navy was to consist of six small battleships, six light cruisers, twelve destroyers, and twelve torpedo boats. The General Staff was abolished and the army restricted to one hundred thousand men. Germany was to remain forever naked to her enemies.

Goaded on by Lord Northcliffe's newspapers, Lloyd George made good on his pledge that Germany be made to bear the full cost of the war—to include the pensions of Allied soldiers. But Wilson's public pledge of no indemnities had first to be circumvented. And someone else would have to persuade Wilson, for the president had come to detest Lloyd George.

"Mr. Prime Minister, you make me sick!" the president blurted, after listening to another shift of position by the "Welsh witch" of John Maynard Keynes's depiction.[22] Keynes, who was with the British delegation, would return home to write *The Economic Consequences of the Peace*, the savage book charging the Allied leaders with having crafted a vindictive peace that must, by crushing Germany with debt, set the stage for a new war.

The British were behind this scheme to include pensions. For as the damage done to the British Isles by air or naval attack was minimal, and the confiscation of Germany's merchant ships had replaced British losses at sea, Britain was entitled to perhaps 1 percent or 2 percent of reparations. If Germany could be made to pay the pensions of millions of British soldiers, however, Britain's share of reparations could soar to more than 20 percent. Including pensions would also triple the reparations bill for Germany.

Lloyd George enlisted South Africa's Jan Smuts, a lawyer one historian calls "the great operator of fraudulent idealism," to persuade Wilson that forcing Germany to fund the pensions of Allied soldiers would not violate his pledge to limit reparations to civilian damage done in the war.[23] An outraged U.S. delegation implored Wilson to veto the reparations bill, arguing that it did not follow logically from any of his Fourteen Points.

"Logic, logic, I don't give a damn about logic," Wilson snarled. "I am going to include pensions."[24] Henry White, one of five members of the official U.S. delegation, reflected the dejection and disillusionment idealistic Americans felt: "We had such high hopes of this adventure; we believed God called us and now we are doing hell's dirtiest work."[25]

In 1920, the Allies would set the final bill for reparations at thirty-two billion gold marks, an impossible sum. Under Article 231 of the treaty, the "war guilt clause," Germany was forced to confess to and accept full responsibility for causing the war and all the damage done. Under Article 227, the Kaiser was declared a war criminal to be arrested and prosecuted.

Forcing the Germans to confess to a historic crime and agree to a lie—that they alone were to blame for the war—was as foolish as it was unjust. Though the Kaiser had been bellicose throughout his reign, by 1914 he had been in power twenty-five years and never fought a war. In the two Moroccan crises, it was he who had backed down. Though he had foolishly given the Austrians a blank check to act against Serbia, when the Austrian archduke was murdered by Serb nationalists on June 28, 1914, by the last days of July, no monarch in Europe was trying more desperately to arrest Europe's plunge to war.

The effect on the German psyche of forcing the nation to confess to a crime Germans did not believe they had committed was poisonous:

> There is no better way to generate hatred than by forcing a person to sign a confession of guilt which he is sacredly convinced is untrue. The wanton humiliation, unprecedented up to that time in the annals of Christendom, created the thirst for revenge which the National Socialists so cleverly exploited.[26]

"The forced admission of German war guilt in the Treaty of Versailles would have been a colossal political blunder even if it had been true: and it was not true,"[27] adds British historian Russell Grenfell.

Today, men do not appreciate what Versailles meant to the Germans, who, triumphant in the east, believed they had laid down their arms and accepted an armistice and peace in the west based on Wilson's Fourteen Points. British Labour leader Sir Roy Denman offers this analogy:

> These terms are difficult to bring home to British readers. But, supposing that Britain had lost the U-boat war in 1917 and Germany had imposed an equivalent peace; it could have meant British recognition that its policy of encirclement [of Germany] had caused the war; confiscation of British colonies and the British merchant fleet; Dover and Portsmouth occupied; the Royal Navy reduced to half a dozen destroyers; south-east England demilitarised; Liverpool a free port, with a corridor under German rule to Harwich; crippling reparations. No post-war British government would have accepted this indefinitely.[28]

THE STARVATION BLOCKADE

WHY DID THE GERMANS SIGN?

Germany faced invasion and death by starvation if she refused. With her merchant ships and even Baltic fishing boats sequestered, and the blockade still in force, Germany could not feed her people. When Berlin asked permission to buy 2.5 million tons of food, the request was denied. From November 11 through the peace conference, the blockade was maintained. Before going to war, America had denounced as a violation of international law and human decency the British blockade that had kept the vital necessities of life out of neutral ports if there were any chance the goods could be transshipped to Germany. But when America declared war, a U.S. admiral told Lord Balfour, "You will find that it will take us only two months to become as great criminals as you are."[29]

U.S. warships now supported the blockade. "Once lead this people into war," Wilson had said in 1917, "and they'll forget there

THE SUCCESS OF CHURCHILL'S STARVATION BLOCKADE

SWEDEN

DENMARK

North
Sea

Baltic
Sea

Kiel
Lübeck
Barnbeck
Messberg
Hamburg

Bremen

NETH.

Charlottenburg   Berlin
Hanover   Brunswick
Munster   Magdeburg
Posen

Essen
Halle Saale
Duisburg
Leipzig
Dresden
Breslau
Dusseldorf
GERMANY
Aachen   Jena   Chemnitz
Cologne
Coblenz

BELG.   Frankfurt

AUSTRIA-HUNGARY

LUX.

Rhine R.

Stuttgart

FRANCE   Nurnberg

Colmar   Munich

Number of deaths attributed to the blockade:	
1915	88,235
1916	121,114
1917	259,627
1918	293,760

SWITZERLAND

ITALY

• Cities in which food riots broke out during 1916

"We are enforcing the blockade with rigour, and Germany is near starvation." —Winston Churchill, to Parliament, March 3, 1919, four months after Germany had signed the Armistice

0 Miles   100   200
0 Kilometers   200

© 2008 Jeffrey L. Ward

ever was such a thing as tolerance."[30] America had forgotten. The blockade was responsible for the deaths of thousands of men, women, and children after the Germans laid down their weapons and surrendered their warships. Its architect and chief advocate had been the First Lord of the Admiralty. His aim, said Churchill, was to "starve the whole population—men, women, and children, old and young, wounded and sound—into submission."[31] On March 3, 1919, four months after Germany accepted an armistice and laid down her arms, Churchill rose exultant in the Commons to declare, "We are enforcing the blockade with rigour, and Germany is very near starvation."[32]

Five days later, the *Daily News* wrote, "The birthrate in the great towns [of Germany] has changed places with the death rate. It is tolerably certain that more people have died among the civil population from the direct effects of the war than have died on the battlefield."[33]

Even the entreaties of "brave little Belgium" for whom the British had gone to war fell on deaf ears. Herbert Hoover, who would be credited with saving a starving Belgium, "spent as much time arguing with the British as with the Germans about getting food to the Belgians," writes U.S. historian Thomas Fleming.

> The "poor little Belgium" of British propaganda meant little to the British admirals and bureaucrats who were sure the Germans would make off with the victuals. . . . Churchill, who favored letting the Belgians starve and blaming the Germans, called Hoover "a son of a bitch."[34]

Americans "have been brought up not to kick a man in the stomach after we have licked him," said Hoover. "We have not been fighting women and children and we are not beginning now."[35] Put in charge of all relief efforts, Hoover wanted to feed the starving Germans. Congress refused.

In February 1919, Congress appropriated $100 million for food, but Germany was not to get a loaf of bread or a bowl of soup.[36] So severe was the suffering that, on March 10, the British Commander on the Rhine publicly urged that food be sent to the population as the specter of starving children was damaging the morale of his troops. General Sir Herbert Plumer's letter was read to the Big Three in Paris:

> Please inform the Prime Minister that in my opinion food must be sent into this area by the Allies without delay. . . . The mortality amongst women, children, and sick is most grave and sickness due to hunger is spreading. The attitude of the population is becoming one of despair, and the people feel that an end by bullets is preferable to death by starvation.[37]

His troops, said General Plumer, could no longer stand the sight of "hordes of skinny and bloated children pawing over the offal from British cantonments."[38] Pope Benedict XV's plea for an end to the blockade was ignored. One visitor to Germany who witnessed it all wrote:

> The starvation is done quietly and decently at home. And when death comes, it comes in the form of influenza, tuberculosis, heart failure or one of the new and mysterious diseases caused by the war and carries off its exhausted victims. In Frankfurt, even as late as March 1920, the funerals never ceased all day.[39]

In 1938, a British diplomat in Germany was asked repeatedly, "Why did England go on starving our women and children long after the Armistice?"[40] "Freedom and Bread" would become a powerful slogan in the ascent to power of the new National Socialist Workers Party.

Decades later, Hoover, a former president and senior statesman, was still decrying the post-Armistice "food blockade" of Germany as "a wicked thrust of Allied militarism and punishment" that constituted "a black chapter in human history."[41]

"Nations can take philosophically the hardships of war. But when they lay down their arms and surrender on assurances that they may have food for their women and children, and then find that this worst instrument of attack on them is maintained—then hate never dies."[42]

"BEASTS THEY ARE"

ON MAY 7, 1919, at Trianon Palace Hotel, Clemenceau, Wilson beside him, handed the Germans the terms of peace: "The hour has struck for the weighty settlement of your account," said Clemenceau. "You have asked for peace. We are ready to give you peace."[43]

As the German foreign minister Ulrich von Brockdorff-Rantzau read his reply to Clemenceau, he refused to stand:

> We can feel all the power of hate we must encounter in this assembly. . . . It is demanded of us that we admit ourselves to be the only ones guilty of this war. Such a confession in my mouth would be a lie. We are far from declining any responsibility for this great world war . . . but we deny that Germany and its people were alone guilty. The hundreds of thousands of non-combatants who have perished since 11 November by reason of the blockade were killed with cold blood after our adversaries had conquered and victory had been assured to them. Think of that when you speak of guilt and punishment.[44]

When he heard this bristling German defiance, "Clemenceau's face turned magenta."[45] Lloyd George snapped the ivory paper knife he was holding and said, "It is hard to have won the war and to have to listen to that."[46]

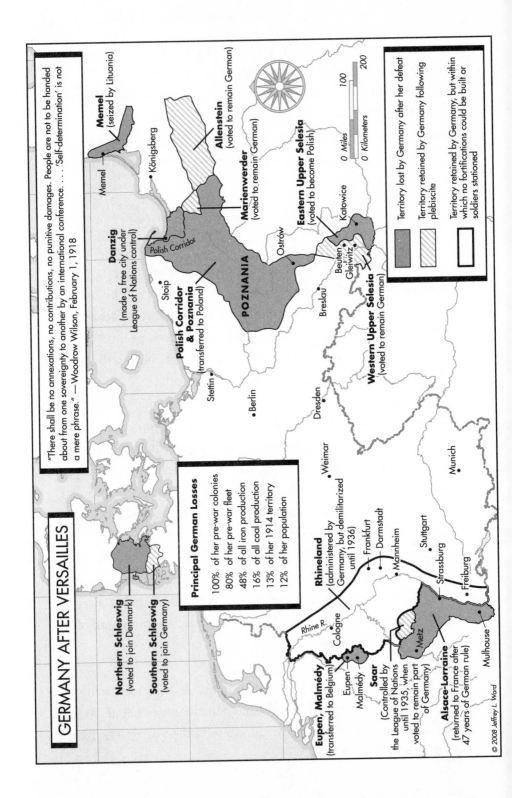

GERMANY AFTER VERSAILLES

Northern Schleswig
(voted to join Denmark)

Southern Schleswig
(voted to join Germany)

"There shall be no annexations, no contributions, no punitive damages. People are not to be handed about from one sovereignty to another by an international conference. . . . 'Self-determination' is not a mere phrase." —Woodrow Wilson, February 1, 1918

Memel
(seized by Lithuania)

Memel

Königsberg

Danzig
(made a free city under League of Nations control)

Polish Corridor

Allenstein
(voted to remain German)

Marienwerder
(voted to remain German)

Polish Corridor & Poznania
(transferred to Poland)

Stoip

Stettin

POZNANIA

Ostrow

Breslau

Eastern Upper Selesia
(voted to become Polish)

Katowice

Beuten
Gleiwitz

Western Upper Selesia
(voted to remain German)

Berlin

Dresden

Weimar

Principal German Losses

100% of her pre-war colonies
80% of her pre-war fleet
48% of all iron production
16% of all coal production
13% of her 1914 territory
12% of her population

Rhineland
(administered by Germany, but demilitarized until 1936)

Frankfurt
Darmstadt

Mannheim

Stuttgart

Strassburg

Freiburg

Munich

Rhine R.

Cologne

Eupen, Malmédy
(transferred to Belgium)

Eupen
Malmédy

Saar
(Controlled by the League of Nations until 1935, when voted to remain part of Germany)

Metz

Alsace-Lorraine
(returned to France after 47 years of German rule)

Mulhouse

0 Miles   100

0 Kilometers   200

Territory lost by Germany after her defeat

Territory retained by Germany following plebiscite

Territory retained by Germany, but within which no fortifications could be built or soldiers stationed

© 2008 Jeffrey L. Ward

Wilson exploded. "What abominable manners . . . the Germans are really a stupid people."[47] "Isn't it just like them?" he whispered to Lloyd George.[48] Said Balfour, "Beasts they were, and beasts they are."[49]

Still, the Germans refused to sign. "What hand would not wither that binds itself and us in these fetters?" said Chancellor Philip Scheidemann.[50] He resigned his office.

But with families starving, Bolshevik uprisings in Munich, Cologne, Berlin, and Budapest, Trotsky's Red Army driving into Europe, Czechs and Poles ready to strike from the east, and Foch preparing to march on Berlin at the head of an American-British-French army, Germany capitulated.

Five years to the day after Gavrilo Princip shot the archduke and his wife in Sarajevo, German delegates signed what Wilson had promised his countrymen would be "peace without victory."

"A huge crowd and two German delegates led like felons into the room to sign their doom" was how an American observer in the Hall of Mirrors that day described it. "[I]t was like the execution of a sentence."[51] The *New York Times's* Charles Selden wrote, "[T]he stillest three minutes ever lived through were those in which the German delegates signed the Peace Treaty today."[52]

The same day, June 28, "the government of the new 'Czechoslovak Democracy' sent a wire to the leaders of Yugoslavia congratulating them on the anniversary of the Sarajevo murder of the archduke and his wife and expressing their hopes of 'similar heroic deeds in the future.' "[53]

By forcing German democrats to sign the Treaty of Versailles, which disarmed, divided, and disassembled the nation Bismarck had built, the Allies had discredited German democracy at its birth.

At Scapa Flow, naval base of the Grand Fleet in the Orkneys, northeast of Scotland, where the High Seas Fleet had been interned, Adm. Ludwig von Reuter, rather than surrender his warships, ordered them scuttled. With a signal from the flagship at noon on June 19,

German sailors pulled the sea cocks, sending ten battleships, nine armored cruisers, eight heavy cruisers, fifty torpedo boats, and one hundred submarines to the bottom.[54] As the unarmed German sailors fled in lifeboats, they were fired on by enraged British sailors.[55] Not until July 12, 1919, did the Allies fully lift the starvation blockade. When Admiral von Reuter returned to Wilhelmshaven in 1920, thousands of Germans thronged the docks to hail him as "the last hero" of the High Seas Fleet.

The Germans felt utterly betrayed—and blamed America.

"President Wilson is a hypocrite and the Versailles Treaty is the vilest crime in history," said the social democrat Scheidemann, who had brought down his government rather than sign.[56] "If these are the peace terms, then America can go to hell," said General Ludendorff.[57]

Men who believe in the rule of law believe in the sanctity of contract. But a contract in which one party is not allowed to be heard and is forced to sign at the point of a gun is invalid. Germany signed the Treaty of Versailles only when threatened that, should she refuse, the country would be invaded and her people further starved.

Though Napoleon's foreign minister Talleyrand had been invited to Vienna to negotiate the peace of Europe, no German had been invited to Paris. Francesco Nitti, the prime minister of Italy when Versailles was signed, in his book *The Wreck of Europe*, expressed his disgust at the injustice.

> In the old canon law of the Church it was laid down that everyone must have a hearing, even the devil: *Etiam diabolus audiatur* (Even the devil has the right to be heard). But the new democracy, which proposed to install the society of the nations, did not even obey the precepts which the dark Middle Ages held sacred on behalf of the accused.[58]

From the hour of signature, the Germans never felt bound. Said *Vorwarts*, the unofficial voice of Berlin, "We must never forget it is only a scrap of paper. Treaties based on violence can keep their validity only so long as force exists. Do not lose hope. The resurrection day comes."[59]

THE RHINELAND

LLOYD GEORGE HAD WANTED a peace that would enlarge the empire, satisfy Northcliffe, have the Jingoes cheering him in the House, and eliminate Germany as a commercial rival and world power. He got it all: the High Seas Fleet, the Kaiser's colonies, the German merchant marine, the promise of full reparations. He could afford to appear magnanimous.

But France had lost 1,375,000 soldiers and millions more were wounded, maimed, or crippled. She demanded full compensation for the ruination of a fourth of the country and terms of peace that would guarantee that Germans would never again attempt what they had done in 1870 and 1914.

Clemenceau wanted to detach all German lands west of the Rhine and create a "Rhenish Rhineland," a buffer state—and to occupy the east bank of the river with Allied troops for thirty years. Poincaré, a Lorrainer, wanted to annex all 10,000 square miles of the Rhineland, as did Foch, who warned, "If we do not hold the Rhine permanently, no neutralization, nor disarmament, nor any kind of written clause can prevent Germany . . . from sallying out of it at will."[60]

Annexing the Rhineland would have put five million Germans and much of Germany's industrial plant under permanent French control. Lloyd George was adamant that no German land be annexed by France. He feared a spirit of revenge would be created in Germany like that created in France by the 1871 loss of Alsace and Lorraine.

Wilson also recoiled at so flagrant a violation of his principle of self-determination. But as the French negotiator André Tardieu argued, to France, such measures were matters of national survival:

> For France, as for Great Britain and the United States, it is necessary to create a zone of safety. . . . This zone the naval Powers create by their fleets, and by the elimination of the German fleet. This zone France, unprotected by the ocean, unable to eliminate the millions of Germans trained to war, must create by the Rhine, by an inter-allied occupation of that river.[61]

What the Channel and Royal Navy were to Britain, what the Atlantic and U.S. Navy were to America, the Rhine and French army were to France, the moat and sword of national survival. "To ask us to give up the occupation [of the Rhine]," said Tardieu, "is like asking England and the United States to give up their fleets of battleships."[62]

France was forced to settle for a fifteen-year occupation. But the price Clemenceau exacted for giving up any claim to the Rhineland was high: an Anglo-American-French alliance. Under a Treaty of Guarantee, America and Britain were to be obligated to come to France's aid should Germany attack her again.

Incredibly, Wilson agreed, though he knew such an alliance violated a cardinal principle of U.S. foreign policy since Washington: no permanent alliances. Moreover, a commitment to go to war for France must be seen as a vote of no confidence in the new League of Nations' ability to maintain the peace by replacing the old balance-of-power politics with the new world's ideal of collective security.

There was also a huge element of impracticality about the Treaty of Guarantee. As the war had demonstrated—when U.S. troops had not begun to enter Allied lines in great numbers until a year after war had been declared—no U.S. army could be raised, trained, and transported across the Atlantic in time to stop a German invasion. The

Treaty of Guarantee thus entailed a permanent commitment by the United States to liberate France. No Senate in 1919 would approve such a commitment, as no U.S. vital interest was involved. President Grant had never thought to intervene when France was invaded in 1870, and, from 1914–1917, as Germans occupied the northeast of France, America had remained neutral. Even Theodore Roosevelt, an enthusiast of U.S. intervention in the war, wrote in 1919, in an article published after his death, "I do not believe in keeping our men on the other side to patrol the Rhine, or police Russia, or interfere in Central Europe or the Balkan peninsula. . . . Mexico is our Balkan peninsula."[63]

Only German U-boats sinking American ships had brought the United States into the war. And the America of 1919 was not going to commit to war for any other country. This was not isolationism. It was a foreign policy tradition of 130 years. Americans went to war when American interests were imperiled. And whose flag flew over Alsace was no vital interest of the United States.

Lloyd George had cooked up this scheme, but built into it an escape hatch. If either the Senate or Parliament refused to approve the Treaty of Guarantee, the other nation was absolved of its commitment. Without a dissenting vote the House of Commons and House of Lords issued France the war guarantee. But the Senate never even took up the treaty. Britain was off the hook. France was left with no security treaty and no buffer state, only a fifteen-year occupation of the Rhineland.

Both banks of the Rhine were to remain demilitarized in perpetuity. But, after 1935, when the occupation was to end, the sole guarantee of their permanent demilitarization would be the French army.

MOST FAVORED NATION

AFTER GERMANY MOUNTED THE scaffold came the turn of the Austro-Hungarian Empire. Under the treaties of St. Germain and

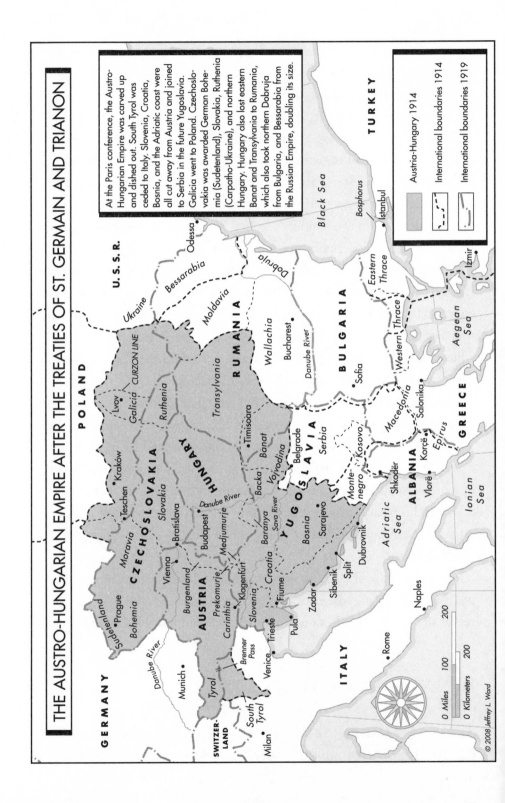

THE AUSTRO-HUNGARIAN EMPIRE AFTER THE TREATIES OF ST. GERMAIN AND TRIANON

At the Paris conference, the Austro-Hungarian Empire was carved up and dished out. South Tyrol was ceded to Italy. Slovenia, Croatia, Bosnia, and the Adriatic coast were all cut away from Austria and joined to Serbia in the future Yugoslavia. Galicia went to Poland. Czechoslovakia was awarded German Bohemia (Sudetenland), Slovakia, Ruthenia (Carpatho-Ukraine), and northern Hungary. Hungary also lost eastern Banat and Transylvania to Rumania, which also took northern Dobruja from Bulgaria, and Bessarabia from the Russian Empire, doubling its size.

Austria-Hungary 1914

International boundaries 1914

International boundaries 1919

© 2008 Jeffrey L. Ward

Trianon, that ancient empire was butchered, cut into pieces to be distributed to the nations that had supported the Allies. Northern provinces went to the new Poland. Czecho-Slovakia, which had emerged as a new nation in 1918 under Thomáš Masaryk, was ceded rule over three and a half million ethnic Germans, three million Slovaks, one million Hungarians, 500,000 Ruthenes, and 150,000 Poles. All resented in varying degrees being forced to live in a nation dominated by seven million Czechs.[64]

Whether to coerce three million Germans to come under a Czech rule most of them despised was fiercely argued at Paris. On March 10, the chief of the field mission for the U.S. delegation, Archibald C. Coolidge, called it a grave mistake and "filed a memorandum in which he proposed a frontier almost the same as that established in 1938 after 'Munich.' "[65]

Coolidge's reasoning was as follows:

> To grant to the Czechoslovaks all the territory they demand would not only be an injustice to millions of people unwilling to come under Czech rule, but would also be dangerous and perhaps fatal to the future of the new State. In Bohemia, the relations between the Czechs and the Germans have been growing steadily worse during the last three months. The hostility between them is now intense. . . . The blood shed on March 3rd [*sic*] when Czech soldiers in several towns fired on German crowds . . . was shed in a manner that is not easily forgiven.[66]

South Africa's Jan Smuts also warned that the Czech lust for land, Hungarian as well as German, might bring disastrous results: "With some millions of Germans already included in Bohemia in the north, the further inclusion of some 400,000 or 500,000 Magyars in the south would be a very serious matter for the young state, besides the grave violation of the principles of nationality involved."[67]

The Big Four did not heed Smuts and Coolidge. They listened instead to Eduard Beneš, the Czech foreign minister who was promising to model Czechoslovakia on the Swiss federation, where minorities would enjoy equal standing and cultural and political autonomy. On the eve of Munich, 1938, Lloyd George would charge Beneš with having deceived the Allies at Paris.

Why did the Czechs succeed at Paris at the expense of their neighbors? First, they had chosen the winning side. Second, their new territories would come at the expense of Germany, Austria, and Hungary, who were to be punished and weakened. "No pity must be shown to Hungary," said André Tardieu, the "Father of Trianon," who chaired the committee dealing with the Austro-Hungarian Empire.[68] Third, Beneš and Masaryk were, like pianist Ignace Paderewski who represented the Poles, great favorites at Paris:

> In Allied eyes, and this is especially true of Woodrow Wilson, T. G. Masaryk had become a George Washington, William the Conqueror and Jeanne d'Arc rolled into one. Masaryk, "the father of his country," the "outstanding democrat and patriot," could do no wrong. His word was accepted as gospel.[69]

Fourth, the Czechs knew what they wanted and were resolute and ruthless in taking it. As Hungary and Austria were reeling in defeat in 1918, Czech troops moved into Slovakia. They then seized the Polish enclave of Teschen, "whose coal heated the foyers and powered the industry of Central Europe from Krakow to Vienna," and occupied German Bohemia, which would come to be known as the Sudetenland.[70] Masaryk told Parliament, "The Germans will have to be satisfied with self-determination of the second class. . . ."[71] Clemenceau supported the Czech seizures.

By the time Masaryk, Beneš, and the Allies were finished, they had created in the new Czechoslovakia the tenth most industrialized nation on earth, having stripped Austria and Hungary of 70 to 80 percent of their industry,

> from china and glass factories to sugar processors . . . to the breweries of Pilzen and the Skoda works producing world-class armaments, locomotives, autos, and machinery. The wealth these companies generated would make Czechoslovakia coveted by Germany and envied by its other, less amply endowed neighbors.[72]

The new nation—one-half Czech, one-fourth German, with Slovaks and Hungarians constituting a fifth of its population—was bordered by four nations (Austria, Germany, Hungary, and Poland) all of which bore deep grievances against her. "[T]he Peace Conference," writes David Andelman in *A Shattered Peace*, "had turned Czechoslovakia into a polyglot highway from Germany to the Balkans . . . with a fifth column in its midst."[73]

South Tyrol, to the bitterness of its two hundred thousand Austrian inhabitants, was turned over to Italy as war booty for switching sides and joining the Allies in 1915. Vienna, seat of one of the greatest empires of Christendom, became the capital of a tiny landlocked country of fewer than seven million.

TRIANON

HUNGARY, HOWEVER, WAS THE "ultimate victim of every sort of prejudice, desire, and ultimate diplomatic and political error of the powers gathered in Paris. It had no real advocate there. . . ."[74]

By the Treaty of Trianon, signed June 4, 1920, Hungary was mutilated, the kingdom reduced from an imperial domain of 125,000 square miles to a landlocked nation of 36,000. Transylvania and the two million Hungarians residing there went to Rumania as a reward for joining the Allies. Slovakia, which a predominantly Catholic Hungary had ruled for centuries, was handed over to the Czechs. Other Hungarian lands went to the Kingdom of Serbs, Croats, and Slovenes. A slice of Hungary was even ceded to Austria.

"Hungary, which might have played a key role in Clemenceau's cordon sanitaire," writes Andelman, "instead became a victim on every side."[75]

The U.S. Congress refused to approve the Treaty of Trianon and in August 1920 signed a separate peace. Hungarians regarded the imposed peace of Trianon as a national crucifixion, the greatest national disaster since the Battle of Mohacs in 1526, which led to a century and a half of Ottoman occupation.

On February 1, 1918, Wilson had told the world:

> There shall be no annexations, no contributions, no punitive damages. People are not to be handed about from one sovereignty to another by an international conference. . . . "Self-determination" is not a mere phrase. . . . Every territorial settlement involved in this war must be made in the interest and for the benefit of the population concerned, and not as part of any mere adjustment or compromise of claims amongst rival States.[76]

What Wilson had promised the world, and the nations that laid down their arms, would not happen, did happen, with his collusion. József Cardinal Mindszenty, primate of Hungary, looked back in his *Memoirs* upon the injustice done his nation and people at Paris:

> Before the 1920 Treaty of Trianon, Hungary comprised almost 109,000 square miles of land. When the treaty was signed, only 35,000 square miles remained. . . . Benes and Masaryk showed fraudulent maps and statistics to the other

delegates at the conference. . . . President Wilson had proclaimed the right of self-determination; but this principle was completely ignored when the Allies lopped off two-thirds of Hungary. No one bothered to consult the people about their wishes.[77]

Of the eighteen million under Hungarian rule in 1910, ten million were taken away. Of the lost ten million, Cardinal Mindszenty estimated that more than three million were of Hungarian nationality. Hungarian bitterness at the Wilsonian peace was as deep as it was in Germany.

At Paris, Germans, Austrians, and Hungarians had no right of self-determination not subject to Allied veto. Germans were handed over to Denmark, Belgium, France, Italy, Czechoslovakia, Poland, and Lithuania without their consent. Plebiscites were granted to peoples who wished to break free of German rule. But in Alsace, Lorraine, Danzig, the Corridor, Memel, Bohemia, and South Tyrol, Germans were denied any plebiscite or voice in choosing the nation to which they wished to belong. Three million Hungarians had been force-marched into new nations. By 1920, 885,000 were under Czech rule, 1.7 million under Rumanian rule, 420,000 under Serb rule. The Little Entente of Rumania, Czechoslovakia, and Yugoslavia was created partly out of fear of a Hungary whose lands and peoples each had torn away.

And though it was promoted by and allied with France, serious statesmen regarded it with scorn, like George Kennan:

The Little Entente, on which the Czechs, with French encouragement, had tried to base their security, had seemed to me an artificial, unwise arrangement founded in the quicksands of the vengeful, emotional, and unrealistic spirit that dominated French policy in the years just after World War I.[78]

As for the newborn nations baptized at Paris, they were almost as multiethnic as the Habsburg Empire, but lacked her history, lineage, and moral authority. Czechoslovakia was but half Czech. Germans, Slovaks, Hungarians, Poles, Ukrainians, and Jews had been handed over to Prague. The Kingdom of Serbs, Croats, and Slovenes contained Bosnian Muslims, Montenegrins, Hungarians, and Bulgarians, the last forcibly transferred to the new kingdom by the Treaty of Neuilly. Poland was a polyglot nation. In a 1931 linguistic census,

> Poles formed only 68.9 per cent of the total population. The Ukrainians with 13.9 per cent, the Yiddish-speaking Jews with 8.7 per cent, the Byelorussians with 3.1 per cent, and the Germans with 2.3 per cent made up nearly one-third of the whole. In specific areas, they constituted a dominant majority.[79]

RUMANIA

LIKE THE CZECHS, the Rumanians would emerge as one of the great winners at Paris. Wedged between the Allies, Serbia, and Czarist Russia, and the Austro-Hungarian Empire, Rumania began the war as a neutral. In August 1916, however, after receiving a secret offer of Transylvania and the Banat, to be taken from Hungary, Bucharest joined the Allies.

Prime Minister Ian Bratianu, who had negotiated the secret treaty, had also been assured of Russian military aid, which never came. By year's end, 1916, Austro-Hungarian and German armies occupied Bucharest. King Ferdinand, Queen Marie, and the government had fled to the protection of the Russians in Bessarabia.

Not until the final weeks of war did Rumania rejoin the struggle. Yet Bratianu and Queen Marie, a granddaughter of Victoria and first cousin of George V, arrived in Paris to demand full payment for having fought on the side of the Allies, though Bucharest had violated

Article V of the 1916 treaty by concluding a separate peace. Between them, Bratianu and Queen Marie succeeded in doubling the size of Rumania. They got Transylvania and the eastern Banat from Hungary, Bessarabia from Russia, northern Dobruja from Bulgaria, and Bukovina from the dismantled Habsburg Empire.

Western Banat went to the Kingdom of Serbs, Croats, and Slovenes—a polyglot nation, 43 percent Serb, 23 percent Croat, 8.5 percent Slovene, 6 percent Bosnian Muslim, 5 percent Macedonian, 3.6 percent Albanian, and the rest a mixture of Germans, Hungarians, Vlachs, Jews, and Gypsies.[80]

So it was that the men of Paris redrew the maps of Europe, and planted the seeds of a second European war.

The winners at Paris were the Czechs, Rumanians, and Serbs. The losers were the Austrians, Germans, Hungarians, Bulgarians, and Russians. The Italians felt cheated of what they had been promised in the Treaty of London. The Poles felt they had been denied Teschen because of favoritism toward the Czechs. Thus was Europe divided between satiated powers, and revisionist powers determined to retrieve the lands and peoples that had been taken from them.

With the treaties of Versailles, St. Germain, Trianon, and Neuilly, the Allies at Paris had made a dog's breakfast of Europe. For America, they had stripped the Great War of any morality. When Wilson came home with a peace that denied the defeated their right of self-determination, made a mockery of his Fourteen Points, honored the secret treaties he denounced, and enlarged the British, French, Italian, and Japanese empires by a million square miles and tens of millions of subjects, Americans concluded that their 116,000 sons died for nothing. In *The World Crisis*, Churchill would express puzzlement as to why the Americans ever went to war.

American historians will perhaps be somewhat lengthy in explaining to posterity why the United States entered the

Great War on April 6, 1917. . . . American ships had been sunk before by German submarines; as many American lives were lost in the *Lusitania* as in all the five American ships whose sinking immediately preceded the declaration of war. As for the general cause of the Allies, if it was good in 1917, was it not equally good in 1914?[81]

"There were plenty of reasons of high policy for [America] staying out in 1917 after waiting so long," Churchill concluded. History has proven him right.

Lloyd George sensed the tragedy the Allies were setting in train. Perhaps with Burke in mind—"Magnanimity in politics is not seldom the truest wisdom"—he retired to Fontainebleau on the last weekend of March and wrote one of the more prophetic documents of the century:

You may strip Germany of her colonies, reduce her armaments to a mere police force and her navy to that of a fifth rate power; all the same, in the end if she feels that she has been unjustly treated in the peace of 1919 she will find means of exacting retribution from her conquerors. . . . Injustice, arrogance, displayed in the hour of triumph will never be forgotten or forgiven. . . .

I am, therefore strongly averse to transferring more Germans from German rule to the rule of some other nation than can possibly be helped. I cannot conceive any greater cause of future war than that the German people, who have certainly proved themselves one of the most vigorous and powerful races in the world, should be surrounded by a number of small states, many of them consisting of people who have never previously set up a stable government for themselves, but each of them containing large masses of Germans clamoring for reunion with their native land.[82]

About the creation of a Polish Corridor, severing Germany in two, Lloyd George warned:

> The proposal of the Polish commission that we should place 2,100,000 million Germans under the control of a people which is of a different religion and which has never proved its capacity for stable self-government throughout its history must, in my judgment, lead sooner or later to a new war in the East of Europe.[83]

Rather than loosen the bonds Bismarck had forged among Germans, the peace of Versailles reinforced a spirit of nationhood. The treaty had defeated its own purpose, writes John Laughland, for it

> allowed the Germans to think of themselves as victims. The debt itself, which obviously fell uniformly on the entire nation, also made the Germans feel solidarity with one another; they became united in their common protest. It made Bavarians and Saxons feel for the territorial losses of Prussia, whereas fifty years previously, such losses would have concerned only Prussians. The tribute which the Germans had to pay to the French thus united them in common resentment. With Germany bordered to the East with nothing but new weak states, this was a fatal combination.[84]

When you strike at a king, you must kill him, Emerson said. At Paris the Allies had scourged Germany and dispossessed her of territory, industry, people, colonies, money—and honor by forcing her to sign the "War Guilt Lie." But they had not killed her. She was alive, united, more populous and potentially powerful than France, and her people were now possessed of a burning sense of betrayal. Novelist Anatole France had written, as he saw victory with America's entry into the war, "Even if beaten, Germany will pride itself on having resisted the entire world; no other people will be so inebriated by their defeat."[85]

The treaty writers of Versailles wrote the last act of the Great War and the first act of the resurrection of Germany and the war of retribution. Even in this hour men saw what was coming: Lloyd George in his Fontainebleau memorandum; Keynes as he scribbled notes for his *Economic Consequences of the Peace*; Foch ("This is not peace, it is an armistice for twenty years"); and Smuts ("This Treaty breathes a poisonous spirit of revenge, which may yet scorch the fair face—not of a corner of France but of Europe)."[86]

Secretary of State Lansing said of the peace he and President Wilson brought home: "[T]he Versailles Treaty menaces the existence of civilization."[87] In Italy, the wounded war veteran and Fascist leader Benito Mussolini warned: "The dilemma is this: treaty revision or a new war."[88] Hans von Seeckt of the German General Staff agreed: "We must regain our power, and as soon as we do, we will naturally take back everything we lost."[89]

Versailles had created not only an unjust but an unsustainable peace. Wedged between a brooding Bolshevik Russia and a humiliated Germany were six new nations: Finland, Estonia, Latvia, Lithuania, Poland, and Czechoslovakia. The last two held five million Germans captive. Against each of the six, Russia or Germany held a grievance. Yet none could defend its independence against a resurrected Germany or a revived Russia. Should Russia and Germany unite, no force on Earth could save the six.

THE FRUITS OF VICTORY

THE BRITISH EMPIRE CAME out of Paris the great beneficiary of the Great War. The Hohenzollern, Romanov, Habsburg, and Ottoman empires had crashed in ruins. The challenge of a Wilhelmine

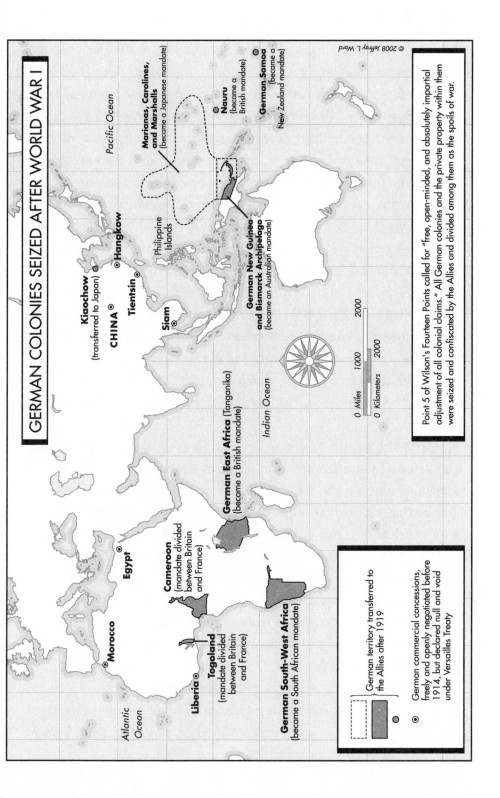

GERMAN COLONIES SEIZED AFTER WORLD WAR I

Kiaochow
(transferred to Japan)

CHINA ◉
⊙ **Hangkow**

Tientsin

Siam ⊙

Pacific Ocean

Marianas, Carolines, and Marshalls,
(became a Japanese mandate)

Philippine
Islands

Nauru
(became a
British mandate)

German Samoa
(became a
New Zealand mandate)

**German New Guinea
and Bismarck Archipelago**
(became an Australian mandate)

*Atlantic
Ocean*

Morocco ◉

Egypt ◉

Liberia ◉

Togoland
(mandate divided
between Britain
and France)

Cameroon
(mandate divided
between Britain
and France)

German East Africa (Tanganika)
(became a British mandate)

Indian Ocean

German South-West Africa
(became a South African mandate)

0 Miles   1000   2000

0 Kilometers   2000

German territory transferred to
the Allies after 1919

⊙ German commercial concessions,
freely and openly negotiated before
1914, but declared null and void
under Versailles Treaty

Point 5 of Wilson's Fourteen Points called for "free, open-minded, and absolutely impartial adjustment of all colonial claims." All German colonies and the private property within them were seized and confiscated by the Allies and divided among them as the spoils of war.

© 2008 Jeffrey L. Ward

Germany that had surpassed British production by 1914 was history. Germany was no longer a great power. The High Seas Fleet, the greatest threat to the Royal Navy since Trafalgar, had committed suicide at Scapa Flow. Britain had taken over Germany's Atlantic cables and most of her merchant fleet to compensate for the loss of 40 percent of her own to U-boats. Germany's islands in the South Pacific had been mandated to Australia and New Zealand. German South-West Africa had gone to South Africa. German East Africa (Tanganyika) had become a British mandate. The Cameroons and Togoland were divided between Britain and France. Mesopotamia and Palestine, taken from the Turks, had gone to Great Britain. Out of the war fought to make the world safe for democracy, the British Empire had added 950,000 square miles and millions of subjects. Said Lord Curzon, "The British flag never flew over more powerful or united an empire than now; Britons never had better cause to look the world in the face; never did our voice count for more in the councils of the nations, or in determining the future destinies of mankind."[90]

After the treaties of Versailles and Sèvres had been imposed on the defeated Germans and Turks, a man could walk from Kuwait to Cairo, turn south, and walk the length of Africa to Cape Town without leaving a British Dominion, colony, or protectorate. The dream of Cecil Rhodes, the Cape-to-Cairo railroad, could now be built without asking for transit rights from any power other than a fellow member of the British Imperial Conference. In 1921, Jan Smuts, now prime minister of South Africa, told his fellow prime ministers that the British Empire "emerged from the War quite the greatest power in the world, and it is only unwisdom or unsound policy that could rob her of that great position."[91]

"When Lloyd George returned from Paris with the Treaty of Victory," wrote Churchill, King George V "took the unprecedented course of . . . driving him in his own carriage to Buckingham Palace. History will not overlook the significance of this act."[92]

THE COST OF VICTORY

BRITISH GAINS, HOWEVER, had not come without costs. The war had proven the disaster Norman Angell had predicted in his 1909 *The Great Illusion.*

> The total number of fatalities for the British empire as a whole was 921,000: the originator of the Imperial War Graves Commission, Sir Fabian Ware, calculated that if the dead were to march abreast down Whitehall the parade past the Cenotaph would last three and a half days.[93]

The highest casualty rate had been among young British officers, striking home with all the leaders of Britain's great parties. The Liberals' Asquith, Labour's Arthur Henderson, and the Irish Nationalists' John Redmond had each lost a son. The Unionists' Bonar Law had lost two. British debt was fourteen times what it had been in 1914. While it appeared to the world that the British Empire had made out wonderfully well, Britain had sustained losses, tangible and intangible, from which she would never recover.

Charles Mee, whose grandfather lost all ten brothers in the war, wrote in his book on Versailles that not only had there been a collapse of the political order in Europe, but

> the war had discredited much of the rhetoric of national pride, honor, and sacrifice, as well as faith in the notions of reason, progress, humanism. Nor did the notions of God, representational art, or Newtonian physics appear to be in such good repair. The "modern" Western civilization that had grown up since the Renaissance was under siege from outside, and from within, and offered scant support to the disintegrating political order.[94]

"A generation had been decimated on the battlefields of Europe," Mee continued. "No one had seen the likes of such slaughter before: the deaths of soldiers per day of battle were 10 times greater than in the American Civil War," heretofore the bloodiest conflict in the history of Christendom.[95]

Then there was her loss of moral authority. How could British and Europeans, who had just concluded four years of butchering one another with abandon, assert a moral superiority that gave them the right to rule other people? With the Turks' defeat of the British at Gallipoli, word had gone out to Asia and the Arab world, as it had after Adowa and Tshushima: Europeans were not invincible. Awe of Western military prowess and power had been irreparably damaged in the eyes of subject peoples. The myth of Western invincibility had been destroyed.

Also, Wilson's sermons on "self-determination" and Lloyd George's hymns to the "rights of small nations" had been heard beyond the German, Austro-Hungarian, and Ottoman empires. The genie of nationalism was out of the bottle. Balfour had promised the Jews a homeland in Palestine. To defeat the Turks, T. E. Lawrence had stirred up the smoldering embers of Arab nationalism. Not a day passed that some popular leader did not arrive in the lobby of Wilson's hotel to plead for independence for a province or colony he had never heard of. At Paris, British diplomat Harold Nicolson spoke of "that sense of a riot in a parrot house."[96] A "chastened Wilson" returned to tell Congress: "When I gave utterance to those words [that "all nations had a right to self-determination"] I said them without the knowledge that nationalities existed, which are coming to us day after day."[97]

The right of all peoples to self-determination, to which the Allies paid homage at Paris, was an ax that would strike the roots of every Western empire. By the time Lloyd George returned to London, Ireland was in revolt. Rebellions had broken out in Egypt, Iraq, and India.

While Germany had been diminished, a more formidable rival had arisen. World financial leadership had passed to a United States that had profited from selling to the Allies while avoiding heavy combat until the summer of 1918. America had shown herself to be a mighty military power, perhaps the greatest. From three hundred thousand men in arms in 1917, she had raised an army of 4 million and transported two million soldiers to France, where they had been decisive in the final victory.

Britain had ceased building warships in 1918. America had just begun. By 1921, the United States had become the first nation in a century to achieve naval parity with Great Britain. And an epidemic of Anglophobia had broken out in America over the belief that the British Empire had gorged itself in a war where 116,000 Americans had made the supreme sacrifice to make the world safe for democracy. Then there were those "six British votes" in the League of Nations: Britain, Australia, New Zealand, South Africa, India, and Canada.

Disillusionment with the treaty Wilson brought home would deepen in the 1920s and 1930s, as all the Allied powers, save Finland, defaulted on their war debts and America fell deep into Depression.

Perhaps the greatest loss Britain suffered was in her standing and credibility with the American people. British propaganda had convinced us the Germans were beasts and we must join the good war for a new world where Prussian militarism would never menace mankind again. But after Versailles enlarged the British Empire by 950,000 square miles, as the Allies walked away from their war debts mocking Uncle Sam as "Uncle Shylock," Americans came to believe they had been hoodwinked and swindled. They came to concur with British historian H.A.L. Fisher: Versailles had "draped the crudity of conquest . . . in the veil of morality."[98]

France and Britain got the peace they had wanted. Twenty years later, they would get the war they had invited. And the next time Britain rang for help, America would take her time answering the call. The Yanks would not be "coming over" until after France had been overrun and Britain thrown off the continent at Dunkirk. Americans' bitterness over the belief they had been played for fools was something the British never understood. I yet recall hearing, as a child in the 1940s, of how the British had cut the cables, how the *Lusitania* had been carrying contraband, how the tales of German atrocities in Belgium had been lies, how the British had sent "Black and Tans" to shoot down Irish patriots, how we had been deceived by "lying British propaganda" into sending our boys into a war "to pull Britain's chestnuts out of the fire."

The revisionist historians of World War I did their work well.

And something new and ominous had come out of the war. The Russia of the Romanovs was gone. Atop the largest nation on earth sat a grisly gang of Bolshevik terrorists committed to world revolution and the destruction of all the Western empires and nations. In March 1920, after a trip to Europe, Churchill, who had been almost alone in urging Allied intervention in Russia, wrote Lloyd George what one historian calls "one of the great prophetic documents of European history."[99]

"Peace with the German people, war on the Bolshevik tyranny" was Churchill's message.[100] "We may," he wrote, "be within measurable distance of a universal collapse and anarchy across Europe and Asia."[101]

> You ought to tell France that we will make a defensive alliance with her against Germany, if, and only if, she entirely alters her treatment of Germany. . . . Next you should send a great man to Berlin to help consolidate the anti-Spartacist anti-Ludendorff elements into a strong left-center block. For this task you must have two levers: first, food and credit, which must be generously accorded in spite of our own difficulties (which otherwise will worsen); secondly, early revision of the Peace Treaty by a Conference to which New Germany shall be invited as an equal partner in the rebuilding of Europe.[102]

What alarmed Churchill was the prospect of civil war in Germany, leading to a dictatorship of Right or Left. Communist coups had briefly succeeded in Budapest and Bavaria, and an attempt had been made to seize power in Berlin. All had been brutally suppressed by German Freikorps.

There was fear that a man of the right like Gen. Erich Ludendorff might sweep aside the democratic regime that had arisen on the Kaiser's abdication but been discredited in many German eyes by having submitted to the Allied diktat at Versailles. In March 1920, the Kapp putsch, a rightist attempt to seize power in Berlin, was blocked only by a general strike called by the Social Democrats. Churchill had perceived the real threat: Germany was now so prostrate she could no longer fulfill her ancient duty—to keep the Russians out of Europe.

Lloyd George's attitude toward Churchill's obsession with Russia was dismissive. When Churchill's name came up over dinner at Lady Astor's, the prime minister became irritable, remarking that Winston "has bolshevism on the brain."[103]

In his memoirs, Lloyd George mocked Churchill's preoccupation with the Bolsheviks, "blaming it on his aristocratic lineage. 'His ducal blood revolted against the wholesale elimination of Grand Dukes in Russia.' "[104]

Yet it is to Churchill's eternal credit that, almost alone among Allied statesmen, he recognized the danger of the regime of Lenin and Trotsky, and, at risk to his relationship with Prime Minister Lloyd George, repeatedly urged Allied intervention to kill the viper in its crib. So prescient was Churchill that his subsequent behavior toward Stalin seems inexplicable.

"A CARTHAGINIAN PEACE"?

THOUGH HE BELIEVED THE "Germans had behaved disgracefully in the war and deserve a hard peace," Prime Minister Smuts argued that this was "no reason why the world must be thrust into ruin."[105] It was he who first branded Versailles a "Carthaginian peace," laying responsibility for the vindictive treaty at the feet of Woodrow Wilson:

> "Making the world safe for Democracy!" I wonder whether in this reactionary peace—the most reactionary since Scipio Africanus dealt with Carthage—he [Wilson] still hears the mute appeal of the people to be saved from the coming war. . . . What a ghastly tragedy this is.[106]

A dissent is in order. Carthage, torched and pillaged, its soldiers put to the sword, its women violated, its children sold into slavery, vanished from history. Germany had suffered, but Germany had survived. Historian Correlli Barnett calls Smuts's characterization of Versailles as a Carthaginian peace "sentimental nonsense." Henry Kissinger, too, regards German complaints over Versailles as "self-pitying nonsense":

> Germany had ignored the Fourteen Points as long as it thought that it had a chance of winning the war, and had . . . imposed a Carthaginian peace on Russia at Brest-Litovsk, violating every one of Wilson's principles. The only reason Germany finally ended the war had to do with pure power calculations—with the American army involved, its final defeat was only a question of time. . . . Germany was exhausted, its defenses were breaking, and Allied armies were about to drive into Germany. Wilson's principles in fact spared Germany much more severe retribution.[107]

Undeniably, there is truth here. For while the stories of raped nuns and Belgian babies being tossed about on bayonets were propaganda lies, the German army in Belgium and France had behaved less like Lee's Army of Northern Virginia than Sherman's army in Georgia. At Brest-Litovsk, Berlin had imposed far more extensive surgery on a Russian empire that was stripped of Finland, Estonia, Latvia, Lithuania, Poland, Ukraine, White Russia (Belarus), and the Caucasus. One-third of Czarist Russia's population, half of her industry, three-fourths of her iron ore, nine-tenths of her coal mines were gone, and the nation was made to pay an indemnity of six thousand million marks.[108]

However, as Erik von Kuehnelt-Leddihn argues, Germany had simply applied to that "prison house of nations," the Russian Empire, the Wilsonian principle of self-determination, permitting its captive peoples to go free.

To understand the German outrage, one must view Versailles through German eyes. As of November 11, 1918, Germans did not see themselves as defeated. German armies were in retreat in the west, but no Allied soldiers stood on German soil. "At the moment of the November 1918 ceasefire in the West," writes German historian Andreas Hillgruber, in the east,

> newspaper maps of the military situation showed German troops in Finland . . . down through Pskov-Orlov-Mogilev and the area south of Kursk, to the Don east of Rostov. Germany had thus secured the Ukraine. . . . In addition, German troops held the Crimea and were stationed in smaller numbers in Transcaucasia.[109]

Also, Germany had accepted an armistice on the basis of Wilson's Fourteen Points, enunciated in his address to Congress January 8, 1918. The fourteen were amended to twenty-four by addresses to Congress, February 11, at Mount Vernon on July 4, and in New York City on September 27. These Twenty-four Points were to serve as the basis of the peace. So Wilson had pledged to the Germans. Under Points Seven and Eight, Germany was to depart Belgium and restore French rights in Alsace-Lorraine lost in 1871.

But where Point 1 called for "open covenants, openly arrived at," South Tyrol, Austrian for six hundred years, was given to Italy under a secret treaty with Britain in 1915, and all German islands in the North Pacific were given to Japan to comply with a secret treaty with Britain in 1917.

Point 2, "absolute freedom of navigation upon the seas . . . in peace and war," except for "international action" to enforce "international covenants," was dropped by Wilson at the insistence of the British.

Point 3 called for "removal of all economic barriers and establishment of an equality of trade conditions among all nations." But Germany was denied the right to enter a customs union with Austria and forced to grant unrestricted Allied access to her markets, while being denied equal access to Allied markets.

Point 4 declared that "national armaments will be reduced to the lowest point consistent with domestic safety." Germany was forced to disarm, but the Allies, while demobilizing their huge armies and reducing the size of their fleets, never fully did. Hitler would use the Allied refusal to match German disarmament to justify German rearmament in 1935.

Point 5 called for the "free, open-minded, and absolutely impartial adjustment of all colonial claims." This was trampled underfoot as the Allies scrambled to seize and confiscate every German colony as well as the private property of German citizens who lived there.

Point 9 read, "A readjustment of the frontiers of Italy should be effected along clearly recognizable lines of nationality." Yet, ceding South Tyrol all the way to the Brenner to Italy, to honor a secret treaty, made Wilson and the Americans appear to the Tyrolese and their Austrian kinsmen as liars and hypocrites.

Point 13 declared an "independent Polish state . . . should include the territories inhabited by indisputably Polish populations." But the Poland created at Paris held captive millions of Germans, Ukrainians, and White Russians, ensuring conflict with Russia and Germany when those nations got back on their feet.

Point 17, enunciated on February 11, 1918, amended on July 4, was the self-determination clause: "The settlement of every question, whether of territory, of sovereignty . . . [or] of political relationship, upon the basis of the free acceptance of that settlement by the people immediately concerned."

On February 11, a Joint Session of Congress had roared its approval as Wilson had declared the principle forever associated with his name:

> National aspirations must be respected; peoples may now be dominated and governed only by their own consent. "Self-determination" is not a mere phrase. It is an imperative principle of action, which statesmen will henceforth ignore at their peril.[110]

Prophetic words, but in dealing with the defeated the statesmen of Versailles not only ignored the "imperative principle," they violated it again and again and again. In a letter home, May 31, 1919, Charles Seymour, head of the Austro-Hungarian division of the American delegation and future president of Yale, described a memorable scene:

> We went into the next room where the floor was clear and Wilson spread out a big map (made in our office) on the floor and got down on his hands and knees to show us what had been done; most of us were also on our hands and knees. I was in the front row and felt someone pushing me, and looked around angrily to find that it was Orlando [Italian premier and leader of the Italian delegation to the conference] on his hands and knees crawling like a bear toward the map. I gave way and he was soon in the front row. I wish that I could have had a picture of the most important men in the world on all fours over this map.[111]

Thus were sown the seeds of the greatest war in the history of mankind.

Point 18 declared that "all well-defined national aspirations shall be accorded the utmost satisfaction . . . without introducing new . . . elements of discord and antagonism that would be likely in time to break the peace of Europe and consequently of the world."

Point 18 is a parody of what was done at Paris.

There was scarcely a promise Wilson made to the Germans at the time of the armistice that was not broken, or a principle of his that he did not violate. The Senate never did a better day's work than when it rejected the Treaty of Versailles and refused to enter a League of Nations where Americans soldiers would be required to give their lives enforcing the terms of so dishonorable and disastrous a peace.

Lloyd George, who had realized all of Britain's ambitions and was, as T. E. Lawrence said, "head and shoulders above anyone else at the peace conference . . . the only man there (in a big position) who was really trying to do what was right," saw what was coming.[112] He returned home triumphant but grim. Awarded the Order of Merit by George V, he said, "We shall have to do the whole thing over again in twenty five years . . . at three times the cost."[113]

The dilemma at Paris was that Allied goals were irreconcilable. No peace could meet Wilson's ideals and Foch's demands. Clemenceau had wanted a truncated, disarmed Germany, weighted down with reparations so heavy she could never rise again to threaten France. Wilson had wanted a peace of no victors, no vanquished. As U.S. historian Thomas Bailey wrote, "The victor can have vengeance, or he may have peace, but he cannot have both" from the same treaty.[114]

At a London dinner party soon after Adolf Hitler had taken power in Berlin, one of the guests asked aloud, "By the way, where was Hitler born?"

"At Versailles" was the instant reply of Lady Astor.[115]

Rising from obscurity to build a mass movement in a demoralized

Germany, Hitler first drew public notice, then attracted ever-larger crowds by delivering again and again a vitriolic speech he titled simply "The Treaty of Versailles."[116]

On April 8, 1945, when Hitler was holed up in his bunker, Germany was smashed and ablaze, and Stalin was at the gates of Berlin, Vienna, and Prague, Churchill, too, in a memo to the Foreign Office traced the origins of the unnecessary war back to Versailles—and Woodrow Wilson:

> This war should never have come unless, under American and modernizing pressure, we had driven the Habsburgs out of Austria and the Hohenzollerns out of Germany. By making these vacuums we gave the opening for the Hitlerite monster to crawl out of its sewer onto the vacant thrones. No doubt these views are very unfashionable.[117]

The men of Versailles had brought home the peace of vengeance the people wanted. Their children would pay the price for their having failed to bring home a peace of justice. That price would be 50 million dead in the war that would come out of the Hall of Mirrors in the Palace of Versailles.

CHAPTER 4

"A Lot of Silly Little Cruisers"

FAR-CALL'D OUR NAVIES melt away . . .[1]
—KIPLING, 1897

IN 1921, BRITAIN WAS STILL the first power on earth, but her strategic situation had deteriorated. Germany was defeated, disarmed, and destitute, but Russia, Britain's ally in the Great War, was gone. America, whose food, munitions, and loans had kept the Allies fighting until two million Yanks arrived in France, had rejected Versailles, refused to join the League of Nations, disarmed, and retreated into neutrality.

Yet Britain still had the most powerful nation in Asia as an ally, and the Anglo-Japanese alliance dating to 1902 had proved its worth in war. Japan had rolled up Germany's possessions in China and the Pacific. Her warships had escorted the Anzac troops to European battlefields. Her naval dominance of the Far East freed up British fleets to deploy in home waters to defend against the High Seas Fleet. Had Japan been hostile, Britain would have been in mortal peril, a point graphically put by Australian prime minister W. H. "Billy" Hughes:

> Look at the map and ask yourselves what would have happened to that great splash of red down from India through Australia down to New Zealand, but for the Anglo-Japanese Treaty. How much of these great rich territories and por-

tions of our Empire would have escaped had Japan been neutral? How much if she had been our enemy? . . . Had [Japan] elected to fight on the side of Germany we should most certainly have been defeated.[2]

CHOOSING BETWEEN FRIENDS

WHEN LLOYD GEORGE HOSTED the Imperial Conference of 1921, the critical issue was whether to renew the Anglo-Japanese treaty. While the treaty conflicted with the League of Nations covenant, which outlawed old-world alliances, more critically, it complicated Britain's "special relationship" with the United States. Secretary of State Charles Evans Hughes had called in the British ambassador to instruct him on how great an impediment the treaty was to Anglo-American comity. America was brazenly demanding the severance of a Britain alliance vital to the security of the Empire in Asia and the Pacific.

London had no illusions about its ally. Lord Curzon considered the Japanese "restless and aggressive . . . like the Germans in mentality. . . . Japan is not at all an altruistic power."[3] Lloyd George felt they "might have no conscience."[4] Yet the benefits of the alliance were apparent. With the Bolsheviks in power in Russia, Britain had as an ally and codefender of India, Australia, New Zealand, Hong Kong, and Singapore, the greatest naval power in the western Pacific. Moreover, the Japanese had been scrupulously faithful.

The problem was the Americans, who were demanding that the Anglo-Japanese treaty be scrapped. "It was one of the most crucial national-strategic decisions England had ever had to reach in her history," writes Correlli Barnett.[5] The Cabinet was divided, as several of its most powerful personalities retained a romantic view of Anglo-American cousinhood:

Churchill was half-American by blood and a life-long romantic about the destiny of the English-speaking peoples,
while Arthur Balfour and Austen Chamberlain had been earlier believers in pan-Anglo-Saxonism. Balfour had visited
America in 1917, and the warmth of his reception had
melted even his frosty detachment.[6]

Canada insisted that U.S. goodwill be maintained, as did Prime
Minister Smuts: "The only path of safety for the British Empire is a
path on which we walk together with America."[7] But Lord Curzon
and Lloyd George wanted to renew the treaty, as did the Foreign Office, Chiefs of Staff, and Pacific Dominions Australia and New
Zealand. Without the Japanese alliance Britain was a third-rate
power in Asia, and should Japan turn on the empire that spurned her,
America would do nothing to save them. The Dutch and French also
had Asian colonies they could not protect against a predatory Japan.
They, too, wanted the alliance renewed.

> Not to renew the alliance . . . carried with it the likelihood
> of changing Japanese forbearance towards the British Em-
> pire into hostility. The British ambassador in Tokyo warned
> indeed that Japan would be so mortified and humiliated by
> British refusal to renew the treaty as to produce an "attitude
> of resentment and a policy of revenge."[8]

Tough-talking "Billy" Hughes asked the critical question: "Is this
Empire of ours to have a policy of its own, dictated by due regard to
its own interests, compatible with its declared ideals . . . or is it to
have a policy dictated by some other Power?"[9]

At Versailles, Hughes had sassed President Wilson to his face.
When Wilson asked if Australia was willing to risk the failure of the
peace conference and a dashing of the hopes of mankind over a few

islands in the South Pacific, Hughes, adjusting his hearing aid, cheer-fully replied, "That's about the size of it, Mr. Wilson."[10]

In Imperial Conference councils, Hughes argued vehemently that the British Empire must not ditch Japan:

> [S]hould we not be in a better position to exercise greater in-fluence over the Eastern policy [of Japan] as an Ally of that great Eastern nation, than as her potential enemy? Now if Japan is excluded from the family of great Western na-tions—and, mark, to turn our backs on the Treaty is cer-tainly to exclude Japan—she will be isolated, her national pride wounded in its most tender spot.[11]

When the Australians were assured that the League of Nations would prevent aggression, they replied that the United States had not joined the League and was not bound by its decisions.

"What is the substantial alternative to the renewal of the Treaty?" asked Hughes. "The answer is, there is none. If Australia was asked whether she would prefer America to Japan as an Ally, her choice would be America. But that choice is not offered her."[12]

Lloyd George wanted to take up the U.S. challenge by standing by the Japanese treaty and building warships. He feared that a Japan expelled from the Western camp might turn to the pariah powers, Germany or Russia. Sir Charles Eliot, Britain's ambassador to Japan, warned of a Tokyo-Berlin axis if the treaty were terminated. But Churchill continued to press the Cabinet to cast its lot with the Americans:

> Churchill, the Secretary of State for War and Air, argued that "no more fatal policy could be contemplated than that of basing our naval policy on a possible combination with Japan against America." Lloyd George retorted by saying that "there was one more fatal policy, namely, one

whereby we would be at the mercy of the United States."[13]

All agreed that if the Americans would offer a U.S.-British alliance to replace the Anglo-Japanese treaty, it should be taken up. But no such offer was on the table. Given the U.S. aversion to alliances—the nation had not entered a formal alliance since the Revolutionary War—America was not going to offer Britain war guarantees for her Asian colonies. U.S. Marines were not going to fight for Hong Kong.

The proper course, argues Barnett, would have been to put the issue straight to the Americans: We will terminate our Anglo-Japanese alliance if you will sign an Anglo-American treaty to defend each other's Pacific and Asian possessions. Otherwise, we will keep the ally we have. Disastrously for Britain, she chose to appease the United States.

"AN ACT OF BREATHTAKING STUPIDITY"

"YOU PROPOSE TO SUBSTITUTE for the Anglo-Japanese alliance and the overwhelming power of the British Navy a Washington conference?" Billy Hughes roared when the Commonwealth Conference agreed to terminate the Japanese alliance and attend a Washington conference to reduce the size and power of the Royal Navy.[14] At that conference, from November 1921 to February 1922, the British were forced to choose. And the decision seemed predetermined, as the British delegation was headed by Balfour, a believer in the myth of the transatlantic cousins striding arm in arm into the future.

At Washington, Britain terminated her twenty-year-old alliance that had proven its worth in the Great War. The Anglo-Japanese treaty was replaced by the Four-Power Treaty, by which America, Britain, France, and Japan agreed to settle their disputes by diplomacy and to respect one another's "rights in relation to their insular possessions and insular Dominions in the region of the Pacific Ocean."[15] The Four-Power Treaty had no enforcement provision.

"We have discarded whiskey and accepted water," said a Japanese diplomat of Tokyo's lost alliance.[16] Britain had done the same.

America's diplomatic victory would prove a disaster for the British Empire. With the termination of the Japanese alliance, Australia and New Zealand ceased to be strategic assets and became liabilities, as Britain now lacked the naval power to defend the two Pacific Dominions. Now alone in Asia, Britain faced a hostile Soviet Union, a xenophobic China, and a bitter Japan. And America had made no commitment to come to the defense of the British Empire in the Far East.

To Japan, the alliance had been her link to the Allies and great powers. It meant she was not isolated in Asia or in the world. She had as her ally the most respected of the world's empires. Writes British historian Paul Johnson,

> [S]o long as Britain was Japan's ally, the latter had a prime interest in preserving her own international respectability, constitutional propriety and the rule of law, all of which Britain had taught her.
>
> That was why the destruction of the Anglo-Japanese alliance by the USA and Canada in 1921–2 was fatal to peace in the Far East. The notion that it could be replaced by the Washington Naval Treaty . . . was a fantasy.[17]

Arthur Herman, biographer of the Royal Navy, concurs. "Only naval ties with Britain kept Japan on a course of international propriety and rule of law, and constrained its thirst for empire."[18] In severing the alliance, Britain had committed "an act of breathtaking stupidity."[19] Japan no longer had an incentive for good behavior. Treated as a pariah, she began to play the part.

The Japanese Foreign Office that failed to win renewal of the

British treaty fell in influence. Japan's military rose. By 1930, "feeling isolated and vulnerable . . . Japan had become a military dictatorship ruled by a clique of imperialist-minded generals and admirals."[20]

"ROLLS ROYCE–ROLLS ROYCE–FORD"

ON THE FIRST DAY of the Washington Conference, Secretary of State Charles Evans Hughes seized the world's imagination with a plan to slash the size of all the great navies of the world. No nation would be more affected than Britain, for whom sea power meant survival. As of November 1918, the Royal Navy was still the world's pre-eminent sea power, with sixty-one battleships, more than the U.S. and French fleets combined, and twice the battleship strength of the combined fleets of Italy and Japan.[21] The Royal Navy deployed 120 cruisers and 466 destroyers, though British admirals felt even this had barely been adequate to defend Britain's empire and trade in a war where Admiral Tirpitz's U-boats had taken so terrible a toll.

But by 1921 the British had not laid a battleship keel in five years. The Americans, however, with Asst. Secretary of the Navy Franklin D. Roosevelt the driving force, had been building ships since war was declared in 1917. After Armistice Day, the United States had laid the keels for ninety-seven destroyers and ten cruisers as part of FDR's drive to make the U.S. Navy the "greatest in the world."[22]

Hughes was calling for a ten-year holiday in shipbuilding and the scuttling of British, U.S., and Japanese capital ships until the three navies reached a 5-5-3 ratio. Britain and the United States would be restricted to 500,000 tons, Japan to 300,000. No warship would be allowed to displace more than 35,000 tons. Hughes's plan spelled an end to the British super-ships.

The Washington Naval Conference, writes James Morris in *Farewell the Trumpets*, was a "surrender by the British Empire . . . of the maritime supremacy which had been its inalienable prerogative, and its surest protection since the Battle of Trafalgar. . . . [T]he Royal Navy was no longer the guarantor of the world's seas, nor even primus inter pares."[23]

> As a result of the treaty the British scrapped 657 ships, with a total displacement of 1,500,000 tons; they included 26 battleships and battlecruisers, among them many a proud stalwart of Beatty's Grand Fleet. Never again would a Fisher at the Admiralty be free to set the standards of the world's navies according to British requirements. No such magnificent fighting ships as Queen Elizabeth, the apex of British naval assurance, were ever again constructed in British dockyards. . . . So ended Britain's absolute command of the seas, the mainstay and in some sense the raison d'être of her empire.[24]

As Admiral David Beatty, the First Sea Lord, who had commanded the battle cruisers at Jutland, listened to the details of Hughes's plan, "he came forward in his chair, 'with the manner of a bulldog, sleeping on a sunny doorstep, who has been poked in the stomach by the impudent foot of an itinerant soap-canvasser.' "[25] The official documents of the naval conference, wrote journalist Mark Sullivan, could not

> convey as much essential fact to the distant and future reader as did the look on Lord Beatty's face . . . when Mr. Hughes, in that sensational opening speech of his, said that he would expect the British to scrap their four great Hoods, and made equally irreverent mention of King George the Fifth.[26]

"Beatty saw the treaty as an abject surrender," writes Arthur Herman, "but the politicians forced him and the Admiralty to swallow this deeply bitter pill."[27]

Japan took her inferior number as a national insult. This looks to us like "Rolls Royce–Rolls Royce–Ford," said one Japanese diplomat. Yet the ratios would enable Japan to construct a fleet 60 percent of Britain's, though Japan had only the western Pacific to patrol while Britain had a global empire.

To induce Japan to accept the inferior number, Britain agreed not to fortify any possession north of Singapore. Equally magnanimous, the United States agreed to no further fortification of the Philippines, Guam, Wake, or the Aleutians. Existing bases could be maintained, but any new or strengthened British base north of the Straits of Malacca or U.S. naval base west of Hawaii was prohibited. The seas around China had been turned into a Japanese lake.

How did the Anglo-Saxon powers now propose to guarantee the Open Door in China? They could not. Barnett regards the Washington Naval Conference as "one of the major catastrophes of English history."[28]

What had happened to Great Britain?

She had been partially converted to the new creed—true security in the modern world lay in parchment, not sea power. So, she had abandoned her policy of maintaining fleets 10 percent stronger than any two rival powers to accept parity with the United States and inferiority to Japan in the western Pacific. The ten-year naval-building holiday would ensure that British ships remained inferior to newer U.S. ships, and that the shipyards, manpower, and skills that had produced the greatest navy the world had ever seen would disappear for lack of contracts. At the same time, Britain had turned her faithful Japanese ally into a bitter enemy.

Instead of having Japan's navy protecting British possessions in Asia, Japan now became their most dangerous predator. "[S]o far as the Western Pacific is concerned, the British Empire is left face to face with Japan; no one else, practically, will be there to intervene," Lord Salisbury explained to the Imperial Conference of 1923.[29] On his return from Washington, Balfour was awarded the Order of the

Garter, the oldest order of chivalry and highest honor a British sovereign can bestow.

Why did Britain capitulate to Harding, Hughes, and the Americans?

Much of the British elite was in thrall to the myth of the Americans as cousins who saw their destiny as one with the Mother Country. This idealized view overlooked a century of hostility—from the Revolution to the *Chesapeake* affair, the burning of Washington, the Battle of New Orleans, Jackson's hanging of the British subjects Arbuthnot and Armbruster on his foray into Florida, the Aroostook War over the border between New Brunswick and Maine, the *Trent* affair, which brought the nations near to war in 1861, Britain's building of Confederate blockade runners and raiders like the *Alabama*, Fenian assaults on Canada, and the 1895 U.S.–British confrontation over Venezuela.

In 1888, when the British minister in Washington, Sir Lionel Sackville-West, was tricked into writing favorably of President Cleveland, this probably cost Cleveland the election and certainly cost Sackville-West his post. To win the Irish-American vote in 1896, the Republicans published a pamphlet, *How McKinley Is Hated in England*.[30] In its 1900 platform, the Republican Party had come close to inserting a pledge to annex Canada.

British elites tended to overlook the tens of millions of Americans of Irish, German, Italian, and East European descent, to whom England was not the Mother Country and the British Empire was no revered institution.

The "special relationship," writes Barnett, was a "British fantasy. It was love in the perfect romantic style, unrequited and unencouraged, yet nevertheless pursued with a grovelling ardour. . . . [T]he myth of the special family relationship had become part of the furniture of the British mind."[31] The British had forgotten the counsel of Palmerston, who had admonished them never to allow emotional attachments to trump national interests:

> It is a narrow policy to suppose that this country or that is to
> be marked out as the eternal ally or the perpetual enemy. . . .
> We have no eternal allies, and we have no eternal enemies.
> Our interests are eternal and perpetual, and those interests it
> is our duty to follow.[32]

There was a second reason why Britain surrendered naval supremacy. The national debt had exploded fourteenfold during the war. Half the national tax revenue was going for interest. Lloyd George feared that if Britain took up the U.S. challenge to her naval supremacy by building warships, Americans would demand immediate payment of her war debts. The Yankees now held the mortgage on the empire.

Third, Wilsonianism, the belief that the blood and horror of the Great War had given birth to a new world where men recognized the insanity of war and were disposed to work together for peace, had rooted itself deep in the British soul. Internationalism and pacifism were the bold new ideas. The wicked old days and ways of militarists, navalists, and power blocs were over. It was the time of the League of Nations.

When the Admiralty began to demand new warships in the 1920s, an exasperated Chancellor of the Exchequer exploded. In a letter of December 15, 1924, to the prime minister that went on "for page after page . . . using every device of statistics and rhetoric to convince [Stanley] Baldwin of the utter impossibility of war with Japan," the Chancellor wrote,

> A war with Japan! But why should there be a war with Japan?
> I do not believe there is the slightest chance of it in our life-
> time. The Japanese are our allies. The Pacific is dominated
> by the Washington Agreement. . . . Japan is at the other end
> of the world. She cannot menace our vital security in any
> way. She has no reason whatever to come into collision with

us. . . . [W]ar with Japan is not a possibility which any reasonable government need take into account.[33]

The Chancellor was Winston Churchill, who wanted the 5-5-3 ratios extended to cruisers, the "basic naval life support system of the empire."[34] Churchill explained his reasoning to Assistant Cabinet Secretary Tom Jones: "We cannot have a lot of silly little cruisers, which would be of no use anyway."[35]

Through the 1920s, Churchill insisted that the "Ten-Year Rule" he had drawn up in 1919 as Secretary of State for War and Air be applied. Each year, the Cabinet would gaze out a decade. If no war loomed, rearmament would be put off another year and disarmament by attrition would proceed. In 1928, the Ten-Year Rule was still being pressed on Baldwin's Cabinet by Chancellor Churchill.

"In the ten years to 1932, the defence budget was cut by more than a third—at a time when Italian and French military spending rose by, respectively, 60 and 55 per cent," writes Niall Ferguson.[36] "By the early 1930s," adds Paul Johnson, "Britain was a weaker naval power in relative terms than at any time since the darkest days of Charles II."[37]

Only weeks after being named Chancellor in 1924, Churchill wrote the secretary to the Cabinet, "asking whether it was not provocative to increase the number of submarines based at Hong Kong from six to twenty-one. 'Suppose the Japanese owned the Isle of Man and started putting 21 submarines there.' "[38]

Two weeks later he [Churchill] wrote to Baldwin saying that to accept the construction demands currently being put forward by the Admiralty "is to sterilize and paralyze the whole policy of the Government. There will be nothing for the taxpayer and nothing for social reform. We shall be a Naval Parliament busily preparing our Navy for some great imminent shock—*Voila tout!*"[39]

The First Sea Lord, Earl Beatty, who had met Churchill at Omdurman and known him as First Lord of the Admiralty, was astounded by the transformation. "That extraordinary fellow Winston has gone mad," he wrote Lady Beatty on January 26, 1925.[40]

Churchill became the great antagonist in Cabinet to a more robust Royal Navy and would remain so until the government fell in 1929. Nor was the navy his only target. Two years into this post, he wrote Clementine, "No more airships, half the cavalry and only one-third of the cruisers."[41] Churchill even dared to risk his chancellorship to win the fight for naval frugality:

> The most dangerous of the disputes for Churchill was over the naval estimates. This was because here he not only performed an extraordinary volte face from his position twelve years before when he had almost broken the Asquith Cabinet with his demand for a larger navy but also in his 1925 demand for a smaller navy took on Baldwin's closest friends within the government.[42]

In 1926, Churchill wrote again that he simply could not imagine "what incentive could possibly move Japan to put herself in the position to incur the lasting hostility of England and run the risk of being regarded as a pariah by the League of Nations."[43] Yet there was such an incentive: Manchuria. In 1931, Japan occupied it. In 1932, Britain finally abandoned Churchill's Ten-Year Rule. But the hour was late and the British position in Asia now perilous to the point of being hopeless. By the early 1930s,

> Australia had only three cruisers and three destroyers, and an air force of seventy planes. New Zealand had two cruisers, and virtually no air force. Canada had four destroyers and an army of 3,600. It had only one military aircraft—on loan from the RAF. Britain was not much more provident so

far as the Far East was concerned. The building of a modern naval base in Singapore had been postponed, at Churchill's urging, for five years.[44]

Correlli Barnett is scathing on Churchill's opposition to British preparedness:

[T]he "ten-year rule" was a calamitous act of policy. . . . It provided the Treasury with a simple and effective weapon for crushing any service demand for research and development. The "ten-year rule" was one of Churchill's least happy contributions to English history, and was to be a major cause of his own difficulties as War Premier after 1940.[45]

Arthur Herman concurs with Barnett on the disastrous five years of Chancellor Winston Churchill.

Churchill applauded rounds of "swinging" budget cuts, which sapped the navy's resources in the 1920s, including cuts in seaman's wages. He had pushed through the Ten Years' Rule and scoffed at the Admiralty's worries that the Washington treaty would "starve" the empire.[46]

THE STIMSON DOCTRINE

JAPAN'S INVASION OF MANCHURIA had been in part defensive. Tokyo feared the rising power of the Chinese Nationalists and the Communists of Mao Tse-tung, backed by Stalin, who had expanded Soviet influence and the Soviet presence in China. Still, the invasion of Manchuria violated both the League of Nations Covenant and the 1928 Kellogg-Briand Pact, which outlawed war as an instrument of national policy. And Japan was a founding member of the League and a signatory to Kellogg-Briand.

Yet, Japan's occupation of Manchuria did not threaten British interests, which lay in central and south China. Had the Anglo-Japanese alliance not been terminated, a *modus vivendi* like the British-French entente of 1904 could have been negotiated. As Britain had recognized France's primacy in Morocco, and France had given up all claims to Suez, Britain could have accepted Japan's special interest in North China, and Tokyo could have agreed to respect British primacy in South China. By recognizing spheres of influence, Britain and Japan could have resolved the crisis. But that was the now-discredited old-world way of realpolitik.

The League of Nations Covenant required members to act against a breach of the peace. But Britain and France, the two members most devoted to the spirit and letter of the Covenant, lacked the power to impose their will on Japan. And sanctions could lead to war, which would be an invitation to Japan to seize British and French possessions in the Far East, as Japan had rolled up Germany's possessions in the Great War. And the Americans would do nothing.

Britain was now face-to-face with the consequences of her folly in severing her Japanese alliance and accepting naval inferiority in the Far East to appease the United States. Because of the shipbuilding holiday imposed at the Washington Conference and Churchill's Ten-Year Rule, the Royal Navy had atrophied.

Where were the Americans for whose friendship Britain had sacrificed Japan? Hoover believed Japan's move into Manchuria was defensive, to protect its empire against a rising China and an encroaching Soviet Union—and no threat to the United States. But Secretary of State Henry Stimson, the Secretary for War under President Taft, was bellicose. "When Stimson in Cabinet meetings began to talk about coercing Japan by all 'means short of actual use of armed force,' the President informed him that this was 'simply the road to war and he would have none of it.' "[47]

Former secretary of state Elihu Root, who had negotiated the Root-Takahira Agreement giving Japan a green light in Manchuria in Theodore Roosevelt's last term, wrote Stimson in protest of his "getting entangled in League [of Nations] measures which we have no right to engage in against Japan," which had the right to protect herself "against the dagger aimed at her heart."[48]

Historian Charles Callan Tansill describes Root as a "realist who did not want war with Japan" and Stimson as "a pacifist who loved peace so much he was always ready to fight for it. He wholeheartedly subscribed to the slogan—perpetual war for perpetual peace."[49]

The energetic Stimson, however, who had come to believe that nonintervention in foreign quarrels was an obsolete policy, responded with the "Stimson Doctrine": The United States would refuse to recognize any political change effected by means "contrary to the covenants and obligations of the Pact of Paris." Initially rebuffed by the British Foreign Office, which did not consider Britain obligated to defend the territorial integrity of China—an ideal that had never been a reality—Stimson soon brought the British around to his view. It was also adopted by the League of Nations. Thus did Stimson put America and Britain on the path to war with Japan.

When the League voted in 1933 to condemn Japan's aggression and demand Manchuria's return to China, Britain voted in favor. Japan walked out. With Hitler now in power in Germany and the specter emerging of a two-front war against Germany and Japan, the British Cabinet began to reconsider the wisdom of having thrown over Japan to appease an America that was now isolationist and indifferent, if not hostile, to British imperial interests. The strongest voice for rapprochement with Japan was that of the new Chancellor of the Exchequer. In a 1934 memorandum, he warned that British failure to neutralize Japan in the event of a European conflict could prove fatal for the empire:

[I]f we had to enter upon such a [European] struggle with a hostile, instead of a friendly, Japan . . . ; if we had to contemplate the division of our forces so as to protect our Far Eastern interests while prosecuting a war in Europe; then not only would India, Hong Kong and Australasia be in dire peril, but we ourselves would stand in far greater danger by a fully armed and organised Germany.[50]

Chancellor Neville Chamberlain would prove a prophet.

The Washington treaty and Ten-Year Rule reduced the real and relative power of the Royal Navy to levels not seen in centuries. By 1931, the British navy was down to 50 cruisers, 120 destroyers, and only 3 new battleships—to police a world empire.[51] The air arm of the Royal Navy, once the largest in the world, had shrunk to 159 planes.[52] On the other side of the world, a bitter ex-ally had four hundred planes in the fleet, and to Britain's four aircraft carriers, Japan had built ten.[53]

Britain's Asian empire was now ripe for the taking. Only the Americans could stop Japan, and the Americans, for whom Britain had thrown over her Japanese ally, were not interested. In 1936, Churchill would look back ruefully upon the historic folly in which he had played a leading role:

What a story of folly is unfolded in the efforts of the United States and Great Britain to tie each other down in naval matters! The two great peaceful sea-Powers have hobbled each other, tied each other's hands, cramped each other's style, with the result that warlike Powers have gained enormous advantages against them both in the Far East and in Europe. Probably no conscious act of those who seek peace, and who have everything to lose by war, has brought war nearer and rendered aggression more possible than the naval limitations which the two great English-speaking nations have imposed upon each other.[54]

In 1948, Churchill, looking back in anger, would lay at the feet of the Americans the blame for the naval disarmament of Britain, for which he, as much as any statesman, was responsible:

At the Washington Conference of 1921, far-reaching proposals for naval disarmament were made by the United States, and the British and American governments proceeded to sink their battleships and break up their military establishments with gusto. It was argued in odd logic that it would be immoral to disarm the vanquished unless the victors also stripped themselves of their weapons.[55]

Yet Churchill had not only gone along with the "odd logic" of naval disarmament by the victorious powers, he had pressed it with "gusto." In *The Gathering Storm,* Churchill blames the United States for forcing Britain to terminate her twenty-year alliance with Japan. This insult to Tokyo led directly to the greatest military disaster in British history: the surrender of Singapore and an army of 80,000 British, Australian, and Indian troops, virtually without a fight, to a Japanese army half that size.

The United States made it clear to Britain that the continuance of her alliance with Japan, to which the Japanese had punctiliously conformed, would constitute a barrier in Anglo-American relations. Accordingly, this alliance was brought to an end. The annulment caused a profound impression in Japan, and was viewed as the spurning of an Asian Power by the Western World.[56]

So wrote Winston Churchill, looking back.

He does not explain why he and his colleagues did not hold fast for the empire and tell the Americans that Great Britain would not throw over a faithful ally who had helped carry the shield of the empire in Asia and the Pacific—unless America was willing to help her hold that shield. It had been at Churchill's insistence that Britain capitulated to the United States. Nor does Churchill explain his zeal in slashing the Royal Navy as Chancellor of the Exchequer, when, as First Lord, he had been its greatest champion.

Two explanations for Churchill's conduct come to mind. The first is Churchill's conviction that the British Lion must ever follow the American Eagle. The second is opportunism. "Anybody can rat," said Churchill of his switch from Unionist to Liberal in 1904 over free trade, "but it takes ingenuity to re-rat." Re-ratting to the Tories in 1924, as the Liberal Party was fading away, he was rewarded with an office second only to Baldwin's. Chancellor of the Exchequer Churchill may have sought to show his gratitude by becoming the most fearless fiscal conservative in the Cabinet. The Royal Navy, the nation, and the empire would all pay a heavy price for his having put budget-cutting ahead of national security.

CHAPTER 5

1935: Collapse of the Stresa Front

AUSTRIA KNOWS THAT she can count on us to defend
her independence as a sovereign state.[1]
— MUSSOLINI, 1934

Next fall I am going to invite Hitler to . . . make Austria
German. In 1934 I could have beaten his army . . . today
I cannot.[2]
— MUSSOLINI, 1937

THE ITALIANS HAD come home from the Paris conference bitter, and they blamed Wilson even more than Lloyd George.

After deserting the Triple Alliance and declaring neutrality in 1914, Rome had been bribed into the war on the Allied side by the British, who offered Rome more than Berlin could. In the secret 1915 Treaty of London, Italy had been promised South Tyrol, Istria, Trieste, northern Dalmatia, most of the Dalmatian Islands, sovereignty over the Dodecanese Islands, and a protectorate over Albania. These lands were to be confiscated from the Austro-Hungarian and Ottoman empires.

Were the Treaty of London to be fully honored, Harold Nicolson had noted, Italy would have been given dominion over "some 1,300,000 Yugoslavs, some 230,000 Germans, the whole Greek population of the Dodecanese, the Turks and Greeks of Adalia, all that was left of the Albanians, and vague areas of Africa."[3] Forced to listen to incessant Italian demands for full payment for having joined the Allies, plus Rome's added demand for the Croatian port of Fiume on the Adriatic, a disgusted Lord Balfour dismissed them as "swine."[4]

Italy had come home from Paris with South Tyrol, Trieste, and Istria, but believed she had been denied the Dalmatian coast and Fiume by Wilson and robbed of her share of the African spoils by Lloyd George.[5] Italy felt cheated, for her sacrifices during the war had included more than four hundred thousand combat deaths.

"Even before he took charge of Italy as the Fascist leader and through the period after 1922," writes the Italian diplomat Luigi Villari, "Mussolini constantly urged a revision of these treaties [Versailles and St. Germain] and predicted a second European war if this was not done."[6] In 1922, however, it was domestic unrest that led to a Fascist march on Rome that brought to power this ex-socialist and war veteran who was determined to gain for Italy that place in the sun denied her at Paris.

Mussolini had been in power for a decade before Hitler ever became Chancellor. During that decade, Il Duce's attitude toward the Nazi leader may be summed up in a single word: contempt. But Hitler's admiration for Il Duce bordered on adulation. As leader of the National Socialist Party in 1927, Hitler had, through the Berlin head of the Italian Chamber of Commerce, requested a signed photograph of Il Duce. Across the memorandum Mussolini scrawled in bold letters, "Request refused."[7]

When Hitler came to power, Mussolini, realizing the Nazis might attempt the violent overthrow of Versailles, imperiling the peace of Europe, proposed a Four-Power Pact. It was among the bolder and more visionary ideas of the era. Britain, France, Italy, and Germany would meet as equals to rectify the injustices of Versailles to avert another war. Il Duce "threw all his energy and enthusiasm into perfection of such a pact in 1933, but it was rejected by France, Britain and the pro-French Little Entente" of Czechoslovakia, Yugoslavia, and Rumania.[8]

Among the statesmen pouring cold water on Il Duce's plan to create a new Concert of Europe was Winston Churchill: "In 1933, Churchill had in the House of Commons vigorously attacked Mussolini's proposal for a four-power pact, the one comprehensive plan set forth in Europe which might have revised postwar treaties in a peaceful manner and held Hitler in check."[9]

SELLING OUT SOUTH TYROL

THE FOREIGN POLICY HITLER would pursue began to take shape within a year of his having taken control of the Nazi Party. His first goal was a Rome-Berlin alliance. Believing that war might be necessary to overturn Versailles, Hitler wanted no repetition of 1914, when Italy, an ally, declared neutrality, then entered the war against Germany. In return for an alliance, Hitler was prepared to surrender all German claims to South Tyrol. Writes biographer Ian Kershaw:

> Already in 1920, before he had heard of Fascism, [Hitler] was contemplating the value of an alliance with Italy. He was determined even then that the question of South Tyrol—the predominantly German-speaking part of the former Austrian province of Tyrol lying beyond the Brenner, ceded to Italy in 1919, and since then subjected to a programme of "Italianization"—would not stand in the way of such an alliance.[10]

Though railing against the injustices of Versailles was a constant theme in his rise to power, Hitler displayed an opportunistic willingness to write off German lands and peoples to avoid wars he did not want and to gather allies for the new German goal: an empire in the east. "Almost alone of Germans, in 1926–27, Hitler did not complain of the Italianisation policies in Alto Adige [South Tyrol], pursued with Mussolini's personal endorsement, and with that Fascist method well defined as the policy of 'open conflicts, openly arrived at,' " writes R.J.B. Bosworth.[11] Hitler would stubbornly admonish friends that any "reconquest of the South Tyrol . . . [is] impossible."[12]

When he took power in 1933, Hitler's readiness to surrender South Tyrol was already being denounced by German and Austrian nationalists as the appeasement of Italy and the abandonment of a Germanic people.

THE MURDER OF DOLLFUSS

HITLER'S FIRST TRIP ABROAD, to meet Mussolini in Venice, June 14, 1934, was "a conspicuous failure."[13] Hitler made a dismal impression. He talked ceaselessly "and what he said was disquieting and repugnant. . . . Hitler made wounding observations on the superiority of the Nordic race and the negroid strain in the Mediterranean peoples."[14]

> Hitler was shy and awkward on his first appearance in a foreign country and the disparity between the two leaders was emphasized by the difference in their appearance: the Duce in his Fascist uniform resplendent among his obedient and acclaiming crowds; and the Fuehrer ill at ease in a badly fitting suit, patent leather shoes, a shabby yellow mackintosh and an old gray felt hat. . . . To the eyes of the Venetians, he might have borrowed his wardrobe from Charlie Chaplin.[15]

Foreign Minister von Neurath, who had advised Hitler on how to dress for his meeting with Mussolini, was never forgiven. Of his visitor, whom he considered a buffoon, Mussolini was contemptuous. He looked like a "plumber in a Mackintosh," Mussolini mocked.[16] "Instead of speaking to me about current problems, he recited . . . from *Mein Kampf,* that boring book which I have never been able to read."[17]

"What a clown this Hitler is," Il Duce told an Italian diplomat.[18] One problem the two had discussed was Austria.

Determined to bring Austria into Germany's orbit, Hitler knew the time was not ripe. Any attempt at Anschluss would be forcibly resisted by Italy, which saw Austria as its buffer state. Hitler was warned by Mussolini not to intervene, and he assured his host he would respect Austrian sovereignty but went no further, for his SS was secretly backing Austrian Nazis in a terror campaign against Chancellor Engelbert Dollfuss.

Mussolini sensed what was about to happen. As early as 1933, he had confided to his son Vittorio, "The saucepan's boiling under poor Dollfuss and it's Hitler who's stoking the fire."[19]

Dollfuss was a fierce nationalist determined to retain the independence of his landlocked nation that had been mutilated by the Treaty of St. Germain. His government has been described as a "repressive single-party dictatorship bearing some distinctly fascist traits."[20] Political parties had been banned. And Dollfuss had not recoiled from using tanks and artillery on rebellious Austrian Social Democrats in a working-class housing project of "Red Vienna" in February 1934.

"Leading Socialists, including their most influential ideologue, Otto Bauer, fled to safety through Vienna's famous underground sewers," writes Richard Evans, author of *The Third Reich in Power.* "Dollfuss now outlawed the Socialists altogether."[21] His real concern was the Nazi Party, banned since July 1933. Dollfuss intended to eliminate it. In Mussolini he had a friend and ally pledged to stand beside him should Germany intervene.

Mussolini had become Dollfuss's patron. On first meeting the Austrian chancellor in 1933, Il Duce had concluded, "Dollfuss in spite of his minuscule size, is a man of ingenuity, possessed of real will. Together, these qualities give a good impression."[22]

Two weeks after Hitler left Venice came the Night of the Long Knives, the "sanguinary liquidation of the S.A. Leader Roehm."[23]

Ernst Roehm was a decorated veteran of the Western Front who had marched beside Hitler in the Munich Beer Hall Putsch and been imprisoned for it. His storm troopers had fought the Nazis' street battles with the Communists. When Hitler came to power, recruits had poured into the SA. Roehm's prestige and power soared. By mid-1934, with his vast army of bully boys, Ernst Roehm was a rival to Hitler and preaching a "second revolution." Hitler was under pressure from President Hindenburg, the German generals, industrialists, and conservatives such as ex-chancellor von Papen, who helped bring him to power, to suppress Roehm's SA. Initially reluctant, Hitler, in the summer of 1934, moved with ruthless efficiency in a lightning purge. Europe was stunned.

Having caught his old comrade in a homosexual tryst, Hitler had him executed, along with scores of brownshirt leaders. The SS used the occasion to settle accounts with ex-chancellor Kurt von Schleicher. He was murdered with his wife at their home. The Night of the Long Knives was the first act of state terror of the Third Reich and revealed the character of Hitler and his regime. To the Nazis, murder was a legitimate weapon to deal with political enemies. Between 150 and 200 people died. Mussolini was shaken. Reading of how Hitler relished the role of executioner of former comrades, Mussolini

> burst into a room in which his sister Edvige was sitting and waved a bundle of newspapers: "He is a cruel and ferocious character and calls to mind legendary characters of the past: Attila. Those men he killed were his closest collaborators, who hoisted him into power. It is as if I came to kill with my own hands, Balbo, Grandi, Bottai . . ."[24]

Il Duce now knew that the Hitler he had considered a buffoon in Venice was a decisive, ruthless, menacing, and formidable figure, unlike any European statesman with whom he had dealt in a decade in power.

Six weeks after Hitler's visit to Venice, 150 Austrian Nazis stormed the chancery in Vienna. Most of the Cabinet, warned in advance, had fled. But the gritty little Dollfuss refused to run. From six inches away, he was shot in the throat. As the celebrating Nazis went on national radio to announce his resignation, Dollfuss, ignored by his killers, bled to death, the only European leader to die a martyr's death resisting Nazism.

Berlin hailed the coup. Whether Hitler knew it was coming remains in dispute. But when word reached him at the Bayreuth Festival in Munich that Dollfuss had died at 6 P.M., that the putsch had been quelled, and that the Nazi assassins were under arrest, Hitler was alarmed. Given the Austrian Nazi hand in the coup, Mussolini might well conclude that Hitler had lied to him.

Late that night, at the home of Wagner's widow, Cosima, who had died in 1930, Hitler appeared nervous. He phoned Berlin, only to be told the German ambassador in Vienna was negotiating for safe passage for the Nazi assassins out of Austria. Hitler shouted that the ambassador had no such instructions. Nearly incoherent with rage, he countermanded Berlin's orders, fired his ambassador in Vienna, and demanded that Franz von Papen, under house arrest since he had narrowly escaped Nazi death squads in the Roehm purge, be flown to Munich. Papen had befriended Dollfuss and warned Hitler about the Austrian Nazis.[25]

Papen found Hitler in a "state of hysterical agitation, denouncing feverishly the rashness and stupidity of the Austrian Nazi Party for having involved him in such an appalling situation."[26]

"We are faced with a new Sarajevo!" Hitler shouted.[27]

Hitler was right to be nervous. Mussolini, who had been hosting Dollfuss's family and had to break the news of his assassination to his wife, was enraged and ordered four divisions to the Brenner. Il Duce sent word to Vienna: If Germany invades, Italy will go to war. In a show of support, Mussolini departed for Austria, where he vented his disgust at Hitler and the Nazis to vice chancellor Prince Ernst Rüdiger von Starhemberg: "It would mean the end of European civilization if this country of murderers and pederasts were to over-run Europe."[28]

Starhemberg recalls Mussolini, eyes rolling, delivering a tirade against the Nazis: "Hitler is the murderer of Dollfuss . . . a horrible sexual degenerate, a dangerous fool."[29] Nazism was a "revolution of the old Germanic tribes of the primeval forest against the Latin civilization of Rome."[30] To Il Duce, Italian Fascism was a world apart from Nazism:

> Both are authoritarian systems, both are collectivist, socialistic. Both systems oppose liberalism. But Fascism is a regime that is rooted in the great cultural tradition of the Italian people; Fascism recognizes the right of the individual, it recognizes religion and family. National Socialism . . . is savage barbarism; the chieftain is lord over life and death of his people. Murder and killing, loot and pillage and blackmail are all it can produce.[31]

Mussolini hoped Britain and France would recognize the danger and form a united front:

> Hitler will arm the Germans and make war—perhaps even in two or three years. I cannot stand up to him alone. . . . I cannot always be the one to march to the Brenner. Others must show some interest in Austria and the Danube basin. . . . We must do something, we must do something quickly.[32]

While Italy had mobilized troops, Britain and France had done nothing. Mussolini was confirmed in his convictions about the decadence of the democracies and "resolved petulantly that he would not again attempt to pull the chestnuts out of the fire for the West."[33]

For Hitler, the failed Austrian coup was a debacle and a humiliation. Writes historian Ernest May, "In foreign newspapers and magazines . . . Hitler saw himself ridiculed. *Punch* pictured Germany as a dachshund cowering before a mastiff labeled, 'Italy.' "[34]

Hitler had to repudiate his fellow Nazis on the other side of the Inn River. Signing a formal agreement that promised no interference in Austria's internal affairs, he dissolved the Austrian Legion, a group that had been training in Bavaria. He even issued an order forbidding Nazis in Germany to have any contact with Nazis in Austria.[35]

Looking back in 1942, Hitler—perhaps exaggerating to impress his listeners—recalled the Austrian Nazis' Vienna coup as far more fraught with peril than any had assumed at the time:

I shall never forget that at the time of the Austrian National Socialist coup d'etat in 1934 . . . [T]he unarmed Germany of the time would have emerged from a struggle against the combined forces of France, Italy and Great Britain in a state of ruin and desolation comparable only to the situation at the end of the Thirty Years' War.[36]

The crisis passed and, in January of 1935, Hitler's Reich received an enormous boost in morale and legitimacy. Writes British historian A.J.P. Taylor,

[T]he Saar—detached from Germany in 1919—held a plebiscite on its future destiny. The inhabitants were mostly industrial workers—Social Democrats or Roman Catholics. They knew what awaited them in Germany: dictatorship, destruction of trade unions, persecution of the Christian churches. Yet, in an unquestionably free election, 90% voted for return to Germany. Here was proof that the appeal of German nationalism would be irresistible—in Austria, in Czechoslovakia, in Poland.[37]

Speaking in Saarbrücken on March 1 of his joy at the Saarlanders' vote to return to the Reich, Hitler, the Versailles amputations in mind, proclaimed, "In the end, blood is stronger than any document of mere paper. What ink has written will one day be blotted out by blood."[38]

With the Saar's return, Hitler prepared his next move. On March 9, 1935, Hermann Göring informed a correspondent of the London *Daily Mail* that the Luftwaffe would become an official branch of the armed forces. The next Saturday, the Nazis announced that Germany was reimposing conscription and calling up 300,000 men to create an army of 36 divisions. This was the first formal breach of Versailles. Hitler reassured the French ambassador he had no designs on the West as he delivered a blazing tirade against Stalin and Bolshevism. The French envoy was soothed. Paris appealed feebly to the League of Nations against this brazen violation of the 1919 peace treaty that had been crafted with France's security foremost in mind.

Britain and France now began to believe Mussolini might be right. With German rearmament under way, and the murder of Dollfuss and the failed Austrian coup in mind, Prime Minister Ramsay MacDonald and French prime minister Pierre Flandin and Foreign Minister Pierre Laval agreed to meet with Mussolini in Stresa on Lake Maggiore from April 11 to 14.

Passed over by many historians, this was a crucial meeting in the interwar period. For in 1935, as Oxford's R. B. McCallum has written, "Italy, with her military force and strong and virile Government, held the balance of power in Europe."[39] At the end of the Stresa conference a communiqué was issued denouncing German rearmament as a violation of Versailles and affirming the three nations' commitment to the principles of Locarno.

THE LOCARNO PACT

THE LOCARNO TREATY OF MUTUAL Guarantee—negotiated in that Swiss town and signed in London in 1925—was the brainchild of German foreign minister Gustav Stresemann. He had suggested to the British that, rather than siding with France against a friendly and democratic Germany by guaranteeing France's border, Britain should guarantee the borders of both nations. As described by historian Correlli Barnett, the Locarno pact was a group of treaties:

> Germany, Belgium and France bound themselves to recognize as inviolable not only their existing mutual frontiers, but also the demilitarisation of the Rhineland. Thus Germany now voluntarily accepted in respect of the Rhineland and her western frontiers what had been imposed on her at Versailles. The three countries further pledged themselves that in no case would they attack, invade or resort to war against one another. All these obligations were guaranteed by Italy and England; in other words, the guarantors were immediately to intervene against a power which broke the treaty by violating the frontier of another. . . . [T]hey were similarly to intervene if Germany violated the demilitarised zone.[40]

Locarno was crucial. For it represented the voluntary acceptance by Berlin of what had been imposed upon Germany at Versailles. On October 16, 1925, a democratic Germany accepted the loss of Alsace-Lorraine, the inviolability of its borders with Belgium and France, and the permanent demilitarization of the Rhineland, and undertook to apply for membership in the League of Nations.

At Locarno, however, the borders of Eastern Europe had gone unmentioned. For no German statesman could accept, in perpetuity, the loss of Memel, Danzig, the Corridor, and the Sudetenland to Lithuania, Poland, and Czechoslovakia, and survive. Writes Taylor:

This was an impossible condition for the German government. Most Germans had acquiesced in the loss of Alsace
and Lorraine; few of them even raised the question until
after the defeat of France in 1940. The frontier with Poland
was felt as a grievance. It might be tolerated; it could not be
confirmed.[41]

How vital to its national security did Britain regard the 1919 Polish–
German borders imposed at Versailles? As Foreign Secretary
Austen Chamberlain, son of Joe and half brother of Neville, who
would win the Nobel Prize for Peace for negotiating Locarno, ex-
plained, the Polish Corridor was a creation "for which no British
Government ever will and ever can risk the bones of a British
Grenadier."[42]

One statesman, however, did favor an "Eastern Locarno" that
would commit the nations of Central and Eastern Europe, including
Russia, backed by Britain and France, to act jointly to stop any German attempt to undo the borders laid down at Paris. He was Louis
Barthou of France. In 1934, French policy toward Hitler's Reich was
in the portfolio of this tough-minded foreign minister and "last sur-
vivor of the staunch old republican politicians of the stripe of
Clemenceau and Poincaré, who had helped guide the country to victory over Germany."[43]

Barthou supported an understanding with Italy, the restoration of
France's alliance with Russia, and firmness toward Hitler. He had
helped to bring the Soviet Union into the League of Nations. Where
Ramsay MacDonald was willing to concede equality of armaments to
Germany, Barthou declared that France would refuse to legalize any
German rearmament contrary to the terms of Versailles, adding,
"France will assure her security by her own means."[44]

Tragically, Barthou was riding beside Yugoslavia's King Alexander
in Marseilles on October 9, 1934, when that monarch was assassinated by a Macedonian terrorist who also shot and wounded Barthou. The king was in France on the first day of a state visit to cement

their alliance against Germany. While the king was being attended to, Barthou, ignored, bled to death.

THE STRESA CONFERENCE

Now, AT STRESA, ten years after Locarno, Britain, France, and Italy had agreed to support the independence and integrity of Austria. But there was a worm in the apple of accord. The British were double-dealing. Mussolini and the French had come prepared to form a united front. But MacDonald and Foreign Secretary John Simon had assured Parliament they would make no commitments at Stresa that would bind Britain to act against Germany.

MacDonald and Simon had both opposed British entry into the war in 1914 and were unwilling to commit Britain to defend any nation in Central or Eastern Europe, or to act with Italy and France, should Hitler commit a new violation of Versailles. As Mussolini biographer Jasper Ridley writes, "In all the discussions between Britain, France and Italy as to how to react to Hitler's breach of the Treaty of Versailles, Simon was the most pro-German and Mussolini the most anti-German."[45]

Britain had also come to Stresa with two cards facedown. She had decided the Rhineland was not a vital British interest and was trolling for an Anglo-German naval agreement that would allow Hitler to breach the Versailles naval restrictions in return for his recognition of Britain's supremacy at sea.[46]

When Flandin declared at Stresa that if Hitler committed one more violation of Versailles, France would mobilize, Mussolini called for even stronger joint action. MacDonald and Simon refused to make any commitment.[47] Concludes historian J. Kenneth Brody,

What had the [Stresa] Conference wrought? The vigorous leadership of Mussolini and the firm determination of France to arrive at concrete courses of action to face up to the German threat contrasted to the British horror of any commitment and Britain's yearning for some kind of arrangement with Germany. The clarity, the logic, the pertinacity, and the force of the Franco-Italian position had been met by British vacillation, hesitancies and obfuscations.[48]

Two days after the Stresa conference ended, however, on April 17, a British-French-Italian resolution condemning German rearmament and conscription as a breach of Versailles was passed by the Council of the League of Nations. The condemnation of Germany was unanimous, with only Denmark abstaining. A committee of thirteen, including Russia, was set up to consider sanctions. The Third Reich was diplomatically isolated.[49]

Having alarmed and united Britain, France, and Italy into forming the Stresa Front against him, Hitler decided the moment was ripe for a peace offensive. On May 21, 1935, he declared to the Reichstag, "What else could I wish for other than calm and peace? Germany needs peace, and wants peace."[50] Hitler went on to reassure Mussolini that "Germany had neither the intention nor wish to annex or incorporate Austria."[51]

THE HITLER-BALDWIN PACT

FOR THE BRITISH, HITLER had prepared a more tempting offer. Alluding to the naval arms race the Kaiser and Admiral Tirpitz had run with the Royal Navy that alienated Britain and propelled her into the 1904 entente with France, Hitler declared:

> The German Government recognizes the overpowering vital importance, and therewith the justification, of a dominating protection for the British Empire on the sea. . . . The German Government has the straightforward intention to

find and maintain a relationship with the British people and state which will prevent for all time a repetition of the only struggle there has been between the two nations.[52]

The London *Times* was ecstatic. Hitler's speech contained "the basis of a complete settlement with a . . . free, equal and strong Germany" and the Fuehrer's words should be taken "as a sincere and well-considered utterance meaning precisely what it says."[53]

Hitler now moved to snap the weak link in the Stresa chain. He wrote his friend, newspaper baron Lord Rothermere. Hinting that a dangerous new Anglo-German naval arms race was in the offing, Hitler told Rothermere he would agree to restrict the new German navy to 35 percent of the Royal Navy, the same fraction France and Italy had accepted at the Washington Conference. The High Seas Fleet had reached 60 percent of the Royal Navy. Hitler knew his history and believed that the challenge of the Kaiser and Admiral Tirpitz to the Royal Navy had assured British hostility in the world war. He did not intend to repeat the blunder. In his letter to Lord Rothermere, Hitler spoke of a broader, deeper entente—between England and Germany:

> Such an agreement between England and Germany would represent the weighty influence for peace and common sense of 120,000,000 of the most valuable people in the world. The historically unique colonial aptitude and naval power of Britain would be combined with that of one of the first military nations of the world.[54]

Stanley Baldwin, who had replaced MacDonald, rose swiftly to the bait. When Hitler's emissary, Joachim von Ribbentrop, arrived in London, he declared the 35 percent figure nonnegotiable. For twenty-four hours, the British balked, and then capitulated. On June 18, 1935, an Anglo-German Naval Agreement was signed permitting

Germany to construct a fleet 35 percent of the Royal Navy and a submarine force equal to Great Britain's. Writes historian Evans, "This rode a coach and horses through the Stresa agreement, concluded only a few months before, and was a major diplomatic triumph for Hitler."[55]

Ribbentrop returned home to a hero's welcome. Paris was as stunned as Moscow. Stalin believed Britain had just given Hitler a green light to build a Baltic fleet strong enough to attack him. From Rome came reports that "Mussolini had nearly gone through the roof of the Palazzo Chigi when he heard about the Anglo-German Agreement," believing that the "British government were so frightened of Hitler that they had lost faith in the League of Nations' ability to prevent war."[56]

To Correlli Barnett, Ribbentrop's demand that Germany be granted, within twenty-four hours, full rights to submarine parity and a fleet one-third the size of the Royal Navy, in violation of Versailles, was a "preposterously arrogant demand."[57] Britain's acceding to it amounted to an "abject surrender" that marked the "consummation of a complete German moral ascendancy over the British . . . disastrous in its results, but even more fateful for the future."[58]

Hitler was elated. A naval agreement meant an alliance was possible. Ever since he had fought the "Tommies" on the Western Front, Hitler had dreamed of an Anglo-German alliance.

Britain had sacrificed both Allied solidarity and principle. A naval treaty with Nazi Germany meant Britain put bilateral relations with Hitler ahead of any reliance on her Stresa Front partners. Having sought her own security in a side deal with Hitler, Britain had undermined the Stresa concept of collective security. "The solidarity of the Stresa Front . . . was destroyed," writes Hitler biographer Alan Bullock. "The British Government, in its eagerness to secure a private advantage, had given a disastrous impression of bad faith."[59] As Ian Kershaw writes, however, to the German people,

Hitler seemed to be achieving the unimaginable. The world . . . looked on in astonishment. Great Britain, party to the condemnation of Germany for breach of treaties, had wholly undermined the Stresa Front, left its allies in the lurch, and assisted Hitler in tearing a further large strip out of the Versailles Treaty.[60]

To Mussolini, the Anglo-German agreement meant Britain was too pacifist to hold a weakened Germany to commitments that en-sured her own security. Perfidious Albion might cut a deal with Hitler behind his back. Rather than rely on such an ally, Il Duce began to consider whether he should cut his own deal first.

Churchill thought the Anglo-German treaty a rotten bargain:

The League of Nations has been weakened by our action, the principle of collective security has been impaired. Ger-man treaty-breaking has been condoned and even extolled. The Stresa front has been shaken, if not, indeed, dissolved.[61]

In coming years, British denunciations of Hitler's moves into the Rhineland and Austria as violations of Versailles would ring hollow in light of her own naval agreement that authorized Hitler to ignore the Versailles limits on warships. British diplomacy would now shatter the Stresa Front altogether and drive Mussolini straight into the arms of Hitler.

ABYSSINIA

THE ROOT OF THE Ethiopia crisis went back to the late nineteenth century.

Following the Berlin conference of 1884–85, which laid down the rules for the partition of Africa, Italy, late to nationhood and empire, had set out on the path trod centuries before by the sea powers that fronted on the Atlantic: Spain, Portugal, England, and France. As all the choicer slices of Africa had been staked out, Italy had to settle for Libya, Somalia, and Eritrea. When Italy attempted to seize the last independent state, Ethiopia, she had taken a thrashing. At Adowa in 1896, the tribal warriors of Ethiopia had slain 4,000 Italian soldiers and perpetrated unspeakable atrocities on the prisoners they had taken. Bismarck had been proven right: "The Italians have a big appetite and poor teeth."[62]

Adowa stuck in Italy's craw, and Mussolini was determined to avenge the humiliation and append to his new Roman empire the last great uncolonized land in Africa. He had an added incentive. In dividing up the Ottoman Empire and distributing Germany's colonies, Britain and France had cut Italy out, though she had lost 460,000 men in the Allied cause. Italy and Mussolini felt these grievances deeply. In December 1934, there occurred a clash on the border between Italian Somaliland and Ethiopia that gave Il Duce his opportunity. According to Luigi Villari,

> In November, 1934, large Ethiopian forces suddenly approached the Italian frontier post at Wal-Wal—an area which had been under Italian rule for many years and to which Ethiopia had never made any claim at all. . . .
>
> On the night of December 4, 1934, the Ethiopians attacked Wal-Wal, but were beaten off after heavy fighting. As the Italians were only one-fifth as numerous as the Ethiopians, it is hardly likely that they would have been the first to attack.[63]

Mussolini now had his casus belli and most of Europe believed Italy would invade. At Stresa, Mussolini had searched for any sign of British-French opposition. In six meetings he heard none. Though banner headlines in the Italian press were trumpeting ITALIAN TROOPS

PASS THROUGH SUEZ CANAL!, the British statesmen at Stresa never mentioned Abyssinia.[64]

"Ramsay MacDonald and Simon could have issued a stern warning to Mussolini at Stresa against Abyssinian aggression," writes Brody. "They chose silence. . . . Simon had the opportunity to warn Mussolini in unmistakable terms. He did not choose to take the opportunity."[65]

As he signed the Stresa communiqué, Mussolini loudly repeated the words of his amendment to the final draft, "peace in Europe."[66] MacDonald and Simon looked at each other and said nothing. Mussolini took this as a signal of Allied assent to his plans for conquest in Africa.[67] Thus did Britain miss an opening that could have saved its alliance with Italy. Writes British diplomat and historian Ivone Kirkpatrick,

> The best chance of inducing Mussolini to compromise over Abyssinia lay in demonstrating that the Stresa Front would otherwise be broken and that maintenance of any effective Stresa front was essential to Italian security. This latter proposition Mussolini was conditioned to accept. The murder of Dollfuss had inflamed him against Germany and he was beginning to be frightened of Hitler.[68]

As the British Empire controlled almost every other piece of real estate in East Africa, Italy's annexation of part or all of Ethiopia posed no threat to Great Britain. And with British flags flying over Hong Kong, Singapore, Malaya, Burma, India, Ceylon, Pakistan, southern Iran, Iraq, Palestine, Egypt, the Sudan, Uganda, Kenya, Tanganyika, Rhodesia, South Africa, Southwest Africa, Togo, the Gold Coast, and Nigeria—not all acquired by peaceful purchase—for Britain to oppose Italy's annexation of Ethiopia might seem hypocritical. To aspiring imperial powers like Italy and Japan, it did. Yōsuke Matsuoka, who had led the Japanese delegation at Geneva, had commented about the centuries-old practice of imperialism: "The Western powers taught the Japanese the game of poker but after acquiring most of the chips they pronounced the game immoral and took up contract bridge."[69]

When a Frenchwoman accosted Churchill to argue that Italy was only doing in Ethiopia what British imperialists had done for centuries, Churchill replied, "Ah, but you see, all that belongs to the unregenerate past, is locked away in the limbo of the old, the wicked days. The world progresses."[70]

Mussolini believed that, as the British-French Entente of 1904 had put Egypt in Britain's sphere and Morocco in France's, Italy, a Stresa partner of the Allies, should be given a free hand in Abyssinia. Moreover, Abyssinia was no ornament of civilization, but

> was itself an empire, ruling subject and often migratory populations by force and terror, behind shifting or indeterminate frontiers. . . . Abyssinia was a primitive African monarchy which practiced slavery; not a modern state at all. It should not have been in the League. The notion that the League had to guarantee its frontiers was an excellent illustration of the absurdity of the covenant which led Senator Henry Cabot Lodge and his friends to reject it. The League should also have been scrapped after the 1931 Manchurian fiasco.[71]

But the League had not been scrapped, Ethiopia was a member, and Wilsonian idealism now had a powerful hold on the British upper class and the national imagination.

How had an African empire that practiced slavery qualified for the League?

Paradoxically, Ethiopia had been brought into the League by Italy in 1923. Rome suspected Britain had designs on the country and wanted to keep it out of the Lion's paws. Indeed, British newspapers had been clamoring for intervention in Ethiopia to abolish slavery, and Britain had been among the least enthusiastic members of the League about admitting so reactionary a state. Ethiopia, upon its admission, had pledged to end slavery, but had never done so.

THE EDEN DEBACLE

As it became clear Mussolini intended to invade Ethiopia, Britain, in June 1935, tried to divert the dictator with a deal. "The carrier of the deal," writes Bosworth, "was Anthony Eden, the elegant, young, ambitious, but nervy British Minister for League of Nations Affairs, a newly minted post unlikely to be applauded in Rome. The offer was of an exchange of territory whereby Italy would gain land in the Ogaden desert, and Ethiopia an outlet to the sea at Zeila in British Somaliland."[72]

Eden was insufficiently briefed and unprepared for his encounter with Mussolini. Brusquely brushing aside the British offer, Il Duce told Eden that Italy would accept nothing less than all the territories that the Ethiopian empire had taken in the last century and "de facto control of the surviving nucleus." Were his demands not met, Mussolini warned, it "would mean the eventual cancellation of Ethiopia from the map." Already, Il Duce maintained, grabbing his statistics from the air, Italy had 680,000 men under arms; a million would be ready soon."[73]

After this verbal beating, the "tender sensibilities of Eden left him with the impression that Mussolini was 'a complete gangster,' the 'Anti-Christ,' a view which never left him."[74] Eden felt personally insulted and humiliated. So enduring was the bad blood between him and Mussolini that when Eden was removed as foreign secretary by Neville Chamberlain, Rome rejoiced.

After the Eden-Mussolini confrontation, the British press, to whom Eden was the personification of the new and higher League of Nations morality in international affairs, turned on Mussolini,

mocking and assaulting him as the world's worst dictator. British socialists, Liberals, and Labour Party members all joined in heaping
abuse on the Italian ruler. Rome-London relations went rapidly
downhill, and in Geneva the League, led by Britain, threatened sanctions if the invasion of Abyssinia went ahead. Isolated, Mussolini decided he had to act quickly.

THE ABYSSINIAN WAR

ON OCTOBER 3, 1935, Italy sent into battle against African
tribesmen a large army equipped with all the weaponry of modern
warfare, including bombers carrying poison gas. It was a slaughter.
Against the Italians' four hundred aircraft, Emperor Haile Selassie
could match thirteen—of which only eight, all unarmed, ever left the
ground. Of his 250,000 troops, only one-fifth had modern weapons.
Against the ruthless Marshal Pietro Badoglio—who had not scrupled
to spray the flanks of his advance with mustard gas, crippling thousands of tribesmen—the Abyssinians never stood a chance.[75]

"Moral indignation was almost universal," writes historian John
Toland:

> How could a civilized nation attack a weak foe forced to bat-
> tle planes and tanks with tribesmen on horseback? Britain
> and America, with conveniently short memories of their
> own pacification programs, were particularly abusive, and
> the former led the campaign in the League of Nations to in-
> voke limited economic sanctions against Italy.[76]

Baldwin's government faced a dilemma. For British ideals now
clashed with British interests. Should Britain avert its gaze from
Ethiopia to keep Italy as a Stresa Front partner against Germany, or
lead the League in branding Italy an aggressor, impose sanctions, and

lose Italy? "What was demanded by fidelity to the high principles of the Covenant of the League of Nations," writes Barnett, "ran clean counter to what was demanded by imperative strategic need."[77]

In January 1935, Barthou's successor Pierre Laval, concerned about Germany, not some tribal fiefdom in Africa, visited Italy and came close to assuring Mussolini that France would not oppose his conquest. In return for Italy's abandonment of all claims to Tunisia and her acceptance of French hegemony there, Mussolini had won from Laval an explicit promise of a "free hand" in Ethiopia. But the British had by now been converted to moralistic internationalism and the principles of the League of Nations.

> So it was that by midsummer 1935 the British had already reached the point where they were admonishing an old friend and ally, a co-guarantor of the Locarno Treaty and a naval power astride their main imperial artery; and doing so in the tone of Dr. Arnold rebuking a boy at Rugby for wickedness and sin.[78]

THE HOARE-LAVAL PLAN

AFTER ITALY INVADED, supported by tribal peoples anxious to end the rule of the Amharic emperor Haile Selassie, who claimed descent from the Queen of Sheba, Foreign Secretary Sam Hoare and France's Laval put together a peace proposal. Italy would take the fertile plains of Ethiopia, the Ogaden. Haile Selassie would retain his mountain kingdom. Britain would compensate Ethiopia for its loss with land and an outlet to the sea. The British Cabinet backed Hoare-Laval and Mussolini was prepared to accept. With peace seemingly at hand, Hoare went on holiday, before heading to Geneva to inform Haile Selassie, King of Kings, Lord of Lords, and Conquering Lion of Judah, that he must give up half his kingdom.

But when the plan leaked in the Paris press, a firestorm erupted over this reward for aggression in violation of the League of Nations Covenant. So hot did the fire burn that Hoare and Laval both had to resign, and London and Paris washed their hands of the Hoare-Laval plan. Sir Roy Denman underscores how political panic and the public uproar over the Hoare-Laval plan caused the British Cabinet to act against vital British interests:

> Had the Cabinet stuck by Hoare it is likely that Mussolini would have accepted the plan. Had [Prime Minister] Baldwin . . . explained robustly the British interest in maintaining Italy as an ally against Germany—the real danger— the massive well-drilled Conservative majority in the House of Commons would not have rebelled. As it was, the Stresa front was broken and the new British Foreign Secretary [Eden] was determined to make the classic mistake of trying to ally himself with Hitler and to oppose Mussolini instead of the reverse.[79]

Richard Lamb underscores the tragedy that came of Britain's failure to stand by Hoare-Laval:

> Mussolini was on the brink of accepting the Hoare-Laval proposals; indeed he had already told Laval that they satisfied his aspirations. His acceptance would have meant the end of the Abyssinian war, and Italy would have happily rejoined the Stresa Front, leaving Hitler isolated.[80]

But with Anthony Eden—still smoldering at his treatment by Mussolini in Rome the previous summer—now foreign secretary, the possibility of a negotiated solution to the crisis among the Great War Allies was gone. Britain led the League in imposing sanctions on Italy. A limited embargo was declared that did not include oil, Rome's critical import, and Britain did not close the Suez Canal to Italian troopships. This produced the worst of all worlds. The sanctions were too weak to compel Mussolini to give up a conquest to which Italy's army had been committed, but they were wounding enough to enrage the Italian people. "The only effect of the sanctions policy," writes Paul Johnson, "was to turn Italy into an enemy."[81] "The only result of this display," wrote Taylor, "was that the Emperor of Ethiopia lost all his kingdom, instead of losing half, as Mussolini had originally intended."[82] Bullock describes how Britain's failure to choose led to total debacle:

> By insisting on the imposition of sanctions, Great Britain made an enemy of Mussolini and destroyed all hope of a united front against German aggression. By her refusal to drive home the policy of sanctions, in face of Mussolini's bluster, she dealt the authority of the League as well as her own prestige a fatal blow, and destroyed any hope of finding in collective security an effective alternative to the united front of the Great Powers against German aggression.[83]

Had Britain closed the Suez Canal to Italian warships and troopships and been willing to engage the Italian fleet, she could have forced Mussolini to quit Abyssinia. But the strategic result would have been the same. To Il Duce, avenging Adowa was a matter of national honor. When Britain and France turned on him, he turned on them. The Stresa Front was dead.

Six months later, when Britain and France sought out Mussolini to stand with them in the Rhineland crisis, the sanctions on Italy were still in effect. By assuming the moral high ground to condemn a land grab in Africa, not unlike those Britain had been conducting for centuries, Britain lost Italy. Her diplomacy had created yet another enemy. And this one sat astride the Mediterranean sea-lanes critical to the defense of Britain's Far Eastern empire against that other alienated ally, Japan.

On July 15, 1936, the League of Nations lifted the sanctions on

Italy. Even Eden had now come around. Finally, in 1938, writes Henry Kissinger, "Great Britain and France subordinated their moral objections to their fear of Germany by recognizing the Abyssinian conquest."[84] By then it was too late. Mussolini had cast his lot with the Hitler he had loathed.

One British Cabinet minister did deliver a "blast of realism" at the "Tennysonian chivalry" of sanctioning Italy over Ethiopia. Said Chancellor of the Exchequer Neville Chamberlain in 1936, recalling Shakespeare's *A Midsummer Night's Dream*, it had been "the very midsummer of madness."[85]

The damage done to Britain's security may be seen by looking back to the Great War. With an army of 1.5 million in France and a navy invincible at sea, Britain had brought Italy, Japan, and the United States into her alliance with France. All were needed to defeat Germany. Now Japan had been cast off to appease America, Italy had been driven into the arms of Germany, and America had retreated into neutrality. And Hitler was about to move.

To appease the Americans, Britain had severed its alliance with Japan and radically reduced the real and relative power of the Royal Navy. Now that navy faced the prospect of war against a German navy in the North Sea and U-boats in the Atlantic, Italy's fleet in the Mediterranean, and a Japanese navy in the Pacific and Indian oceans that was growing in carriers and battleships as Tokyo cast off the restrictions of the Washington and London naval agreements.

Luigi Villari's 1956 *Italian Foreign Policy Under Mussolini* is a defense of Italian policy and an explanation of how Mussolini was driven into the arms of the Nazi dictator he despised. But even British historians concede Britain's folly in the Abyssinian crisis, and many blame the same man. Wrote Villari:

> More than any other Englishman he [Eden] was responsible
> for blocking any successful effort to attain relatively perma-
> nent peace between the two World Wars and for thus expos-

ing England to an "unnecessary war" which "liquidated" the main portions of the British Empire, subjected Britain to many years of austerity after the War, and reduced it to the status of a second-rate world power.[86]

Privately, Churchill shared a low regard for the Kennedyesque Eden. On Eden's elevation to Foreign Secretary, he wrote Clementine, "Eden's appointment does not inspire me with confidence. . . . I expect the greatness of his office will find him out. . . . I think you will now see what a lightweight Eden is."[87]

Italy, now friendless and alone in the League, enduring sanctions that had begun to bite, seeking friends, turned to Germany. On January 7, 1936, von Hassel, Hitler's ambassador in Rome, reported that Mussolini regarded Stresa as "dead and buried" and wanted to improve relations: "If Austria as a formally quite independent state were . . . in practice to become a German satellite, he would have no objection."[88]

On November 1, in Milan, Mussolini proclaimed the Rome-Berlin Axis. In 1937, Italy would adhere to the Anti-Comintern Pact of Germany and Japan, established to resist subversion by the Comintern, or Communist International, centered in Moscow. For the League of Nations, the crisis in Abyssinia was the end of the line. A.J.P. Taylor writes,

> Fifty-two nations had combined to resist aggression; all they accomplished was that Haile Selassie lost all his country instead of only half. Incorrigible in impracticality, the League further offended Italy by allowing Haile Selassie a hearing at the Assembly; and then expelled him for the crime of taking the covenant seriously. Japan and Germany had already left the League; Italy followed in December 1937. . . . When foreign powers intervened in the Spanish civil war, the Spanish government appealed to the League.

The Council first "studied the question"; then expressed its "regrets" and agreed to house the pictures from the Prado . . . at Geneva.[89]

By the time of Munich 1938, Hitler had his alliance with Italy. He would seal it on the eve of war by ordering the German population of South Tyrol transferred to the Reich. Germans who adopted Italian surnames and agreed to assimilate could remain. This ethnic "self-cleansing," this sellout of his Austrian kinsmen, was done by Hitler to demonstrate good faith to his Axis partner. South Tyrol was expendable to Hitler. But Ethiopia was not expendable to Britain. Thus did Britain lose Ethiopia—and Italy.

CHURCHILL AND MUSSOLINI

WHERE DID CHURCHILL STAND on Abyssinia?

Historian Richard Lamb writes that in the House of Commons, the now backbencher Churchill "argued with passion that sanctions must be taken against Italy if Mussolini violated the Covenant of the League of Nations by attacking Abyssinia."[90] William Manchester contradicts him: "Churchill's steady eye was still fixed on Germany. Compared with Hitler's Reich, he had told Parliament, Ethiopia was 'a very small matter.' "[91] On July 11, 1935, Churchill had warned against getting too far out in front in urging the League to punish Italy. We ought not to become, said Churchill,

> a sort of bell-wether or fugleman to gather and lead opinion in Europe against Italy's Abyssinian designs. . . . We must do our duty, but we must do it only in conjunction with other nations. . . . We are not strong enough—I say it advisedly—to be the law-giver and the spokesman of the world.[92]

Churchill thought Ethiopia a matter of honor for the League, and the League a vital instrument of collective security against Hitler. But he did not believe Ethiopia was a matter of morality: "No one can keep up the pretence that Abyssinia is a fit, worthy, and equal member of a league of civilized nations."[93] To Churchill, Abyssinia was a "wild land of tyranny, slavery, and tribal war."[94] And there were far more serious concerns. "In the fearful struggle against rearming Nazi Germany I could feel approaching," Churchill later wrote, "I was most reluctant to see Italy estranged, and even driven into the opposite camp."[95]

On October 1, 1935, hours before the Italian army marched, Churchill expressed his feelings about the folly of alienating an old ally that had fought beside Britain in the Great War:

> I am very unhappy. It would be a terrible deed to smash up Italy, and it will cost us dear. How strange it is that after all those years of begging France to make up with Italy, we are now forcing her to choose between Italy and ourselves. I do not think we ought to have taken the lead in such a vehement way. If we had felt so strong on the subject we should have warned Mussolini two months before.[96]

British leaders willing to appease Mussolini to keep him as an ally would be derided as the Guilty Men in the title of leftist Michael Foot's 1940 book savaging the Tory appeasers. But Churchill had been among them. From the first time he met Mussolini, Churchill seemed taken with the Fascist dictator. Emerging from a talk with Il Duce in 1927, Churchill, then still Chancellor of the Exchequer, told the press,

> I could not help being charmed . . . by Signor Mussolini's gentle and simple bearing and by his calm, detached poise in spite of so many burdens and dangers. . . . If I were Italian, I

am sure I would have been with you from beginning to end in your struggle against the bestial appetites of Leninism."[97]

Churchill went on to praise Fascism's contribution to the world and the struggle against Bolshevism:

> I will . . . say a word on the international aspect of Fascism. Externally your movement has rendered a service to the whole world. . . . Italy has shown that there is a way of fighting the subversive forces which can rally the mass of the people, properly led, to value and wish to defend the honour and stability of civilized society. She has provided the necessary antidote to the Russian poison.[98]

Writes Churchill biographer Robert Payne,

> With an unusual blindness, even in those times when the blind were leading the blind, Churchill continued to hold Mussolini in high esteem. The man he was later to call "Hitler's utensil" belonged to the company of "great men" to be admired, placated and helped on their way. When Mussolini invaded Abyssinia in October, 1935, Churchill staunchly defended him: The Abyssinians were as primitive as the Indians and deserved to be conquered. While the invasion was taking place, Churchill was holidaying pleasantly in Barcelona and North Africa.[99]

A week before the Italian army invaded Ethiopia, Churchill was hailing Mussolini as "so great a man and so wise a leader."[100]

Two years after Mussolini had embraced Hitler, Churchill was still proclaiming the genius of Rome's Fascist dictator: "It would be a dangerous folly for the British people to underrate the enduring position in world-history which Mussolini will hold; or the amazing qualities of courage, comprehension, self-control and perseverance which he exemplifies."[101] In December 1940, when Britain was at war with Italy, Churchill, in an address to the Italian people, again said of Mussolini, "That he is a great man I do not deny."[102]

A.J.P. Taylor, looking back at the fraudulence of Fascism and the "vain, blundering boaster without ideas or aims" Mussolini had been, wondered at the character of British statesmen, Churchill included:

> Ramsay MacDonald wrote cordial letters to Mussolini—at the very moment of Matteoti's murder; Austen Chamberlain and Mussolini exchanged photographs; Winston Churchill extolled Mussolini as the saviour of his country and a great European statesman. How could anyone believe in the sincerity of Western leaders when they flattered Mussolini in this way and accepted him as one of themselves?[103]

When Ramsay MacDonald returned from his first meeting with Il Duce, he was so effusive in his praise for the achievements of Fascism and Mussolini, one colleague remarked, "There is nothing more for the British Prime Minister to do but to don the Black Shirt in the streets of London."[104]

Still, what was the proper course for a disarmed Britain, confronted with an atavistic act of aggression by a friendly Italy? If one believed Hitler was a mortal peril and Italy a valuable ally against a greater menace, Britain ought to have put League of Nations morality on the shelf. "Great Britain's leaders should have confronted Hitler and conciliated Mussolini," Kissinger writes. "They did just the opposite; they appeased Germany and confronted Italy."[105]

Where did this leave Britain in January of 1936?

Let Correlli Barnett have the last word on the consequences of putting League of Nations morality above vital security interests. After Abyssinia and the collapse of the Stresa Front,

> England, a weakly armed and middle-sized state, now faced not one, not two, but three potential enemies: enemies

inconveniently placed so as to threaten the entire spread of empire from the home country to the Pacific. And the third and most recent potential enemy in the Mediterranean and Middle East, was the entirely needless creation of the British themselves as Eden himself admitted to the House of Commons in November 1936, in recalling that the "deterioration in our relations with Italy was due to the fulfillment of our obligations under the Covenant; there had never been an Anglo-Italian quarrel so far as our country was concerned."[106]

CHAPTER 6

1936: The Rhineland

A NATION OF seventy millions of people suffers, but it does not die.[1]
> —MATTHIAS ERZBERGER TO MARSHAL FOCH
> *November 11, 1918*

I assure the House that it is the appeasement of Europe as a whole that we have constantly before us.[2]
> —ANTHONY EDEN, 1936

WITH THE BREAKUP OF the Stresa Front and the falling-out of the Allies over Abyssinia, Hitler saw his opening to secure his French frontier—before he renewed the *Drang nach Osten*, the ancient German drive to the east.

Under Versailles, Germany west of the Rhine had been demilitarized, as had the bridgeheads and an area fifty kilometers east of the river. In the Rhineland, German troops, armaments, or fortifications were forbidden. This was to give France time and space to meet any attack inside Germany rather than in Alsace. A demilitarized Rhineland meant that, at the outbreak of war, the French army could march in and occupy the Ruhr, the industrial heartland of Germany. The Rhineland was to France what the Channel was to England.

Under Versailles, France had the right to occupy the Rhineland until 1935. But at British insistence, and as a gesture of goodwill to the German democrats facing nationalist pressure, French troops had been pulled out in 1930, five years ahead of schedule. One British historian calls this withdrawal a "strategic catastrophe."[3]

> The French military frontier had been brought back from the Rhine and its bridgeheads to the French national frontier. There was no longer a military presence physically to prevent Germany from sending in troops to re-occupy and re-militarise what had now become a strategic No-Man's-Land. The integrity of the de-militarised zone, upon which the security of France and the Low Countries so depended, rested now either on Germany's good faith, or, in default of that hitherto fragile safeguard, upon the readiness and willingness of the French to march forward and turn invading German forces out again—a major military operation, indeed an act of war.[4]

France had abandoned vital strategic terrain. Should the Germans, in belligerency or ingratitude, remilitarize the Rhineland, France would have to go to war to take back what had been given to her at Versailles. Had France consulted her security interests rather than her British allies, the French army would have stood on the Rhine the day Hitler took power. But, in 1936, the Rhineland had been free of French troops for half a decade.

Hitler knew that Western statesmen and peoples nurtured a sense of guilt over Versailles and he intuitively sensed how to play upon that guilt. He would first identify an injustice of Versailles, or a new threat to a disarmed Germany. Then, playing the aggrieved party, he would announce what seemed a proportionate response, protesting all the while that he was acting only in self-defense or to assert Germany's right to equality of treatment. To soothe Allied fears, Hitler tied his response to an olive branch.

The issue that triggered Hitler's boldest assault on the terms of

Versailles was a vote in the French Chamber of Deputies to approve an anti-German pact between France and Bolshevik Russia, Germany's mortal enemy. Rising in Kroll Opera House that fateful Saturday, March 7, 1936, Hitler declared that if France and Stalin's Russia were ganging up on Germany, he had a sworn duty to act in defense of the Fatherland. Ian Kershaw describes Hitler's speech that was broadcast to the nation:

> After a lengthy preamble denouncing Versailles, restating Germany's demands for equality and security, and declaring his peaceful aims, a screaming onslaught on Bolshevism brought wild applause. This took Hitler into his argument that the Soviet-French pact had invalidated Locarno.[5]

Under the Locarno pact, Germany, France, and Belgium accepted as inviolate the borders laid down at Versailles. Germany had accepted the loss of Alsace and Lorraine and agreed to the permanent demilitarization of the Rhineland. And, under Locarno, Britain and Italy had agreed to defend those borders against "flagrant aggression."[6]

Unlike Versailles, which Germany had signed only under a threat of having Marshal Foch march on Berlin, Locarno had neither been negotiated nor signed under duress. German democrats had proposed the idea to Great Britain. Austen Chamberlain had won the Nobel Peace Prize for negotiating Locarno, as had Gustav Stresemann, the German foreign minister. In Allied eyes, Locarno—not Versailles, which Hitler denounced with endless invective—was the real guarantee of peace. For Hitler had himself accepted Locarno.

Thus, when Hitler rose to speak at Kroll Opera House on that fateful day, he began by charging that France had just violated the Locarno pact that Berlin had faithfully observed for ten years by entering an alliance with Soviet Communists—against Germany. And Hitler had a strong case. Any Franco-Soviet security pact implied a French commitment to attack Germany should Germany go to war with

Stalin. And any French attack must come through the Rhineland. When the French Chamber of Deputies approved the Soviet mutual security pact on February 27, opponents of the treaty had made Hitler's precise point: The French-Soviet treaty violates Locarno.

Thus, after reciting arguments heard a week before in the Chamber of Deputies, Hitler paused—and continued:

> Germany regards itself, therefore, as . . . no longer bound by this dissolved [Locarno] pact. . . . In the interest of the primitive rights of a people to the security of its borders and safeguarding of its defence capability, the German Reich government has therefore from today restored the full and unrestricted sovereignty of the Reich in the demilitarized zone of the Rhineland.[7]

The Nazis lifted the roof off Kroll Opera House. The six hundred Reichstag deputies, "all appointees of Hitler, little men with big bodies and bulging necks and cropped hair and pouched bellies and brown uniforms and heavy boots, little men of clay in his fine hands, leap to their feet like automatons, their right arms upstretched in the Nazi salute, and scream 'Heil's.' "[8] "When the tumult eventually subsided," writes Kershaw,

> Hitler advanced his "peace proposals" for Europe: a non-aggression pact with Belgium and France, demilitarization of both sides of the joint borders; an air pact; non-aggression treaties, similar to that with Poland, with other eastern neighbors; and Germany's return to the League of Nations. Some thought Hitler was offering too much.[9]

As France's ambassador, André François-Poncet, wryly put it, "Hitler struck his adversary in the face, and as he did so declared: 'I bring you proposals for peace!' "[10]

Thus did Hitler—as a few lightly armed German battalions moved across the Rhine bridges, with bands playing, to the cheers of the crowds—assure the world of the defensive character of his operation. He had coupled the German army's return to the Rhineland after seventeen years with an offer to negotiate a nonaggresion pact with France and to rejoin the League of Nations.

Hitler had originally set 1937 as the date to send his army across the Rhine bridges, but had come to believe Germany must act sooner, as he feared Soviet and Allied rearmament would make a later move even more risky.[11] While his generals had not opposed remilitarization—a strategic necessity if the Reich was to have freedom of action—some questioned his timing. At a February 27 lunch with Göring and Goebbels where the Rhineland had been the topic, Goebbels had summed up, "Still somewhat too early."[12] The German army was unprepared to resist the French army. Minister of War General Blomberg was said to be nearly paralyzed with fear over the French reaction. Walking out of Kroll Opera House after Hitler's speech, William Shirer encountered the minister. "I ran into General Blomberg. . . . His face was white, his cheeks twitching."[13] Hitler would describe Blomberg as having behaved like a "hysterical maiden."[14]

Looking back, Western men profess astonishment the Allies did not strike and crush Hitler here and now. Why did they not eliminate the menace of Hitler's Reich when the cost in lives would have been minuscule, compared with the tens of millions Hitler's war would later consume?

BEHIND THE ALLIED INACTION

AMERICA IGNORED HITLER'S MOVE because she had turned her back on European power politics. Americans had concluded they had been lied to and swindled when they enlisted in the Allied cause in

1917. They had sent their sons across the ocean to "make the world safe for democracy," only to see the British empire add a million square miles. They had been told it was a "war to end wars." But out of it had come Lenin, Stalin, Mussolini, and Hitler, far more dangerous despots than Franz Josef or the Kaiser. They had lent billions to the Allied cause, only to watch the Allies walk away from their war debts. They had given America's word to the world that the peace imposed on Germany would be a just peace based on the Fourteen Points and Wilson's principle of self-determination, then watched the Allies dishonor America's word by tearing Germany apart, forcing millions of Germans under foreign rule, and bankrupting Germany with reparations.

For having been deceived and dragged into war, Americans blamed "the Merchants of Death"—the war profiteers—and the British propagandists who had lied about raped Belgian nuns and babies being tossed around on Prussian bayonets. By the 1930s, Americans, in the worst depression in their history, which had left a fourth of all family breadwinners out of work, believed they had been played for fools and gone to war "to pull England's chestnuts out of the fire" and make the world safe for the British Empire.

America was resolved never again to ignore the wise counsel of the Founding Fathers to stay out of foreign wars. With the outbreak of war in Abyssinia in 1935 and the League of Nations debating sanctions on Italy, a Democratic Congress passed and FDR signed the first of three neutrality acts to ensure that America stayed out of any new European war. At Chautauqua, on August 14, 1936, five months after Hitler's Rhineland coup, FDR spoke for America as he thundered his anti-interventionist and antiwar sentiments:

> We shun political commitments which might entangle us in foreign wars; we avoid connection with the political activities of the League of Nations. . . . [W]e are not isolationists, except insofar as we seek to isolate ourselves from

war. . . . I have seen war. . . . I have seen blood running from the wounded. I have seen men coughing out their gassed lungs. I have seen the dead in the mud. I have seen cities destroyed. . . . I hate war.[15]

Americans saw no vital U.S. interest in whether German soldiers occupied German soil, on the other side of the Atlantic, 3,500 miles from the United States. They had a Depression to worry about. But why did Britain and France do nothing?

The British had concluded that Keynes and the other savage critics of Versailles had been right in accusing the Allies of imposing a Carthaginian peace on Germany in violation of the terms of armistice. Britain was now led by decent men with dreadful memories and troubled consciences, who were afflicted with guilt over what had been done.

No one wanted another European war. The horrors of the Western Front had been described in the poems and memoirs of those who had survived the trenches. The crippled and maimed were still visible in British cities, begging in the streets. The graves and war memorials were fresh. Few now believed it had been worth it. Three of the great houses of Europe had fallen, four empires had collapsed, nine million soldiers had perished. And what had it all been for? Ten years after the guns had fallen silent, a moving epitaph of the Great War had been penned by that most bellicose of leaders in the War Cabinet, the former First Lord of the Admiralty. Wrote Winston Churchill:

Governments and individuals conformed to the rhythm of the tragedy, and swayed and staggered forward in helpless violence, slaughtering and squandering on ever-increasing scales, till injuries were wrought to the structure of human society which a century will not efface, and which may conceivably prove fatal to the present civilization. . . . Victory was to be bought so dear as to be almost indistinguishable from defeat. It was not to give even security to the victors. . . . The most complete victory ever gained in arms has failed to solve the European problem or to remove the dangers which produced the war.[16]

When visiting French foreign minister Flandin asked what Britain would do if France marched against the German battalions in the Rhineland, Baldwin told him: "[I]f there is even one chance in a hundred that war would follow from your police action I have not the right to commit England. England is simply not in a state to go to war."[17] A.J.P. Taylor describes how Baldwin explained Britain's impotence:

Tears stood in [Baldwin's] eyes as he confessed that the British had no forces with which to support France. In any case, he added, British public opinion would not allow it. This was true: there was almost unanimous approval in Great Britain that the Germans had liberated their own territory. What Baldwin did not add was that he agreed with this public opinion. The German reoccupation of the Rhineland was, from the British point of view, an improvement and a success for British policy.[18]

Baldwin believed and hoped Hitler's ambitions might be directed to the east. In July of 1936, he met with a deputation of senior Conservatives that included Churchill.

Baldwin told them that he was not convinced that Hitler did not want to "move east," and if he did, "I should not break my heart." If there was any "fighting in Europe to be done," Baldwin would "like to see the Bolshies and the Nazis doing it."[19]

A measure of the moral unreadiness of Britain for war may be seen in the mind-set of George V in the Abyssinian crisis. To Foreign

Secretary Sam Hoare the king had spoken in anguish, "I am an old man. I have been through one world war. How can I go through another? If I am to go on you must keep us out of this one."[20] When warships were dispatched to the Mediterranean to prepare for action against the Italian navy, George V had been even more emphatic as he poured out his heart to Lloyd George: "I will not have another war. I will not. The last one was none of my doing and if there is another one and we are threatened with being brought into it, I will go to Trafalgar Square and wave a red flag myself rather than allow this country to be brought in."[21] Behind the king's anguish, writes Andrew Roberts, was a sense that it was "considered axiomatic that another war would spell doom for the British Empire."[22]

> The royal family, which had watched the stock of monarchies diminishing after European wars, had acquired highly developed antennae for survival. The Franco-Prussian War of 1870 had led to the fall of the French imperial throne. By the end of the Great War the imperial crowns of Russia, Germany and Austria-Hungary lay in the dust.
>
> The Second World War was to destroy the thrones of Italy, Albania, Bulgaria, Romania and Yugoslavia, so it was understandable that the British royal familiy should have embraced appeasement.[23]

Also, many in Britain now believed that France and her huge army were a greater threat to the balance of power than Germany. Some even welcomed Hitler's buildup—to check France. Others admired how Hitler had revived a crushed nation. And the chickens of Abyssinia had come home to roost.

> [T]he Germans had chosen their moment well. English chivalry over Abyssinia had shattered the Stresa front. . . . Relations between England and her Locarno guarantor,

Italy, were at present as hostile as it was possible for them to be, short of outright war. England was now in the absurd situation of having to consult Italy about the German aggression at a time when she was acting as the ringleader at Geneva in attempts to thwart Italy's ambition in Abyssinia.[24]

Lloyd George not only opposed any British-French military action in the Rhineland, he called on his colleagues to try to see the world from Germany's point of view. Even before this latest pact between Paris and Moscow, Germany was encircled by French alliances that included Belgium, Poland, Rumania, Czechoslovakia, and Yugoslavia. Now Germany faced a Stresa Front of Italy, France, and Britain and a new Franco-Soviet alliance that imperiled the most important industrial area of Germany, the undefended Ruhr. Lloyd George implored Parliament to see Germany's dilemma and forcefully argued Hitler's case in the House of Commons:

> France had built the most gigantic fortifications ever seen in any land, where, almost a hundred feet underground you can keep an army of over 100,000 and where you have guns that can fire straight into Germany. Yet, the Germans are supposed to remain without even a garrison, without even a trench. . . . If Herr Hitler had allowed that to go on without protecting his country, he would have been a traitor to the Fatherland.[25]

After commending Hitler for having reoccupied the Rhineland to protect his country, Lloyd George received an invitation—to Berchtesgaden. Out of that meeting, the ex–prime minister emerged "spellbound by Hitler's astonishing personality and manner."[26] "He is indeed a great man" were Lloyd George's first words, as he compared *Mein Kampf* to the Magna Carta and declared Hitler "The Resurrection and the Way" for Germany.[27]

In an interview with the *News-Chronicle* on his return to England, Lloyd George assured his countrymen, "Germany has no desire to attack any country in Europe . . . Hitler is arming for defence and not for attack."[28] Asked what he thought of Germany having become a dictatorship, the old prime minister responded, "Hitler has done great things for his country. He is unquestionably a great leader . . . a dynamic personality."[29]

Nor was Lloyd George alone among British statesmen in being taken with Hitler. Eden had met with Hitler in 1934 and written his wife, "Dare I confess? . . . I rather liked him."[30] John Simon, Eden's predecessor as foreign secretary, described Hitler to King George as "an Austrian Joan of Arc with a moustache."[31]

In 1937, three years after the Night of the Long Knives murders of Roehm and his SA henchmen, two years after the Nuremberg Laws had been imposed on the Jews, one year after Hitler had marched into the Rhineland, Churchill published *Great Contemporaries*. He included in it his 1935 essay "Hitler and His Choice." In this profile, Churchill expresses his "admiration for the courage, the perseverance, and the vital force which enabled [Hitler] to challenge, defy, conciliate, or overcome, all the authorities or resistances which barred his path."[32]

"Those who have met Herr Hitler face to face," wrote Churchill, "have found a highly competent, cool, well-informed functionary with an agreeable manner, a disarming smile, and few have been unaffected by a subtle personal magnetism."[33] Hitler and his Nazis had surely shown "their patriotic ardor and love of country."[34] Churchill went on to conclude:

> We cannot tell whether Hitler will be the man who will once again let loose upon the world another war in which civilization will irretrievably succumb, or whether he will go down in history as the man who restored honour and peace of mind to the great Germanic nation. . . . [H]istory is replete

with examples of men who have risen to power by employing stern, grim, and even frightful methods but who, nevertheless, when their life is revealed as a whole, have been regarded as great figures whose lives have enriched the story of mankind. So may it be with Hitler.[35]

Churchill concluded his essay on a hopeful note: "We may yet live to see Hitler a gentler figure in a happier age."[36]

In September of 1937, Churchill wrote of Hitler "in a clearly placatory tone that . . . sits extremely ill with his image as the mortal foe of Nazism":

One may dislike Hitler's system and yet admire his patriotic achievement. If our country were defeated I hope we should find a champion as indomitable to restore our courage and lead us back to our place among the nations.[37]

Thus did even the Great Man believe about Hitler, a year after he reentered the Rhineland, and years after Dachau was established, Versailles overthrown, Roehm and the SA leaders murdered on Hitler's orders and with his personal complicity, and the anti-Semitic laws enacted. About the reoccupation of the Rhineland, biographer Roy Jenkins finds Churchill strangely unconcerned:

On March 7 Hitler sent his troops into the demilitarized Rhineland, thereby defying Locarno as well as Versailles. Churchill's initial reaction was muted. He telegraphed to Clementine that day, merely telling her that nothing was settled (by which he meant his inclusion in the government). . . . [H]e did speak on the Tuesday [March 10] but in a curiously tentative and low-key way, never mentioning the Rhineland. . . . Despite his hindsight [in *The Gathering Storm*, 1948] Churchill was far from being rampageously strong on the Rhineland issue at the time. . . . [There was no] indication that Churchill thought irreversible disaster had struck either himself or the country.[38]

In his fortnightly letter of March 13, 1936, "Britain, Germany and Locarno," republished in his 1939 collection of columns *Step by Step*, Churchill commended French restraint: "Instead of retaliating by armed force, as would have been done in a previous generation, France has taken the proper and prescribed course of appealing to the League of Nations."[39]

The best solution to the Rhineland crisis, Churchill wrote, would be a beau geste by Adolf Hitler—to show his respect for the sanctity of treaties.

> But there is one nation above all others that has the opportunity of rendering a noble service to the world. Herr Hitler and the great disconsolate Germany he leads have now the chance to place themselves in the very forefront of civilization. By a proud and voluntary submission, not to any single country or group of countries, but to the sanctity of Treaties and the authority of public law, by an immediate withdrawal from the Rhineland, they may open a new era for all mankind and create conditions in which German genius may gain its highest glory.[40]

Since the Allies are unwilling to use military power to enforce the terms of Locarno, Churchill is saying here, Hitler should do the noble thing voluntarily: withdraw all troops from the Rhineland, and thereby earn the goodwill and gratitude of the civilized world.

Nor did Britain's elite seem concerned by Germany's reoccupation of the Rhineland. Lord Lothian famously quipped, "The Germans, after all, are only going into their own back-garden."[41] Was it "flagrant aggression," a violation of Locarno requiring Britain to act, for Germans to walk into their "own back-garden"? "It was as if the British had reoccupied Portsmouth," echoed Bernard Shaw.[42] Foreign Secretary Eden assured Britons, "There is, I am thankful to say, no reason to suppose that Germany's present actions threaten hostilities."[43] Secretary for War Duff Cooper, who would resign as First Lord over Munich, told the German ambassador the British public "did not care 'two hoots' about the Germans reoccupying their own territory."[44]

WHY WAS FRANCE PARALYZED?

IT IS FRANCE'S CONDUCT that is inexplicable. The Rhineland bordered on Alsace. Its importance to French security had been recognized at Versailles by Foch and Poincaré, who wanted to annex it, and by Clemenceau, who wanted to convert it into a buffer state. Only after Wilson and Lloyd George offered France a Treaty of Guarantee, an American-British guarantee to come to the aid of France were she attacked again by Germany, had Clemenceau agreed to settle for a fifteen-year occupation and its permanent demilitarization. If the Wehrmacht was in the Rhineland, it was not America or Britain face-to-face with a Germany of seventy million led by a vengeful Adolf Hitler. It was France.

"What was called for on that crucial Saturday of March 7, 1936," writes William Shirer, "was a police action by the French to chase a few German troops who were parading into the Rhineland—this was clear even to a correspondent in Berlin that weekend."[45]

Why, when Hitler had sent in only three lightly armed battalions, with orders to withdraw immediately if they met resistance, did France, with the most powerful army in the world, not march in, send the Germans scurrying back over the Rhine bridges, and restation French troops on the river? Decisive action, warranted by Versailles and Locarno, to which Britain was signatory and which she would have had to back up, might have prevented World War II. The Poles and Czechs had indicated that, if France acted, they would be with her. Even Austria supported her. Why did France not act?

First, the French recalled 1923, when they had marched into the Ruhr to force Germany to pay the war reparations imposed at Versailles, on which the Germans were defaulting. The French move so disgusted the United States that the Americans pulled out their occupation troops and brought them home. Most of the world had denounced France. The Germans had gone on strike. Paris had gotten a black eye in world opinion.

Second, by January 1930, when she acceded to a British request to vacate the Rhineland by midyear, in a concession to German democracy, France had adopted a Maginot Line strategy, named for Minister of War André Maginot, and begun to build vast defensive fortifications on her eastern border, a Great Wall in front of Alsace-Lorraine. Militarily, the Rhineland was now no-man's-land. By making the Maginot Line her defense line, France had ceded the Rhineland to Germany. By adopting the Maginot Line strategy and mentality, wholly defensive in character, France had signaled to all of Europe, including her allies to the east, in the clearest way possible, that she would fight only if invaded and only a defensive war. The message of the Maginot Line was that any European nation east of the Rhine was on its own.

As the French government debated military action, it called in the army commander in chief. General Maunce Gamelin asked the ministers if they were aware Hitler had a million men under arms and 300,000 already in the Rhineland and that any move to retake the territory would require general mobilization. This was an absurd exaggeration of Nazi strength. Gamelin added that the French army was understrength because the politicians had failed to provide the needed resources. As this was only six weeks before a general election, the Cabinet reacted with shock and horror. Gamelin did muster thirteen divisions near the German border, but they did not cross it.

"The forty-eight hours after the march into the Rhineland were the most nerve-racking in my life," Hitler later said. "If the French had then marched into the Rhineland, we would have had to withdraw with our tails between our legs."[46] He need not have been alarmed, for Hitler was dealing with defeatist leaders of a morally defeated nation. At Nuremberg, General Jodl would testify, "Considering the situation we were in, the French covering army could have blown us to pieces."[47] Added Shirer,

> It could have—and had it, that almost certainly would have been the end of Hitler, after which history might have taken quite a different and brighter turn than it did, for the dictator could never have survived such a fiasco. Hitler himself admitted as much. "A retreat on our part," he conceded later, "would have spelled collapse."[48]

Churchill, in his war memoirs, adopts the same view that, had the French army entered the Rhineland and run the German battalions out, the German generals might have rebelled and overthrown Hitler: "[T]here is no doubt that Hitler would have been compelled by his own General Staff to withdraw, and a check would have been given to his pretensions which might well have proved fatal to his rule."[49]

Historian Ernest May ridicules Churchill's contention. "Not a scrap of evidence supports such a story" of German generals ready in 1936 to oust Hitler for overreaching in the Rhineland, May writes: "Neither Fritsch nor Beck evidenced serious misgivings."[50] Hitler was far more popular in 1936 than he had been in 1934, and there had been no move against him after the Vienna debacle. There is no logical reason "to suppose that a setback in the Rhineland in 1936 would have had any worse effect on Hitler's standing with the German public than the setback in Austria in 1934."[51]

How great a strategic setback was the Rhineland debacle?

For France the failure to oppose the German reoccupation of the demilitarized zone was a disaster, and one from which all the later ones of even greater magnitude followed. The two Western democracies had missed their last chance to halt, without the risk of a serious war, Nazi Germany. . . .

The whole structure of European peace and security set up in 1919 collapsed. The French alliances with the countries to the east of Germany were rendered useless. As soon as Hitler had fortified the Rhineland, the French army, even if it found more resolute generals, would no longer be able to achieve a quick penetration of Germany to aid the Eastern allies if they were attacked.[52]

Seeing France's paralysis, Belgium's King Leopold III, who had succeeded his father, the heroic Albert, in 1934, declared neutrality and scrapped the Franco-Belgian alliance of 1920—"with the optimism of the imprudent little pigs, 'This policy should aim resolutely at keeping us apart from the quarrels of our neighbors.' "[53]

As the Maginot Line ended at Belgium, France's northern border was now as exposed as it had been in 1914, when French generals had to watch and wait as von Kluck's armies drove through Belgium. "In one stroke," writes British military historian Alistair Horne, "the whole of her Maginot Line strategy lay in fragments."[54]

France would blame Britain for not backing her up when French diplomats went to London to ask for support for military action. But as Churchill wrote, this is an "explanation but no excuse . . . since the issue was vital to France."[55] Under Versailles and Locarno, France had the right to expel the German battalions that were in the Rhineland in violation of both treaties. And the British were obligated to assist her militarily. What France should have done was act and force Britain's hand. Britain would have had to back up the French army. But the French army did not move, so Britain was off the hook.

Once he had the Rhineland, Hitler began to construct his West Wall, the Siegfried Line. Its significance was recognized by Churchill. "[I]t will be a barrier across Germany's front door, which will leave her free to sally out eastward and southward by the back door."[56] On April 6, 1936, Churchill observed that the rising Rhineland fortifications

> will enable the German troops to be economised on that line, and . . . enable the main force to swing round through Belgium and Holland. Then look East. There the consequences of the Rhineland fortifications may be more immediate. . . . Poland and Czechoslovakia, with which must be associated Yugoslavia, Roumania, Austria and some other countries, are all affected very decisively the moment that this great work of construction has been completed.[57]

Week by week, the West Wall rose, Germany grew stronger, and the locus of action shifted farther and farther away, and French willingness to die for distant lands eroded. The significance of the lost moment is captured by Shirer:

> France's failure to repel the Wehrmacht battalions and Britain's failure to back her up in what would have been nothing more than a police action was a disaster for the West from which sprang all the later ones of even greater magnitude. In March 1936 the two Western democracies were given their last chance to halt, without the risk of a serious war, the rise of a militarized, aggressive, totalitarian Germany, and in fact—as we have seen Hitler later admitting—bring the Nazi dictator and his regime tumbling down. They let the chance slip by.

> For France it was the beginning of the end.[58]

All of France's Eastern allies—Russia, Czechoslovakia, Yugoslavia, Rumania, Poland—grasped the significance of Hitler's coup. If France would not fight in the Rhineland to guarantee her own security, would she order hundreds of thousands of French soldiers to their deaths against a German West Wall—to save the peoples of Central Europe? The German foreign minister, Konstantin von Neurath, explained the new strategic reality to William Bullitt, the U.S. ambassador to France who had called on him in Berlin: "As soon as our [West Wall] fortifications are constructed and the countries of Central Europe realize that France cannot enter German territory at will, all those countries will begin to feel very differently about their foreign policies and a new constellation will develop."[59]

The new reality would soon assert itself and all Europe would realize its implications. With Belgium now neutral, France must now extend the Maginot Line to the Channel. With Hitler's West Wall rising, France could no longer march into the Rhineland and seize the Ruhr on behalf of her allies in Central Europe. With Mussolini now aligned with Hitler, no power could intervene directly to halt Hitler's inevitable next move—turning Austria into a vassal state. After Austria must come the turn of Czechoslovakia and Poland, both of which held large German populations as anxious to join the Reich as the Saarlanders had been. "The evacuation of the Rhineland led therefore to a calamitous weakening of France's defensive position," writes Correlli Barnett. "Perhaps more serious, it removed the last positive French hold over Germany."[60]

On March 29, 1936, Hitler held a plebiscite on his decision to send the Wehrmacht in to restore German sovereignty to the Rhineland. Ninety-nine percent of the German people voted to approve his tearing up of the Versailles Treaty and repudiation of the Locarno pact.[61]

March 1936 was the crucial moment of the postwar era. Versailles was dead. Locarno was dead. Stresa was dead. The League was on life support. The Allies had lost the last chance to stop Hitler without war. "The reoccupation of the Rhineland marked the watershed between 1919 and 1939," writes Alistair Horne. "No other single event in this period was more loaded with dire significance. From March 1936, the road to France's doom ran downhill all the way."[62]

And the road to Vienna lay open to Hitler.

As an awakened Churchill observed late in that month of March in which Hitler had sent his battalions across the Rhine: "An enormous triumph has been gained by the Nazi regime."[63] Added Prime Minister Baldwin in April, "With two lunatics like Mussolini and Hitler, you can never be sure of anything. But I am determined to keep the country out of war."[64]

CHAPTER 7

1938: Anschluss

GERMAN-AUSTRIA MUST RETURN to the great German mother-country. . . . Common blood belongs in a common Reich.[1]
> —ADOLF HITLER, 1925
> *Mein Kampf*

The hard fact is that nothing could have arrested what actually happened [in Austria]—unless this country and other countries had been prepared to use force.[2]
> —NEVILLE CHAMBERLAIN, 1938

AT THE PARIS CONFERENCE, an amputated, landlocked Austria of 6.5 million had asked Allied permission to enter into a free-trade zone with a starving Germany. Permission denied. In April and May of 1921, plebiscites on a union with Germany were held in the North Tyrol and at Salzburg: "The votes in the former were over 140,000 for the Anschluss and only 1,794 against. In Salzburg, more than 120,000 voted for union, and only 800 against. This was twelve years before Hitler became Reichsführer."[3]

Permission again denied. For the statesmen at Paris did not wish to unify Germans, but to divide them, and to undo the post-1870 alliance of Bismarck's Germany and the Habsburgs. Under the treaties of Versailles and St. Germain, even a customs union between Austria and Germany was forbidden—without the approval of the League of Nations. This gave Britain, France, and Italy veto power over trade between the two defeated Germanic nations.

In 1931, hard hit by depression, Germany again asked for permission to form an Austro-German customs union. The idea was the brainchild of Chancellor Heinrich Brüning. But President Eduard Beneš of Czechoslovakia and Britain, France, and Italy vetoed it. Historian Richard Lamb, a veteran of the British Eighth Army, views the Allied veto of that customs union as a grave blunder that was to have "dire consequences for both the German and Austrian economies"; and, he argues, "the resulting economic distress contributed to the rapid rise of the Nazis to power in Germany."[4] Alan Bullock concurs. The Czech-Italian-French veto of the Austro-German customs union

> not only helped to precipitate the failure of the Austrian Kreditanstalt and the German financial crisis of the summer but forced the German Foreign Office to announce on September 3 that the project was being abandoned. The result was to inflict a sharp humiliation on the Brüning government and to inflame national resentment in Germany.[5]

Robert Vansittart of the British Foreign Office had warned British leaders that "Brüning's government is the best we can hope for; its disappearance would be followed by a Nazi avalanche."[6] Vansittart's warning was ignored.

Brüning resigned. He was succeeded as chancellor by Franz von Papen, who implored the Allies, given Germany's economic crisis in the Great Depression, to wipe the slate clean of war reparations. But the new Chancellor of the Exchequer, Neville Chamberlain, refused, and demanded another four billion marks. In negotiations, Chamberlain magnanimously settled for three, to the cheers of Parliament. When the German negotiators returned home they were "met at the railway station by a shower of bad eggs and rotten apples."[7] Papen warned the Allies that if German democrats "were not granted a single diplomatic success, he would be the last democratic chancellor in Germany. He got none."[8]

In 1938, Hitler would succeed where the Allies had ensured that the German democrats would fail. "Magnanimity in politics is not seldom the truest wisdom," Burke had admonished his countrymen.[9]

THE HITLER-HALIFAX SUMMIT

HISTORIANS TODAY SEE IN Hitler's actions a series of preconceived and brilliant moves on the chessboard of Europe, reflecting the grand strategy of an evil genius unfolding step by step: rearmament of the Reich, reoccupation of the Rhineland, Anschluss, Munich, the Prague coup, the Hitler-Stalin Pact, blitzkrieg in Poland, the Rommel-Guderian thrust through the Ardennes, seizure of the Balkans, and Barbarossa, the invasion of Russia. This is mythology. While Hitler did indeed come to power with a "vision" of Versailles overturned and a German-dominated Europe, most of his actions were taken in spontaneous reaction to situations created by his adversaries. Hitler "owed all his successes to his tactical opportunism," wrote Sir Nevile Henderson.[10] Henderson was right. Surely this was true of the Anschluss.

For two years after German troops reoccupied the Rhineland, Hitler made no move in Europe. "Until 1938, Hitler's moves in foreign policy had been bold but not reckless," writes biographer Ian Kershaw.[11]

> From the point of view of the Western powers, his methods were, to say the least, unconventional diplomacy—raw, brutal, unpalatable; but his aims were recognizably in accord with traditional German nationalist clamour. Down to and including the Anschluss, Hitler had proved a consummate nationalist politician.[12]

Despite his braggadocio about German military superiority, Hitler knew his forces were inferior to the Royal Air Force and French army, if not to the Czechs and Poles. But he sensed that if he were patient, then, as the conservative German establishment had invited him to become chancellor, the Allies, full of guilt over Versailles and horrified at the prospect of another war, would come to offer him what he wanted. Hitler had read the Allies right.

In 1937, Lord Halifax, who was close to Baldwin's successor, the new prime minister Neville Chamberlain, was invited to Germany for a hunt with Hermann Göring, the legendary air ace who had succeeded Manfred von Richthofen as commander of the "Flying Circus" when the Red Baron had been shot down. When Halifax accepted, a second invitation came from Ambassador Ribbentrop—as Halifax told Eden—to "call upon the Leader at his Bavarian hideaway, 'Berchtergaden, or wherever the place is.' "[13] The Cabinet agreed that Halifax should go. But the Hitler-Halifax meeting almost ended before it began, in disaster.

As the immensely tall Halifax was driven up to Berchtesgaden, he could only see, looking down out of the window of his car, the shiny patent-leather shoes and black-trousered pants legs of the man at his car door. Emerging from his limousine, Lord Halifax started to hand his hat and coat to the footman. Only after an agitated Neurath had hissed in his ear, "Der Fuehrer! Der Fuehrer!" did Halifax realize this was Adolf Hitler.[14]

A diplomatic debacle had been narrowly averted.

Throughout the meeting, Hitler remained in a foul mood. After lunch, Halifax brought up his experiences as viceroy of India, where he had urged a policy of conciliation. Hitler, who had just related how *Lives of a Bengal Lancer* was his favorite film, and compulsory viewing for the SS to show "how a superior race must behave," rudely interrupted him.[15]

"Shoot Gandhi!"[16]

A startled Halifax fell silent, as Hitler went into a rant:

"Shoot Gandhi! And if that does not suffice to reduce them to submission, shoot a dozen leading members of Congress; and if that does not suffice, shoot 200 and so on until order is established."[17]

"During this tirade," writes biographer Andrew Roberts, citing a diplomat present, Halifax, a lay leader in the Anglican Church, "gazed at Hitler with a mixture of astonishment, repugnance and compassion. He indicated dissent, but it would have been a waste of time to argue."[18]

Early in the meeting, however, Halifax had delivered a crucial message on behalf of Chamberlain. Singling out Austria, Czechoslovakia, and Danzig, Halifax told Hitler that if "far-reaching disturbances" could be avoided, all of Germany's grievances from Versailles, in Central Europe, could be resolved in Germany's favor.[19] Halifax had told Hitler what he had hoped to hear. Britain would not go to war to prevent an Anschluss with Austria, transfer the Sudetenland to the Reich, or return of Danzig. Indeed, Britain might be prepared to serve as honest broker in effecting the return of what rightfully belonged to Germany, if this were all done in a gentlemanly fashion.

Hitler had just been handed a road map for the peaceful incorporation of the German peoples of Central Europe into the Reich, if only he would avoid those "far-reaching disturbances." Writes A. J. P. Taylor,

> Halifax's remarks . . . were an invitation to Hitler to promote German nationalist agitation in Danzig, Czechoslovakia, and Austria; an assurance also that this agitation would not be opposed from without. Nor did these promptings come from Halifax alone. In London Eden told Ribbentrop: "People in England recognized that a closer connection between Germany and Austria would have to come about sometime."[20]

Why was Halifax conveying such a message?

Chamberlain had come to believe that, by tearing people and provinces away from Germany at the point of a gun, the Allies had made historic and terrible blunders in 1919. And the new prime minister was ready to rectify these injustices, if Hitler would agree that it would be done diplomatically. Chamberlain believed the peace of Europe depended upon Germany being restored to her rightful role as a coequal Great Power on the continent.

The message Halifax conveyed at the Berghof underscores a crucial point in the history of this era: Hitler's agenda was no surprise or shock to European statesmen. All of them knew that any German nationalist would demand the same rectifications and adjustments of the frontiers laid down at Versailles. The claims Hitler would make were known in advance and largely assented to by the elites of Europe as the preconditions of peace. Berlin's drive to restore its ties to its former Vienna ally and effect the return of the Sudetenland, Danzig, and Memel to Germanic rule were not unanticipated demands in the chanceries of Europe. They knew what was coming.

In his 1940 memoir *Failure of a Mission*, Nevile Henderson, the British ambassador in Berlin in 1937, wrote of the Halifax visit, "Hitler cannot but have been—and in fact, so I heard, was—impressed by the obvious sincerity, high principles, and straightforward honesty of a man like Lord Halifax."[21] Historian B. H. Liddell Hart saw it differently: "[T]he German documents reveal that Hitler derived special encouragement from Lord Halifax's visit in November 1937."[22]

The day following his visit to the Berghof, Lord Halifax arrived at Karinhall, the vast estate and game preserve of Göring, where he found its proprietor decked out "in brown breeches and boots all in one, a green leather jerkin and a belt from which was hung a dagger in a red leather sheath, completed by a green hat topped by a large chamois tuft."[23] Put at ease by his host's comical appearance, Halifax wrote down his impression of the hero of the Great War who now headed the Luftwaffe:

> I was immensely entertained at meeting the man himself. One remembered at the time that he had been concerned with the "clean-up" in Berlin on June 30, 1934 [the Night of

the Long Knives] and one wondered how many people he had been, for good cause or bad, responsible for having killed. But his personality, with that reserve, was frankly attractive, like a great schoolboy . . . a composite personality— film star, great landowner interested in his estate, Prime Minister, party manager, head gamekeeper at Chatsworth.[24]

Lord Halifax, reported his friend Henry "Chips" Channon, had "liked all the Nazi leaders, even Goebbels, and he was much impressed, interested and amused by the visit. He thinks the regime absolutely fantastic."[25]

THE HITLER-SCHUSCHNIGG SUMMIT

WITH ENGLAND'S BLESSING TO bring Austria into Germany's sphere, if done peacefully, Hitler was left with but one problem: how to get the Austrians to agree. Austrian Chancellor Kurt von Schuschnigg would provide Hitler his opportunity.

"A devout Catholic and intellectual, a decent man with little vanity or driving ambition," a veteran of the Great War, Schuschnigg had arrested the Nazis involved in the plot against Dollfuss, hanged the two who fired the fatal shots, and had himself become chancellor in 1934.[26] On July 11, 1936, he had entered into a "Gentlemen's Agreement" with Berlin. Vienna was to "maintain a policy based on the principle that Austria acknowledges herself to be a German state," and Berlin recognizes "the full sovereignty of the Federal State of Austria" and agrees not to interfere in her internal affairs.[27] Respectable pro-Nazis were to be permitted in politics and government, but Nazis were to end political agitation and street action. A Committee of Seven was set up to carry out the terms of the Gentlemen's Agreement. Hitler wanted no repetition of the abortive 1934 coup.

"It was a bad bargain," writes Manchester. "Secret clauses" of the

Gentlemen's Agreement "stipulated the muzzling of the Viennese press and amnesty for Nazi 'political prisoners' in Austrian jails— many of them storm troopers convicted of murdering Jews and critics of the Fuhrer."[28]

Austria's Nazis ignored the agreement and continued to plot the overthrow of Schuschnigg. In January 1938, Austrian police raided the Committee of Seven headquarters and discovered plans there for a Nazi coup. Hitler had assured Mussolini there would be no Anschluss and, according to historian Taylor, he "knew nothing of these plans, which had been prepared despite his orders. . . . [T]he Austrian Nazis were acting without authority."[29]

An indignant Schuschnigg called in Ambassador Papen and showed him the evidence of Nazi violations of the Gentlemen's Agreement. Papen, who had just been relieved of his Vienna post, had had his own clashes with the Austrian Nazis and was not amused to learn that they had planned to assassinate him as a provocation, while disguising themselves as members of Schuschnigg's Fatherland Front. Papen suggested Schuschnigg take up the matter directly with Hitler.

At this time, Hitler was in the grip of a political crisis and personal scandal. He had stood up on January 12 at the wedding of Minister of War Blomberg, after which it was discovered that Frau Blomberg had been a Berlin prostitute with a police record and had posed for pornographic photographs, taken by a Jew, with whom she had been living at the time. As Richard Evans writes, Hitler was mortified to the point of paralysis:

> Alarmed at the ridicule he would suffer if it became known that he had been witness to the marriage of an ex-prostitute, Hitler plunged into a deep depression, unable to sleep. . . . It was, wrote Goebbels in his diary, the worst crisis in the regime since the Roehm affair. "The Leader," he reported, "is completely shattered."[30]

"Blomberg can't be saved," noted Goebbels. "Only the pistol remains for a man of honour. . . . The Fuhrer as marriage witness. It's unthinkable. . . . The Fuhrer looks like a corpse."[31] Writes Kershaw, "Scurrilous rumours had it that Hitler took a bath seven times" the day after he was told "to rid himself of the taint of having kissed the hand of Frau Blomberg."[32] The following day, he was heard muttering, "If a German Field-Marshal marries a whore, anything in the world is possible."[33]

Blomberg resigned. The generals favored as his replacement army commander in chief Colonel-General von Fritsch. But Fritsch was regarded by the Nazis as even less reliable than Blomberg. So Heinrich Himmler, head of the SS, gathered or fabricated evidence that Fritsch was a homosexual who had used a Berlin rent-boy known as "Bavarian Joe." Hitler set up a meeting in his private library at the Reich Chancellery with Fritsch, the prostitute Otto Schmidt, and Göring. Schmidt and General Fritsch stuck by their contradictory stories. Unconvinced of his innocence, Hitler decided that Fritsch, too, must go.

Meanwhile, Hjalmar Schacht, architect of Germany's recovery from the Great Depression, had resigned, and Hitler was trying to bury the news by sweeping his Cabinet clean of all the old conservatives, including Neurath and Papen. As Hitler was casting about for a way to divert public attention from the lurid Blomberg and Fritsch scandals and the resignation of Schacht, Papen came to him with the recommendation that he invite Schuschnigg to Berchtesgaden. Hitler seized it. Set up a meeting at once, he told Papen.

On February 12, Schuschnigg arrived at Berchtesgaden, intending to play the victim who had faithfully adhered to the Gentlemen's Agreement, only to see it blatantly violated by treacherous Austrian Nazis. Hitler did not wait to hear him out. He exploded, addressing Austria's chancellor as "Herr Schuschnigg" and berating him for having been first to violate their 1936 agreement. "The whole history of Austria," Hitler ranted, "is just one uninterrupted act of high treason.

That was so in the past and remains so today."[34] Hitler then proceeded to issue his own demands.

> Germany would renew its full support of Austria's sovereignty if all imprisoned Austrian National Socialists, including the assassins of Dollfuss, were set free within three days and all dismissed National Socialist officials and officers were reinstated in their former positions. In addition, Artur Seyss-Inquart, the leader of the moderate Pan-German faction, was to be appointed Minister of Interior with full, unlimited control of the nation's police forces; a "moderate" Austrian Nazi was to be Minister of Defense.[35]

Vienna was also to coordinate its economic and foreign policies with Berlin. Schuschnigg replied that he lacked the authority to make such commitments, which would mean an end to Austrian sovereignty. He wished to return to Vienna and consult with President Miklas and his Cabinet. Hitler continued to rant, called his generals in and out of the room to intimidate the Austrian chancellor, then sent Schuschnigg away for two hours to reflect on the consequences should he refuse the Fuehrer's demands.

Though bullied brutally, Schuschnigg returned to Vienna with a deal. Seyss-Inquart got the security post, but Germany condemned the Austrian Nazis and Hitler made good on his promise to remove the worst of the lot. The Nazi underground leader in Austria, Captain Josef Leopold, was called before Hitler and denounced as "insane."[36] Other Austrian Nazis were expelled and also berated by Hitler, who conceded in his notebook, "This Schuschnigg was a harder bone than I first thought."[37]

By mid-February the Austrian crisis was over. The German army units demonstrating on the border had stood down and Hitler had informed the Reichstag, "Friendly co-operation between the two countries has been assured. . . . I would like to thank the Austrian

Chancellor in my own name, and in that of the German people, for his understanding and kindness."[38]

"When a snake wants to eat his victims," snorted Churchill, "he first covers them with saliva."[39]

SCHUSCHNIGG RELIGHTS THE FUSE

HITLER HAD NOT ABANDONED his plan to convert Austria into a satellite, but believed this should and would come about through an "evolutionary solution."[40] Austria would drop like ripe fruit, for, with Italy now an Axis power, she was isolated, had nowhere else to go, and the Allies had neither the will nor the power to prevent her eventual merger with the Reich. As for Austria's Nazis, Hitler was incensed that they had again disrupted and imperiled his "evolutionary solution."

But while the crisis appeared over, it was not. For Schuschnigg, like Dollfuss a man of courage, seethed over the abuse at the Berghof and relit the fuse. After consulting Mussolini on March 7, who warned him he was making a mistake—*"C'é un errore!"*— Schuschnigg, on March 9 in Innsbruck, announced that on Sunday, March 13, a plebiscite would be held to decide, finally and forever, whether the country wished to remain a "free, independent, social, Christian and united Austria—*Ja oder Nein?*"[41]

Twenty thousand Tyroleans had roared their approved, but Prince Starhemberg had not. "This means the end of Schuschnigg," the ex–vice chancellor told his wife. "Let us hope it is not the end of Austria. Hitler can never allow this."[42]

Hitler was stunned. As Kerhsaw writes,

The German government was completely taken aback by Schuschnigg's gamble. For hours, there was no response from Berlin. Hitler had not been informed in advance of Schuschnigg's intentions, and was at first incredulous. But his astonishment rapidly gave way to mounting fury at what he saw as a betrayal of the Berchtesgaden agreement.[43]

Schuschnigg had ordered a vote in four days where Austrians would choose between Christianity and Nazism, Austria and Germany, Schuschnigg and Hitler. To Hitler, Schuschnigg had broken their Berchtesgaden agreement and bellowed a defiant "No!" to his vision of an "evolutionary solution" and eventual union of Germany with the land of his birth. Moreover, after winning the grudging backing of the socialist unions and Marxists for the plebiscite, Schuschnigg's government believed it would sweep between 65 percent and 70 percent of the Austrian vote.[44]

After the army scandals and Cabinet debacle, Hitler could not abide humiliation at the hands of Schuschnigg. Yet neither he nor the army had prepared for a campaign against Austria. Hitler called in General Wilhelm Keitel and told him to make ready to invade. Keitel remembered that the army had drawn up an "Operation Otto" plan in the event Otto von Habsburg attempted to regain the Austrian throne. "Prepare it!" Hitler ordered.[45] When Keitel got to army headquarters, he found that Operation Otto was a theoretical study. No German army plans existed for an invasion of Austria.

Hitler called his generals to Berlin and ordered all troops anywhere near Austria to proceed to the border and be prepared to invade on March 12. Leaving Göring in command in Berlin, Hitler departed to lead his army into the land of his birth.

RETURN OF THE NATIVE

HITLER KNEW FROM THE Dollfuss affair that Mussolini might react violently. Through Prince Philip of Hesse, who flew by special plane to Rome, Hitler sent a letter to Il Duce explaining the confrontation with Schuschnigg and proffering a naked bribe. Said

Hitler, "I have drawn a definite boundary . . . between Italy and us. It is the Brenner."[46]

Hitler was telling Mussolini that if given a free hand in Austria, South Tyrol was Italy's forever. To corral seven million Austrians, Hitler was prepared to sell out two hundred thousand Tyrolese who had been his countrymen.

On March 11, Germany closed its border with Austria and, on Göring's orders, the pro-Nazis in Schuschnigg's government demanded the March 13 plebiscite be canceled. Schuschnigg phoned Mussolini. Il Duce did not take his call. Nor did Paris respond. The Radical government of Camille Chautemps, in power for only a year and in financial straits, had just resigned. Former premier Léon Blum, at the instigation of the president, was trying to form a new government to deal with the Austrian crisis when the Anschluss was proclaimed. When Göring sought out the Czechs for their reaction to any German move into Austria, the Czechs assured Göring they would not mobilize. The British ambassador in Berlin, Henderson, agreed with Göring that "Dr. Schuschnigg had acted with precipitate folly."[47]

For Prime Minister Chamberlain, news of the imminent invasion came at an awkward moment. He and Halifax were hosting a farewell lunch at 10 Downing Street for Ambassador Ribbentrop, who had just been named by Hitler to replace Neurath as foreign minister. Ribbentrop had been assuring his British hosts the Austrian situation was calm, when a telegram arrived from Schuschnigg informing Chamberlain that the German army was at his border and asking "for immediate advice of his Majesty's Government as to what he should do."[48]

Shaken, Chamberlain suggested that he, Ribbentrop, and Halifax repair to his study "for a private word."[49] Halifax was incensed. But Ribbentrop soothed the British leaders, assuring them he knew nothing of an invasion and perhaps this was a false report. Yet, if true, Ribbentrop added, might it not be the best way to resolve the matter?

Chamberlain instructed Halifax to wire Schuschnigg: "His

Majesty's Government cannot take responsibility of advising the Chancellor to take any course of action which might expose his country to dangers against which His Majesty's Government are unable to guarantee protection."[50] The Austrians were on their own.

Abandoned and alone, Schuschnigg canceled the plebiscite. But this was no longer sufficient. Göring, who was managing the crisis by telephone, demanded that Austria replace Schuschnigg with Seyss-Inquart. President Miklas refused. Göring told Seyss-Inquart to declare himself chancellor and invite the German army in to restore law and order. But before Seyss-Inquart's telegram arrived in Berlin calling on Germany to intervene, Hitler's army was in Austria. On the morning of March 12, Seyss-Inquart wired Berlin to say that, as he was in charge in Vienna, the invasion should be halted. Göring told him this was now impossible.

As Hitler's army pushed into Austria, Prince Philip phoned from Rome: "I have just returned from the Palazzo Venezia. Il Duce took the news very well indeed. He sends his very best regards to you."[51] Hitler was ecstatic. On and on he burbled to the prince:

> [P]lease tell Mussolini that I shall never forget this. . . . Never, never, never! Come what may! . . . And listen—sign any agreement he would like. . . . You can tell him again. I thank him most heartily. I will never forget him! . . . Whenever he should be in need or in danger, he can be sure that I will stick with him, rain or shine—come what may—even if the whole world would rise against him—I will, I shall—"[52]

This commitment Hitler would keep. His faithfulness to Mussolini would be a principal cause of Germany's defeat and his own downfall.

On March 13, the day of Schuschnigg's plebiscite to decide if Austria should remain an independent nation, Hitler arrived in the hometown of his boyhood. As Gen. Heinz Guderian, who stood beside him in Linz, relates, tears ran down Hitler's cheeks; "this was certainly not play-acting."[53]

In Vienna, Hitler recalled for one reporter a day years before when, following a blizzard, he and five down-and-outers hired themselves out to shovel snow. By chance, they were assigned to sweep the sidewalk and street in front of the Imperial Hotel on a night when the Habsburgs were entertaining inside. Said Hitler, bitterness and resentment pouring out:

> I saw Karl and Zita step out of their imperial coach and grandly walk into this hotel over the red carpet. We poor devils shoveled the snow away on all sides and took our hats off every time the aristocrats arrived. They didn't even look at us, although I still smell the perfume that came at our noses. We were about as important to them, or for that matter to Vienna, as the snow that kept coming down all night, and this hotel did not even have the decency to send a cup of hot coffee to us. . . . I resolved that night that someday I would come back to the Imperial Hotel and walk over the red carpet in that glittering interior where the Hapsburgs danced. I didn't know how or when, but I have waited for this day and tonight I am here.[54]

"I can only describe him as being in a state of ecstasy," von Papen wrote.[55] And it was while in that state, in an utterly unexpected decision, that Hitler declared the annexation of Austria.

Göring, who had brilliantly and brutally managed the crisis, may have been the instigator of Anschluss. Seeing the Wehrmacht welcomed without a shot being fired, and how wildly the crowds received Hitler, he sent a courier by plane to the Fuehrer: "If the enthusiasm is so great, why don't we go the whole hog?"[56]

Hitler did. Seyss-Inquart was instructed to resign, as Austria was now a province of Germany. His twenty-four hours as chancellor were up. For seven years, Austria ceased to exist and became the Ost-mark, the East Mark, the ancient bulwark of Europe against the hordes of Asia.

Mussolini had not expected Hitler to annex Austria. "Floored" by the news, he railed about "that damned German," but then recognized reality.[57] After forty-eight hours of silence, he sent a congratulatory message. Again Hitler replied, "Mussolini, I shall never forget this."[58]

A fortnight before the Anschluss, Göring was a guest in Warsaw of Col. Jozef Beck, the foreign minister who had taken over on the death of Pilsudski. As the two walked into dinner, "they passed an engraving of John Sobieski, the Polish king coming to the rescue of the besieged city of Vienna in 1683. Beck drew Göring's attention to the title: 'Don't worry,' he remarked, 'that incident will not recur.' "[59]

In a year, Beck's turn would come.

It bears repeating. In 1934, an Austrian chancellor, Dollfuss, died a hero's death resisting Nazism, the only European leader to give up his life fighting Hitlerism from 1933 to 1939. In 1938, his successor, Schuschnigg, took a desperate gamble to break Austria forever free of the Reich. He failed, and spent the next seven years in a Nazi prison for defying Hitler. Austria capitulated because she was facing a Germany ten times her size and had been abandoned by all who could have helped her stay free—Poland, Czechoslovakia, Italy, France, and Great Britain.

As the German army entered Vienna, the world awakened to two realities. First, the vaunted Wehrmacht, 70 percent of whose tanks and armored vehicles broke down on the roads, was in no condition to fight a major war. Second, the cheering crowds showed that Hitler was wildly popular in his home country:

> The scenes of enthusiasm according to a Swiss reporter who witnessed them "defied all description." An English observer of the scene commented, "To say that the crowds which greeted [Hitler] along the Ringstrasse were delirious with joy is an understatement." Hitler had to appear repeatedly on the balcony of the Hotel Imperial in response to continued shouts of "We want to see our Fuhrer."[60]

On April 10, the Anschluss was submitted to a vote of the Austrian people. Fully 99 percent voted in favor. Some historians consider this a fair reflection of Austrian sentiment by then, but, if that was true, why had Hitler been so fearful of Schuschnigg's plebiscite?

There is surely truth in the sharp note Churchill wrote to Hitler idolater Unity Valkyrie Mitford, who had compared sitting next to Hitler like "sitting beside the sun" and who told Churchill that 80 percent of all Austrians were pro-Hitler. "It was because Herr Hitler feared the free expression of opinion that we are compelled to witness the present dastardly outrage."[61]

Yet, as Taylor writes, Schuschnigg, not Hitler, precipitated the crisis with his call for a plebiscite in four days to dramatize Austria's separation from Germany.

> The belief soon became established that Hitler's seizure of Austria was a deliberate plot, devised long in advance, and the first step toward the domination of Europe. This belief was a myth. The crisis of March 1938 was provoked by Schuschnigg, not by Hitler. There had been no German preparations, military or diplomatic. Everything was improvised in a couple of days—policy, promises, armed force.[62]

Taylor and Henderson are correct that Hitler had responded to Schuschnigg's initiative. Yet it must not be forgotten that absorption of Austria into the Reich he now ruled conformed to Hitler's vision from the time of *Mein Kampf.* Unlike the British Empire, which Lord Palmerston famously said had been "acquired in a fit of absentmindedness," a Germanic empire existed in the mind of Hitler before it ever came to be. True, he was an opportunist, but he also knew where he wished to go. As of 1938, Hitler had taken what he wanted in the south, Austria, and let go of what he had always been willing to trade away: South Tyrol.

For his Anschluss with Austria, however, Hitler would pay a price. His use of raw military power to overrun and annex a small neighbor stunned Europe. The Germans were no longer walking into their own back garden. Many who had been prepared to work with Hitler for redress of grievances dating to Versailles now began to think of standing up to him. Hitler had Austria, but Germany had lost any moral high ground it had held as the victim of Versailles. Moreover, the abominable public mistreatment of the Jews of Vienna by Austrian Nazis was reported across Europe and America. CBS's William Shirer called it an "orgy of sadism."[63] The Anschluss was not an unmitigated triumph for the Third Reich.

Why did Britain and France sit paralyzed? Why did they not act to stop the Anschluss? Consider the situation they confronted.

Though naked aggression, invading Austria was not a premeditated act Hitler had been carefully plotting for months, or even weeks. After reoccupying the Rhineland in March 1936, Hitler had not made a move on the European chessboard for two years. There had been no confrontations with the Allies.

Moreover, Austria was not an ally of Britain or France. She shared no common border with them. She had offered no resistance. From start to finish, the invasion did not last seventy-two hours. In town after town, thousands had cheered Hitler's arrival in his native land. Mussolini shared a border with Austria and, in the 1934 crisis, had marched four divisions to the Brenner. But due to the British, French, and League of Nations sanctions of 1935, Italy was no longer a Stresa Front partner but Hitler's ally in the Rome-Berlin axis.

The Anschluss was a clear violation of Versailles, but the British had negotiated an Anglo-German naval treaty in 1935, which also violated the terms of Versailles. And if Britain and France had failed to resist German rearmament or German remilitarization of the Rhineland, a direct threat to France, why fight over a German Anschluss with an Austria of seven million Germans, who had no border with France?

And how would the Allies resist the Anschluss? Had Britain sent an ultimatum to Hitler to get out of Austria and Hitler rejected it, how would Britain and France fight a war for Austrian independence? Britain had no draft and no army to send to France. The French army was dug deep inside the Maginot Line. How would they wage war on Germany? By a bombing campaign that would cause German bombs to rain down in retaliation on London and Paris?

And if Austria and Germany wished to unite—99 percent of each nation would vote in favor of unification in April—on what moral and political ground could Britain and France stand to deny Austrians the right of self-determination that they had preached to the world at Versailles? Should they declare war and, after countless dead, defeat Germany, what would they do with Austria—if the Austrians had fought beside the Germans? Separate the nations again? A war to oppose Anschluss would mean a war to reimpose Versailles. But Chamberlain and Halifax believed Versailles had been a blunder, because Germans and Austrians had been denied the right of self-determination granted to Poles and Czechs. Faced with Anschluss, the Allies were militarily hamstrung and morally paralyzed.

Halifax had supported Versailles, but he and Chamberlain had come to believe that Germany had been wronged and peace required the righting of those wrongs. They believed that Germans under Czech and Polish rule in 1938 should be granted the same right of self-determination extended to Poles and Czechs under German and Austro-Hungarian rule in 1919. They believed that addressing Germany's valid grievances and escorting her back into Europe as a Great Power with equality of rights was the path to the peace they wished to build. Their problem was this: If they assisted Hitler in gathering into the Reich all Germans who wished to be part of the Reich, they would be helping to remake Germany into what she had been in 1914, the dominant power in Europe. But the ruler of Germany was now Adolf Hitler, and should he turn aggressor, as his words in *Mein Kampf* portended, he would be a graver threat than the Kaiser, who had almost conquered Europe. For Italy, Japan, and Russia, Britain's allies in the Great War, were all now potential enemies. And America was gone from Europe.

Through the 1930s, British principles clashed with British interests. Chamberlain, Halifax, the Cabinet, and Parliament believed that rectifying the wrongs of Versailles and granting Germans the right of self-determination was essential for any lasting peace. However, self-determination for Germans meant an Anschluss with Austria, and the amputation of German peoples and their ancestral lands from France's allies Poland and Czechoslovakia. Some Britons, including Churchill, believed Britain should go to war, if necessary, to prevent the restoration of a Bismarckian Reich in Central Europe that encompassed Austria. European security, they believed, trumped any German claim to severed lands or lost peoples.

Chamberlain and Halifax had to ask: If they fed this tiger, would it turn on them and devour them? Perhaps Britain should have killed the cub. But that issue was now academic, for the opportunity had passed in the time of MacDonald and Baldwin. "The watershed between the two world wars extended over precisely two years," writes Taylor. "Post-war ended when Germany reoccupied the Rhineland on March 7, 1936; prewar began when she annexed Austria on March 13, 1938."[64]

After the Anschluss, Chamberlain wrote his sister to tell her that he planned to say to Hitler "it is no use crying over spilt milk and what we have to do now is consider how we can restore the confidence which you have shattered."[65] Chamberlain now mulled over an offer to Hitler of the return of some of the former German colonies in Africa.

> The Prime Minister still saw the return of colonies as a powerful gesture which it was hoped would calm down Germany's expansionist ambitions in central and south-eastern Europe. Halifax seemingly placed even more emphasis on this point, having articulated the belief that colonial concessions were the only vital question between Britain and Germany.[66]

It is a mark of the distance British leaders had traveled from reality that the prime minister and foreign minister entertained the idea, in March 1938, that Hitler might be diverted from his vision of restoring German lands and peoples in the east of Europe by the return of the Cameroons or Togoland.

Where was Churchill at the time of Anschluss?

In the Commons debate of March 14, Churchill called for a warning to be sent to Hitler that if he invaded any other country, Britain would intervene to stop him.[67] On March 24, he rose in Parliament and in a speech full of foreboding—"a kind of terror," Robert Payne writes—spoke of the retreat of British power since the rise of Hitler:

I have watched this famous island descending incontinently, fecklessly, the stairway which leads to a dark gulf. It is a fine, broad stairway at the beginning, but after a bit the carpet ends. A little farther on there are only flagstones, and a little farther on still these break beneath your feet. . . . Now the victors are vanquished, and those who threw down their arms in the field and sued for an armistice are striding on to world mastery.[68]

CHAPTER 8

Munich

You have only to look at the map to see that nothing
we or France could do could possibly save Czechoslovakia from being overrun by the Germans if they wanted
to do it.[1]
> —Neville Chamberlain
> *March 1938*

If you have sacrificed my nation to preserve the peace of
the world, I shall be the first to applaud you. But, if not,
gentlemen, God help your souls.[2]
> —Jan Masaryk, Czech ambassador,
> *to Chamberlain and Halifax, 1938*

On September 30, 1938, after a private meeting at Hitler's
apartment, the prime minister flew home from Munich to Heston
aerodrome. Emerging from his plane smiling, Neville Chamberlain
waved aloft the declaration he and Hitler had signed that morning.

"I've got it!" he shouted to Lord Halifax. "I've got it!"[3] "Here is a
paper which bears his name."[4]

Drafted by Chamberlain and Sir Horace Wilson, three sentences
long, the Munich Accord read: "We, the German Fuehrer and Chancellor and the British Prime Minister . . . regard the agreement
signed last night and the Anglo-German Naval Agreement, as

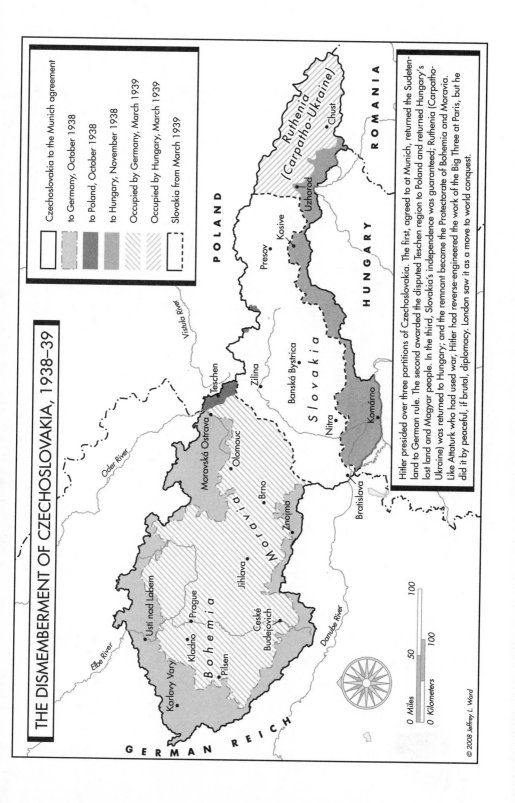

THE DISMEMBERMENT OF CZECHOSLOVAKIA, 1938–39

Legend:

- Czechoslovakia to the Munich agreement
- to Germany, October 1938
- to Poland, October 1938
- to Hungary, November 1938
- Occupied by Germany, March 1939
- Occupied by Hungary, March 1939
- Slovakia from March 1939

GERMAN REICH

POLAND

HUNGARY

ROMANIA

Bohemia: Karlovy Vary, Ústí nad Labem, Kladno, Prague, Pilsen, Jihlava, České Budějovice

Moravia: Moravská Ostrava, Olomouc, Brno, Znojmo

Teschen, Zilina, Banská Bystrica, Nitra, Komárno, Bratislava

Slovakia: Presov, Kosive

Ruthenia (Carpatho-Ukraine): Uzhorod, Chust

Elbe River, Oder River, Vistula River, Danube River

0 Miles 50 100
0 Kilometers 100

Hitler presided over three partitions of Czechoslovakia. The first, agreed to at Munich, returned the Sudetenland to German rule. The second awarded the disputed Teschen region to Poland and returned Hungary's lost land and Magyar people. In the third, Slovakia's independence was guaranteed; Ruthenia (Carpatho-Ukraine) was returned to Hungary; and the remnant became the Protectorate of Bohemia and Moravia. Like Atatürk who had used war, Hitler had reverse-engineered the work of the Big Three at Paris, but he did it by peaceful, if brutal, diplomacy. London saw it as a move to world conquest.

© 2008 Jeffrey L. Ward

symbolic of the desire of our two peoples never to go to war with one another again."[5]

At the request of George VI "to come straight to Buckingham Palace so that I can express to you personally my most heartfelt congratulations on the success of your visit to Munich," Chamberlain was driven to the palace to receive the gratitude of his sovereign.[6] Though the trip was only nine miles, so dense were the crowds it took an hour and a half.[7]

"Even the descriptions of the papers give no idea of the scenes in the streets as I drove from Heston to the Palace," wrote Chamberlain. "They were lined from one end to the other with people of every class, shouting themselves hoarse, leaping on the running board, banging on the windows, and thrusting their hands into the car to be shaken."[8]

At Buckingham Palace, Chamberlain and his wife were invited by the King to "join him on the balcony . . . as a token of the 'lasting gratitude of his fellow countrymen throughout the Empire.' "[9] "It was . . . the first time a ruling monarch had allowed a commoner to be acknowledged from the balcony of Buckingham Palace."[10] Thus did George VI and his queen render a royal blessing to appeasement. Beside his sovereign, the prime minister "stood there smiling, the most popular man in the world, more universally acclaimed than any statesman has ever been."[11] From the palace, Chamberlain was driven to 10 Downing Street, where another throng awaited, singing over and over, "For He's a Jolly Good Fellow." From the window at Number 10, Chamberlain, in the shortest, most famous speech he would ever deliver, declared, "My good friends, this is the second time in our history that there has come back from Germany to Downing Street peace with honour. I believe it is peace for our time."[12]

"Peace with honour" was the phrase Disraeli had used when he returned from Berlin after redrawing the map of Europe with Bismarck. "Peace in our time," from the Anglican Book of Common Prayer, was the title of a 1928 collection of speeches by Neville

Chamberlain's half brother Austen, the architect of the Locarno pact and winner of the Nobel Prize for Peace. "In repeating the phrase," writes a British historian, "Neville believed that he had completed his late brother's unfinished business: the pacification of Europe."[13]

When French Premier Edouard Daladier flew home from Munich, he was stunned to see a huge throng gathered at Le Bourget. He circled the field twice, fearful the crowd was there to stone him for having capitulated to Hitler and betrayed France's Czech allies by forcing them to surrender the Sudetenland. Daladier was astonished to find the crowd rejoicing and waving him home as a hero of peace.

Across the Atlantic, FDR, who had bid Chamberlain Godspeed on his Munich mission with the cryptic telegram "Good Man!," wanted to share the glory.[14] Undersecretary of State Sumner Welles went on national radio, where he referred to "steps taken by the President to halt Europe's headlong plunge into the Valley of the Shadow of Death."[15] Credit for Munich, Welles told the nation, must go to Franklin Roosevelt: "Europe escaped war by a few hours, the scales being tipped toward peace by the President's appeal."[16]

In a letter to Canada's Mackenzie King, Roosevelt wrote, "I can assure you that we in the United States rejoice with you, and the world at large, that the outbreak of war was averted."[17] A week later, FDR wrote to Ambassador William Phillips in Rome, "I want you to know that I am not a bit upset over the final result [Munich Agreement]."[18]

The *New York Times* echoed FDR: "Let no man say that too high a price has been paid for peace in Europe until he has searched his soul and found himself willing to risk in war the lives of those who are nearest and dearest to him."[19] Declared the New York *Daily News:* "[Hitler] has made a significant gesture towards peace. . . . Now is the time for haters of Hitler to hold their harsh words."[20]

The British press outdid the Americans. The morning after the prime minister's return, the London *Times*'s story began: "No conqueror in history ever came home from a battlefield with nobler laurels."[21] Margot Asquith, widow of the prime minister who had led

Britain into the Great War, called Chamberlain the greatest Englishman who had ever lived.[22] Old ladies "suggested that Chamberlain's
umbrella be broken up and pieces sold as sacred relics."[23] From exile
in Holland, the Kaiser wrote Queen Mary of his happiness that a catastrophe had been averted and that Chamberlain had been inspired
by heaven and guided by God Himself.[24] The clerics rejoiced.

> The Church of England responded very largely as if the
> men of Munich had been guided by Almighty God. "You
> have been enabled to do a great thing in a great way at a
> time of almost unexampled crisis. I thank God for it,"
> wrote [the Archbishop of Canterbury] Cosmo Lang to
> Chamberlain. There were services of thanksgiving in all
> the churches and cathedrals of England on the next Sun-
> day. In Lincoln Cathedral, the dean held the congregation
> spellbound "by ascribing the turn of events to God's won-
> derful providence."[25]

On October 2, Chamberlain wrote the Archbishop of Canter-
bury, "I sincerely believe that we have at last opened the way to that
general appeasement which alone can save the world from chaos."[26]

To Western peoples, familiar with shuttle diplomacy, Chamberlain's journey to Germany may seem routine. But as Graham Stewart
writes,

> No British Prime Minister had ever intervened in this man-
> ner before. Indeed, Chamberlain had never been in an aero-
> plane before, let alone one making a trip to the heart of
> Europe. Chamberlain was to be the first British Prime Min-
> ister to set foot in Germany for sixty years.[27]

Not all joined the celebration. The *Daily Telegraph* was caustic
and cutting: "It was Mr. Disraeli who said that England's two greatest

assets in the world were her fleet and her good name. Today we must console ourselves that we still have our fleet."[28]

Duff Cooper resigned as First Lord of the Admiralty.

"This is hell," Harold Nicolson said to Churchill, who muttered in reply, "It is the end of the British Empire."[29] Listening in Parliament as Chamberlain was feted as the Prince of Peace, Churchill was heard to say in a sarcastic aside, "I never knew Neville was born in Bethlehem."[30]

On October 5, Churchill rose in the House. "We have sustained a total and unmitigated defeat," he began.[31]

"Nonsense!" cried Lady Astor.[32]

Churchill continued with an address of great foreboding:

All is over. Silent, mournful, abandoned, broken, Czechoslovakia recedes into the darkness. . . . We have passed an awful milestone in our history, when the whole equilibrium of Europe has been deranged and . . . the terrible words have for the time being been pronounced against the Western democracies: "Thou art weighed in the balance and found wanting."

This is only the beginning of the reckoning. This is only the first sip, the first foretaste of a bitter cup which will be proffered to us year by year unless, by a supreme recovery of moral health and martial vigor, we rise again and take our stand for freedom as in the olden times.[33]

Yet Churchill could not contain his awe and envy at Hitler's audacity and nerve. On October 4, one day before his mighty address to the Commons, he wrote of Britain's need to replicate "the spirit of that Austrian corporal" who had bested the British statesmen at Munich:

It is a crime to despair. We must learn to draw from misfortune the means of future strength. There must not be lacking in our leadership something of the spirit of that Austrian corporal who, when all had fallen into ruins about him, and when Germany seemed to have sunk for ever into chaos, did not hesitate to march forth against the vast array of victorious nations, and has already turned the tables so decisively upon them.[34]

Chamberlain, however, must have sensed he had not really brought home "peace for our time." In the triumphal ride to Buckingham Palace, he had confided to Halifax, "All this will be over in three months."[35]

THE VICTOR

ACROSS THE NORTH SEA, Adolf Hitler was sullen and silent. As an Austrian, he despised the Czechs' mongrel state that had come out of the Paris peace conference and then allied itself with archenemy France and the detested Bolshevik regime. He hated Beneš and had wanted to crush his regime in a lightning war and ride in triumph through Prague. Munich had robbed him of his moment. He had the Sudetenland, but to the world it was only because Chamberlain permitted him to take it. Chamberlain was the hero of Munich who had been cheered by throngs of Germans on his trips to Berchtesgaden, Godesberg, and Munich, for the Germans, too, wanted peace and believed he had come to preserve it.

"That senile old rascal," Hitler raged at his ministers. "If ever that silly old man comes interfering here again with his umbrella, I'll kick him downstairs and jump on his stomach in front of photographers."[36]

Munich has been called the greatest diplomatic disaster in history. It was also a strategic disaster. By surrendering the Sudetenland, which held Czechoslovakia's mountain fortifications, Prague's Maginot Line was lost. Hitler would confide to Dr. Carl Burckhardt, the League of

Nations High Commissioner for Danzig, how astonished he had been by the strength of the Czech defenses:

> When after Munich, we were in a position to examine Czechoslovak military strength from within, what we saw of it greatly disturbed us; we had run a serious danger. The plan prepared by the Czech Generals was formidable. I now understand why my generals urged restraint.[37]

Six months after Munich, the remnant of Czecho-Slovakia—the name had been hyphenated after Munich on the demand of the Slovaks—was occupied by Hitler, and the thirty-five Czech divisions prepared in September of 1938 to fight to hold the Sudetenland vanished. Paul Johnson describes the Nazi windfall:

> As Churchill who perceived the military significance of the capitulation better than anyone pointed out in the Munich debate (5 October 1938), the annexation of Austria had given Hitler an extra twelve divisions. Now, the dismantling of Czech military power released a further thirty German divisions for action elsewhere.
>
> In fact the shift was worse than this. The Czechs' forty divisions were among the best-equipped in Europe: when Hitler finally marched in he got the means to furnish equivalent units of his own, plus the huge Czech armaments industry. The "turnaround" of roughly eighty divisions was equivalent to the entire French army.[38]

There is evidence that the ex–chief of the German General Staff Ludwig Beck, his successor Franz Halder, Admiral Wilhelm Canaris, and other officers were so alarmed at the prospect of war with Czechoslovakia and France, and possibly Russia and Britain, they had planned to arrest Hitler, Himmler, Göring, and Goebbels, but held off after learning Chamberlain was coming to Germany. American historian Ernest May writes:

> In 1938, General Beck had ended up advocating that the army seize power. Halder had backed him. Preparations were being made for army units from the Berlin military district to seize the Chancellery when news arrived of Chamberlain's surprise flight to Berchtesgaden. The plans for a coup were put on hold and then, after Munich, practically ceased.[39]

U.S. historian Charles Callan Tansill supports this version, contending a putsch had been prepared for September 28, when word came that Chamberlain and Daladier would fly to Munich on the twenty-ninth. Writes Tansill, " '[T]he old man with the umbrella' had scared off an immediate shower in favor of the wild tempest of World War II."[40]

Munich gave Hitler another year to build up his Panzers and erect his West Wall. "Finally and most important of all," writes Shirer, "the Western democracies lost Russia as an ally."[41] A Soviet diplomat who had considered an alliance with Britain and France remarked after Munich, "We nearly put our foot on a rotten plank. Now we are going elsewhere."[42]

About the character of Hitler and the folly of Munich, Churchill was right. And Chamberlain and Halifax have gone down in history as two of the Guilty Men in the 1940 book indicting the Tory governments of the 1930s. "Appeasement had been designed by Chamberlain as the impartial redress of justified grievances," writes Taylor. "It became a capitulation, a surrender to fear. This was Chamberlain's own doing."[43]

Few today defend Chamberlain. And appeasement has become a synonym for cowardly surrender to evil that leads to desperate war. As Churchill said to the prime minister, home from Munich: You were given a choice between dishonor and war. You chose dishonor, you will have war.

But why did the British in the autumn of 1938, from palace to pulpit, from Parliament to press, celebrate Chamberlain as a miracle worker of peace? Why was Munich a diplomatic triumph unequaled by a British prime minister since Lloyd George came home from Versailles? What persuaded Britain to break up Czechoslovakia to appease Adolf Hitler?

WHY MUNICH?

WHY DID CHAMBERLAIN GO to Munich? What could he have hoped to accomplish by brokering the transfer to Hitler of a Sudetenland that held the mountain fortifications of Czechoslovakia, loss of which would put Prague at the mercy of Berlin?

To answer these questions we must go back to 1919. At Paris, 3.25 million German inhabitants of Bohemia and Moravia had been transferred to the new Czechoslovakia of Tomáš Masaryk and Eduard Beneš in a flagrant disregard of Wilson's self-proclaimed ideal of self-determination. Asked why he had consigned three million Germans to Czech rule, Wilson blurted, "Why, Masaryk never told me that!"[44]

H. N. Brailsford, England's leading socialist thinker on foreign policy, had written in 1920 of the Paris peace: "The worst offence was the subjection of over three million Germans to Czech rule."[45] Austrian historian Erik von Kuehnelt-Leddihn describes the polyglot state the men of Paris had created:

The Czechs numbered 47 percent of the population of Czechoslovakia. It was only by "annexing" the Slovaks, much against their expressed will, into a hyphenated nation which had never existed historically that they suddenly became a "majority." In fact, there were more Germans (24.5 percent) in Czechoslovakia than Slovaks. But by clever gerrymandering devices the Czechs maintained a parliamentary majority and exercised an oppressive rule which drove the German minority (inexactly called "Sudeten Germans") into a rebellious and disloyal nationalism that would evolve into national socialism.[46]

Masaryk and Beneš, who had demanded the breakup of the Austro-Hungarian Empire on the principle of self-determination for Czechs, ran a state that was a living contradiction of the principle. For Czechs now ruled Germans, Hungarians, Slovaks, Poles, and Ruthenians, who constituted half the population and had never been consulted about being ceded to Prague. Czechoslovakia was a multiethnic, multilingual, multicultural, Catholic-Protestant conglomerate that had never before existed.

Less than a year after the Paris treaties that created Czechoslovakia, leaders of the German and Hungarian minorities in the new state had begun angrily to petition the League of Nations:

> More than five million Germans, Magyars, and people of other nationalities have not a single representative in this National Assembly, and all claims advanced by them have been waived aside by the Czechs. All the fundamental laws concerning the Constitution, and the language to be used in the administration, as regards social reform, the expropriation of land, etc., have been determined by this arbitrarily formed National Assembly without a single German-Bohemian or Magyar having been allowed a voice.[47]

From 1920 to 1938, repeated petitions were sent to the League by the repressed minorities of Czechoslovakia.[48] By 1938, the Sudetendeutsch were agitating to be rid of Czech rule and become part of the new Reich. In a fair plebiscite, 80 percent might have voted to secede. On the eve of the 1938 crisis, Lloyd George blamed the impending disaster on the duplicity of Beneš, who had not kept his word given at Paris: "Had the Czech leaders in time, and without waiting for the menacing pressure of Germany, redeemed their promise to grant local autonomy to the various races in their Republic on the lines of the Swiss Confederation, the present trouble would have been averted."[49]

European statesmen by 1938 had concluded that severing the ethnic Germans in the Sudetenland from Vienna had been a blunder that must be corrected. Neither Chamberlain nor his Cabinet was willing to go to war to deny Sudeten Germans the right to self-determination or keep them under an alien Czech rule. But there were complications. The first was France.

As we have seen, at Paris in 1919, Marshal Foch had wanted to annex the Rhineland and Clemenceau wanted to make it a buffer state. Wilson and Lloyd George had refused, but made a counteroffer: a U.S.-British-French alliance. Should Germany attack France again, America and Britain would fight at her side. But the Senate had refused to take up Wilson's security treaty and the British had then exercised their right to back out. France was left with no security treaty and no buffer state.

Paris had sought to compensate for the loss of a security treaty with America and Britain, and loss of her former Russian ally to Bolshevism, by negotiating defense pacts with the Little Entente of Rumania, Yugoslavia, and Czechoslovakia. By 1938, France was thus obligated to come to the defense of Czechoslovakia. But if a war between France and Germany broke out over Czechoslovakia, Britain must surely be drawn in.

Thus, as the Sudeten crisis unfolded, Chamberlain believed Britain must become involved diplomatically to address the valid German grievances and prevent a Franco-German war. The prime minister viewed the prospect of another Great War with horror. The war of 1914–1918 had cost the lives of 700,000 British soldiers, among them his beloved cousin Norman.

Why did Britain not let Paris play the hand? Why not stay out of the crisis and let the French force their Czech allies to give up the Sudetenland? Eden's biographer, David Carlton, explains. Chamberlain and his Cabinet

> were driven to the conclusion . . . that there was a serious risk, as in 1914, of the French Government going to war over an eastern European quarrel and thereby causing a conflict in western Europe from which the British could not afford to remain aloof. Accordingly, Chamberlain gradually and reluctantly came to take charge of the crisis. . . . Then, during September, the British Prime Minister assumed the responsibility of negotiating with Hitler and coercing the Czechs into surrender.[50]

So it was that Neville Chamberlain made three trips to Germany in September 1938: first to Berchtesgaden, then to Bad Godesberg, finally to Munich. But who and what precipitated the crisis of September 1938?

BENEŠ HUMILIATES HITLER

WHAT CAUSED HITLER TO turn with sudden ferocity on the Czechs and President Eduard Beneš, and risk war with Britain and France so soon after his triumph in Austria?

The triggering event occurred two months after Anschluss, while Hitler was still celebrating. Rumors began to fly of an imminent German invasion of Czechoslovakia. The rumors were false, and there is reason to believe the Czechs had planted them with the knowledge of Beneš, who ordered mobilization. As the rumors ricocheted around

Europe, London warned Berlin that Britain would not sit still for an invasion. Paris and Moscow renewed their commitments to Prague. Hitler was suddenly in a major crisis not at all of his own making.

Confronted by a united Europe, Hitler was forced to renounce any intent to invade Czechoslovakia. German officers escorted British military advisers along the Czech border to prove there were no preparations for war. When no attack came, the Czechs bragged and brayed about how they had forced Hitler to back down, showing the world how to face down the bully. "It was apparent to Hitler that Beneš had precipitated the crisis to humiliate Germany," wrote Tansill. "To be falsely accused by Czech officials was to Hitler the supreme insult."[51]

> [Hitler] convinced himself, Jodl reported, that he had suffered a loss of prestige, and nothing could put him in a blacker, uglier mood. Swallowing his pride, he ordered the foreign office in Berlin to inform the Czech Minister in Berlin on Monday, May 23, that Germany had no aggressive intentions toward Czechoslovakia and that the reports of German troop concentrations on her borders were without foundation. . . .
>
> Hitler, it was believed in the West, had been given a lesson by the firmness of the other great European powers and by the determination of the small one that seemed threatened.[52]

The Fuehrer was now gripped by "a burning rage to get even with Czechoslovakia and particularly with President Beneš, who, he believed, had deliberately humiliated him."[53] He called in his generals and ranted: "It is my unshakeable will that Czechoslovakia shall be wiped off the map."[54] Hitler ordered up Case Green, the plan for invading Czechoslovakia, and rewrote it to read, "It is my unalterable decision to smash Czechoslovakia by military action in the near future."[55] What did Hitler mean by "in the near future"? Keitel explained in a covering letter: "Green's execution must be assured by October 1, 1938 at the latest."[56] Henderson believed that the Czech provocation and exploitation of the May crisis, and the ridicule that was heaped upon Hitler for backing down to the Czechs, led directly to Munich:

> The defiant gesture of the Czechs in mobilizing some 170,000 troops and then proclaiming to the world that it was their action which had turned Hitler away from his purpose was . . . regrettable. But what Hitler could not stomach was the exultation of the press. . . . Every newspaper in America and Europe joined in the chorus. "No" had been said and Hitler had been forced to yield. The democratic powers had brought the totalitarian states to heel, etc.
>
> It was, above all, this jubilation which gave Hitler the excuse for his . . . worst brain storm of the year, and pushed him definitely over the border line from peaceful negotiation to the use of force. From May 23rd to May 28th his fit of sulks and fury lasted, and on the latter date he gave orders for a gradual mobilization of the Army.[57]

Many "advocates of appeasement" considered the phony crisis of May "a grave blunder and blamed President Beneš for his 'provocative' action, while Chamberlain determined never to run so grave a risk of war again," writes Hitler biographer Alan Bullock.[58]

> For a week [Hitler] remained at the Berghof in a black rage, which was not softened by the crowing of the foreign Press at the way in which he had been forced to climb down. Then, on May 28, he suddenly appeared in Berlin and summoned another conference at the Reich Chancellery. . . . Spread out on the table in the winter garden was a map, and on it Hitler sketched with angry gestures exactly how he

meant to eliminate the State which had dared to inflict this humiliation on him.[59]

Foolish as was the fake crisis created by Prague in May 1938, it must be seen in the same light as Schuschnigg's rash plebiscite. Both were desperate cries of imperiled prey who sensed the predator was close at hand.

Yet by painting the phony crisis of May 1938 as a showdown where Hitler had capitulated to their brave defiance, Czechoslovakia and Beneš set in motion the events that would lead to Munich, the end of Czechoslovakia, and Herr Beneš fleeing for his life.

WHY NOT TELL HITLER "NO!"?

WHY DID CHAMBERLAIN NOT reject Hitler's demands? Why did Britain not elect to fight, rather than abandon the Czechs?

First, as he had written his sister, Chamberlain "didn't care two hoots whether the Sudetens were in the Reich, or out of it."[60] He did not believe that maintaining Czech rule over three million unhappy Germans was worth a war. As the British saw the German demands as reasonable, they came to see the Czechs as obdurate. Nevile Henderson, the British envoy in Berlin, thought it necessary, in the interests of peace, to be "disagreeable to the Czechs," for they were a pigheaded race and President Beneš "not the least pig-headed among them."[61]

Many British believed justice was on the German side. The Sudeten Germans, a privileged minority in the Austro-Hungarian Empire, hated the Prague regime and had no loyalty to a nation where they were second-class citizens. Under Wilson's principle of self-determination, they should have been left under Vienna. Granted a plebiscite, like the people of Schleswig and the Saar, the Sudetendeutsch would have voted to stay with Austria or join their

German kinsmen. But this had been unacceptable to the Allies at Paris, especially the French, who had been operating on the principles of realpolitik. Wilsonian principles be damned, France was determined to separate Germans from Germans. And from the standpoint of France's security, the Allies had been right. Graham Stewart explains their dilemma:

> Self-determination had been a great cry of the liberal diplomat for a century, but strategic necessities prevented the Sudeten question being framed in these singularly uncomplicated terms. If the Sudetenland, much of which was mountainous, was absorbed into the German Reich, then the remaining rump Czech state would become virtually indefensible against invasion.[62]

Strict application of the principle of self-determination would have meant that all Germans in Eupen, Malmédy, Alsace, Lorraine, South Tyrol, Austria, the Sudetenland, Danzig, the Corridor, and Memel must be allowed to secede and join the Reich. But that would resurrect a Germany more populous and potentially powerful than that of the Kaiser.

At Paris, the principles the Allies professed clashed with the security interests they had come to protect. They resolved the question with no small cynicism and hypocrisy, granting self-determination to peoples who wished to be free of German rule, while denying it to Germans. Wilsonian self-determination was sacrificed on the altar of realpolitik and French security. The problem now was that Adolf Hitler was singing Wilson's song, demanding that Germans in the Sudetenland be granted the same right of self-determination that had been granted at Paris to Poles and Czechs. By 1944, Walter Lippmann realized the insanity of Versailles in elevating the principle of self-determination to infallible doctrine:

To invoke the general principle of self-determination, and to make it a supreme law of international life was to invite sheer anarchy. . . .

None knew this better than Adolf Hitler himself: the principle of self-determination was his chief instrument for enlarging the Reich by annexation, and for destroying from within the civil unity of the states he intended to attack. Hitler invoked this principle when he annexed Austria [and] dismembered Czechoslovakia."[63]

What also made the prospect of a war for Czechoslovakia repellent to Chamberlain was that he believed that, as a people, Czechs were "not out of the top-drawer."[64] As he memorably told the nation on the eve of Munich, when war seemed inevitable,

How horrible, fantastic, incredible it is that we should be digging trenches and trying on gas masks here because of a quarrel in a faraway country between people of whom we know nothing. . . .

However much we may sympathize with a small nation confronted by a big and powerful neighbor, we cannot in all circumstances undertake to involve the whole British Empire in a war simply on her account. If we have to fight, it must be on larger issues than that.[65]

In 1914, Britain had gone to war to save France, and the British had followed Asquith, Churchill, and Grey in when Belgium was violated. But while France and Belgium were just across the Channel, the Czechs were in Central Europe. Why should British soldiers die so Czechs could hold on to three million unhappy ethnic Germans who had lived under Habsburg or Hohenzollern rule for centuries? Thus British principles (supporting the right of self-determination) and British policy (building a permanent peace by rectifying the injustices of Versailles) seemed to dictate pressuring Beneš to give the Sudetenland to Germany, where the Sudetenlanders wished to be.

Thus it was that Munich was regarded, as historian Taylor wrote in 1961, as "a triumph for all that was best and most enlightened in British life; a triumph for those who had preached equal justice between peoples, a triumph for those who had courageously denounced the harshness and short-sightedness of Versailles."[66]

Finally, Britain lacked the military power and strategic reach to save Czechoslovakia, and Chamberlain knew it. As he wrote to his sister,

> The Austrian frontier is practically open; the great Skoda munitions works are within easy bombing distance of the German aerodromes; the railways all pass through German territory; Russia is a hundred miles away. Therefore we could not help Czechoslovakia—she would simply be a pretext for going to war with Germany. That we could not think of unless we had a reasonable prospect of beating her to her knees in a reasonable time, and of that I see no sign.[67]

In September 1938, Britain was utterly unprepared for war. She had two combat divisions ready for battle in England, none in France, no draft, no Spitfires, and no allies save a reluctant France. Only five of her twenty-seven fighter squadrons were equipped with the new Hurricanes. The RAF "cannot at the present time be said to be in any way fit to undertake operations on a major war scale," the Air Ministry concluded.[68]

General Ironside, inspector-general of overseas forces, confided, "Chamberlain is of course right. We have not the means of defending ourselves and he knows it. . . . We cannot expose ourselves now to a German attack. We simply commit suicide if we do."[69] "In the circumstances," warned Lord Gort, the new chief of the Imperial General Staff, "it would be murder to send our forces overseas to fight against a first-class power."[70]

Even John Lukacs, who regards Churchill as the savior of Western civilization, believes he was wrong in thinking Britain and France could have saved the Czechs by going to war in the fall of 1938:

> Churchill was wrong. It would have been disastrous for the Western democracies to go to war in October of 1938. He may have been right morally speaking; practically, he was wrong. . . .
>
> He was wrong, too, in his conviction that in 1938 Stalin's Russia would have gone to war on the side of the Czechs. He wrote this as late as 1948, in volume 1 of his *Second World War.* Yet Stalin was even less inclined to honor his military pact with the Czechs than were the French.[71]

Churchill was also wrong in his wild exaggeration of the martial spirit and fighting prowess of the Czech army. On September 15, two weeks before Munich, Churchill wrote:

> Inside the Czechoslovakian Republic there is an absolute determination to fight for life and freedom. All their frontiers, even that opposite Austria, are well fortified and guarded by a strong and devoted army. . . . [T]he Czechoslovakian army is one of the best equipped in the world. It has admirable tanks, anti-tank guns and anti-aircraft artillery. This resolute people have long prepared themselves for the ordeal.[72]

This was hyperbole. After Munich, when Britain and France told the Czechs to let the Sudetenland go, the Czechoslovakian army folded without firing a shot. Herr Beneš fled.

WHERE FDR STOOD AT MUNICH

COULD BRITAIN HAVE RELIED on America had she defied Hitler?

In September 1938, the month of Munich, FDR disabused Europe of any such notion: "Those who count on the assured aid of the United States in case of a war in Europe are totally mistaken. . . . To include the United States in a Franco-British front against Hitler is an interpretation that is 100 percent false."[73] That month, America informed France that, in the event of war, America could not, under the Neutrality Act, transfer to her the warplanes she had already purchased. FDR's message: This is your war, not ours.

Britain's lack of an army, France's lack of will, and lack of support from America, Australia, Canada, and South Africa meant Britain and France could not prevail against Germany. In May 1938, in the unkindest cut of all, Belgian troops maneuvered on the French frontier, as the Belgian foreign minister put it, to "show you that if you come our way in order to support Czechoslovakia, you will run up against the Belgian army."[74]

Even should Britain and France together fight Germany to a standstill in France, what would be the purpose of the war? To restore the status quo ante and return the Sudeten Germans to a Czech rule 80 percent of them wished to be rid of? That would only replicate the folly of Versailles and set the stage for yet another crisis. As the British minister in Prague, Basil Newton, wrote, should Britain go to war, the most that could be accomplished was to "restore after a lengthy struggle a status quo which had already proved unacceptable and which, even if restored, would probably again prove unworkable."[75]

The brutal truth: The Sudeten Germans wanted to be reunited with their kinsmen and could not forever be denied. And as Britain now believed the decision to deliver them to Prague had been a blunder, why fight a war to perpetuate a blunder? Neither the British nation nor empire, wrote Henderson, would have supported war on

Germany to deny Germans the right of self-determination the Allies had so loudly preached at Paris.[76]

Chamberlain had another motive in going to Munich. He believed the key to peace lay in addressing the grievances of Germany and rectifying the wrongs of Versailles, and he wanted to be the British statesman who restored Germany to her rightful position as a Great Power and converted her into a partner in peace. If this required the return of all German lands and peoples, should they wish to return, Chamberlain would facilitate it, if done peacefully. This is why historian Taylor came in 1961 to plea-bargain on behalf of the appeasers he had opposed at the time of Munich:

> Historians do a bad day's work when they write the appeasers off as stupid or as cowards. They were men confronted with real problems, doing their best in the circumstances of their time. They recognized that an independent and powerful Germany had somehow to be fitted into Europe. Later experience suggests that they were right.[77]

Had Hitler gone about the in-gathering, by negotiation and plebiscite, of all the lost peoples and provinces of Germany and Austria—the Saar, the Rhineland, the Sudetenland, Danzig, the Corridor, Memel—Britain would have accommodated him. A war to block the unification of the Germans in a national home would not have been acceptable to the British people. Wilson had preached his doctrine of self-determination all too well.

Nor was Chamberlain alone in this conviction. While appeasement is today a synonym for craven cowardice in the face of evil, appeasement as a policy predated Chamberlain. As Andrew Roberts writes in his biography of Halifax, "Although today it is considered shameful and craven, the policy of appeasement once occupied almost the whole moral high ground. The word was originally synonymous with idealism, magnanimity of the victor and the willingness to right wrongs."[78]

Henderson described appeasement as "the search for just solutions by negotiation in the light of higher reason instead of by resort to force."[79] Eden, a four-year veteran of the trenches and the toast of the League of Nations Union, who had lost two brothers in the war, described his policy as "the appeasement of Europe as a whole."[80] By appeasement, Eden meant

what liberal opinion had endorsed since Versailles—the removal of the causes of war by the remedy of justified grievances. Thus Eden acquiesced in Germany's remilitarization of the Rhineland in 1936. True, it was a violation of the Versailles Treaty—but who now defended its one-sided and obsolescent provisions, denying Germany full control of its own territory? True, it had been achieved by force—but who wanted to take back from Hitler what would otherwise have been conceded to him across the conference table with a handshake from a smiling Eden?[81]

WHY DID FRANCE NOT FIGHT?

BELATEDLY, FRANCE HAD AWAKENED to the realization that her eastern allies might not be strategic assets at all, but potentially lethal liabilities. Having lost her great ally, Czarist Russia, France had looked on Poland, Czechoslovakia, and Yugoslavia as new allies who would fight on her side if Germany invaded Alsace. She now began to realize that France could be dragged into a war with Germany to defend them. The French had always asked, "How can our eastern allies help us?" not "How can we help them?"

France was in another dilemma. Her British assurances took effect only if she acted defensively. But to protect her eastern allies, she had to go on the attack. Her insurance policies thus canceled each other out. If she attacked Germany to aid Poland or Czechoslovakia, she lost

Britain. If she remained inside the Maginot Line to await a German attack, she abandoned and lost her eastern allies, whom one historian dismissed as three small hens penned up with a large fox harboring a grievance. Wrote historian Correlli Barnett brutally but accurately, "The French system of alliances . . . rested on strategic nonsense."[82]

By the 1930s, German and British assessments of Versailles and the requirements of peace had converged. Hitler argued that Germany had been dealt with unjustly at Versailles after she laid down her arms. Chamberlain did not disagree. Writes Ernest May,

> Abhorring Lloyd George, the British prime minister who was partly accountable for the Versailles Treaty, Chamberlain adopted every chapter of the "revisionist" critique. He believed that emotion had ruled in the 1919 peacemaking, that Germans have been wronged in ways harmful to the world economy and dangerous both politically and economically. He deemed Hitler's grievances real and Hitler's demands not unreasonable.[83]

The British people, too, wished to right the wrongs of Versailles. If that meant granting self-determination to the German-speaking peoples of the Sudetenland, they approved. Appeasement of a Germany they now believed to have been wronged was broadly supported. But with appeasement came the old insoluble problem—and several new ones.

First, restoration of German lands and peoples to the Reich, even if done by plebiscite, meant reconstituting the Germany of Bismarck and the Kaiser that almost defeated a coalition of Britain, France, Russia, Japan, Italy, and the United States. Second, restoring lost German provinces and peoples meant that two allies of France, Czechoslovakia and Poland, must undergo amputation. How were Britain and France to persuade Czechoslovakia to surrender the Sudetenland or Poland to give up Danzig?

The third problem with appeasement was that the new chancellor of Germany was no Ebert, Stresemann, or Brüning. The Hitler of *Mein Kampf* had made it starkly clear that overturning Versailles and bringing Germans home to the Reich was not the end of his life's mission. Having let slip the chance to accommodate German democrats, Britain and France now had to deal with a coarse, brutal German dictator who had cold-bloodedly executed the comrades who had helped hoist him to power.

The Allies had been warned of what they were inviting. But they had not listened. Shortly before his death, "exhausted and disillusioned," Gustav Stresemann, the widely respected German foreign minister, summed up his dealings with the Allies: "I gave and gave and gave until my followers turned against me. . . . If they could have granted me just one concession, I would have won my people. But they gave nothing. . . . That is my tragedy and their crime."[84]

Thus, long before he flew to Munich for his final meeting, Chamberlain had come to believe that keeping the Sudeten Germans under a Czech rule they despised was not worth a war. And even should Britain go to war, she could not prevent German annexation of the Sudetenland. So, to make a virtue of necessity, he would fly to Munich and effect the peaceful transfer. While there, he would persuade Hitler that German grievances for the return of peoples who wished to belong to the Reich could be met, if only Hitler would renounce force. "Halifax had already visited Germany and had assured Hitler that Danzig, Austria, and Czechoslovakia could be settled in Germany's favour, provided that there were no 'far-reaching disturbances.' "[85]

Finally, after Hitler annexed the Sudetenland, Britain, France, and Germany would guarantee the remnant of Czechoslovakia in which Hitler had professed no interest. An Eastern Locarno. But this guarantee raised a logical question. If Britain and France could not prevent amputation of the Sudetenland, how could they prevent Hitler from overrunning the remnant of Czechoslovakia after it had been stripped of its mountain fortifications, should he decide to occupy that as well?

Thus did Chamberlain volunteer to officiate at the peaceful transfer of the Sudetenland to Germany—rather than have Hitler take it by force.

CHURCHILL'S ALTERNATIVE

AT THE TIME OF MUNICH, Churchill was frozen out of Chamberlain's Cabinet but still in Parliament and a voice heard not only in England but in Germany and the world. And the more insistent the demands of Hitler, the wider and more attentive his audience.

What alternative did Churchill offer?

Self-determination be damned! Rather than force the Czechs to give up the Sudetenland, Britain should go to war. Yet, in Churchill's position, there was a contradiction. If Britain was as inferior to Germany in airpower as he had proclaimed, and she had no army in Europe, how could she win Churchill's war? How could Britain, with two divisions that could be sent to France, stop fifty German divisions from overrunning a Czechoslovakia bordered on three sides by Germany and that harbored a fifth column of three million ethnic Germans? Churchill's answer: an alliance with Stalin.

But no Western statesman had been more eloquent than Churchill in excoriating Bolshevism. He had described the 1917 decision of the German General Staff to transport Lenin in the famous sealed train from Switzerland across Germany as comparable to having introduced a "plague bacillus" into Russia, adding, "[I]n the cutting off of the lives of men and women, no Asiatic conqueror, not Tamerlane, not Jengiz Khan, can match the fame" of Lenin.[86]

Since Lenin's death, Stalin had surpassed him in mass murders that included the forced starvation of the Ukrainians and the Great Terror that began with the torture, show trials, and executions of his revolutionary comrades and went on to consume hundreds of thousands of lives. Was Churchill willing to ally the Mother of Parliaments with this monster?

If Churchill's assessment of Hitler's character and Munich were spot-on, his strategic alternative—bring the Red Army into Europe to stop him—appalled Chamberlain, who despised and distrusted the Bolsheviks more than the Nazis and Fascists. Forced to choose between Nazi Germany and Stalin's Soviet Union controlling Eastern and Central Europe, he would have preferred the former. "Better Hitler than Stalin" was a sentiment shared by leaders of all the nations bordering on Stalin's empire: Finland, Estonia, Lithuania, Latvia, Poland, Rumania. They had all heard the screams from over the border. Living next door, they had none of the romantic illusions about a "brave new world" held by British Labourites and American liberals.

By Munich, when the number of Hitler's victims still numbered in the hundreds, Stalin had murdered millions in his "prison house of nations" stretching from Ukraine to the Pacific. Chamberlain also believed any alliance with Russia meant certain war with Germany, a war from which Hitler or Stalin would emerge as master of Eastern and Central Europe. Neither result, Chamberlain thought, was worth Britain's fighting another horrific European war. Here, too, argues Taylor, Chamberlain and the appeasers were prescient:

> Again the appeasers feared that the defeat of Germany would be followed by a Russian domination over much of Europe. Later experience suggests that they were right here also. Only those who wanted Soviet Russia to take the place of Germany are entitled to condemn the "appeasers"; and I cannot understand how most of those who condemn them are now equally indignant at the inevitable result of their failure.[87]

In 1938, Chamberlain perceived clearly and correctly the probable outcome of a war with Nazi Germany that Churchill would not perceive until 1944 and 1945. The only force that could save Czechoslovakia in September 1938 was the Red Army. But how does bringing the Bolsheviks' Red Army into Czechoslovakia save Czechoslovakia?

Nor were the Poles or Rumanians willing to let the Red Army tramp through to save the Czechs. They believed—rightly, it turned out—that if the Red Army came into Europe, it would not go home and they would lose their freedom. Eastern and Central Europe preferred the risks of a German invasion to the certain horrors of a Russian rescue.

But if Chamberlain's strategic assessment was right and Britain's vital interests dictated staying out of a war for the Sudetenland, why was Munich a disaster? Why is Chamberlain virtually without defenders?

THE GODESBERG MEETING

CHAMBERLAIN'S FAILURE LAY NOT in his refusal to take Britain to war with Germany over the Sudetenland. There he was right. His failure was in how he behaved at Munich and after Munich.

The prime minister made three trips to Germany that September to persuade Hitler to agree to a plebiscite and the peaceful transfer of the Sudetenland to the Reich. On his first, to Berchtesgaden, he had received Hitler's demands and taken them back to England, where he won Cabinet acceptance. Chamberlain then returned to meet Hitler at Bad Godesberg, to report on the success of his mission to London.

This meeting was held in a hotel kept by one Dreesen, a backer of the Nazi cause. As Henderson relates, it was at Dreesen's hotel that

Hitler "had taken the decision for the 'blood bath' of June 1934, and it was thence that he flew with Goebbels to Munich for the arrest and execution of Roehm."[88]

At Godesberg, Chamberlain was shaken by the new truculence and intransigence of Hitler. The Fuehrer announced that acceding to his earlier demands was now insufficient. He threatened an immediate occupation of the Sudetenland and war should he meet resistance. Chamberlain replied that Britain could not accept an outcome imposed by naked force. When Neville Chamberlain returned with Hitler's new demands, the Cabinet rejected them. The French rejected them. The Czechs rejected them.

As Chamberlain did not want the error of 1914 repeated, where the Kaiser and Bethmann-Hollweg were still uncertain, in the final hours before war, whether Britain would fight, he sent Sir Horace Wilson to read Hitler a clear message. If Germany invaded, and the Czechs resisted, and France honored her word to Prague, Britain would fight at France's side in a new European war. Facing Hitler directly, Wilson read him this message:

> The French Government has told us that in the case of a German attack against Czechoslovakia it will faithfully fulfill its obligations. If in carrying out these obligations deriving from its treaties, France became actively engaged in hostilities against Germany, the United Kingdom would feel obliged to come to her aid.[89]

In *Dark Summer*, Gene Smith describes Hitler's reaction as Wilson slowly read to him Chamberlain's note.

"So! That settles it!" shouted Hitler. "Now I will really smash the Czechs."[90] Hitler's interpreter Paul Schmidt had never seen him so out of control. "That old shit-hound must be crazy if he thinks he can influence me in this way," Hitler said of Chamberlain.[91]

A shaken Wilson replied that his prime minister was only inter-

Above left: Lord Salisbury. **"Isolation is much less dangerous than the danger of being dragged into wars which do not concern us."** *(Getty)*

Above right: Otto von Bismarck. **"[Germany] has hay enough for her fork."** *(Getty)*

Right: Sir Edward Grey. **"If we are engaged in war, we shall suffer but little more than we shall suffer if we stand aside."** *(Getty)*

David Lloyd George. **"I never want to be cheered by a war crowd."** *(Getty)*

Prime Minister H. H. Asquith. **"Winston . . . has got on all his war paint. . . . The whole thing fills me with sadness."** *(Getty)*

Churchill as First Lord of the Admiralty. **"My God! This is living History. . . . I would not be out of this glorious delicious war for anything the world could give me."** *(Getty)*

Below left: Kaiser Wilhelm II. **"It is not I who bears the responsibility for the disaster which now threatens the entire civilized world."** *(Getty)*

Below right: King Edward VII. **"He is Satan. You cannot imagine what a Satan he is."**—Kaiser Wilhelm II *(Getty)*

Admiral Tirpitz. **"This war is really the greatest lunacy ever committed by the white races."** *(Getty)*

Below: (Left to right) Lloyd George, Clemenceau, Wilson. **"Those three all-powerful, all-ignorant men . . . carving continents with only a child to lead them."** —Arthur Balfour *(Getty)*

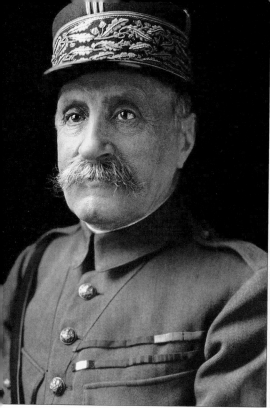

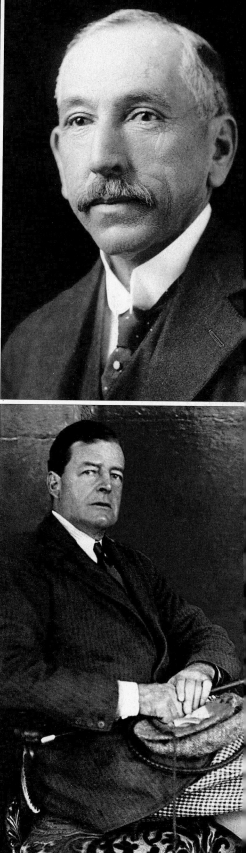

Above left: Marshal Ferdinand Foch. **"This is not peace, it is an armistice for twenty years."** *(Getty)*

Above right: Prime Minister William "Billy" Hughes of Australia. **"You propose to substitute for the Anglo-Japanese alliance and the overwhelming power of the British Navy a Washington conference?"** *(Corbis)*

Right: First Sea Lord Earl Beatty. **"That extraordinary fellow Winston has gone mad."** *(Corbis)*

Arthur Balfour at the Washington Naval Conference (second from right). **Severing the Anglo-Japanese alliance "was an act of breathtaking stupidity."** —U.S. historian Arthur Herman *(Getty)*

Winston Churchill as Chancellor of the Exchequer. **"A war with Japan! . . . I do not believe there is the slightest chance of it in our lifetime."** *(Getty)*

Mussolini and Hitler in Venice, June 1934. **"What a clown this Hitler is."**—Benito Mussolini (*Library of Congress*)

Austrian Chancellor Engelbert Dollfuss. **"Hitler is the murderer of Dollfuss . . . a horrible sexual degenerate, a dangerous fool."**—Benito Mussolini, August 1934 (*Getty*)

King George V. **"I will not have another war. I will not. The last one was none of my doing."** *(Getty)*

Prime Minister Stanley Baldwin. **"With two lunatics like Mussolini and Hitler, you can never be sure of anything. . . . I am determined to keep the country out of war."** *(Getty)*

Below: (Left to right) Foreign Minister Pierre Laval of France, Mussolini, Prime Minister Ramsay MacDonald of Great Britain, and French prime minister Pierre-Étienne Flandin at Stresa, Italy, 1935. **"The Stresa front has been shaken, if not, indeed dissolved."**—Winston Churchill, 1935 *(Corbis)*

Foreign Secretary Anthony Eden. **"[T]he greatness of his office will find him out. . . . I think you will now see what a lightweight Eden is."**
—Winston Churchill
(Getty)

Hitler and Lord Halifax at Berchtesgaden.
"Shoot Gandhi!"
—Adolf Hitler

Austrian Chancellor Kurt Schuschnigg. **"This Schuschnigg was a harder bone than I first thought."** —Adolf Hitler *(Getty)*

Hermann Göring. **"[H]is personality . . . was frankly attractive, like a great schoolboy."** —Lord Halifax, 1937 *(Getty)*

(Left to right) Chamberlain, Daladier, Hitler, and Mussolini in Munich. **"I got the impression that he was a man who could be relied upon when he had given his word."**—Chamberlain on Hitler, September 1938 *(Getty)*

Chamberlain at Heston Aerodrome, 1938. **"I've got it! I've got it! Here is a paper which bears his name."** *(Getty)*

Czech president Eduard Beneš. **Hitler was gripped by "a burning rage to get even . . . with President Beneš, who, he believed, had deliberately humiliated him."** —historian William Shirer *(Getty)*

Colonel Jozef Beck of Poland. **"If Beck was at fault as a diplomat, the fault lay . . . in his naïve belief in the sincerity of Allied guarantees and assurances."** —historian Norman Davies *(Getty)*

Below: (Left to right) Count Ciaro, Lord Halifax, Chamberlain, and Mussolini in January 1939. **"These . . . are the tired sons of a long line of rich men, and they will lose their empire."**—Benito Mussolini *(Corbis)*

Hitler in Prague, March 1939. **"It is the greatest triumph of my life! I shall enter history as the greatest German of them all!"** *(Getty)*

Below left: Sir Nevile Henderson (left) and Hermann Göring. **"It was the final shipwreck of my mission to Berlin. . . . Hitler had crossed the Rubicon."** *(Getty)*

Below right: Virgil Tilea, Romania's minister in London. **Instigator of panic.** *(Getty)*

Adolf Hitler on the eve of war, September 1939. **"The last thing that Hitler wanted to produce was another great war."**—B. H. Liddell Hart *(Getty)*

Moscow, 1942.
CHURCHILL: "Have you forgiven me?"
STALIN: "It is not for me to forgive. It is for God to forgive." *(Corbis)*

"If our country were defeated, I hope we should find a champion as indomitable to restore our courage and lead us back to our place among the nations." —Churchill on Hitler, 1937 *(Getty)*

Man of the Century? "Historians are apt to judge war ministers less by the victories achieved under their direction than by the political results which flowed from them. Judged by that standard, I am not sure that I shall be held to have done very well." *(Getty)*

ested in peace. At this, Hitler shouted, "The comments of his ass-kissers do not interest me. . . . All that interests me are my people who are being tortured by that dirty ——— Beneš. I will not stand it any longer! It is more than a good German can bear! Do you hear me, you stupid pig?"[92]

Hitler shouted that the Germans "were being treated like nig-gers; one would not dare treat even Turks like that."[93]

That night, in a speech at the Sportspalast that Alan Bullock calls a "masterpiece of invective which even he never surpassed," Hitler gave a catalog of his diplomatic achievements—from his pact with Poland, to the Anglo-German Naval Treaty, to the renunciation of Alsace-Lorraine, the friendship with Italy, the peaceful annexation of Austria.[94] "And now before us stands the last problem that must be solved and will be solved. It is the last territorial claim which I have to make in Europe, but it is the claim from which I will not recede, and, God willing, I will make good."[95]

With the Czech allegations of his cowardice in the May crisis in mind, Hitler now turned the new crisis into a test of manhood be-tween himself and Eduard Beneš:

Now two men stand arrayed one against the other: there is Herr Benes, and here am I. We are two men of a different make up. In the great struggle of the peoples, while Herr Benes was sneaking about through the world, I as a decent German did my duty. And now today I stand over against this man as a soldier of my people. . . . The world must take note that in four and a half years of war, and through the long years of my political life, there is one thing which no one could ever cast in my teeth: I have never been a coward. Now I go before my people as its first soldier, and behind me—this the world should know—there marches a different people from that of 1918.

We are determined![96]

Hitler had overreached.

Though the democracies were not strong enough to defeat him, they suddenly seemed ready to fight. At Chamberlain's direction, First Lord Duff Cooper ordered mobilization of the fleet.[97] France and Czechoslovakia began to mobilize. Their armies would outnumber Hitler's two-to-one. Mussolini was doing nothing to pin down French divisions on the Italian border. "What Hitler did know," writes Shirer, "was that Prague was defiant, Paris rapidly mobilizing, London stiffening, his own people apathetic, his leading generals dead against him, and that his ultimatum [to the Czechs to accept] . . . the Godesberg proposals expired at 2 P.M. the next day."[98]

On September 27, an event in Berlin caused Hitler to reconsider and back away from war. Nevile Henderson describes it in his memoirs:

A chance episode had . . . produced a salutary revulsion in Hitler's mind. In the afternoon of that Tuesday, a mechanized division had rumbled through the streets of Berlin and up the Wilhelmstrasse past the Chancellor's window. For three hours Hitler stood at his window, and watched it pass. The Germans love military display, but not a single individual in the streets applauded its passage. The picture which it represented was almost that of a hostile army passing through a conquered city. Hitler was deeply impressed. At that moment he realized for the first time that the cheers of his sycophants in the Sportspalast were far from representing the true spirit and feelings of the German People.[99]

Hitler was heard to mutter, "I can't wage war with this nation yet."[100] Bluff called, Hitler sat down and wrote to Chamberlain, urging him not to give up his efforts for a peaceful resolution.

On September 28, as he spoke in the House of Commons of how "horrible, fantastic, incredible that we should be digging ditches and

trying on gas masks because of a quarrel in a far-away country between people of whom we know nothing," the prime minister was
interrupted. He stopped speaking, read a note, and then, in what
Harold Nicolson said was one of the most dramatic moments he
ever witnessed, Chamberlain announced: "Herr Hitler has just
agreed to postpone his mobilisation for twenty-four hours and meet
me in conference with Signor Mussolini and Signor [*sic*] Daladier at
Munich."[101]

For a while there was silence and then the whole House of Commons broke into ecstatic cheering and sobbing. Churchill went up to
Chamberlain and said to him, sourly, "I congratulate you on your
good fortune. You were very lucky."[102]

On that third and final trip to Munich, according to aides present, Hitler was surly, angry, rude, brusque. Lord Dunglass, the future prime minister Sir Alec Douglas-Home, described it as the
worst experience of his career. Never had he expected to see a British
prime minister treated in the manner that Adolf Hitler treated
Neville Chamberlain.[103]

Which raises the question still unanswered by history.

How could Chamberlain believe that by getting the signature of
such a man on a three-sentence statement, he had created a bond of
trust and he and Hitler would now work together for peace in Europe? When Hitler said the Sudetenland was his last territorial demand, did Chamberlain think he had given up Danzig and Memel?
Given *Mein Kampf,* Hitler's record as a leader of street thugs who had
attempted a putsch in Bavaria, his Night of the Long Knives, his
trashing of Locarno, his warmongering at Godesberg, his crudity at
Munich, why did Chamberlain trust him not to do what he had
boasted repeatedly he intended to do?

Chamberlain was right in believing the Sudetenland not worth a
war. He was wrong in believing that by surrendering it to Hitler he
had bought anything but time, which he should have used to rally
Britain. A good man who wanted peace, he deceived himself into

believing he had achieved it. Instead of returning home and report-
ing that, while war had been averted, Britain must prepare for the
worst, Chamberlain came home boasting that he had brought back
"peace for our time." Devastating to his reputation in history, Chamberlain then presented himself to the nation as the only leader who
really understood and could deal with Hitler.

Chamberlain staked his place in history on his assessment that
Hitler was a man he could do business with and trust to keep his
word. Returning from Berchtesgaden, he had told Parliament: "In
spite of the hardness and ruthlessness I thought I saw in his face, I got
the impression that here was a man who could be relied upon when
he had given his word."[104]

After Godesberg, Chamberlain assured the Cabinet that Hitler
"would not deliberately deceive a man whom he respected and with
whom he had been in negotiation."[105]

Thus did Chamberlain permit himself to be made history's fool.
Thus did he morally disarm his people, who were so desperate to
avoid war they were ready to be deceived. By reveling in the celebration of Munich, Chamberlain disarmed himself. He could not now
say what had to be said. He could not now do what had to be done:
tell the nation it must sacrifice and prepare, for war with Germany
was now a possibility and, if British vital interests were imperiled, a
certainty. But having declared he had brought home "peace for our
time," how could Chamberlain ask the British to sacrifice to finance
the weapons of war? As Sir Harold Nicolson mused, "It is difficult to
say: 'This is the greatest diplomatic achievement in history, therefore
we must redouble our armament in order never again to be exposed
to such humiliation.' "[106] Chamberlain had put all Britain's eggs in
one basket and handed it to Hitler, who, within hours of Munich, was
cursing him for having robbed him of the pleasure of smashing the
Czechs and exacting vengeance upon Beneš.

Chamberlain was a perfect foil for Hitler—and for Churchill,
who, in the euphoria of Munich, declared that Britain had concluded

a shameful betrayal and Hitler would digest the Sudetenland and be back for more: "We have sustained a great defeat without a war, the consequences of which will travel far with us. We have passed an awful milestone in our history. And do not suppose that this is the end. This is only the beginning."[107]

In January 1939, Chamberlain went to Rome to confer with the Italian dictator he had met at Munich. He returned satisfied that he had established a rapport. He had asked Il Duce for his thoughts on Hitler. In the Cabinet minutes, Chamberlain described the Duce's response:

[He, Mussolini] had never taken the opportunity offered to him, but had remained throughout absolutely loyal to Herr Hitler. The Prime Minister said that at the time he had been somewhat disappointed at this attitude, but on reflection he thought that it reflected credit in Signor Mussolini's character.[108]

Chamberlain thought it a "truly wonderful visit."[109] In describing his British guests to his son-in-law, Foreign Minister Count Ciano, Mussolini had taken away another impression: "These men are not made of the same stuff as the Francis Drakes and the other magnificent adventurers who created the empire. These, after all, are the tired sons of a long line of rich men, and they will lose their empire."[110]

THE FAILURE OF APPEASEMENT

HAD THE BALDWIN-CHAMBERLAIN POLICY of redressing grievances and accommodating legitimate demands been adopted by Britain before 1933, when Germany was ruled by democrats, it might have worked. With their face cards stripped from their hands by

Allied magnanimity, Hitler and the Nazis might never have come to power. But once they did, and began to bang the table, Germans concluded it was Allied fear of Hitler and of them that made them so reasonable now. What doomed Chamberlain's policy was that, in Hitler and his Nazi cohorts, he was confronted by hard, coarse men, full of resentment, who preferred brutality to get what they wanted, who relished humiliating the weak, and whose ambitions extended beyond what Britain could assent to. Hitler knew he would prevail at Munich, said Henderson, for he had put himself in his adversaries' shoes. Henderson describes Hitler's thinking:

> In September . . . [Hitler] had not believed that . . . the French nation would be ready to fight for the Czechs or that England would fight if the French did not. He argued as follows: Would the German nation willingly go to war for General Franco in Spain, if France intervened on the side of the Republican Government at Valencia? The answer that he gave himself is that it would not; and he was consequently convinced that no democratic French Government would be strong enough to lead the French nation to war for the Czechs. That was the basis of his calculations, and his policy was in accordance therewith.[111]

Hitler's calculation proved correct. The German generals who were near panic over the prospect of a war over the Sudetenland were discredited.

Though Czechoslovakia had a powerful army, Beneš, abandoned by the British and French, did not order it to resist. Unlike Schuschnigg, who remained in Vienna to face Hitler's wrath, Eduard Beneš fled.

With Austria and the Sudetenland now his, Hitler in 1938 had added ten million Germans to the Reich without firing a shot. It was a Bismarckian achievement. Yet it is a myth to say Munich led directly to World War II. It was a diplomatic debacle, but it was not why Britain went to war.

The casus belli of World War II emanated from a decision, six months later, that would drag England into a six-year death struggle at the wrong time, in the wrong place, for the wrong reason. That decision would prove the greatest blunder in British history.

CHAPTER 9

Fatal Blunder

[THE DICTATORS] HAVE HAD good cause to ask for
consideration of their grievances & if they had asked
nicely after I appeared on the scene they might already
have got some satisfaction.[1]
— NEVILLE CHAMBERLAIN,
February 1939

AS THE FALL OF 1938 slipped into winter, Chamberlain continued to defend his Munich accord. His Christmas cards bore a picture of the plane that had carried him to Munich.[2] But the bloom was
off the rose. A poll in October revealed that 93 percent of the British
did not believe that Hitler had made his last territorial demand in
Europe.[3]

After the Godesberg ultimatum, the Czechs had been ready to
fight. France had begun to mobilize. First Lord Duff Cooper, at
Chamberlain's direction, had called out the fleet. It was Hitler who
had backed away from his ultimatum and agreed to a third meeting—
at Munich. Though realpolitik may have dictated telling the Czechs
that Britain could not fight for the Sudetenland, the British, a moral
people, came to be ashamed of what they had done. And public opinion soon took a hard turn against Germany.

On November 7, seventeen-year-old Herschel Grynszpan, whose
family had been ordered deported from Hamburg to Poland with
twenty thousand other Jews—when Warsaw threatened to cancel

their passports, leaving them stateless in Germany and thus Berlin's responsibility—walked into the German embassy in Paris and shot Third Secretary Ernst vom Rath. When Rath died two days later, all hell broke loose in the Reich.

On the night of November 9–10, Nazi storm troopers went on a rampage, smashing windows, looting Jewish shops, burning synagogues, beating and lynching Jews. Scores perished. Hundreds were assaulted in what would be known as Kristallnacht, the night of broken glass, the greatest pogrom in Germany since the Middle Ages.

Kristallnacht was a shameful crime and a historic blunder. Much of the goodwill garnered by the 1936 Berlin Olympics and Munich, which the democracies still believed had averted war, was washed away. The United States called its ambassador home. "Nazi treatment of the Jews," wrote Taylor, "did more than anything else to turn English moral feeling against Germany, and this moral feeling in turn made English people less reluctant to go to war."[4]

Some historians claim Kristallnacht, shocking, revolting, and stupid as it was, evoking only disgust and contempt for Germany in the West, was not ordered by Hitler but was the work of Goebbels, his propaganda minister. But moral responsibility rests with Hitler. For those who carried out the rampage were not punished, Goebbels was not fired, and the German Jews were forced to pay a billion marks to clean up the damage.

"The bestial wave of anti-Semitism which Goebbels unleashed in Germany during November completed the route of the appeasers," writes Paul Johnson. "During the winter of 1938–9 the mood in Britain changed to accept war as inevitable."[5]

POLAND'S TURN

As CHAMBERLAIN WAS BASKING in his triumph, Hitler had turned to the next item on his menu. On October 24, Foreign Minister

Ribbentrop made a surprise offer to Polish ambassador Jozef Lipski. If Warsaw would permit the "reunion of Danzig with the
Reich" and consent to Germany's building of "an extra-territorial
motor road and railway line" across the Corridor, Berlin would
leave Warsaw in control of the economic and railway facilities in
Danzig and guarantee Poland's frontiers.[6] With the issues of
Danzig and the Corridor resolved, Ribbentrop told Lipski, a "joint
policy towards Russia on the basis of the anti-Comintern pact"
could be adopted.[7] Ribbentrop was offering the Poles a Berlin-
Warsaw alliance against Russia.

Ribbentrop had reason to expect a positive response. Like Hungary, Poland had joined in the dismemberment of Czechoslovakia
after Munich. As Hitler seized the Sudetenland, the Poles, "like a
carrion fish swimming in the wake of a shark," seized the coal-rich
region of Teschen.[8] Also, Danzig was 95 percent German. Before
Versailles, the town had never belonged to Poland. Danzig had been
detached from Germany at Paris and declared a Free City to be administered by a High Commissioner appointed by the League of Nations to give Poland a port on the Baltic. As the Poles were now
developing their own port, Gdynia, and could continue to use Danzig, Warsaw no longer needed to rule Danzig. Moreover, the 350,000
Danzigers were agitating for a return to Germany.

The Corridor had also been cut out of Germany at Versailles.
This slice of land now severed East Prussia from Berlin and was
Poland's corridor to the Baltic Sea. Mistreatment of the 1.5 million
Germans still living in the Corridor was bitterly resented. On the issues of Danzig and the Corridor, the German people were more bellicose than Hitler, who wanted the return of Danzig but did not want
war. What Hitler sought was a Polish-German alliance, modeled on
the Rome-Berlin axis.

A bit of history. By 1933, Marshal Jozef Pilsudski, the Polish hero
of the Great War, was dictator. His August 1920 victory that hurled
Trotsky's army back from Warsaw had been compared by the British

ambassador in Berlin to Charles Martel's triumph at Tours. As the Hammer of the Franks saved Europe from Islam, Pilsudski had saved Europe from Bolshevism.

In Hitler Pilsudski saw a mortal threat. In early 1933, when Hitler became chancellor, Pilsudski massed five Polish army corps on his western border and "sounded out Paris about a joint application of pressure against Hitler while the Nazi regime was still insecure."[9] Pilsudski intended to kill the infant Nazi regime in its cradle.

"[T]here is plenty of evidence to suggest that Pilsudski seriously considered a preventive war against Hitler if only the western powers had shown themselves willing," writes Norman Davies.[10] German historian Hillgruber adds that these " 'preventive war' designs came to nothing because of France's immobility in foreign affairs. Thereupon Pilsudski himself undertook a rapprochement with Hitler in May 1933."[11]

Taking the measure of his French ally, Pilsudski decided his country would be better served by a ten-year nonaggression pact with Hitler. It was signed in January 1934. Hitler had removed the first foreign threat to his rule. The first and best opportunity to deal preemptively with the man who had laid out his vision in *Mein Kampf* had passed by.

Half a decade later, Hitler wanted Poland in his Anti-Comintern Pact. The fiercely anti-Bolshevik, anti-Russian, Catholic Poles seemed natural allies in a crusade to eradicate Communism. As an Austrian, Hitler did not share the Prussian bias against Poles. The role he had in mind for Poland was that of partner in his New Order in Europe. Italy, and eventually Hungary and Rumania, would accept this role. To Hitler's astonishment, Poland refused.

"In the early days of 1939," writes U.S. historian Charles Callan Tansill, "Hitler believed that [Polish Foreign Minister] Beck was so well versed in the principles of Realpolitik that he would be glad to go hand in hand with the Nazi leaders in a joint search for plunder that was weakly guarded by the broken-down states of Europe."[12]

Hitler believed Beck was a man he could do business with. So it would seem, for, as Manchester writes,

> No one questioned Jozef Beck's ability. His remarkable diplomatic skills had led to his appointment, at the age of thirty-eight, as Poland's foreign minister. Respected for his intellect and powerful will, he was also distrusted—even detested—for his duplicity, dishonesty, and, in his private life, depravity. In Rome, where he had spent an extended visit-cum-vacation, the Princess of Piedmont had said of him that he had the "sort of face you might see in a French newspaper as that of a ravisher of little girls."[13]

But Beck rebuffed Ribbentrop's offer. For, after their 1920 victory over the Red Army, the Poles considered themselves a Great Power. They were not. Writes A.J.P. Taylor,

> [T]hey . . . forgot that they had gained their independence in 1918 only because both Russia and Germany had been defeated. Now they had to choose between Russia and Germany. They chose neither. Only Danzig prevented cooperation between Germany and Poland. For this reason, Hitler wanted to get it out of the way. For precisely the same reason, Beck kept it in the way. It did not cross his mind that this might cause a fatal breach.[14]

Chamberlain also believed Danzig should be returned. As Taylor wrote, "The British cared nothing for Danzig, or, if they did, sympathized with the German case."[15] Lord Halifax considered Danzig and the Corridor "an absurdity."[16] Indeed, of all the German claims to lost lands, the claim to Danzig was strongest. It had always been a German city. Its population was 95 percent German. Any plebiscite would have produced a 90 percent vote to return to the Fatherland.

And Britain had no objection to Danzig's return, as long as it came about peacefully through negotiation, not violently through military force. On Danzig, the basic British and German positions were almost identical. Both wanted its peaceful return to Germany.

But the Poles adamantly refused to negotiate.

Hitler invited Beck to Berchtesgaden on January 5, 1939. There, in terms unlike those he had used on Schuschnigg, Hitler explained that if Danzig was returned, it could remain under Polish economic control. He impressed on Beck that a connection "with East Prussia was as vital a matter for the Reich as the connection with the sea was for Poland."[17] Ribbentrop "hinted very heavily" to Beck "that Polish concessions over Danzig could be compensated at Slovakia's expense"[18]

"On Hitler's part it was a remarkably moderate demand," writes the British historian Basil Liddell Hart.[19] But, again, Beck rebuffed Hitler. Hitler offered to guarantee Poland's borders and accept permanent Polish control of the Corridor, if Beck would simply agree to the return of Danzig and the construction of a German rail-and-road route across the Corridor. Beck again refused. So matters stood in March 1939, when the rump state of Czechoslovakia suddenly began to collapse and fall apart, as Hitler had warned Chamberlain at Berchtesgaden it would. By Chamberlain's own notes of that first meeting, Hitler had said that, once the Sudeten Germans were free of Prague, the Hungarians, Poles, and Slovaks left inside the multiethnic state would also secede.[20] Indeed, agents of the Reich were stoking the fires of secession, subverting the Czech state.

As Hitler had predicted, planned, and promoted, the disintegration of Czechoslovakia began as soon as Munich had been implemented. Slovakia and Ruthenia, or Carpatho-Ukraine, a hotbed of Ukrainian nationalism, set up parliaments. Hungary, which had lost Slovakia to Prague in the Treaty of Trianon, asked Hitler to mediate a border dispute.

"[B]y the Vienna Award of November 2, 1938, Ribbentrop and Ciano, the Italian Foreign Minister, assigned a sizable portion of southern Slovakia to Hungary."[21] Hungary also had designs on Ruthenia, a slice of which it had already received, including the city of Kosice, in the Vienna Award. But when Budapest began to move on the remnant in mid-November, Hitler sent an ultimatum. The annexation of Ruthenia by Hungary would be regarded as an unfriendly act. Budapest backed off.

By New Year's Day 1939, Germany, Poland, and Hungary had all taken bites out of Czechoslovakia to reclaim lost kinsmen, and the ethno-nationalists of Slovakia and Ruthenia were agitating for independence.

In March, the remnant of Czechoslovakia fell apart.

On March 7, Czech president Emil Hacha dismissed the Ruthenian government.

On March 10, following a rancorous quarrel between Czechs and Slovaks over the latter's push for independence, Emil Hácha ousted the Slovak prime minister, Father Tiso, occupied Bratislava, and forcibly installed a new government loyal to Prague.

On March 11, Tiso fled to Vienna and appealed to Berlin for protection.

On March 13, Tiso met Hitler, who told him if he did not declare immediate independence, Germany would not interfere with Hungary's forcible reannexation of all of Slovakia. Budapest was moving troops to the border of both Slovakia and Ruthenia.

On March 14, Slovakia declared independence. "Ruthenia quickly followed and this action dissolved what was left of the Czech state."[22]

The same day, Hungary, told by Hitler it could move on Ruthenia but must keep hands off the rest of Slovakia, occupied Ruthenia, establishing a border between Poland and Hungary both had sought. Admiral Horthy "was delighted and sent Hitler a fulsome telegram of gratitude."[23]

Stationed in Prague, George Kennan saw it coming. As he wrote in early March 1939, after visiting Ruthenia, "[S]omehow or other, and in the not too distant future, the unwieldy remnant of what was once Ruthenia will find its way back to the economic and political unit in which it most naturally belongs, which is Hungary."[24]

Thus, at the expense of Prague, Hitler had brought the Germans of Bohemia and Moravia back under German rule, and appeased four nations. Hungary had the Vienna Award of the Hungarian lands and peoples in Slovakia and regained control of Ruthenia. Slovakia had independence and freedom from Prague, and a promise of German protection from Hungary. Poland had gained the coal-rich region of Teschen and a new border with a friendly Hungary. And Hitler had done Stalin a huge favor, for Ruthenia was ablaze with Ukrainian nationalism and Horthy would put the fire out. Historian John Lukacs notes that George Kennan was among the few to see in Hitler's partition of Czechoslovakia something no one else saw:

> Hitler's tacit consent to let Ruthenia (also called Carpathian Ukraine) go to Hungary was significant because it indicated that, whether temporarily or not, Hitler now dropped the promotion of Ukrainian nationalism that had been directed against the Soviet Union. We know (or ought to know) that this was but a first step in the direction of an eventual accord between Hitler and Stalin.[25]

Rapprochement with Stalin may have been in Hitler's mind by early 1939.

President Hacha asked to see Hitler. Elderly and sick, he was invited to Berlin and accompanied by his daughter, to whom Ribbentrop presented a bouquet at the train station. Hitler sent a box of chocolates.

After 1 A.M., Hacha was ushered in to see the Fuehrer, who bullied him for three hours, telling him the Wehrmacht and Luftwaffe were preparing to strike his country. After Hacha suffered an apparent heart attack, German doctors revived him. Just before 4 A.M., Hacha signed a statement by which he "confidently placed the fate of the Czech people and country in the hands of the Fuehrer of the German Reich."[26] As he left the Chancellery at 4:30, his foreign minister Chvalkovsky said to him, "Our people will curse us, and yet we have saved their existence. We have preserved them from a horrible massacre."[27]

Hacha would serve Hitler faithfully through the end of the war. As British historian Donald Cameron Watt writes, "[Hitler] was remarkably kind (for him) to the Czech Cabinet after the march into Prague, keeping its members in office for a time and then paying their pensions."[28]

As Hitler stayed up into the morning to savor his triumph with aides, his physician, Dr. Morell, interrupted to say that had it not been for him, there might have been no communiqué. "Thank God," said Morell, "that I was on the spot and in time with my injections."[29]

"You go to hell with your damn injections," Hitler bellowed. "You made the old gentleman so lively that for a moment I feared he would refuse to sign!"[30]

Emerging from the negotiations, Hitler ecstatically told his two middle-aged secretaries: "Children, quickly, give me a kiss! Quickly!"[31] The ladies bussed him on both cheeks, as Hitler exclaimed: "It is the greatest triumph of my life! I shall enter history as the greatest German of them all!"[32]

Indeed, as of that night, Hitler had brought the Saar, Austria, and the Sudetenland under Berlin's rule, made Bohemia and Moravia protectorates of the Reich, overthrown the detested Versailles regime in Central Europe, and raised Germany from the depressed and divided nation of 1933 to the first economic and military power in Europe— in six years without firing a shot. He was a figure in German history to rival Bismarck. But Hitler could say, as Bismarck could not, that he had done it all with diplomacy and without bloodshed.

On March 15, Hitler entered Prague. Hungary marched into Ruthenia. The Ruthenians appealed to Berlin. Hitler said "No!" On the afternoon of the fourteenth, German troops had occupied the vital strategic area of Ostrava to preempt an expected Polish move.

Thus the Munich agreement, altarpiece of Chamberlain's career, pillar of his European policy, lay in ruin. "It was the final shipwreck of my mission to Berlin," wrote Henderson. "Hitler had crossed the Rubicon."[33]

> Up till that March . . . the German ship of state had flown the German national flag. On those Ides of March, its captain defiantly hoisted the skull and crossbones of the pirate, and appeared under his true colors as an unprincipled menace to European peace and liberty.[34]

Historians mark Hitler's march into Prague as the crossroads where he started down the path of conquest by imposing German rule on a non-Germanic people. The "destruction of Czechoslovakia," writes Kissinger, "made no geopolitical sense whatever; it showed that Hitler was beyond rational calculation and bent on war."[35]

But did it? And war with whom? From the vantage point of Hitler, raised in Linz near the Czech border when both were ruled from Vienna, it appeared far different from the way it did in London or Washington. And the motives behind Hitler's actions in the Czech crisis of March remain in dispute. Here is Taylor's take, half a century ago:

> All the world saw this as a culmination of a long-planned campaign. In fact, it was the unforeseen by-product of developments in Slovakia; and Hitler was acting against the Hungarians rather than against the Czechs. Nor was there anything sinister or premeditated in the protectorate over Bohemia. Hitler, the supposed revolutionary, was simply reverting in the most conservative way to the pattern of previous centuries. Bohemia had always been a part of the Holy Roman Empire; it had been part of the German Confederation between 1815 and 1866; then it had been linked to German Austria until 1918. Independence, not subordination, was the novelty in Czech history. . . .

Hitler took the decisive step in his career when he occupied Prague. He did it without design; it brought him slight advantage. He acted only when events had already destroyed the settlement of Munich. But everyone outside Germany, and especially the other makers of that settlement, believed that he had deliberately destroyed it himself.[36]

Taylor here seems too benign. While historians disagree on whether Hitler harangued the old man, there is no doubt he threatened Hacha with bombing and invasion if he did not sign away his country. Michael Bloch, the author of *Ribbentrop*, writes that Hitler was no passive observer to the breakup of the country after Munich. "Hitler's plan was to provoke a civil war in Czecho-Slovakia, by secretly encouraging secessionist movements in Slovakia and Ruthenia: German troops would then intervene to 'restore order.' "[37]

Bullock, too, contradicts Taylor, contending that, after Munich, Hitler began a campaign of subversion to liquidate the independent Czecho-Slovak state. German archives document the pressure Hitler put on Prague. What were Hitler's motives?

The German Army was anxious to replace the long, straggling German-Czech frontier, with a short easily-held line straight across Moravia from Silesia to Austria. The German Air Force was eager to acquire new air bases in Moravia and Bohemia. The seizure of Czech Army stocks and of the Skoda arms works, second only to Krupp's, would represent a major reinforcement of German strength.[38]

Moreover, Hitler had long "detested" Czechoslovakia as both a "Slav state . . . and one allied with the Bolshevik arch-enemy and with France."[39]

A deep-seated hatred of the Czechs—a legacy of his Austrian upbringing (when rabid hostility towards the Czechs had been endemic in the German-speaking part of the Habsburg Empire)—added a further personal dimension to the drive to destroy a Czechoslovakian state allied with the arch-enemies of Germany: the USSR in the east and France in the west.[40]

Whatever triggered the crisis or motivated Hitler, it was a blunder of historic magnitude and utterly unnecessary. Having lost the Sudetenland, and now facing a hostile breakaway Slovakia to the east and Germans to the north, west, and south, Prague was already a vassal state. Why send in an army and humiliate a British prime minister who had shown himself willing to accommodate Hitler's demands for the return of German territories and peoples, if Hitler would only proceed peacefully?

For little gain, Hitler had burned his bridges to the political leaders of a British Empire he had sought to befriend and who were prepared to work with him for redress of grievances from Versailles. Hitler now had the Skoda arms works. But he had also made a bitter enemy of Great Britain.

CHAMBERLAIN'S ABOUT-FACE

As HITLER RODE INTO Prague, Chamberlain initially reaffirmed his policy of appeasement. On March 15, he rose in the Parliament to say that the British guarantee to preserve the integrity of Czechoslovakia, given after Munich, was no longer binding, for the state of Czechoslovakia no longer existed. The government's position, the prime minister told the House, has

> radically altered since the Slovak Diet declared the independence of Slovakia. The effect of this declaration put an end by internal disruption to the State whose frontier we had proposed to guarantee and His Majesty's government cannot accordingly hold themselves bound by this obligation.[41]

"It is natural that I should bitterly regret what has now occurred," Chamberlain went on, "but do not let us on that account be deflected from our course. Let us remember that the desire of all the peoples of this world still remains concentrated on the hopes of peace."[42]

MP Harold Nicolson recorded in his diary that the "feeling in the lobbies is that Chamberlain will either have to go or completely reverse his policy. Unless in his speech tonight, he admits that he was wrong, they feel that resignation is the only alternative. All the tadpoles are beginning to swim into the other camp."[43]

Halifax now began to take command of British policy toward the Reich. He informed the prime minister that his speech of March 15 would no longer do. And there now began to transpire the events that would lead to the decision that would change the history of the world.

On March 16, Rumania's minister in London, Virgil Tilea, ran to the Foreign Office to warn that he had learned "from secret and other sources" that the Nazis planned to overrun Hungary and "disintegrate Rumania in the same way as they had disintegrated Czechoslovakia . . . establishing a German protectorate over the whole country."[44] Hitler's objective: the Ploesti oil fields. Noting the "extreme urgency" of Britain taking a stand against this imminent "threat," Tilea asked for a loan of ten million pounds to strengthen Rumania's defenses.[45]

No such German plans or preparations existed. Berlin had no border with Rumania or any quarrel with Rumania, and was negotiating a trade treaty to be signed in a week. Consulted by London, Bucharest emphatically denied it had received any ultimatum and refused to back up its ambassador.

Yet Tilea spread his wild story through the diplomatic corps and on March 17 "called on Lord Halifax in a state of considerable excitement."

As Halifax listened intently, Tilea

poured forth a story of imminent German action against Romania, of economic demands presented as a virtual ultimatum. What would Britain do? If Romania fought, would Britain support her? Would Britain draw a line beyond which Hitler must not go? . . . He again asked for a loan to enable Romania to buy armaments from Britain.[46]

The British government believed Tilea.

Writes Manchester, "It was Tilea who suggested that Britain's position might be strengthened if Poland joined them as a third ally. Halifax and Chamberlain found the prospect appealing."[47]

On March 17 came the first sign of a major policy shift. In a speech in his home city of Birmingham, Chamberlain, to rising applause, charged Hitler with "a flagrant breach of personal faith." Bitterly reciting Hitler's words at Munich—"This is the last territorial claim I have to make in Europe. . . . I shall not be interested in the Czech state anymore and I can guarantee it. We don't want any Czechs any more"—Chamberlain declaimed: "Is this the last attack upon a small state or is it to be followed by another? Is this in fact a step in the direction of an attempt to dominate the world by force?"[48]

On March 21, hosting Daladier, Chamberlain discussed a joint front with France, Russia, and Poland to act together against aggressive German behavior. Chamberlain had drafted the proposal. The four nations were to agree "immediately to consult together as to what steps should be taken to offer joint resistance to any action which constitutes a threat to the political independence of any European state."[49]

Beck torpedoed the joint front. The Poles feared Russia more than Germany. "With the Germans we risk losing our liberty," Polish marshal Eduard Smigly-Rydz told the French ambassador, "with the Russians we lose our soul."[50] Even Halifax appreciated Poland's reluctance to rely on Russia for her security: "An intelligent rabbit would hardly be expected to welcome the protection of an animal ten times its size, whom it credited with the habits of a boa constrictor."[51]

The same day, March 21, during a stop-off in Berlin on his return from Rome, Lithuania's foreign minister was invited in to see Ribbentrop. The Lithuanian was given an ultimatum: Return Memel now or the Fuehrer "would act with lightning speed." Memel was the East Prussian city of 150,000 that Lithuania had seized from a disarmed Germany in 1923. Its people were clamoring to return to Germany. Having seen what happened to the Czechs, the Lithuanian foreign minister needed no further prodding.

On March 22, Memel was reannexed by the Reich.

On March 23, the German army marched in.

On March 24, a seasick Hitler, who had sailed across the Baltic in the pocket battleship *Deutschland,* rode in triumph through the newest city of the Reich and addressed a delirious throng in the Staadtheater.

On March 26 came another shock. German-Polish talks on Danzig had broken down.

On March 29, Ian Colvin, a twenty-six-year-old *News-Chronicle* correspondent in Berlin with excellent sources inside Hitler's regime, came to London with "hair-raising details of [an] imminent [Nazi] thrust against Poland."[52] Like Tilea's report, Colvin's was a false alarm.

Four days earlier, March 25, Hitler had issued a secret directive to his army commander in chief: "The Fuehrer *does not* wish to solve the Danzig question by force. He does not wish to drive Poland into the arms of Britain by this."[53] Hitler did not want war with Poland, he wanted an alliance with Poland. But Halifax and Chamberlain believed Colvin and feared that Beck might cut a deal with Hitler, which was what Hitler had in mind—a deal, not a war. Immediately after the meeting with Colvin, as Chamberlain wrote to his sister, "we then and there decided" Poland must be guaranteed.[54]

Thus, on March 30, an astonished Colonel Beck received the British ambassador, who inquired whether Warsaw would object if Britain gave an unconditional guarantee of Poland's independence in the event of an attack by Germany. Beck accepted.

On March 31, 1939, Chamberlain rose in the House of Commons to make the most fateful British declaration of the twentieth century:

> I now have to inform the House that . . . in the event of any action which clearly threatened Polish independence and which the Polish Government accordingly considered it vital to resist with their national forces, His Majesty's Government would feel themselves bound at once to lend the Polish Government all support in their power. They have given the Polish Government an assurance to that effect.[55]

In words drafted by Halifax, Neville Chamberlain had turned British policy upside down.[56] The British government was now committed to fight for Poland. With this declaration, writes Ernest May,

> a government that a half-year earlier had resisted going to war for a faraway country with democratic institutions, well-armed military forces, and strong fortifications, now promised with no apparent reservations to go to war for a dictatorship with less-than-modern armed forces and wide-open frontiers.[57]

"Englishmen who possessed strategic vision were, with few exceptions, appalled," writes Manchester.[58]

"This is the maddest single action this country has ever taken," MP Robert J. G. Boothby told Churchill.[59]

We are undertaking "a frightful gamble," said Lloyd George.[60] Told by Chamberlain the pact with Poland would deter Hitler, the former prime minister "burst out laughing."[61] If the British army general staff approved this, said Lloyd George, they "ought to be confined to a lunatic asylum."[62]

Liddell Hart agreed. The Polish guarantee was "foolish, futile, and provocative . . . an ill-considered gesture [that] placed Britain's destiny in the hands of Polish rulers, men of very dubious and unstable judgment."[63]

Chamberlain's "reversal was so abrupt and unexpected as to make war inevitable," wrote Liddell Hart:

> The Polish Guarantee was the surest way to produce an early explosion, and a world war. It combined the maximum temptation with manifest provocation. It incited Hitler to demonstrate the futility of such a guarantee to a country out of reach from the West, while making the stiff-necked Poles even less inclined to consider any concession to him, and at the same time making it impossible for him to draw back without "losing face."[64]

To dramatize his protest of Chamberlain's folly, Liddell Hart resigned as military correspondent for the *Times*.[65]

Duff Cooper, who had resigned as First Lord in protest of Munich, wrote in his diary, "Never before in our history have we left in the hands of one of the smaller powers the decision whether or not Britain goes to war."[66]

Sir Alexander Cadogan, Permanent Undersecretary at the Foreign Office, echoed Lloyd George, calling the guarantee a "frightful gamble."[67]

"The whole point is that we cannot save these eastern nations," Sir Maurice Hankey, retired secretary of the Committee of Imperial Defense, wrote Ambassador Phipps in Paris.[68]

Half a century later, Sir Roy Denman called the war guarantee to Poland of March 31 "the most reckless undertaking ever given by a British government. It placed the decision on peace or war in Europe in the hands of a reckless, intransigent, swashbuckling military dictatorship."[69]

Nevile Henderson reported from Berlin that Germans were telling him Chamberlain had made the same blunder as the Kaiser in

July 1914. He had given Poland a "blank check" to start a European war.[70] As for the French, "they thought the British pledge madness and endorsed it only because they had no alternative."[71] The gravest problem with the war guarantee, writes Paul Johnson, was that

> the power to invoke it was placed in the hands of the Polish government, not a repository of good sense. Therein lay the foolishness of the pledge: Britain had no means of bringing effective aid to Poland yet it obliged Britain itself to declare war on Germany if Poland so requested.[72]

The legendary military strategist and historian Major-General J.F.C. Fuller, in *The Second World War*, related a comment he heard from a veteran American newspaperman in Germany:

> When in Berlin, shortly after the guarantee was given, I asked a well-known American journalist what he thought of it. His answer was: "Well, I guess your Mr. Prime Minister has made the biggest blunder in your history since the Stamp Act." Further he said, and he had known Poland for thirty years, "There is no reason why you should not guarantee a powder factory so long as the rules are observed; but to guarantee one full of maniacs is a little dangerous."[73]

One statesman, however, thought the war guarantee a splendid idea. Declared Winston Churchill to Parliament: "The preservation and integrity of Poland must be regarded as a cause commanding the regard of all the world."[74] There is, Churchill added, "almost complete agreement" now between the prime minister and his critics: "We can no longer be pushed from pillar to post."[75]

"This approached a blanket endorsement," says Manchester.[76] "It is also fair to add that within a week Winston was raising doubts about the Polish guarantee."[77]

Indeed, four days after Chamberlain handed Poland the war

guarantee, the rashness and potential consequences of the act seemed to have sunk in on Churchill. He wrote publicly that Polish concessions to Hitler on Danzig and the Corridor might still be welcomed: "There is . . . no need for Great Britain and France to be more Polish than the Poles. If Poland feels able to make adjustments in the Corridor and at Danzig which are satisfactory to both sides, no one will be more pleased than her Western allies."[78]

Unfortunately, now that Warsaw had her war guarantees from the two great Western democracies, any Polish concessions were out of the question.

Nine years later, in *The Gathering Storm*, Churchill would cover his spoor by expressing amazement at the audacity and rashness of Neville Chamberlain's radical reversal of British policy:

> And now . . . Great Britain advances, leading France by the hand to guarantee the integrity of Poland—of that very Poland which with hyena appetite had only six months before joined in the pillage and destruction of the Czechoslovak State. . . .
>
> Moreover, how could we protect Poland and make good our guarantee? . . . Here was a decision taken at the worst possible moment and on the least satisfactory ground, which must surely lead to the slaughter of tens of millions of people.[79]

To call Churchill's 1948 words disingenuous is understatement. By March 1939, he had been hounding Chamberlain for a year to draw a line in the sand and go to war if Hitler crossed it. Now Chamberlain had done what Churchill had demanded—threatened Germany with war over Poland. The guarantee to Poland, which Churchill had applauded, would force Britain to declare war on Germany five months later.

Yet here is Churchill in 1948 asking in feigned innocence:

"[H]ow could we protect Poland and make good our guarantee?" Answer: There was no way Britain could protect Poland, and there was no plan to protect Poland. But though that war guarantee "must surely lead to the slaughter of tens of millions of people," Churchill, in the spring of 1939, had applauded it. Why? Because, as he put it in his inimitable style,

> [I]f you will not fight for the right when you can easily win without bloodshed; if you will not fight when your victory will be sure and not too costly; you may come to the moment when you have to fight with all the odds against you and only a precarious chance of survival. There may even be a worse case. You may have to fight when there is no hope of victory, because it is better to perish than live as slaves.[80]

Churchill's 1948 depiction of Britain's situation on the day of the war guarantee to Poland is absurd. On March 31, 1939, Britain was not facing a "precarious chance of survival." Hitler had neither the power nor desire to force Britons to "live as slaves." He wanted no war with Britain and showed repeatedly he would pay a price to avoid such a war. It was the Poles who were facing imminent war with "only a precarious chance of survival." It was the Poles who might end up as "slaves" if they did not negotiate Danzig. That they ended up as slaves of Stalin's empire for half a century, after half a decade of brutal Nazi occupation, is a consequence of their having put their faith in a guarantee Chamberlain and Churchill had to know was worthless when it was given.

Liddell Hart, in his history of World War II, comes close to charging Churchill with rank intellectual dishonesty for his crude attempt to foist all responsibility for the "fatally rash move"—the guarantee to Poland—onto the dead prime minister.[81] Of Churchill's reflections in 1948 on that war guarantee of March 31, 1939, Liddell Hart writes:

It is a striking verdict on Chamberlain's folly written in hindsight. For Churchill himself had, in the heat of the moment, supported Chamberlain's pressing offer of Britain's guarantee to Poland. It is only too evident that in 1939 he, like most of Britain's leaders, acted on a hot-headed impulse, instead of with the cool-headed judgment that was once characteristic of British statesmanship.[82]

Historian Gene Smith writes that to a world "seeing Armageddon in the offing," it appeared "that the pledged word of the West, of democracy, of the future, was in the hands of the unstable and irresponsible leaders of a country . . . no less authoritarian, nationalistic, totalitarian and racially intolerant than Germany and Italy."[83]

The war guarantee to Poland tied Britain's "destiny to that of a regime that was every bit as undemocratic and anti-Semitic as that of Germany," adds Niall Ferguson.[84]

Thus did Neville Chamberlain, who never believed Britain had any vital interest in Eastern Europe, become the first British prime minister to issue a war guarantee to Eastern Europe. Nowhere in British diplomatic history is it possible to discover a more feckless and fateful act. The guarantee to Poland, writes Luigi Villari, was "the most disastrous single diplomatic move" of the interwar era.[85]

> It rendered the second World War almost inevitable, for a quarrel between Germany and Poland, even if capable of a peaceful settlement, might now be converted into Armageddon at the caprice of whoever happened to be in power in Poland at the time. . . . Chamberlain, by no means a warmonger, had evidently been driven into this act of madness by the followers of Churchill and the Labourites whose program was to make war inevitable.[86]

Paul Johnson calls the guarantee a "hysterical response" to what had happened in the previous two weeks, and describes the panic that gripped Neville Chamberlain and turned that statesman into a Hotspur.

> The German occupation of Prague . . . followed swiftly by the seizure of Memel from Lithuania, six days later, convinced most British people that war was imminent. Fear gave place to a resigned despair, and the sort of craven, if misjudged, calculation which led to Munich yielded to a reckless and irrational determination to resist Hitler at the next opportunity, irrespective of its merits.[87]

In his book on that fateful year September 1938 to September 1939, *How War Came*, historian Donald Cameron Watt writes of the astonishing gamble the prime minister had just taken:

> Mr Chamberlain . . . left no option whatever for the British Government. If the Poles took up arms, then Britain fought too. The decision, war or peace, had been voluntarily surrendered by Chamberlain and his Cabinet into the nervous hands of Colonel Beck and his junta comrades-in-arms. It was unprecedented. It was also unconstitutional. It is also clear that Chamberlain . . . did not understand what he had done.[88]

Halifax, who had been alarmed by the sensational reports of Colvin, played the pivotal role in having a Cabinet meeting called to deal with the nonexistent crisis. Writes historian Graham Stewart:

> Intelligence reports backing up Colvin's claim that Hitler was poised to invade Poland particularly concentrated Halifax's mind. Requesting and being granted an emergency meeting of the Cabinet, he argued for issuing an immediate British guarantee to Poland in the hope of making Hitler rethink a quick strike. Here was an example of sudden

events bouncing a government into action contrary to its long-term strategy.[89]

Thus did the British government, in panic over a false report about a German invasion of Poland that was neither planned nor prepared, give a war guarantee to a dictatorship it did not trust, in a part of Europe where it had no vital interests, committing itself to a war it could not win. Historian Johnson's depiction of Chamberlain's decision as reckless and irrational is an understatement.

To assess the recklessness of the guarantee, consider:

In the Great War, Britain, France, Russia, Italy, Japan, and the United States together almost failed to prevent Germany from occupying Paris. Now, without Russia or America, and with Japan and Italy hostile, Britain and France were going to keep the German army out of Warsaw. Writes British historian Capt. Russell Grenfell, "[A] British guarantee of Poland against Germany was about as capable of implementation as a guarantee of Mexico against the United States."[90]

"When one keeps in mind that the British Government could not put one soldier in the Polish Corridor in the event of war between Poland and Germany, the dubious quality of this Chamberlain assurance is clearly evident," writes Tansill.[91] As for Colonel Beck, "By turning his back on Hitler he invited a swift destruction that no European power could avert."[92]

Kissinger agrees. Britain's "drawing the line made . . . little sense in terms of traditional power politics," for the "seizure of Prague [had] changed neither the balance of power nor the foreseeable course of events."[93]

To British historian Peter Clarke, the war guarantee to the Poles, after the British had abandoned the Czechs along with their army and mountain fortifications, was an act of sheer irrationality: "If Czechoslovakia was a faraway country, Poland was further; if Bohemia could not be defended by British troops, no more could

Danzig; if the democratic Czech Republic had its flaws, the Polish regime was far more suspect."[94]

In defense of the Polish guarantee, Henderson wrote in his memoir:

[A]fter Prague no nation in Europe could feel itself secure from some new adaption of Nazi racial superiority and jungle law. In twelve months Germany had swallowed up Austria, the Sudeten Lands, and Czechoslovakia. Verbal protests were so much waste paper; and a firm stand had to be taken somewhere and force opposed by force; otherwise, in the course of the intoxication of success, Hitler, in the course of another twelve months, would continue the process with Poland, Hungary, and Rumania. The principles of nationalism and self-determination, which had served Hitler to create Greater Germany . . . had been cynically thrown overboard at Prague and world dominion had supplanted them. If peace were to be preserved, it was essential that it should be made crystal clear what limit Germany would not go without provoking England to war.[95]

Nothing in this passage explains why it was Britain's duty to fight and die for Poland, which, as Churchill reminds us in his war memoir, had joined in the rape of Czechoslovakia. Henderson himself, in the last days of August, would urge a deal on Danzig. And while Poland had reason to fear "Nazi racial superiority and jungle law," Britain did not. She had no vital interest in Eastern Europe to justify a war to the death with Germany and no ability to wage war there. A German march to the east might imperil Stalin's Russia; it did not imperil Chamberlain's Britain. And if preserving peace was Britain's goal, was a threat to set Europe ablaze if Hitler clashed with the Poles the way to preserve it? Six months earlier, Chamberlain had written to his sister that he had been reading a life of

George Canning and agreed with that nineteenth-century states-man that "Britain should not let the vital decision as to peace or war pass out of her hands into those of another country."[96] Yet Chamberlain had now done exactly that. Writes William Shirer:

> Now, overnight, in his understandably bitter reaction to Hitler's occupation of the rest of Czechoslovakia, Chamberlain . . . had undertaken to unilaterally guarantee an Eastern country run by a junta of politically inept "colonels" who up to this moment had closely collaborated with Hitler, who like hyenas had joined the Germans in the carving up of Czechoslovakia and whose country had been rendered militarily indefensible by the very German conquests which Britain and Poland had helped the Reich to achieve.[97]

A.J.P. Taylor describes how Beck received word that Great Britain would defend Poland to the death:

> The [British] ambassador read out Chamberlain's assurance. Beck accepted it "between two flicks of the ash off his cigarette." Two flicks; and British grenadiers would fight for Danzig. Two flicks; and the illusory great Poland, created in 1919, signed her death warrant. The assurance was unconditional: the Poles alone were to judge whether it should be called upon. The British could no longer press for concessions over Danzig.[98]

Two flicks of the ash off the colonel's cigarette and the fate of the British Empire and fifty million people was sealed.

"In such panicky haste," writes Barnett, "did the British finally and totally reverse their traditional eastern European policy by giving to Poland the guarantee."[99] What did this tough-minded chronicler of Britain's decline think of the guarantee?

Yet it was an incautious guarantee. It was unconditional; it was up to the Poles, not the British, to decide when and whether the time had come to fight. It was one-sided; for Poland was not asked to give a reciprocal assurance.

The circumstances in which so fateful a guarantee was given, together with the rashness and looseness of its wording, serve to show that, although Chamberlain and his colleagues had at last recognised what kind of game they were playing, it did not follow that they could play it very well.[100]

How rash a commitment the war guarantee to Poland was may be seen by considering the balance of power on the day it was given. As of April 1, 1939, Britain and France retained an advantage in naval power over Germany, Italy, and Japan. On land, where any war to defeat Germany must be fought, the French were outmanned two-to-one by the Germans, who were conscripting soldiers from a far larger population. The British situation was hopeless.

On land, as of 1 April, France and Britain were now overwhelmingly out-numbered. Britain herself could put no divisions at all into the field in Europe by the eighteenth day after mobilization, but 3 in Egypt. France would initially field 54 divisions (including one armoured and five mobile) to Germany's 96 (including five armoured); and later 76 to 106. Italy could field a total of 76 divisions.[101]

Looking back at century's end, Roy Denman saw the guarantee to Poland as the fatal blunder that led to the collapse of the British Empire. The war guarantee, he writes, was

an even greater British folly [than Munich]. . . . The fear that after Poland Hitler would have attacked Britain was an illusion. As he had made clear in *Mein Kampf*, Hitler would have marched against Russia. As it was, Britain was dragged into an unnecessary war, which cost her nearly 400,000 dead, bankruptcy, and the dissolution of the British Empire.[102]

Again, in Denman's prose the phrase appears: "an unnecessary war."

WHY DID BRITAIN DO IT?

WHY DID CHAMBERLAIN, who never believed Britain had a vital interest in Eastern Europe, give the first war guarantee in British history to Eastern Europe?

Deceived and betrayed by Hitler, his Munich pact made a mockery, Chamberlain appears to have acted out of shame and humiliation at having been played for a fool, out of fear of Tory backbenchers who had turned against Munich in disgust, and out of panic that Hitler was out to "dominate the world."

"It is impossible," writes Liddell Hart, "to gauge what was the predominant influence on his impulse—the pressure of public indignation, or his own indignation, or his anger at having been fooled by Hitler, or his humiliation at having been made to look a fool in the eyes of his own people."[103]

Lloyd George believed that Chamberlain's "hare-brained pledge" had been an impulsive reaction to his humiliation:

> Hitler having fooled him, he felt he must do something to recover his lost prestige, so he rushed into the first rash and silly enterprise that entered his uninformed mind. He guaranteed Poland, Roumania and Greece against the huge army of Germany. . . .
>
> I denounced it as sheer madness to give such a pledge in the absence of military support from Russia.[104]

In his 1976 book *March 1939: The British Guarantee to Poland*, Simon Newman concludes that "the critical decisions in March 1939 were made in an atmosphere of panic, humiliation, and moral hysteria. A frantic urgency to do something—anything—replaced calm consideration of the alternatives."[105]

In *Six Crises*, Richard Nixon warns that "the most dangerous period" in any crisis is "the aftermath. It is then, with all his resources spent and his guard down, that an individual must watch out for dulled reactions and faulty judgment."[106]

Chamberlain thought a war guarantee to Poland might block a Polish-German deal, force Hitler to think about a two-front war, give Britain an ally with fifty-five divisions, and enable Britain to avoid the alliance with Stalin being pressed upon him by Churchill, Lloyd George, and the Labour Party. Newman believes the prime mover behind the guarantee was Halifax, who had come to believe that if Hitler continued with his bloodless victories, Germany would dominate Europe economically and no longer be at the mercy of a British blockade. That would mean Britain's end as a world power. When the German-Rumanian Trade Treaty was announced on March 24, Halifax feared Poland would also strike a deal. Rather than have Poland become a partner of Germany, Newman argues, Halifax preferred war. He pushed the guarantee on Chamberlain to stiffen the Polish spine, knowing the guarantee would harden Polish resistance to any deal over Danzig. Halifax preferred war, and the sacrifice of Poland to Hitler's war machine, to seeing Britain yield her preeminence in Europe and the world. By March 1939, writes Newman, war with Germany had become

> the only real alternative to Britain's relegation to second-class status. As Halifax described this dilemma to the Foreign Policy Committee, the choice was between "doing nothing" which would mean a "great accession of Germany's strength and a great loss to ourselves of sympathy

and support" and "entering into a devastating war." He [Halifax] preferred the latter course.[107]

Andrew Roberts credits Halifax with being the decisive force behind the guarantee. After Hitler entered Prague, Halifax told the Cabinet, "The real issue was Germany's attempt to obtain world domination."[108]

Yet, Halifax admitted, "there was probably no way in which France and ourselves could prevent Poland and Roumania from being overrun."[109]

Knowing Poland could not be saved from a Nazi onslaught and occupation, Halifax nevertheless wanted to give Poland a war guarantee, which he knew could precipitate a suicidal Polish policy of defiance.

For Halifax, writes Roberts,

> the issue had long moved beyond the rights and wrongs of individual claims and towards the "great moralities" which he had declared his willingness to fight for at the time of Munich. The fear which materialized in late March was that Poland might disclaim Danzig and allow herself to be neutralized in return for not fighting, thus chalking up yet another bloodless coup for Hitler.[110]

Rather than see Poland return Danzig to the Reich, Halifax preferred that Poland fight Germany to the death in a war Halifax knew Poland could not win, because the British could not help. To Halifax, Poland's suicide was preferable to having Hitler chalk up "yet another bloodless coup." The Holy Fox appears to have had no reservations about pushing Poland to its death in front of Hitler's war machine—to exhibit "his willingness to fight for . . . the 'great moralities.' "

Such is the morality of Great Powers.

WAS CHAMBERLAIN MISUNDERSTOOD?

What Chamberlain's war guarantee wrought was the bloodiest war in all of history. But what was its literal meaning to the prime minister who had issued it?

As one inspects Chamberlain's words of March 31, they do not bind Britain to fight for Danzig or the Corridor. It is not a commitment to defend the territorial integrity of Poland. It is only a commitment to repel an attack "which clearly threatened Polish independence."

What was Chamberlain up to? Graham Stewart explains:

> The Polish guarantee was not intended to make war with Germany inevitable. . . . On the contrary, the commitment was intended to give Britain leverage in forcing Poland to come to terms with Hitler's demands over the Danzig and Corridor questions. In this way, Hitler could be satisfied without Poland being subjected either to a full-scale invasion (forcing a Europe-wide war) or succumbing to a treaty that reduced her to vassal status.[111]

In a letter to his sister, April 3, Chamberlain concedes as much. The guarantee of March 31, he wrote, was "unprovocative in tone, but firm, clear but stressing that the important point (perceived alone by the *Times*) that what we are concerned with is not the boundary of States, but attacks on their independence. And it is we who will judge whether this independence is threatened or not."[112]

What had the *Times* written for which the prime minister had given its editor such high marks for his perceptiveness and insight?

On April 3, an alarmed Churchill rose in the House to point to a "sinister passage in the *Times*'s leading article on Saturday [April 1], similar to that which foreshadowed the ruin of Czechoslovakia."[113] Saturday was the day following Chamberlain's declaration. In that editorial by *Times* editor Geoffrey Dawson, the limited nature of the war guarantee is discerned and defined. Here is Manchester:

> Dawson had written: "The new obligation which this country yesterday assumed does not bind Great Britain to defend every inch of the present frontiers of Poland. The key word in the statement is not 'integrity' but 'independence.' " The prime minister's statement, the editorial continued "involves no blind acceptance of the status quo. . . . This country . . . has never been an advocate of the encirclement of Germany, and is not now opposed to the extension of Germany's economic pressure and influence, nor to the constructive work she may yet do for Europe."[114]

Dawson had either been privately informed or had ferreted out the truth. Appeasement was not dead! Chamberlain had not declared that Britain would fight to keep Danzig from Germany, only that Britain would fight for Poland's "independence." Chamberlain was signaling Hitler that the return of Danzig was not opposed by Britain and she would go to war only if he tried to destroy Poland as an independent nation. The British war guarantee had not been crafted to give Britain a pretext for war, but to give Chamberlain leverage to persuade the Poles to give Danzig back.

Chamberlain seems to be signaling his willingness for a second Munich, where Poland would cede Danzig and provide a road-and-rail route across the Corridor, but in return for Hitler's guarantee of Poland's independence—so there would be no repeat of the Czech debacle.

Unfortunately, the diplomatic subtlety was lost on Hitler. To him, and to the world, it appeared that a now-defiant prime minister had drawn a line in the sand and warned Hitler not to cross it. To Hitler this was a virtual ultimatum: If you try to take back Danzig, you will be at war with Britain.

Donald Watt describes how Hitler received the news:

Then on March 31 came the news of the British guarantee to Poland, clearly involving British support for the Polish position over Danzig. As the news reached Hitler, he was sitting in front of the great marble table in the new Reichs Chancellery. With clenched fists he hammered on its marble top, enraged. . . . "I will brew them a devil's drink," he shouted.[115]

The Poles, too, read Chamberlain's declaration as a solemn British commitment to stand by them in their resolve never to return Danzig. From that day forward, the Poles refused even to discuss Danzig with Germany.

ALTERNATIVES TO THE WAR GUARANTEE

WHAT ELSE COULD Great Britain have done? So it is asked.

Her prime minister had been humiliated and the Munich accord treated as a scrap of paper. Hitler had imposed Nazi rule on a non-Germanic people. He had smashed the only democracy in Central Europe and was on the road to conquest. He had to be stopped, and Britain and France, as the greatest democracies in Europe, had a moral duty to stop him.

So runs the argument for the war guarantee to Poland.

Hitler's ambitions will be dealt with in a subsequent chapter. Let us deal here with the question: What else could Chamberlain have done after Hitler seized Prague? What was the alternative to giving a war guarantee to Poland?

Quite simply, it was not to give a war guarantee to a nation wedged between Nazi Germany and Bolshevik Russia. By 1939, Britain and France no longer had the power to save any nation of Eastern Europe, if ever they did, and they did not save any. As W. H. Chamberlin argued half a century ago:

[T]here was an alternative to the policy which the British and French governments followed after March 1939. This alternative would have been to write off eastern Europe as geographically indefensible, to let Hitler move eastward, with the strong probability that he would come into conflict with Stalin. Especially in light of the Soviet aggressive expansion that has followed the war, this surely seems the sanest and most promising course western diplomacy could have followed.[116]

Hanson Baldwin, military writer for the *New York Times*, seconded Chamberlin:

There is no doubt whatsoever that it would have been to the interest of Britain, the United States, and the world to have allowed—and, indeed, to have encouraged—the world's two great dictatorships to fight each other to a frazzle. Such a struggle, with its resultant weakening of both Communism and Nazism, could not but have aided in the establishment of a more stable peace. It would have placed the democracies in supreme power in the world, instead of elevating one totalitarianism at the expense of the other and of the democracies.[117]

In 1995 in *Missed Chances*, Sir Roy Denman, who considered the war guarantee an "even greater folly" than Munich, echoed the late American historian:

If Chamberlain had not committed the two monumental blunders of his personal involvement and then humiliation in the Czechoslovak affair and then the guarantee to Poland—if he had backed isolation on these issues but accompanied it with a firm emphasis on rearmament and drawn a realistic line in the sand, Britain, the sea routes, the Empire, France and the Channel ports, then he would have faced a rising tide of doubt and discontent in the press and more eloquent speeches by Churchill, but would have had no serious difficulty in carrying with him a massive House of Commons majority in favour of staying out of a German-Polish war. Churchill would never have become Prime Minister. Germany, after Poland, would have turned on Russia.[118]

BY MARCH 1939, France, having failed to keep the Wehrmacht out of the Rhineland, had lost her military superiority over Germany and adopted a Maginot Line strategy. Paris would have welcomed Britain's recognition that an Eastern Europe of new nations that had been ruled by czars, kings, or emperors before 1918 could not be defended, and the two Allies should draw Denman's "realistic line in the sand" before France and the Channel ports.

What else could Chamberlain have done after Hitler's Prague coup? Tell Britons the truth: Hitler was not to be trusted and he was on the march. Chamberlain could have imposed conscription, stepped up the production of aircraft, begun buying munitions from the United States, and waited. Rather than commit Britain to a war she could not win, he could have done what Truman did when another ruthless totalitarian seized an indefensible Prague. Adopt a policy of containment.

When I wrote in *A Republic, Not an Empire* that this was the proper course, and sent the book to a man I admired, I received a letter in return. I have "read extensively" into your book, wrote George F. Kennan. You and I, he continued, "have a large number of views in common, and some of them, particularly those on the history of American foreign policy, ones on which not many others would share with us."[119] Kennan went on:

[Y]ou make a strong case, in my view, for the thesis that the British guaranty to Poland . . . was neither necessary nor wise. The British government could not improve anything by offering to the Poles a support they were quite unable to give. They would have done better to shut up, to rearm as speedily as possible, and to avoid further formal commitments of any sort, while waiting the further turn of events.[120]

So wrote George Kennan, sixty years after Chamberlain issued the war guarantee that changed the history of Britain, its empire, and the world. But instead of a tough-minded appraisal of British vital interests, and what was needed to defend them, Chamberlain, with Churchill egging him on, now began to hand out British war guarantees across the continent of Europe.

CHAPTER 10

April Fools

For the Polish Corridor, no British government
ever will or ever can risk the bones of a British grenadier.[1]
— Austen Chamberlain, 1925

STUNNED AND STUNG by the British war guarantee to Poland,
Hitler took it as a direct challenge to him and to Germany, and executed his own volte-face. Wrote F. H. Hinsley in his 1951 *Hitler's
Strategy:* "[T]he Anglo-Polish Declaration not only forced [Hitler's]
hand, but also led him to lose his head."[2]

Within hours, he had ordered up plans for Case White, the invasion of Poland. "The first direction for planning this operation, with
September 1 as the suggested date, was issued by General Keitel,
Hitler's Chief of Staff, on April 3, three days after the announcement
of the guarantee to Poland."[3]

Before March 31, "it had been Nazi policy to offer Poland the
role of a satellite ally in an ultimate move against the Soviet Union,"
writes historian William Henry Chamberlin.[4] Indeed, in late March,
Hitler had issued a strict directive that he *did not want* the Danzig
issue settled by force.

As the war guarantee stood British policy on its head, it had the
same effect on German policy. The two nations, neither of which
wanted war with the other, were now on a collision course to war.
False intelligence and a false reading of Hitler's intentions had caused
Britain to panic and issue the war guarantee. A false reading of
British motives and intentions had caused Hitler to start the ball

rolling toward war with Poland, which now meant war with Britain and France.

Spines stiffened by their British alliance, the Poles now became even more intransigent. From March to August, to the amazement of a British Cabinet that believed Danzig should be returned to Germany, the Poles refused even to discuss the city with Berlin. By rejecting negotiations, Colonel Beck was deciding not only the fate of Poland but of Europe and the British Empire.

> At the greatest cross roads in all history, [Colonel Beck] rejected a ride in the German war machine that promised Poland power and plunder as a satellite state. Instead, he and the Polish Cabinet followed the lead of Chamberlain and chose the road that led to war with Germany and the consequent destruction of the Polish State.[5]

On April 6, Chamberlain had the Foreign Office issue a declaration that Britain and Poland were "prepared to enter into an agreement of a permanent character," a security pact requiring each nation to declare war, if the other were attacked.[6] In one week, "Beck had pushed Poland far down the road to war and national destruction. Such a policy pointed directly to disaster."[7]

On Good Friday, April 7, it was Chamberlain's turn to be jolted. Italy invaded Albania and sent King Zog packing.

Mussolini's attitude toward Hitler has been described as "that of a cat who had given birth to a tiger."[8] Jealous of Hitler's Prague coup, Il Duce

> complained to Ciano: "every time Hitler occupies a country he sends me a message." He [Mussolini] dreamed of creating an anti-German front, based on Hungary and Yugoslavia. By the evening he had recovered his temper: "we cannot change our policy now. After all, we are not political whores."[9]

Mussolini did not sulk long. Three weeks after Hitler motored into Prague, Mussolini sent his army into Albania, setting off alarms in Paris and London. Was Greece next? Was Rumania next?

Chamberlain took the invasion of Albania personally. He wrote to his sister Hilda that Mussolini had behaved "like a sneak and a cad. He has not made the least effort to preserve my friendly feelings."[10]

Saturday morning, Churchill telephoned Chamberlain to urge him to call an Easter Sunday emergency session of Parliament and to launch an invasion of the Greek island of Corfu. "Hours now count to recover the initiative in diplomacy," said Churchill.[11] He knew his history. When an Italian delegation, sent to deal with an Albanian border dispute, had been assassinated on Greek soil, August 27, 1923, Mussolini had bombarded Corfu and landed marines until retribution was exacted. Churchill was anticipating Mussolini's next move and urging preemption.

Paris was receiving its own intelligence that Rumania was next on the Nazi menu and an attack imminent. Stealing a march on Chamberlain, who had led with the British guarantee to Poland, Daladier informed the British that France was issuing war guarantees to Rumania and Greece. "Though some officials in Whitehall questioned the wisdom of these additional guarantees," writes Ernest May, "Chamberlain and his Cabinet decided to go along with Daladier."[12]

Chamberlain explained that he did not think it important to distinguish among states being guaranteed or to make calculations about whether a particular state could be protected by Britain and France. "The real issue," he said, "was that, if Germany showed signs that she intended to proceed with her march for world domination, we must take steps to stop her. . . . We should attack Germany not in order to save a particular victim but in order to pull down the bully."[13]

Chamberlain here makes three assumptions. The first is that any further German attempt to reclaim lost peoples or provinces meant a "march for world domination." The second is that it was Britain's duty to "stop" Hitler in Central and Eastern Europe, where no British army had ever fought before. The third is that Britain had the strength "to pull down the bully."

Chamberlain had lost touch with reality. He began handing out war guarantees all over Europe. Barnett compares him to a "bankrupt passing out dud checks." On April 13, Chamberlain "informed a startled House of Commons that His Majesty's Government had decided to guarantee the frontiers of Greece, Turkey and . . . Rumania."[14] British foreign policy had become one of wild improvisation. Writes Shirer,

> Stung, as he was, by Hitler's deceit, the peace-loving Prime Minister now proceeded recklessly to add guarantees to other countries in Eastern Europe that felt threatened by Nazi German ambitions. . . .
>
> How could Britain, it was asked in Paris, help Poland or Rumania—or for that matter, France—when it had no army?[15]

Here is a list of the war guarantees the British government issued in that springtime of madness in 1939:

> On March 23, Britain declared she would intervene militarily to stop any German attack on Holland, Belgium, or Switzerland.
> On March 31, the British gave the war guarantee to Poland.
> On April 13, Britain gave war guarantees to Rumania and Greece.
> On May 12, Britain concluded a treaty of mutual assistance with Turkey.[16]

When one considers that in April of 1939 Britain had no draft and only two divisions ready for combat in France, this is an astonishing list of security guarantees. It was at this point that Lloyd George exploded:

Without Russia, these three guarantees to Poland, to Rumania and to Greece are the most reckless commitments that
any country has ever entered into. . . . These are demented . . . madness. . . . did the General Staff advise the
Government before they entered into these commitments . . . ? If they ever did, they ought to be removed from
the War Office and confined to a lunatic asylum.[17]

In a conversation with Churchill on April 6, Lord Halifax agreed that
Yugoslavia might also be a worthy recipient of a war guarantee. But,
as Andrew Roberts writes, Lord Halifax "may have wondered whether
he had gone too far . . . when the Liberian Ambassador solemnly requested a British guarantee of Liberia."[18]

Seeing his nation declare its readiness to fight wars to defend
regimes across Europe, many of which were holding land to which
they had no valid title, other than in the unjust peace of Paris, historian E. H. Carr wrote, "[T]he use or threatened use of force to maintain the status quo may be morally more culpable than the use or
threatened use of force to alter it."[19]

Two-thirds of a century later, these war guarantees still call forth
the words Lloyd George used, "madness" and "demented." From
1914 to 1918, Britain and France, with millions of soldiers, had
barely been able to keep the German army out of Paris. Two million
Americans had been needed to crack the German lines. Now, with a
tiny fraction of the British army of 1918, with former allies Russia,
Japan, and Italy now hostile, and with America now neutral, Britain
was handling out war guarantees not only to Belgium and Holland,
but also to Poland and Rumania.

"While Chamberlain was busily engaged in extending promises
of aid that he could not possibly deliver," wrote Tansill, "Hitler was
preparing for war."[20]

On April 12 the chief of the German General Staff had a talk
with the American chargé d'affaires in Berlin. He was not

backward in intimating that "unless fewer obstacles were placed in the way of Germany's eastern expansion it would be necessary for Hitler to end the opposition . . . in the West."[21]

On April 24, Hitler announced the termination of his Anglo-German Naval Agreement and, more ominously, of his nonaggression pact with Poland. Message to Beck: Rather than return Danzig and join us against Stalin, you intend to keep our city and have joined England against us. Poland will pay for your rejection of our offer of friendship and alliance.

SECOND THOUGHTS AT NUMBER 10

EVEN BEFORE HITLER HAD announced the scrapping of the naval pact, however, Chamberlain was having second thoughts about his alliance with Poland. Indeed, he had begun to regret it. For, on April 3, just three days after Chamberlain issued the war guarantee, Jozef Beck, "swaggering, chain-smoking and leering at young women," arrived in London, where Chamberlain and Halifax pressed him to join in a war guarantee to Rumania.[22] Thanks to Tilea's wild reports, the Cabinet had concluded that Rumania was Hitler's immediate target.

Beck flatly refused his British allies.

Any Polish guarantee to Rumania, Beck told his startled hosts, would precipitate an alliance between Germany and Hungary that would threaten Poland, and Poles were not going to die for Transylvania or the Ploesti oil fields. Chamberlain suddenly began to realize the rash and reckless decision he had made.

"[T]he more he listened to Beck," writes Manchester, "the more alarmed he became. Chamberlain—apparently grasping for the first time the implications of Britain's commitment to Warsaw—expressed anxiety that a German invasion of Poland might involve Great Britain."[23] Exactly. And yet:

On 6 April, the Polish and British delegates agreed on the
terms of what amounted to a mutual security pact. . . . The
terms of the final agreement were as follows:
a) If Germany attacks Poland His Majesty's Government in
the United Kingdom will come at once to the help of
Poland. . . .
c) Reciprocally, Poland gives corresponding assurances to
the United Kingdom.[24]

Goaded by Halifax, stampeded by Tory backbenchers and a jingo
press into issuing his war guarantee, Chamberlain would get the war
he never wanted, and Churchill would get the war he had sought to
bring about. To them both belongs the responsibility for what happened to Britain. But what Chamberlain did to the Poles, issuing a
war guarantee he knew was worthless, was far worse than what he had
done to the Czechs. At least he had told the Czechs the truth: Britain
would not fight for the Sudetenland. But Poles put their trust in their
war guarantee and security pact with Great Britain. They were repaid
for that trust with abandonment and half a century of Nazi and Soviet barbarism.

"In 1938," writes A.J.P. Taylor, "Czechoslovakia was betrayed. In
1939, Poland was saved. Less than one hundred thousand Czechs
died during the war. Six and a half million Poles were killed. Which
was better—to be a betrayed Czech or a saved Pole?"[25]

After six years of war, Warsaw had been reduced to rubble.
Prague was barely touched, "almost the only European capital to escape any serious measure of aerial destruction."[26] Eduard Beneš, who
had fled after Munich, would say from his palace in Prague at war's
end: "Is it not beautiful? The only central European city not destroyed. And all my doing."[27]

In May 1945, little that was beautiful remained of Warsaw.

Trusting in Britain and France, the Poles defied Hitler and refused to negotiate. Had they known the truth—Britain and France
would abandon them—the Poles might have accepted the return of

Danzig to the Germans, whose city it had always been. Historian Norman Davies accuses the British leaders of deceiving the Poles into making their defiant stand:

> The British Prime Minister must surely have known that in terms of practical assistance to Poland nothing was in fact possible. His purpose in making this gesture, unparalleled in the whole course of British history, was to deter Hitler, not to assist the Poles. He knew perfectly well that the British forces did not have the means available, either in men, ships, or planes, to intervene in Central Europe, and that he could not count automatically on the French Army to march on his behalf. Hitler smelt the phoney nature of the Guarantee.[28]

The British guarantee to Poland that solidified Polish determination to fight Nazi Germany in suicidal defiance, in anticipation of British military assistance Neville Chamberlain knew would never come, was the most cynical act in British history.

On April 28, 1939, there appeared an opening for a settlement of the Danzig dispute. "Hitler for the first time published the terms on which he was prepared to come to an agreement with Poland. They were widely recognized as mild."[29] Alan Bullock describes Hitler's offer to Poland of April 28:

> With Poland, too, Hitler declared, he had been only too anxious to reach a settlement. Poles and Germans had to live side by side, whether they liked it or not, and he had never ceased to uphold the necessity for Poland to have access to the sea. But Germany also had legitimate demands, for access to East Prussia and for the return of the German city of Danzig to the Reich. To solve the problem, Hitler had made an unprecedented offer to Poland, the terms of which he

now repeated, with the careful omission of the German invitation to join in a bloc directed against Russia.[30]

Hitler also declared that the London-Warsaw pact of April 6 had destroyed the basis of the Anglo-German Naval Agreement and of the Hitler-Pilsudski agreement of 1934. He renounced both. However, as Bullock writes, Hitler "was careful to add . . . that the door to a fresh agreement between Germany and Poland was still open, and that he would welcome such an agreement, provided it was upon equal terms."[31]

On May 5, Colonel Beck rose in the Polish Diet and rejected both the German version of negotiations and Hitler's offer to start anew. Still, the German press "was kept under restraint."[32] As the French ambassador in Berlin wrote to Paris, the Germans were serenely confident Britain and France would persuade the Poles to negotiate on Danzig, as the Allies surely realized that "Danzig is not worth a European war."[33]

Nothing happened. No one talked. After Hitler's April 28 offer, "there were no further negotiations with the Poles before the outbreak of war and none with the British until the middle of August."[34]

And so London, Paris, Berlin, and Warsaw all drifted on toward the greatest cataclysm in human history.

The British ambassador in Berlin, Nevile Henderson, "thoroughly upset" that he had not known of this offer that Hitler had made to Beck, wrote in anguish to Chamberlain's close adviser, Sir Horace Wilson:

I must . . . admit that I regard Hitler's proposals as a fair basis of negotiation and in my innermost heart I regard the Poles as exceedingly unwise to make enemies of Germany and as dangerous allies for us. The Prague coup has affected our whole outlook towards Hitler but it has not altered the merits of the Danzig-Corridor case in themselves. I may be wrong but I am personally convinced that there can be no permanent peace in Europe until Danzig has reverted to Germany. The Poles cannot be masters of 400,000 Germans in Danzig—ergo Germany must be. I am sorry that I feel that way, but I fear that we are again on a bad wicket as we were over the Sudeten.[35]

Beck would refuse even to discuss Danzig with the Germans, and the British would refuse to press Beck to negotiate. Hitler thus concluded that Britain was behind Poland's intransigence, and that Britain was committed to war to prevent Danzig's return. The conclusion is understandable. The conclusion was wrong. For Chamberlain still believed Germany's case for Danzig was her strongest territorial claim and favored the return of the city, if only Hitler would go about it peacefully—which was exactly what Hitler, at that point, was still trying to do.

In the final fateful week of August 1939, as Hitler desperately cast about for a way to keep Britain out of his war with Poland, British leaders were desperately casting about for a way to convince the Poles to effect a peaceful return of Danzig to Germany.

It was the war guarantee—that guaranteed the war.

CHAPTER 11

"An Unnecessary War"

WAR WINS NOTHING, cures nothing, ends nothing. . . . [I]n war there are no winners, but all are losers.[1]
— NEVILLE CHAMBERLAIN, 1939

My only fear is that some bastard will propose a peace conference.[2]
— ADOLF HITLER, 1939

R EALITY SOON INTRUDED on Britain after the war guarantee had been gratuitously given to Colonel Beck. If the Allies were to have any hope of saving Poland, the Red Army was indispensable. So began the six-month courtship of the men Churchill in 1919 had called the "foul baboonery of Bolshevism . . . a pestilence more destructive of life than the Black Death or the Spotted Typhus."[3] No sooner had the courtship begun, however, than Chamberlain came face-to-face again with the old arguments against any alliance with Stalin's Russia—to save Poland.

First, Britain had no vital interest either in Danzig or the Corridor, and Germany had as strong a claim to Danzig and the Corridor as France had had to Alsace and Lorraine. As Lloyd George had written years before,

The British people . . . would not be ready to be involved in quarrels which might arise regarding Poland or Danzig. . . .

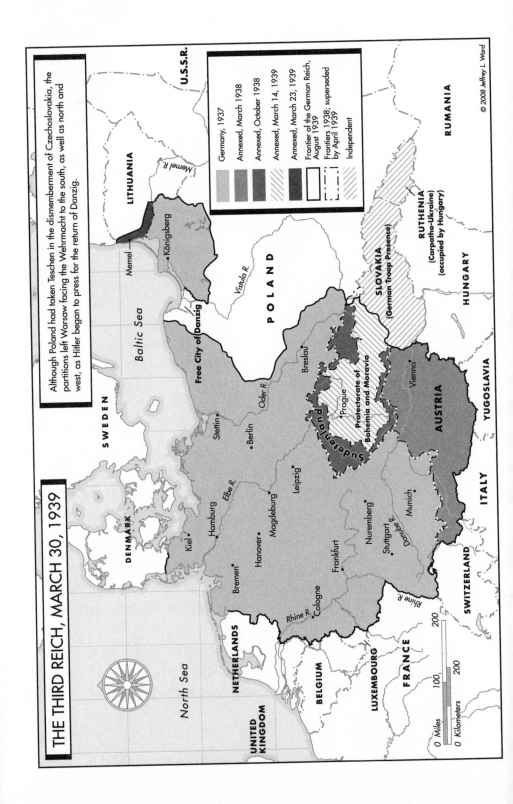

THE THIRD REICH, MARCH 30, 1939

Although Poland had taken Teschen in the dismemberment of Czechoslovakia, the partitions left Warsaw facing the Wehrmacht to the south, as well as north and west, as Hitler began to press for the return of Danzig.

Legend:
- Germany, 1937
- Annexed, March 1938
- Annexed, October 1938
- Annexed, March 14, 1939
- Annexed, March 23, 1939
- Frontier of the German Reich, August 1939
- Frontiers 1938; superseded by April 1939
- Independent

© 2008 Jeffrey L. Ward

U.S.S.R.

LITHUANIA

Memel R.

Königsberg

Memel

Baltic Sea

SWEDEN

DENMARK

Kiel

Hamburg

Bremen

Hanover

Cologne

Rhine R.

Frankfurt

Stuttgart

Danube R.

Nuremberg

Munich

Magdeburg

Leipzig

Berlin

Elbe R.

Stettin

Free City of Danzig

Vistula R.

Oder R.

Breslau

POLAND

Prague

Sudetenland

Protectorate of Bohemia and Moravia

SLOVAKIA
(German Troop Presence)

RUTHENIA
(Carpatho-Ukraine)
(occupied by Hungary)

Vienna

AUSTRIA

HUNGARY

RUMANIA

YUGOSLAVIA

ITALY

SWITZERLAND

FRANCE

LUXEMBOURG

BELGIUM

NETHERLANDS

UNITED KINGDOM

North Sea

0 Miles 100 200

0 Kilometers 200

The British people felt that the populations of that quarter of Europe were unstable and excitable; they might start fighting at any time and the rights and wrongs of the dispute might be very hard to disentangle.[4]

On April 13, 1933, two months after Hitler assumed power, Churchill himself had declared in Parliament:

Many people would like to see, or would have liked to see, a little while ago—I was one of them—the question of the Polish Corridor adjusted. For my part, I should certainly have considered that to be one of the greatest practical objectives of European peace-keeping diplomacy.[5]

A second argument against a Russian alliance was that Chamberlain believed he had read Stalin right:

I must confess to the most profound distrust of Russia. . . . I distrust her motives, which seem to me to have little connection with our ideas of liberty, and to be concerned only with getting everyone else by the ears. Moreover, she is both hated and suspected by many of the smaller states, most notably Poland, Rumania and Finland.[6]

Third, the nations wedged between Russia and Germany feared a Red Army rescue more than a German invasion. They had heard the screams of Stalin's victims.[7]

Fourth, as a condition of alliance, Moscow was demanding the right to impose protectorates over Estonia, Lithuania, and Latvia and to march into Poland and Rumania to meet the German army. No European nation would agree to this.

Fifth, if Moscow were to commit to war if Hitler attacked Poland, Stalin wanted full reciprocity: a British commitment to go to war if Hitler attacked the Soviet Union.

The British were now in the box Chamberlain had sought to avoid. Men of honor, they could not let Stalin, whose record of mass murder far exceeded Hitler's as of 1939, march into the Baltic countries. That would surrender millions of innocent people to a terrorist regime, a crime far worse than Munich. At least the Sudetendeutsch had wanted to join the Reich. The Baltic peoples feared and hated Stalin. Events would show they were justified in their fears. William Henry Chamberlin describes the strategic and moral dilemma Chamberlain now confronted:

> Whether the Soviet Union would have entered the war even if its demands had been granted is doubtful. But it was politically and morally impossible to accede to these demands. For this would have amounted to conceding to Stalin that very right of aggression against weaker neighbors which was the ostensible cause of fighting Hitler. Such glaring inconsistencies may be tolerated in war, as the records of the Teheran and Yalta conferences testify. But the coercion of friendly powers to part with sovereignty and territory was impossible in time of peace.[8]

Nor could Britain commit to war to defend a Bolshevik state whose very reason for existence was the destruction of Christianity and Western civilization. Why should a single British soldier die to save a Stalinist regime whose departure from the earth all decent men would celebrate? Yet, in a supreme irony of the twentieth century, Britain's greatest champion of an alliance with Stalin turned out to be that same Churchill who had championed the Allied intervention to strangle Bolshevism in its crib and who had been England's most ferocious and eloquent anti-Communist. In a September 1936 column, "Enemies to the Left," written after the show trials of the Bolshevik Old Guard, Churchill wrote, "What is the meaning and effect in this oppressive scene of the Moscow executions?"[9]

Churchill answered his own question. Stalin's regime, he wrote, had taken on the same anti-Semitic and nationalistic features as Hitler's.

Many people unable to be shocked at the expiation of these miscreants who have blithely sent uncounted thousands of good men to their doom, were nonetheless sickened at the elaborate farce of their trial. Its technique throws a gleam of intimate light upon the mysterious nature of a Communist state. . . . We see the gulf between the Communist mentality and the wider world.

The second point to notice is that these victims were nearly all Jews. Evidently the Nationalist elements represented by Stalin and the Soviet armies are developing the same prejudices against the Chosen People as are so painfully evident in Germany. Here again extremes meet, and meet on a common platform of hate and cruelty.[10]

What stance should Britain take toward the twin evils of Nazism and Bolshevism and the Stalin-Trotsky split? In "The Communist Schism," published in October 1936, Churchill gave his answer:

We ought to arm night and day in conjunction with other friendly countries and make ourselves independent of all these monstrous and fathomless intrigues. The stronger we are, the more upright and free-spoken, the less danger will there be of the civilised and normal nations being drawn into the quarrels of cruel and wicked forces at either extreme of the political gamut.[11]

Wise counsel. Would that the Western democracies had taken it. Yet five months before the Hitler-Stalin Pact exploded upon the world, Churchill was assuring his country that Stalin's Russia was a mighty force for peace upon whom East Europeans could rely: "The loyal attitude of the Soviets to the cause of peace, and their obvious interest in resisting the Nazi advance to the Black Sea, impart a feeling of encouragement to all the Eastern States now menaced by the maniacal dreams of Berlin."[12]

THE COURTSHIP OF STALIN

HITLER WON THE COMPETITION for Stalin's hand for a reason: They were brothers under the skin, amoral political animals with blood on their hands who would unhesitatingly betray nations or crush peoples to advance state or ideological interests. In the Ribbentrop-Molotov pact, Hitler conceded that Stalin's slice of Europe would include Finland, Estonia, Latvia, eastern Poland, Bessarabia, and, later, Lithuania and Northern Bukovina. Stalin would sell Hitler the food and raw materials needed to crush the democracies and repatriate to Hitler all anti-Nazi Germans in his new territories or any who sought refuge there. It was a transaction between two regimes entailing what Auden had called the "conscious acceptance of guilt in the necessary murder."[13]

Hobbled by scruples, Britain and France took months to negotiate with Molotov and Voroshilov. They got nowhere. Ribbentrop and Molotov negotiated the most famous (and infamous) pact in history in twenty-four hours. One hitch came up in the negotiations: Stalin demanded two Latvian port towns. Ribbentrop requested a recess. Gene Smith describes:

> Ribbentrop agreed to everything, but when Stalin expressed an interest in the Latvian warm-weather ports of Libau and Windau, he said he would have to consult the Leader. . . . [Ribbentrop] put in a call to Hitler and told him of the Russian request that the Latvian ports be assigned to their sphere of interest. Hitler sent an orderly for an atlas, looked

at the map of the Baltic coastline, noted that the ports were a stone's throw from East Prussia, but told Ribbentrop to tell Stalin he was welcome to them.[14]

Hitler could be magnanimous in granting Stalin custody of what Stalin would one day have torn from him.

The news of the Hitler-Stalin pact of August 23, 1939, shook the world. Militarily, it was directed at Poland; strategically, at London. Hitler believed his pact, which put Russia at Germany's side in a war on Poland, would jolt Britain awake to reality. Poland was surrounded. Poland was indefensible. Poland was lost. It made no sense for Britain to declare war to defend a doomed nation. Confident Britain would now back away from its war guarantee, Hitler assured his comrades, "Our enemies are little worms. . . . I saw them at Munich."[15]

To Hitler's astonishment, Chamberlain countered his pact with Stalin with a British Mutual Assistance Pact with Beck.

Thus, on August 25, 1939, hours before the scheduled August 26 attack, Hitler called off his invasion for a week. Not only had Britain affirmed its commitment to Poland, Mussolini had, the same day, weaseled out of his Pact of Steel pledge to go to war. Italy's ambassador and Foreign Minister Ciano were imploring Il Duce not to let Italy be dragged into a war that threatened national ruin for Hitler, who had never consulted Mussolini on his pact with Stalin or on the steps he was taking to war. Chief of the German General Staff Halder wrote in his diary that Hitler was "considerably shaken" by the two events.[16] " 'The Italians are behaving just like they did in 1914,' fumed Hitler. He canceled the marching orders, and the invasion ground to a halt just before it reached the Polish border."[17]

LAST WEEK OF PEACE

THUS BEGAN THE FINAL week's countdown to the bloodiest war in all of history, with Chamberlain and Halifax searching, as the hours slipped away, for a way to accommodate Hitler's demand for Danzig, as Hitler and Göring sought some way to avoid war with Britain. By August 30, the British were pressing the Poles to agree to Ribbentrop's final offer: a Polish plenipotentiary sent to Berlin in twenty-four hours with full powers to negotiate the return of Danzig.

The Poles said, "No!"

Behind Polish defiance lay the lesson of Czechoslovakia. Six months after Prague surrendered the Sudetenland, the multiethnic country had come apart. Poland, too, was a multiethnic country, with Germans, Balts, Ukrainians, and Jews unhappy under Polish rule. If the Poles agreed to give back Danzig, would not the Germans in the Corridor and Silesia, and perhaps the Ukrainians, too, demand the right to secede? What would happen then? Even without their war guarantee, the Poles might have concluded: Better to go down fighting than suffer the fate of the Czechs. And so the Poles rejected the final German offer of August 30.

Was this final Hitler-Ribbentrop offer—to effect the return of Danzig to Germany but let Poland retain its economic rights in the city, and to hold a plebiscite in the Corridor to decide its future—a Nazi ploy to give Britain an escape hatch from its war guarantee? Of course. But was it also a serious offer?

Henderson believed that a Polish plenipotentiary in Berlin on August 30 could have stopped the invasion. Had Poland formally received the offer, Chamberlain would have insisted it be taken up in negotiations. Hitler would then have had his excuse for calling off the invasion. His generals, up to the hour they crossed the frontier, believed Hitler would find a way to retrieve Danzig and avoid war. But the Poles refused to send a negotiator. They had confidence in themselves as a warrior people and trusted in their British guarantee. "Colonel Beck missed the bus to Berlin and Poland paid in terms of a fourth partition."[18] As Marshal Foch predicted, the next war would break out over the Polish Corridor.[19]

For that war one man bears full moral responsibility: Hitler.

A self-described "barbarian" who mocked Christian concepts of morality, he was content to take responsibility before history. Crushing Poland to restore land and peoples to the Reich and to realize Germany's manifest destiny was no more immoral to him than riding down Dervishes at Omdurman was immoral to Churchill.

AN ALTERNATIVE TO WAR?

B**UT THIS WAS NOT** only Hitler's war. It was Chamberlain's war and Churchill's war, and it is the conduct of the British statesmen that concerns us here. Was this the time, the place, and the cause for Britain to fight?

Kissinger contends that Britain was swept into war on a wave of righteous revulsion: "After Germany occupied Czechoslovakia, British public opinion would tolerate no further concessions; from then on, the outbreak of the Second World War was only a matter of time."[20]

But no war is inevitable until it has begun. What made a European war "only a matter of time" was not Hitler's occupation of Prague but Britain's guarantee to Poland. Had there been no war guarantee, Poland, isolated and friendless, might have done a deal over Danzig and been spared six million dead. Had there been no war guarantee of March 31, there would have been no British declaration of war on September 3, and there might have been no German invasion of France in May 1940, or ever. For there was nothing inevitable about Hitler's war in the west.

> The fear that after Poland Hitler would have attacked Britain was an illusion. As he had made clear in *Mein Kampf*, Hitler would have marched against Russia. As it was, Britain was dragged into an unnecessary war, which cost her nearly 400,000 dead, bankruptcy and the dissolution of the British empire.[21]

When deterrence failed and Britain was faced with an obligation to declare a war it could not win, to honor a war guarantee it should not have given, on behalf of a nation it could not save, what should Britain have done? Barnett addresses that question:

> [T]he British guarantee to Poland had entirely failed of its deterrent purpose. Was it therefore still in England's interest to fulfill it? Poland herself could not be saved. . . . [N]o general discussion even took place in the Cabinet as to whether it would be expedient to fulfill the British guarantee to Poland. There were no prolonged and anguished debates such as had taken place during the Czechoslovakian crisis.[22]

Barnett suggests that, given the costs of a European war and the impossibility of saving Poland, the Cabinet should have considered not declaring war, even after Hitler invaded Poland. That would have been seen as a betrayal of Poland and Chamberlain's government may have fallen. But if Chamberlain believed, as he told U.S. Ambassador Joe Kennedy, that Poland's cause was lost and war an act of suicidal revenge in which millions must die, ought he not to have resigned rather than lead his country into such a war?

In the last days of August, Britain seemed fatalistic, resigned to war. An anti-Hitler German diplomat, Ulrich von Hassel, wrote in his diary, "The government in London, whose ambassador did everything to keep the peace, gave up the race in the very last days and adopted a kind of devil-may-care attitude."[23]

But Hitler and Ribbentrop were desperately seeking a way to avoid war with Britain. Here is Hitler's interpreter describing the scene when the Leader was told Britain had sent an ultimatum and would declare war in two hours:

> There was complete silence. Hitler sat immobile, gazing before him. He was not at a loss, as was afterwards stated, nor did he rage as others allege. He sat completely silent and un-

moving. After an interval . . . he turned to Ribbentrop: ". . . What now?" asked Hitler with a savage look, as though implying that his Foreign Minister had misled him about England's probable reaction. Ribbentrop answered quietly: "I assume that the French will hand in a similar ultimatum within the hour."[24]

Interpreter Schmidt withdrew to the anteroom and informed the others of the British ultimatum: "Göring turned to me and said: 'If we lose this war, then God have mercy on us.' Goebbels stood in a corner, downcast and self-absorbed. Everywhere in the room I saw looks of grave concern."[25]

Hitler and his high command believed war with Britain represented their own failure, which underscores the point Albert Speer made: "From [my] observations I deduced that this initiation of real war was not what Hitler had projected."[26]

That Hitler wanted no war with Britain is evident from his final directive of August 31, in which he ordered the attack on Poland the following morning, September 1:

The responsibility for the opening of hostilities in the West should rest unequivocally with England and France. . . . The German land frontier in the West is not to be crossed at any point without my express consent. The same applies to war-like actions at sea or any which may be interpreted as such. . . . Defensive measures on the part of the Air Force should at first be exclusively confined to the warding-off of enemy air attacks on the frontier of the Reich.[27]

Writes Hillgruber, "[T]he European war that came on September 3 was as incomprehensible as it was contrary to his [Hitler's] aims."[28]

Germans reacted as their leaders did. Shirer was in the Wilhelms-platz when news of Britain's declaration of war blared out on the loudspeakers. "Some 250 people were standing there in the sun.

They listened attentively to the announcement. When it was finished there was not a murmur. They just stood as they were before. Stunned."[29]

By the second day of war, however, September 2, the Germans had broken through the Polish defenses. The Poles were publicly calling on their British allies to declare war and attack Germany from the west. But to the astonishment of many, no action came. For Neville Chamberlain yet hoped that Hitler might agree to a conference to avert a European war. On the evening of September 2, at 7:30 P.M., Chamberlain rose in the House and spoke hopefully of such a conference. He sat down—to a stunned silence. The House had expected an announcement that an ultimatum was being sent to Berlin. As Labour leader Arthur Greenwood rose to reply to the prime minister, Tory backbencher Leo Amery shouted across to Greenwood, "Speak for England!"

When he departed the Commons that night, Neville Chamberlain

> was told that Tory backbenchers would rise in revolt if the government did not immediately carry out its threat to declare war. Twelve Cabinet members met in caucus in the chambers of Chancellor of the Exchequer Sir John Simon. They agreed to warn Chamberlain that his government could not survive another day of delay, regardless of what France did. Shortly before midnight, Chamberlain gathered his Cabinet and accepted a vote for war.[30]

On September 3, the day Britain declared war, Neville Chamberlain, "looking crumpled, despondent and old," broadcast to his nation in words that echoed Sir Edward Grey, twenty-five years before: "Everything that I have worked for, everything that I have hoped for, everything that I have believed in during my public life has crashed into ruins."[31]

"It seemed," said Eden, "rather the lament of a man deploring his own failure than the call of a nation to arms."[32] Yet one U.S. historian writes: "This note of melancholy was distinctly appropriate to the occasion. British and French statesmanship had been outmaneuvered by Soviet. What could easily have been a German thrust against the Soviet Union had been deflected against the West."[33]

The threat of a mutiny in conservative ranks that night of September 2 had forced Chamberlain, at 11:30 P.M., to assemble his Cabinet and direct Henderson to see Ribbentrop at 9 A.M.—to give Germany two hours to declare it was withdrawing from Poland or face war. His own House had forced on Chamberlain the war he never wanted. Seven weeks into that war, Chamberlain wrote his sister, "I was never meant to be a war leader."[34] He was right. As biographer Ian Macleod wrote, "He should have resigned on the outbreak of war."[35]

As of September 1939, "Britain had only four or five divisions ready for action, which was minuscule compared to the French and German armies, which each numbered about 100 divisions."[36] Looking back on the British decision to declare a war it had neither the ability to wage nor an idea of how to win calls to mind Lord Kitchener's remark in 1914: "No one can say my colleagues in the Cabinet are not courageous. They have no Army and they declared war against the mightiest military nation in the world."[37]

POLAND ABANDONED

WHEN GERMANY INVADED POLAND on September 1, six months after Warsaw received its war guarantee, not one British bomb or bullet had been sent to Poland. No British credit had been extended. Britain still lacked the power to come to Poland's aid. And Britain had made no plans to come to Poland's aid. The Poles, however, facing the first blitzkrieg, or lightning war, awaited the promised Allied offensive.

General Ironside had told the Poles that German bombing raids on Poland would be answered by British bombing raids on Germany.[38] Within hours of the declaration of war, British bombers were in the air—dropping leaflets over Germany. Warsaw was bombed by the Luftwaffe while Bomber Command ineffectually struck at German naval targets in the North Sea.

General Gamelin had assured the Poles that within fifteen days of a German attack, forty divisions, the "bulk of the French Army," would be hurled against the Reich.[39] "[T]he French general staff concluded a military agreement with its Polish counterpart on May 19," writes Hillgruber, "that called for a French offensive with approximately 40 divisions against the German western border on the fifteenth day of a European war."[40]

No French offensive ever came. As the German armies rampaged across Poland, the French army entered a few German towns, withdrew, and burrowed into the Maginot Line. The Poles learned that they had been chips sacrificed in an attempt to bluff Hitler. The bluff had been called. There was nothing to back it up. Poland had been deceived. Poland had been abandoned. When an offensive did come in the west, it would be five years later and led by Americans who would halt at the Elbe. And the Poles, who had endured five years of Nazi occupation, would endure forty-five years of Soviet tyranny.

Chamberlain had known all along his guarantee was worthless. He had confided as much to Joe Kennedy, who wrote in his diary, "[Chamberlain] says the futility of it all is the thing that is frightful; after all they cannot save the Poles; they can merely carry on a war of revenge that will mean the destruction of the whole of Europe."[41]

"The still-accepted idea that while the German armies were fighting in Poland, an Allied ground offensive across the so-called Siegfried Line would not only have been possible but decisive is groundless," writes historian John Lukacs, "it was not possible because it was not planned, and it was not planned because it was not possible."[42]

"The British stand in September 1939 was no doubt heroic," writes Taylor, "but it was heroism mainly at the expense of others."[43]

When Stalin attacked Poland on September 17, there was no British declaration of war on Russia. The war guarantee covered only a German attack. Indeed, Churchill saw a bright side to Stalin's attack on Britain's bleeding ally. "Hitler's path to the east is closed," he exclaimed.[44]

"If Beck was at fault as a diplomat," writes Davies, "the fault lay not in his . . . suspicions of Hitler and Stalin, but in his naive belief in the sincerity of allied guarantees and assurances."[45]

Whatever the sins of Colonel Beck, of the Poles it must be said: Unlike the British and French, they rejected both Hitler and Stalin. Unlike the Czechs and the Austrians, they went down fighting and behaved more honorably than did the nations upon whom they had so unwisely relied. Again, Davies:

> The [Polish] colonels were not going to bow and scrape to an ex–Austrian corporal. Their instinct was to fight, and to go down fighting. Every single Polish official who had to deal with Nazi and Soviet threats in 1939 had been reared on the Marshal's moral testament: "To be defeated but not to surrender, that is victory."[46]

After dividing Poland with Stalin, Hitler turned west to deal with the nations that had declared war on him. On May 10, 1940, he launched his blitzkrieg through the Low Countries and into the Ardennes. In three weeks, the British army had been hurled off the continent. In six weeks, France had fallen. The Wehrmacht was at the Pyrenees.

PRIMARY BENEFICIARY

The British-French war guarantee to Poland would result in defeat and disaster for all three nations. But there would be one great beneficiary.

Consider the hellish situation Stalin faced in March 1939. A pariah state with a reputation for mass murder and an archipelago of slave-labor camps, the USSR was isolated from the Western democracies, hated and feared by its neighbors, and threatened by Nazi Germany and by Japan in the Far East. Stalin knew a goal that motivated the man who wrote *Mein Kampf* and now ruled Germany was the extermination of Bolshevism.

He had watched Hitler annex Austria, carve the Sudetenland out of Czechoslovakia, turn Bohemia and Moravia into protectorates and Slovakia into an ally, retake Memel, and begin to move on Poland—without a shot being fired. Stalin knew: After Poland, his turn would come. That would mean a Nazi-Bolshevik war in which he must face Germanic power alone.

On March 31, 1939, came deliverance. Britain and France declared they would fight for Poland, the buffer state between Russia and Germany. British Tories had become the guarantors of Bolshevism. Moscow had been given free what Stalin would have paid a czar's ransom for.

Within days, the Allies had given a war guarantee to Rumania. Now any German attack through Poland or Rumania, against Russia, would cause Britain and France to declare war on Germany before Hitler could reach him. And war between Nazi Germany and Britain and France would weaken all three and fertilize the ground for Communist revolution in all three nations. Stalin's relief and joy can only be imagined.

British and French emissaries soon arrived to offer Stalin an alliance. Typhoid Mary was suddenly the most courted lady in Europe. But without any commitment of his own, Stalin already had the benefit of an alliance with Britain. The Polish war guarantee, wrote Henderson, "relieved Russia of all fear of German aggression against herself, and instead of being obliged any longer to consider her own safety, she could now afford to think only of her personal advantage."[47]

All the British emissaries could offer Stalin was an alliance to fight

Hitler. They could not offer him the Baltic states and half of Poland. Hitler could. All Stalin need do was join Hitler in a partition of Poland, as Russian czars and Prussian kings had done in centuries past.

At Ribbentrop's request, and as a sign of his good faith, Stalin agreed to deport to the Reich four thousand Germans living in Russia. Between one thousand and twelve hundred of them were German Communists.

The world over, Communists professed to be sickened by the Hitler-Stalin pact. How could the world leader of international Communism crawl into bed with the Nazi monster? But Stalin would have been a fool not to take Hitler's offer. His pact with Hitler allowed him to occupy and bolshevize six Christian nations and gave the Red Army two years to prepare for the coming war with Germany. Writes Hillgruber,

> Stalin's decision of August 1939 . . . put the Soviet Union in the most favorable position it had enjoyed since its creation in 1917. In place of the conception of "capitalist encirclement" that had dominated its policy, there emerged an appreciation of its position as a great power, respected and indeed wooed by all of the participants in the war, its political weight waxing as the war continued and absorbed the energies of the combatant nations.[48]

Had Britain never given the war guarantee, the Soviet Union would almost surely have borne the brunt of the blow that fell on France. The Red Army, ravaged by Stalin's purge of senior officers, might have collapsed. Bolshevism might have been crushed. Communism might have perished in 1940, instead of living on for fifty years and murdering tens of millions more in Russia, China, Korea, Vietnam, and Cuba. A Hitler-Stalin war might have been the only war in Europe in the 1940s. Tens of millions might never have died terrible deaths in the greatest war in all history.

CHAPTER 12

Gruesome Harvest

IF WAR SHOULD COME . . . nothing is more certain than that victor and vanquished alike would glean a gruesome harvest of human misery and suffering.[1]
— NEVILLE CHAMBERLAIN, JULY 31, 1939

ON JUNE 18, 1940, Churchill declared in one of his most memorable addresses, "Let us therefore brace ourselves to do our duties and so bear ourselves that, if the British Empire and its Commonwealth last for a thousand years, men will still say, 'This was their finest hour.' " One British historian has another perspective on his country in its critical hour:

> The plight of the summer of 1940 . . . marked the consummation of an astonishing decline in British fortunes. The British invested their feebleness and isolation with a romantic glamour—they saw themselves as latter-day Spartans, under their own Leonidas, holding the pass for the civilised world. In fact, it was a sorry and contemptible plight for a great power, and it derived neither from bad luck, nor from the failures of others. It had been brought down upon the British by themselves.[2]

The statements of Churchill and Correlli Barnett do not conflict. The summer of 1940 was among the finest hours of the British people. But they themselves were responsible for their perilous situation.

MILITARY DEATHS, MAJOR POWERS, WORLD WARS I AND II		
	WWI	**WWII**
Russia [USSR]	1.8 million	10.7 million
Germany	2.0 million	5.5 million
France	1.375 million	212 thousand
Habsburg Empire	1.1 million	n/a
UK & Dominions	921 thousand	491 thousand
Italy	460 thousand	301 thousand
USA	116 thousand	417 thousand

For each dead serviceman, three or four were wounded. Figures do not include millions of dead from the influenza epidemic after WWI or millions of civilian and military dead in nations of Eastern and Central Europe and the Balkans fought over by Hitler and Stalin in WWII.

VICTORS AND VANQUISHED

AFTER DUNKIRK, WITH THE FALL of France imminent, Mussolini saw history passing him by: "I can't just sit back and watch the fight. When the war is over and victory comes I shall be left empty-handed!"[3]

"Mussolini had long been champing at the bit to grab a piece of French territory as well as a crumb of the glory," writes Alistair Horne. "He told Marshal Badoglio: 'I need only a few thousand dead to ensure that I have the right to sit at the peace table in the capacity of a belligerent.' "[4]

When the French government fled Paris for Bordeaux, Mussolini, still seething over the League of Nations sanctions, declared war on Britain and invaded France, evoking FDR's riposte: "On this tenth day of June, 1940, the hand that held the dagger has stuck it into the back of its neighbor."[5]

To Churchill, who had lauded Mussolini as "so great a man and so wise a ruler," Il Duce had suddenly become Hitler's:

little Italian accomplice, trotting along hopefully and hungrily at his side. . . .

This whipped jackal Mussolini, who to save his own skin has made of Italy a vassal state of Hitler's empire, goes frisking up at the side of the German tiger with relish not only of appetite—that could be understood—but even of triumph.[6]

That fall, Mussolini's armies invaded Egypt and Greece, where they quickly floundered. To rescue his ally, Hitler sent armies into the Balkans and North Africa. Thus, by June 1941, Hitler occupied Europe west to the Pyrenees and south to Crete. These conquests had come about not because of some Hitlerian master plan, but because of a war with Britain that Hitler had never wanted, and an invasion of Greece by Mussolini that Hitler had opposed.

As Hitler's armies drove deep into the Soviet Union in the summer of 1941, Nazi Germany soon occupied all the lands on which the Kaiser's army had stood on November 11, 1918. This was the apogee of Nazi power. Except for Spain, Portugal, Sweden, and Switzerland, almost all of Europe was under either German occupation or a pro-Nazi regime.

Six months after invading the Soviet Union, however, Hitler had been stopped in the east and had declared war on the United States. Nazi Germany was doomed. She would take three years to die and take down millions with her. Germany would be destroyed and Fascism forever disgraced. But the price would be scores of millions dead and the devastation of Europe. And the peace of 1945, Stalin's peace east of the Elbe, would make Jan Smuts's "Carthaginian peace" of 1919 appear magnanimous. The true winners of the greatest war in history would be the two powers that continue to celebrate V-E Day.

America. Last of the great powers to go to war, the United States emerged as the first nation on earth, unrivaled in the air or at sea, with the fewest casualties, four hundred thousand dead, relative to her population. Save for Pearl Harbor and the Aleutians, the homeland had been unmolested. Americans had liberated Italy, France,

Belgium, Holland, and the Philippines. The battles of Midway and Normandy, of Iwo Jima and the Bulge, would become the stuff of legend. For Americans, it became "the Good War." Leadership of the West would pass forever from Britain and Europe to the United States and the twentieth century would be the American Century.

The Soviet Union. While Russia lost millions of soldiers and civilians and suffered devastation, Stalin emerged from the war as the most powerful czar in history, with the Red Army occupying Berlin, Vienna, and Prague. In the aftermath, Communist parties loyal to Stalin would vie for power in Paris and Rome and Communist revolutionaries would help tear down the empires of the West. In 1949, Stalin would treble the subject peoples of Communism as China fell to the armies of Mao Tse-tung, converting America's wartime ally into Stalin's partner in world conquest. In 1949, too, Stalin's scientists, with stolen American technology, exploded an atomic bomb.

For almost all the other nations and people of Europe, the war would prove more a disaster than a triumph.

Britain. From Norway to France, to Greece, Crete, to Libya, Britain lost every battle with the Germans—until El Alamein in 1942. She would end the war with four hundred thousand dead and a Pyrrhic victory, and never again be great. Churchill had devoted his life to three causes: the preservation of the empire, keeping socialism at bay, and preventing any hostile power from dominating Europe. By July of 1945, all three had been lost and Churchill dismissed by the people he had led to victory.

"I have not become the King's First Minister in order to preside over the liquidation of the British Empire," Churchill declared in 1942.[7] By 1946, liquidation had begun. By 1947, India, crown jewel of the empire, was gone and Britain had transferred her duties to Greece and Turkey to help stop Communist aggression to Truman's America. Poland, the nation for which Britain had gone to war, nine other Christian nations, and Albania were now in the death grip of Stalin.

"We killed the wrong pig," Churchill is said to have muttered.

STALIN'S EUROPEAN EMPIRE, 1945

Annexed by Stalin, 1940

Countries under Soviet control, 1945

Occupied by U.S., U.K., USSR

Iron curtain

FINLAND

NORWAY

Karelian
Peninsula

ESTONIA

SWEDEN

U.S.S.R.

LATVIA

North
Sea

Baltic
Sea

DENMARK

LITHUANIA

Belarus

EAST
GERMANY

POLAND

WEST
GERMANY

CZECHOSLOVAKIA

Ukraine

Northern
Bukovina

AUSTRIA

Bessarabia

HUNGARY

ITALY

ROMANIA

YUGOSLAVIA

Black
Sea

Adriatic Sea

BULGARIA

ALBANIA

GREECE

TURKEY

0 Miles 100 200

0 Kilometers 200

"It has been ironically said that the British brought Hailé Selassié back to Addis Ababa in order to bring the Russians into Vienna, Berlin, and Port Arthur. Let us hope they are pleased with the result." —Luigi Villari, Italian diplomat

© 2008 Jeffrey L. Ward

By 1948, Palestine was gone and Britain was surviving on Marshall Plan aid. In 1956, President Eisenhower ordered Great Britain, which had invaded Suez to overthrow Nasser, to get out of Egypt. Threatening to sink the pound if Britain did not depart, Ike brought down the government of Churchill's heir, Anthony Eden. By Churchill's death in 1965, the empire had vanished and Britain was applying for admission to a Common Market dominated by Germans and the France of an ungrateful Charles de Gaulle, who vetoed British entry.

What had all the "blood, sweat, toil and tears" produced?

In Eastern and Central Europe, Hitler's rule had given way to Stalin's. Pax Britannica had given way to Pax Americana. And for this the British Empire had sacrificed itself. Yet there was this notable success: Britain had restored Ethiopia's emperor to his throne. Said one caustic critic, "It has been ironically said that the British brought Hailé Selassié back to Addis Ababa in order to bring the Russians into Vienna, Berlin and Port Arthur."[8]

France would be occupied for four years, the Vichy era marked by widespread collaboration. French Indochina would be overrun by Japan. By war's end, Syria and Lebanon were gone. In 1954, the French, defeated at Dienbienphu, were run out of Vietnam by General Giap and Ho Chi Minh. In 1962, France was driven out of Algeria by the terror tactics of the FALN. North Africa was gone and France's sub-Sahara empire was crumbling.

Denmark, Norway, Luxembourg, Belgium, and **Holland** would endure four years of Nazi occupation. The Dutch East Indies, lost to Japan in 1941, were taken into receivership by a despotic Japanese collaborator named Sukarno.

Poland, trusting in her war guarantee, suffered hundreds of thousands of dead resisting the Nazi-Soviet onslaught in September 1939. The Polish officer corps would be massacred by Stalin's NKVD in killing fields like Katyn Forest. Poland would be occupied five years by Nazis and become the site of such horrors as Treblinka and Auschwitz. Poland's Home Army, at the urging of the Red Army on the far side of the Vistula, would rise in Warsaw in 1944. And as that Red Army looked on, refusing to help, the Polish Home Army and Warsaw's civilian population would suffer losses as heavy as 9/11 every day for two months, and finally be annihilated by the Wehrmacht and the SS.[9]

"The cream of Poland's patriotic and democratic youth had been eliminated," writes one historian.[10] Poland's Catholic population would be decimated, her Jews virtually exterminated. Poland would lose six million people and fifty years of freedom. Writes historian Norman Davies, "Poland's reliance on Churchill . . . proved worthless."[11]

The British-French war guarantee of March 31, 1939, that brought Britain, France, and Poland into an alliance against Germany ended in calamity for all three. Britain would have to be rescued and France liberated by the Americans. Poland would be abandoned, first to Hitler then to Stalin.

"The Western Allies entered that war with a two-fold object," wrote Liddell Hart. "The immediate purpose was to fulfill their promise to preserve the independence of Poland. The ultimate purpose was to remove a potential menace to themselves, and thus ensure their own security. In the outcome, they failed in both purposes."[12] By war's end, Britain "had become a poor dependent of the United States."[13]

Germany would end the war occupied, in total ruin, with millions of civilians dead from the carpet bombing of the Allies and the reprisals of the Red Army. In one of the great exoduses of human history, thirteen to fifteen million Germans would be driven out of lands their ancestors had lived on for centuries. Two million would perish in the long orgy of rape and revenge. The problem of German minorities in European countries would be solved by exterminating some and "ethnically cleansing" the rest. Of the Stalinized states of Central and Eastern Europe it may be said: They were now more ethnically pure than they had been before the war.

Italy would be bombed and invaded by Anglo-American forces and Mussolini executed by Communist Partisans, his body hanged upside down with that of his mistress Clara Pettacci in a Milan gas station. Well before the war's end, his New Roman Empire had vanished.

The Baltic republics, Lithuania, Latvia, and Estonia, seized by Stalin in June 1940 as his plunder from his pact with Hitler, would suffer untold horrors, with the cultural, political, religious, and intellectual leaders of the three tiny nations disappearing forever in the labor and death camps of the Gulag Archipelago.

Czechoslovakia, Hungary, Rumania, Bulgaria, Yugoslavia, Albania, and eastern Germany would end up as captive nations of a new Soviet Empire, ceded to Stalin by Churchill and FDR. They would suffer half a century of tyranny at the hands of the political criminals who ruled Eastern Europe for the Politburo.

Most of the fighting and dying in the bloodiest of all wars, to bring down Hitler's Reich, was done on the Eastern Front. As Davies writes, "The Third Reich was largely defeated not by the forces of liberal democracy, but by the Red Army of another mass-murdering tyranny. The liberators of Auschwitz were servants of a regime that ran an even larger network of concentration camps of its own."[14]

Measured by the size of the armies, the scope of the battles, and the length of the casualty lists, World War II was less a war between Fascism and freedom than a war between Nazism and Bolshevism. Hitler lost, Stalin won.

Of the Little Entente of Czechoslovakia, Rumania, and Yugoslavia, which in February 1933 had declared itself the "Fifth Great Power" in Europe, Villari writes: "When it came to a showdown in 1939, the combination utterly failed to save its members from invasion, devastation and wholesale massacre, ending up in slavery for all three under a blood-thirsty Communist regime, of the Stalinist variety in two of them, of a Titoist variety in the third, but both equally oppressive and abominable."[15]

There was another consequence of "The Good War."

HITLER'S POGROM

FOR WHAT HAPPENED TO the Jews of Europe, Hitler and his collaborators in the unspeakable crimes bear full moral responsibility. The just punishment for people who participate in mass murder is death, be it in a bunker or on a gallows. The Nazi murderers got what they deserved. But was the Holocaust inevitable? Could it have been averted?

Clearly, hatred of Jews was a defining characteristic of the Nazi Party from birth. *Mein Kampf,* written while Hitler was imprisoned at Landsberg after the Beer Hall Putsch in 1923, is saturated in it.

Within weeks of Hitler's taking power came the Reichstag fire, which led to Dachau and the other camps to hold enemies of the regime. In 1935, Hitler imposed the Nuremberg Laws, discriminating against Jews in every walk of life. Yet though viciously anti-Semitic, Hitler's Reich had not gone genocidal. Nazi policy had been to make Jewish lives so miserable in Germany that the Jews would leave.

Six weeks after Munich, however, came Kristallnacht. Synagogues were torched, Jewish businesses smashed and ransacked, and Jews attacked, brutalized, and lynched. Before Kristallnacht, half of the Jewish population had fled Germany. Of those who remained, perhaps half fled after the night of terror of November 9–10, 1938. Fortunately, they were gone when the curtain fell on September 1, 1939.

Three months after Kristallnacht, on the sixth anniversary of his assumption of power, January 29, 1939, Hitler, in a speech to the Reichstag, publicly threatened the Jews of Europe. America, Britain, and France, he charged, "were continually being stirred up to hatred of Germany and the German people by Jewish and non-Jewish agitators."[16] Hitler then issued his threat:

> In the course of my life I have often been a prophet, and have usually been ridiculed for it. . . . I will once more be a prophet: If the international Jewish financiers in and outside

Europe should succeed in plunging the nations once more into a world war, then the result will not be the Bolshevization of the earth, and thus the victory of Jewry, but the annihilation of the Jewish race in Europe.[17]

The mass deportations and destruction of the Jews of Europe, however, did not begin in 1939 or 1940. They began after Hitler invaded Russia, June 22, 1941, when the Einsatzgruppen trailed the Wehrmacht into the Soviet Union exterminating Bolsheviks, commissars, and Jews. Writes Ian Kershaw, "[T]he German invasion of the Soviet Union triggered the rapid descent into full-scale genocide against the Jews."[18]

Not until January 1942, after Hitler had been at war two and a half years, invaded Russia, declared war on the United States, and begun to sense disaster, was the infamous Wannsee Conference held.

In February 1942, after that conference, Goebbels wrote ominously in his *Diaries*, "World Jewry will suffer a great catastrophe. . . . The Fuehrer realizes the full implications of the great opportunity offered by this war."[19]

On March 7, 1942, the ominous phrase "a final solution of the Jewish question" appears in *The Goebbels Diaries*.[20]

On March 27, 1942, after describing the deportations lately begun from Poland's ghettos, Goebbels writes chillingly, "Fortunately, a whole series of possibilities presents itself for us in wartime that would be denied us in peacetime. We shall have to profit by this."[21]

The same day, Goebbels refers back to Hitler's threat of January 1939, adding, "[T]he fact that Jewry's representatives in England and America are today organizing and sponsoring the war against Germany must be paid for dearly by its representatives in Europe—and that's only right."[22]

From this chronology, the destruction of the European Jews was not a cause of the war but an awful consequence of the war. Had there been no war, would there have been a Holocaust at all?

In *The World Crisis*, Churchill, the Dardanelles disaster in mind, wrote: "[T]he terrible Ifs accumulate." If Britain had not issued the war guarantee and then declared war on Germany, Hitler might never have invaded France. Had he not, Mussolini would never have invaded France or Greece, or declared war on England.

With no war in the west, all the Jews of Norway, Denmark, Holland, Belgium, Luxembourg, France, Italy, Yugoslavia, and Greece might have survived a German-Polish or Nazi-Soviet war, as the Jews of Spain, Portugal, Sweden, and Switzerland survived.

But because Britain issued the guarantee to Poland and declared war on Germany, by June 1941 Hitler held hostage most of the Jews of Western Europe and the Balkans. By 1942, after invading Ukraine, Byelorussia, the Baltic states, and Russia, he held hostage virtually the entire Jewish population of Europe.

Yet neither the Allies nor the Soviets were focused on the potential fate of the hostages Hitler held. At Casablanca in 1943, Churchill and FDR declared their war aim was "unconditional surrender." At Quebec in 1944, Churchill and FDR approved the Morgenthau Plan calling for the destruction of all German industry. Goebbels used the Morgenthau Plan to convince Germans that surrender meant no survival. Annihilation of their hostages was the price the Nazis exacted for their own annihilation.

WHAT MIGHT HAVE BEEN

LOOKING BACK, WOULD IT not have been better to tell the Poles the truth—that Britain and France could not save them? And hence Beck must decide if it was worth war with Germany to hold a town of 350,000 Germans clamoring to return to the Reich?

Was Danzig worth a war? Was Poland worth a war, if there was no way to save Poland? Comes the reply: The war was never about Danzig. It was never about Poland. The war was fought to stop Hitler, the most demonic ruler ever to walk this Earth, whose crimes are unequaled in the annals of man. To destroy such a monster and eradicate his satanic regime, to prevent his gaining "mastery of the world," any price, including tens of millions dead and the devastation of World War II, was worth it. The Good War was the great crusade against Nazism and Fascism, and if the British Empire had to perish to end this evil before it consumed the world, the British Empire died in the noblest of causes. So argues Niall Ferguson:

> By the time Churchill became Prime Minister in 1940, the most likely alternatives to British rule were Hirohito's Greater East Asia Co-Prosperity Sphere, Hitler's Thousand Year Reich and Mussolini's New Rome. . . . It was the staggering cost of fighting these imperial rivals that ultimately brought down the British Empire. . . . [T]he Empire was dismantled . . . because it took up arms for just a few years against far more oppressive empires. It did the right thing, regardless of the cost.[23]

"In the end," writes Ferguson, "the British sacrificed [their] Empire to stop the Germans, Japanese and Italians from keeping theirs," and it was this inevitably Pyrrhic victory that makes the sacrifice of her empire "so fine, so authentically noble."[24]

But is this really how it happened? Was the sacrifice of the empire done willingly as an act of martyrdom? Or was it rather the result of British blundering on a colossal scale?

As for "Mussolini's New Rome," the British had courted Il Duce for years and had formally recognized Italy's conquest of Ethiopia and her rights in Libya and Eritrea before the war began. Indeed, before his excoriation of Mussolini for joining Hitler's attack on France, Churchill had been ever effusive in his praise of the greatness of Il Duce. And Britain did not declare war on Mussolini. Mussolini declared war on Britain on June 10, 1940.

As for Japan, it was as barbarous an empire as modernity had seen. But Japan had been Britain's ally before London terminated the Anglo-Japanese treaty in 1922, not out of moral revulsion, but because the Americans demanded it. In the mid-1930s, after Japan's invasion of Manchuria, Neville Chamberlain was urging a rapprochement with Tokyo so Britain would not have to fight both Japan and Germany. And Britain did not go to war to bring down Japan's empire. Japan attacked first—and America crushed Japan. And Japan's empire—Manchuria, China, North Korea, Indochina— ended up in the empire of Stalin and his heirs, under the rule of Mao, Kim Il Sung, Ho Chi Minh, and Pol Pot, whose victims would far exceed in number those of imperial Japan.

Britain surely played an indispensable role in bringing down Hitler and liberating Western Europe, but it was a supporting role. It was the Red Army that tore the guts out of the Werhrmacht. D-Day in France did not come until three years after Hitler's invasion of Russia. As Norman Davies writes,

> Proportions . . . are crucial. Since 75%–80% of all German losses were inflicted on the eastern front it follows that the efforts of the western allies accounted for only 20%–25%. Furthermore, since the British army deployed no more than 28 divisions as compared with the American army's 99, the British contribution to victory must have been in the region of 5%–6%. Britons who imagine that "we won the war" need to think again.[25]

And before Britain's declaration of war on Germany brought Hitler's army west, Western Europe did not need liberating. As for Eastern and Central Europe, they were "liberated" by Stalin.

Had Britain not declared war on Germany, perhaps Hitler, after taking back Danzig, would have turned west and overrun France as he did in 1940, then stormed into Yugoslavia, Greece, and North Africa as he did in 1941. But why? And what would have been lost had Britain and France never given the war guarantee to Poland, but rearmed and waited to see if Hitler would ever attack Western Europe?

Even had Hitler come west after crushing Stalin's Soviet Union, how could it have been worse than it was for the Jews? Or the Gypsies? Or the Slavs? Or the Christians, tens of millions of whom would die and one hundred million of whom would end up slaves in an empire that was the most brutal and barbaric enemy Christianity had ever known? Had Britain not given the war guarantee, and not declared war over Poland, Western Europe might have avoided war altogether. And was the war worth it? Let us give the last word to Churchill. Three years after the victory, he wrote in *The Gathering Storm:*

> The human tragedy reaches its climax in the fact that after all the exertions and sacrifices of hundreds of millions of people and of the victories of the Righteous Cause, we have still not found Peace or Security, and we lie in the grip of even worse perils than those we have surmounted.[26]

What did Churchill mean by "even worse perils" than Nazism and Hitler? He meant Stalinism and Stalin, a mass murderer whose victims exceeded even those of Hitler. By 1948, all of Stalin's promises about elections had been broken and he was crushing all opposition to communist tyranny in the eleven countries now in his grip, including Czechoslovakia, for which Churchill had wanted to go to war, and Poland, for which Churchill had demanded Britain go to war.

If the West faced "even worse perils" in 1948 than in 1939, what had it all been for? Yes, Hitler was dead and Nazism exterminated, but at a cost of 50 million lives. And Britain had lost four hundred thousand men, and was broken and bankrupt. The empire had lost scores of thousands more dead and was collapsing. India, the crown jewel, was already gone. Stalin's Red Army loomed over Europe.

Stalinist parties were grasping for power in Italy and France. Mao's armies were moving from victory to victory in China. And the Americans had gone home.

On May 13, 1940, in his first address to the House as prime minister, Churchill declared: "You ask, What is our aim? I can answer in one word. It is victory, victory at all costs."[27] Churchill was true to his word. As we shall see, it was he alone who refused to consider any agreement to end the war at Dunkirk. It was he who rejected Hitler's offer of peace in July 1940.

On May 21, 1937, according to Churchill, at the German embassy he had warned Ribbentrop, "Do not underrate England. She is very clever. If you plunge us all into another Great War, she will bring the whole world against you like last time."[28]

Churchill made good on his threat, holding on until the Americans came in. But that meant the war would last five years after Dunkirk, and all Europe would lie in ashes. Wrote Tory historian Alan Clark in 1993:

> The war went on far too long, and when Britain emerged the country was bust. Nothing remained of assets overseas. Without immense and punitive borrowings from the US we would have starved. The old social order had gone forever. The empire was terminally damaged. The Commonwealth countries had seen their trust betrayed and their soldiers wasted.[29]

"Victory at all costs" proved costly indeed. Yet, horrendous as the cost was, it had to be paid. So we are told. For Hitler, as Henderson wrote, was out to "rule the earth."[30] But if he was out to rule the earth, and war was the only way to stop him, we must ask:

Where did Hitler declare his determination to destroy the British Empire and "rule the earth"? How was a nation of Germany's modest size and population to conquer the world? Was there no way to contain Hitler but declare a war in which, as Chamberlain told Joe Kennedy, millions must die? What were Hitler's real ambitions?

CHAPTER 13

Hitler's Ambitions

THE LAST THING that Hitler wanted to produce was another great war.[1]
—B. H. LIDDELL HART

The one thing [Hitler] did not plan was the great war, often attributed to him.[2]
—A.J.P. TAYLOR

WHEN HITLER TOOK POWER in 1933, not all Englishmen were ignorant of the character of the man who had attempted the Munich Beer Hall Putsch and written *Mein Kampf*. Sir Horace Rumbold, the British ambassador in Berlin, a man wiser than those who would succeed him, wrote in his valedictory dispatch to London of April 26, 1933, that Hitler

> starts with the assumption that man is a fighting animal; therefore the nation is a fighting unit, being a community of fighters. . . . A country or race which ceases to fight is doomed. . . . Pacifism is the deadliest sin. . . . Intelligence is of secondary importance. . . . Will and determination are of the highest worth. Only brute force can ensure the survival of the race.[3]

Hitler believes, wrote Rumbold, "It is the duty of government to implant in the people feelings of manly courage and passionate hatred. . . . The new Reich must gather within its fold all the scattered German elements in Europe. . . . What Germany needs is an increase in territory."[4]

With the mass arrest of Communists after the Reichstag fire, the concentration camp established at Dachau, the murders by the SS during the Night of the Long Knives, the kind of men the Allies were dealing with in the new Germany was known by 1934. Even Mussolini had been shaken. But the issue of this chapter is not that Hitler was crude, cruel, and ruthless, or that the barbarism his Nazi regime degenerated into was rivaled only by Stalin, Mao, and Pol Pot, but whether Hitler ever sought war with the West.

Looking back at each of the crises before 1939 and how he responded, the answer would seem to be "No." In 1934, Hitler had been nearly hysterical that the Austrian Nazis, who had assassinated Dollfuss, would drag him into a confrontation with Mussolini. He disowned the coup and the Nazi plotters and pledged to make amends.

Hitler described the days of March 1936, when he sent three lightly armed battalions into the Rhineland with orders to pull out immediately if they met French resistance, as the "most nerve-racking moment" of his life.

In March 1938, it was not Hitler who precipitated the Austrian crisis, but Schuschnigg with his call for a plebiscite in four days so Austria could vote permanent independence of Germany. Hitler did not even have an invasion plan prepared. When Mussolini sent word he would not interfere if Hitler sent his army in, Hitler was almost hysterical with gratitude and relief.

In September 1938, after his second meeting with Chamberlain, at Bad Godesberg, where Hitler had threatened to invade and seize what he wanted of Czechoslovakia, and the British, French, and Czechs began to mobilize, Hitler rushed a conciliatory letter to Chamberlain, urging him not to give up his search for peace. He grasped Mussolini's proposal for a third meeting at Munich. It was Hitler who backed down after Godesberg.

In August 1939, when, after the Ribbentrop-Molotov pact exploded on the world, Chamberlain reaffirmed his alliance with Poland, a stunned Hitler put off his invasion a week to find a way out of a war with Britain. When the British ultimatum came on September 3, Hitler turned an angry face at Ribbentrop: "What now!" If Hitler were out to conquer the world, would he not have worked out his plans for conquest with his only major ally, Mussolini, who weaseled out of his Pact of Steel commitment in the week before Hitler went to war?

Hitler never wanted war with Britain. As his naval treaty showed—accepting a Kriegsmarine one-third the size of the Royal Navy, then declining to build up to the limits allotted—he had always been willing to pay a high price to avoid it. His dream was of an alliance with the British Empire, not its ruin. In August 1939, his generals expected, his people hoped, and Hitler believed he could still do a deal.

But if Hitler did not seek war with the British Empire, how could he have been out to conquer the world? What was Hitler's real agenda?

HITLER'S AMBITIONS

ABOUT HITLER'S AMBITIONS, historians yet disagree. Some insist his ambitions were global: to conquer Europe, invade Britain, and build a naval and air armada to confront America for mastery of the world. Others argue that Hitler's plans for conquest were primarily and perhaps only in the east.

To discern his ambitions, there are several sources: Hitler's words, beginning with *Mein Kampf* and even before, the shape of the forces he constructed for war, what he did and did not do given his opportunities, and the plans Hitler wrote down but never implemented.

On some issues all agree. Hitler's first goal was absolute power in Germany. A second was to overturn the Versailles Treaty that denied

Germany equality of rights, especially the right to rearm. A third was to restore lands severed by Versailles and bring Germans home to the Reich. A fourth was the *Drang nach Osten*, the drive to the east to carve out a new German empire. Finally, Hitler intended to cleanse Germany of Jews, smash Bolshevism, and make himself a man of history like Frederick the Great and Bismarck. The anti-Semitism in which *Mein Kampf* is steeped was his most consistent conviction. As German historian Andreas Hillgruber, among other historians, contends, to Hitler the Jews and Bolsheviks were one and the same enemy:

> The conquest of European Russia, the cornerstone of the continental European phase of his program, was thus for Hitler inextricably linked with the extermination of these "bacilli," the Jews. In his conception they had gained dominance over Russia with the Bolshevik Revolution. Russia thereby became the center from which a global danger radiated, particularly threatening to the Aryan race and its Germanic core.[5]

Once he attained power, however, Hitler, like Lenin and Stalin, would subordinate ideology to raison d'état, as in the volte-face toward Russia in early 1939 and the Molotov-Ribbentrop pact that August. And when Hitler did move on Russia in 1941, his motivation was not ideology.

THE LESSONS OF DEFEAT

HAVING FOUGHT FOUR YEARS on the Western Front, Hitler had formed indelible ideas as to why Germany had lost the war. While the Nazis ranted and railed against the "November criminals" of 1918 and the "stab in the back," Hitler was not such a fool as to swallow whole his own Nazi Party propaganda. The German army had been defeated by the Allies in the west in 1918. And because Germany was defeated in France, all the fruits of her victory over Russia in the east had been taken from her, and the humiliation of Versailles imposed.

The crucial lesson Hitler drew from defeat was that Germany must never again fight a two-front war. By 1917, Germany was at war with Britain, France, and America in the west, Italy to the south, and Russia to the east, with Japan and the British Empire having seized her colonies in Africa, Asia, and the Pacific. Hitler believed the two-front war had been a historic blunder that must never be repeated. Again, Hillgruber:

> Together with his prewar Vienna period and postwar Munich years, the war provided . . . Hitler with his formative experiences. It made him recognize the impossibility of a German victory in a war where Germany was pitted against both the continental power, Russia, and the British Empire, let alone the two Anglo-Saxon sea powers. His memory was alive with the hopelessness of Germany's predicament surrounded by enemies in a Central European bastion . . . in a world war in which the superior economic and armaments potential of the hostile coalition would ultimately tell.[6]

Second, Hitler knew the longer a war went on, the weaker Germany became relative to her potential enemies. While Germany's population of seventy million—eighty million after Anschluss and absorption of the Sudeten Germans—was approaching that of Britain and France combined, it was dwarfed by the 458 million in the British Empire, the 197 million of a Soviet Union that stretched across a dozen time zones, and the 140 million Americans, whose productive power exceeded that of Britain, France, and Germany combined.

On the eve of war, Hitler's domain, even with the Saar, Austria, and the Sudetenland added to it, covered about 260,000 square miles—to the United States's 3.6 million, the USSR's 8.5 million, and the British Empire's 14 million square miles. Should these three powers unite, Hitler knew, their manpower and resources would dwarf what Germany could command in Central Europe. A European power, not yet a world power, Germany lacked the resources and productive capacity to fight a world war. Outside of Europe, in North and South America, Africa, the Middle East, South Asia, Australia, China, and the Pacific, Germany was an inconsequential force. Hitler understood this.

Hitler had also concluded that the Kaiser's decision to build a High Seas Fleet to challenge the Royal Navy had been an act of monumental folly. The appearance of German battleships in the North Sea drove Britain into the 1904 entente with France, which brought her into war against Germany in 1914. Had Admiral Tirpitz and the Kaiser not challenged the Royal Navy, sword and shield of the empire, Britain would have had far less reason to fear Germany and to align with her old enemies France and Russia.

And what good had the High Seas Fleet done for Germany? It had not stopped the British Expeditionary Force from crossing the Channel to defeat the Schlieffen Plan. It had proved incapable of defending Germany's colonies. It had failed to break the blockade that had starved Germany into submission. It had ventured out for battle once, at Jutland in 1916, retired to port, and, in 1919, was escorted to Scapa Flow by the Royal Navy, where it committed suicide.

This led to a third lesson Hitler took from the war. Germany could not defend overseas colonies against the Anglo-Saxon sea powers. Her colonies would always be hostages to the British and U.S. fleets. If Germany went to war again with the Anglo-Saxon powers, she must expect to lose any overseas possessions and endure another starvation blockade. Thus, before any new war was undertaken, Germany must achieve economic self-sufficiency in Europe.

Autarky is a word that recurs often in Hitler's talk. By autarky, Hitler meant Germany must find within defensible borders all the resources needed to sustain her at war. Never again could Germany rely on imports. British and U.S. warships would intercept them and starve her out, as they had in the Great War. Hitler, writes Hillgruber, "believed he would succeed in creating an autarkic, blockade-proof and defensible sphere that would grant Germany real autonomy . . . for all time. In short, he would create a German world power to stand beside the other world powers."[7]

Hitler's conclusions: Since an overseas empire was indefensible, the new German empire must be created not in Africa or Asia but in Central and Eastern Europe, where Royal Navy warships and American fleets could not reach. In the second volume of *Mein Kampf,* published in 1926, Hitler lays out his agenda with great clarity.

> Germany either will be a world power or there will be no Germany. And for world power she needs that magnitude which will give her the position she needs in the present period, and life to her citizens.
>
> And so we National Socialists consciously draw a line beneath the foreign policy tendency of the pre-War period. We take up where we broke off six hundred years ago. We stop the endless German movement to the south and west of Europe, and turn our gaze to the land in the east. At long last we break off the colonial and commercial policy of the pre-War period, and shift to the soil policy of the future.
>
> If we speak of soil in Europe today, we can primarily have in mind only Russia and her vassal border states.[8]

Here is the polestar of Hitler's ambition. Biographer Ian Kershaw writes that Hitler reached this conclusion even before *Mein Kampf:*

> By early 1922 . . . Hitler had abandoned any idea of collaboration with Russia. He saw no prospect of Russia looking only eastwards. Extension of Bolshevism to Germany would prove an irresistible urge. . . . Only through the destruction of

Bolshevism could Germany be saved. And at the same time this—through expansion into Russia—would bring the territory which Germany needed. During the course of 1922— perhaps reinforced towards the end of the year by contact with the arch-expansionist Ludendorff—the changed approach to future policy towards Russia was consolidated.[9]

HITLER'S DREAM ALLIANCE

ADOLF HITLER WAS AS dedicated to Nazism as Lenin and Stalin were to Bolshevism. Yet all three would sacrifice ideology for reasons of state.

Lenin signed on to the Brest-Litovsk treaty of 1918 that tore his empire to pieces. He reined in Trotsky's permanent revolution lest it imperil the state. He introduced a New Economic Policy in 1921, introducing market forces, when rebellion threatened the regime. Stalin colluded with Nazi Germany in return for the Baltic states and half of Poland. Hitler would abandon South Tyrol to Italy for an alliance with Rome and cede all claims to Alsace and Lorraine rather than risk another war in the West over the lost provinces.

As Hitler showed in the murder of Roehm and the SA leaders who helped bring him to power, he could be a cold-blooded opportunist who, to cement the loyalty of the army, would assent to the execution of his oldest comrades. U.S. historian David Calleo writes: Hitler was "highly pragmatic about means . . . always prepared to drop ideology when it suited him."[10]

A.J.P. Taylor and other historians contend that Hitler's foreign policy was more traditional and in ways less ambitious than that of the Kaiser, who saw Germany as a great sea power, a colonial power, a global power. Hitler did not rule out a return of lost colonies in Africa, but this was never where his ambitions or interests lay.

"Hitler was more moderate than his predecessors in that he did not aspire to colonies overseas nor to territorial gains in Western Europe, though naturally his modesty diminished when the chance of such gains actually matured," wrote Taylor.[11]

To Hitler, Great Britain was Germany's natural ally and the nation and empire he most admired. He did not covet British colonies. He did not want or seek a fleet to rival the Royal Navy. He did not wish to bring down the British Empire. He was prepared to appease Britain to make her a friend of Germany. Where the Kaiser had grudgingly agreed in 1913 to restrict the High Seas Fleet to 60 percent of the Royal Navy, Hitler in 1935 readily agreed to restrict his navy to 35 percent. What Hitler ever sought was an allied, friendly, or at least neutral Britain.

Conversing in 1922 with a publisher friendly to the Nazi party, Hitler "ruled out the colonial rivalry with Britain that had caused conflict before the First World War." Said Hitler, "Germany would have to adapt herself to a purely continental policy, avoiding harm to English interests."[12]

"By late 1922," Kershaw writes, "an alliance with Britain, whose world empire he admired, was in [Hitler's] mind. This idea had sharpened in 1923 when the disagreements of the British and French over the Ruhr occupation became clear."[13]

Having fought the "Tommies" on the Western Front, he admired their martial qualities. Nor was Churchill unaware of "Hitler's notorious Anglomania and his almost servile admiration of British imperialism. . . ."[14]

Hitler biographer Alan Bullock summarizes his grand strategy:

In *Mein Kampf* Hitler had written: "For a long time to come there will be only two Powers in Europe with which it may be possible for Germany to conclude an alliance. These Powers are Great Britain and Italy." The greatest blunder of the Kaiser's government—prophetic words—had been to quarrel with Britain and Russia at the same time: Germany's future lay in the east . . . and her natural ally was Great Britain, whose power was colonial, commercial and naval, with no territorial interests on the continent of Europe. "Only by alliance with England was it possible (before 1914) to safeguard the rear of the German crusade. . . . No sacrifice should have been considered too great, if it was a necessary means of gaining England's friendship. Colonial and naval ambitions should have been abandoned."[15]

The dream of an Anglo-German alliance would stay with Hitler even when he was at war with Great Britain:

Even during the war Hitler persisted in believing that an alliance with Germany . . . was in Britain's own interest, continually expressed his regret that the British had been so stupid as not to see this, and never gave up the hope that he would be able to overcome their obstinacy and persuade them to accept his view.[16]

Sir Roy Denman came to the same conclusion:

Hitler . . . had no basic quarrel with Britain. Unlike William II, he had no wish from the outset to rival the British navy, nor covet the British Empire. His territorial aims were in Central and Eastern Europe and further east. He could never understand why the British constantly sought to interfere.[17]

After the British escape at Dunkirk, because of his own "stop order" to his armored units not to advance into the undefended city, Hitler told Martin Bormann he had purposely spared the British army so as not to create "an irreparable breach between the British and ourselves."[18]

"The blood of every single Englishman is too valuable to be shed," Hitler told his friend Frau Troost. "Our two people belong together racially and traditionally—this is and always has been my aim even if our generals can't grasp it."[19]

On June 25, 1940, after the fall of France, Hitler telephoned Goebbels to lay out the terms of a deal with England. Britain's empire was to be preserved, but Britain would return to Lord Salisbury's policy of "splendid isolation" from the power politics of Europe. Here is the entry from Goebbels's diary:

> The Fuhrer . . . believes that the [British Empire] must be preserved if at all possible. For if it collapses, then we shall not inherit it, but foreign and even hostile powers take it over. But if England will have it no other way, then she must be beaten to her knees. The Fuhrer, however, would be agreeable to peace on the following basis: England out of Europe, colonies and mandates returned. Reparations for what was stolen from us after the World War.[20]

What Hitler was demanding after his triumph in the west in 1940 was restoration of what had been taken from Germany at Versailles.

In his postwar book *The Other Side of the Hill*, Liddell Hart relates a conversation Hitler had at Charleville, after Dunkirk, with General von Rundstedt and two of his staff, Sodenstern and Blumentritt. The latter told Liddell Hart the conversation had come around to Great Britain:

> He [Hitler] then astonished us by speaking with admiration of the British Empire, of the necessity for its existence and of the civilisation that Britain had brought into the world. . . . He compared the British Empire with the Catholic Church—saying they were both essential elements of stability in the world. He said that all he wanted from Britain was that she should acknowledge Germany's position on the Continent. The return of Germany's lost colonies would be desirable but not essential, and he would even offer to support Britain with troops if she should be involved in any difficulties anywhere. . . . He concluded by saying that his aim

was to make peace with Britain, on a basis that she would regard compatible with her honour to accept.[21]

As the Battle of Britain was under way, on August 14, 1940, Hitler called his newly created field marshals into the Reich Chancellery to impress upon them that victory over Britain must not lead to a collapse of the British Empire:

> Germany is not striving to smash Britain because the beneficiaries will not be Germany, but Japan in the east, Russia in India, Italy in the Mediterranean, and America in world trade. This is why peace is possible with Britain—but not so long as Churchill is prime minister. Thus we must see what the Luftwaffe can do, and wait a possible general election.[22]

Hitler is here telling his military high command that the air war over England, the Battle of Britain, was not designed to prepare for invasion but to bring down Churchill. From his actions in the west, from 1933 through 1939, there is compelling evidence Hitler wanted to see the British Empire endure. And if he did not wish to bring down the British Empire, how can it be argued that Hitler was out to conquer the world?

Though Hitler had exploited popular clamorings in the Sudetenland, Danzig, and Memel for a return to the Reich, he never stoked the fires of revanchism in the lands Germany lost to the west. Northern Schleswig had gone to Denmark, Eupen and Malmédy to Belgium, Alsace and Lorraine to France. Before September 1939, Hitler offered to guarantee the French-German border. He knew that to try to take back Alsace-Lorraine meant war with France, which meant war with Britain. If the price of a neutral or friendly Britain was giving up German claims to the lands lost to the West at Versailles, Hitler was prepared to pay it.

Well into the war, Hitler held on to his impossible dream of an Anglo-German alliance. To Hitler the British were a superior race and fit partner for the Germans, preferable even to his Asian ally, Japan. Denman retells a story from February of 1942:

> Hitler was returning from Berlin to his East Prussian head-quarters when Ribbentrop made his way along the swaying train with the news that the British had just surrendered Singapore. He had dictated a gloating announcement. Hitler tore it up. "We have to think of centuries," he said. "Who knows, in the future the Yellow Peril may be the biggest one for us."[23]

THE KRIEGSMARINE

IF HITLER ENVISIONED WAR with Britain, he would have built a navy capable of challenging Britain's. He never did.

"The Navy—what need have we of that?" Hitler said in 1936. "I cannot conceive of a war in Europe which will hang in the balance because of a few ships."[24] "When Hitler invaded Poland on 1 September 1939," writes F. H. Hinsley, the history lecturer at Cambridge, in his 1951 book *Hitler's Strategy,*

> Germany was not ready for a major war at sea. The German surface fleet consisted of no more than 2 old battleships, 2 battle-cruisers, 3 pocket battleships, 8 cruisers and 22 destroyers. . . . [O]nly 57 German U-boats had been built by 1939; and only 26 of these were suitable to Atlantic operations. . . . [O]nly 8 or 9 [of these U-boats] could be kept in the Atlantic at a time.[25]

Liddell Hart, who assisted Hinsley with his book, writes:

> [Hitler] did not even build up his Navy to the limited scale visualized in the Anglo-German Naval Treaty of 1935. He

constantly assured his admirals they could discount any risk of war with Britain. After Munich, he told them that they need not anticipate a conflict with Britain in the next six years at least. Even in the summer of 1939, and as late as August 22, he repeated such assurances—if with waning conviction.[26]

A.J.P. Taylor concurs with Hinsley and Liddell Hart. Though a German attack at sea presented a graver threat to Britain's survival than the Luftwaffe, Taylor—with only slightly different statistics—writes:

> Here, too, the Germans were badly prepared. At the outset of war they had only twenty-two ocean-going U-boats and few trained crews. Hitler did not authorize new construction until July 1940 and cut it down again in December when the army prepared to attack Soviet Russia.[27]

Churchill, who had returned as First Lord of the Admiralty, confirms Germany's dearth of sea power to combat the Royal Navy. When war broke out in September 1939, Churchill writes,

> the German navy had only begun their rebuilding and had no power even to form a line of battle. Their two great battleships, *Bismarck* and *Tirpitz*, were at least a year from completion. . . . Thus there was no challenge in surface craft to our command of the seas. . . . Enemy shipping, as in 1914, virtually vanished almost at once from the high seas. The German ships mostly took refuge in neutral ports, or, when intercepted, scuttled themselves.[28]

Hitler's navy was that of a Germany whose ambitions lay on land. Had he ever planned to invade England, he would have built troopships, landing barges, and transports to ferry tanks and artillery across the Channel—and warships to escort his landing craft, provide fire support for the invasion, and keep the Royal Navy out of the Channel while his invasion force was crossing. He did none of this.

LOOKING EASTWARD

THERE IS OTHER EVIDENCE that Hitler never intended to invade Western Europe. Before World War I, the German General Staff had adopted the Schlieffen Plan, which entailed a massive German offensive through Belgium. Because German war strategy was to take the offensive from day one, the Kaiser built no new defensive fortifications to match the great French forts of Toul and Verdun. Hitler, however, for three and a half years after his army entered the Rhineland, invested huge sums and tens of millions of man-hours of labor constructing his West Wall. On September 1, 1939, his engineers were frantically completing it. Asks Taylor: If Hitler was all along planning an invasion of France, why did he, at monstrous cost, build purely defensive fortifications up and down the Rhineland? The Kaiser never built a Siegfried Line, because Moltke's army of 1914 planned to attack on the first day of war.

Even after Britain and France had declared war on Germany, Hitler confided to his inner circle, "[I]f we on our side avoid all acts of war, the whole business will evaporate. As soon as we sink a ship and they have sizable casualties, the war party over there will gain strength."[29] After Poland had surrendered, Hitler, on October 6, 1939, made a "peace offer" to Britain and France; it "was turned down without hesitation."[30]

"Even when German U-boats lay in a favourable position near the battleship *Dunkerque*, he [Hitler] refused to order an attack," wrote Albert Speer.[31] Other strategic decisions make sense only if Hitler's true ambitions lay in the east. After overrunning France, Hitler stopped at the Pyrenees. He asked Franco for passage through Spain to attack Gibraltar. Denied, he abandoned the idea. He did not demand that France turn over its battle fleet, the fourth largest in the world, as Germany had been forced to do in 1918. He did not demand France's North African colonies. He did not demand access to French bases in the Middle East to threaten Suez. He visited Paris, saw the Eiffel Tower, went home, and began to plan the invasion of Russia, preliminary orders for which went out in July 1940—before the Battle of Britain had even begun.

Hitler also issued the "stop order" to his Panzers, letting the British army escape at Dunkirk. His occupation of Britain's Channel Islands was benign compared to the horrors in the east. While Hitler reannexed Alsace and Lorraine after June 1940, the peace terms he imposed on France were more generous than those the Allies had imposed on Germany in 1919. None of this represented magnanimity. In the New Order in Europe, Hitler wanted Marshal Petain as an ally, as he had wanted Colonel Beck as an ally.

On August 10, 1939, three weeks before the attack of Poland, Hitler summoned the League of Nations High Commissioner for Danzig, Dr. Carl Burckhardt, to the Eagle's Nest the next day. Writes Kershaw, this "was a calculated attempt to keep the West out of the coming conflict."[32] Hitler gave Burckhardt this message, intended for British ears:

> Everything that I undertake is directed against Russia; if the West is too stupid and too blind to understand this, then I will be forced to reach an understanding with the Russians, smash the West, and then turn all my concentrated strength against the Soviet Union. I need the Ukraine so that no one can starve us out again as in the last war.[33]

Historian John Lukacs suggests Burckhardt's quotation is suspect. Indeed, it seems incredible that Hitler would reveal his intention to smash the Soviet Union and seize Ukraine to a Swiss diplomat, who would be relating what he had been told as soon as he got down from the Eagle's Nest.[34]

Henry Kissinger, however, cites Burckhardt and writes that this is

> certainly an accurate statement of Hitler's priorities: from
> Great Britain he wanted non-interference in continental
> affairs, and from the Soviet Union he wanted Lebensraum,
> or living space. It was a measure of Stalin's achievement
> that he was [able] to reverse Hitler's priorities, however
> temporarily.[35]

Kissinger might have added, "and a measure of Britain's failure."
American historian W. H. Chamberlin is even more damning of
British diplomacy:

> From every standpoint, military, political and psychological,
> it would have been far more advantageous if Hitler's first
> blows had fallen on Stalin's totalitarian empire, not on
> Britain, France and the small democracies of the West. . . .
> [O]n the basis of available evidence, the failure of Britain
> and France to canalize Hitler's expansion in an eastward di-
> rection may reasonably be considered one of the greatest
> diplomatic failures in history.[36]

Though Bismarck had maintained good relations with Russia, the
Drang nach Osten, or drive to the east, was embedded deep in German
history. While infinitely more savage in the means he employed,
Hitler's *Ostpolitik* did not differ in its ultimate goals from that of Hindenburg and Ludendorff. The lands Hitler coveted were not terra
incognita. They had been occupied by the German army as of
Armistice Day 1918.

Nor had Britain been greatly alarmed in 1918 at German gains in
the east at the expense of Russia. Some Allied statesmen were willing
to let the Kaiser keep his eastern conquests if he would restore the
status quo ante in Belgium and France. In November 1917, after the
Germans and Austrians had broken the Italian lines at Caporetto and

Bolsheviks had seized power in Petrograd and sued for peace, some British statesmen wanted to end the war. They suggested offering the Germans an eastern empire, including Ukraine, if the Kaiser would agree to give up his lost African and Pacific colonies and retire from Belgium and France. Jan Smuts, fearing the war could last until 1920, signed on. In short, British statesmen in 1917 and 1918 were prepared to offer the Kaiser's Germany the same dominance in Eastern Europe they went to war to deny to Hitler's Germany in 1939.[37]

Here, then, is the unwritten bargain Hitler had on offer to Britain in 1939. France and Belgium could keep the lands given to them at Versailles—Malmédy, Eupen, Alsace, and Lorraine. But Germany would take back the German lands and peoples given to the Czechs and Poles in violation of Wilson's principle of self-determination. Germany would concede the democracies' dominance west of the Rhine if they would cease interfering in the east. Why Britain would reject this, Hitler could never understand. He believed a Germany prepared to confront and block Bolshevism should cause rejoicing in the capitalist West.

Thus, when the Allies refused to give Hitler his free hand in the east and threatened war if he moved on Poland, Hitler decided to offer a deal to Stalin. Stalin greedily accepted. Thus the Allies got war, while Stalin got Finland, the Baltic republics, half of Poland, and two years to prepare for the inevitable Nazi attack. Stalin used those two years to build the tanks, planes, and guns, and conscript the troops that stopped Hitler at Leningrad, Moscow, and Stalingrad. Thus did British diplomatic folly succeed only in getting Western Europe overrun and making Eastern Europe safe for Stalinism.

DID HITLER WANT THE WORLD?

HITLER HAD TO BE stopped, it is argued, because he wanted the world. After defeating Russia, he would have turned west, overrun

France, and starved Britain. Then would have come the turn of the United States—and America would have had to face Nazi Germany and Imperial Japan alone. British statesmen believed this. After Czechoslovakia fell to pieces in mid-March 1939 and Hitler motored into Prague to make it a protectorate of the Reich, Chamberlain asked aloud: "Is this in fact a step in the direction of an attempt to dominate the world by force?"[38]

Halifax wrote that "the lust of continental or world mastery seemed to stand out in stark relief."[39] Henderson agreed: "The principles of nationalism and self-determination . . . had been cynically thrown overboard at Prague and world dominion had supplanted them."[40]

But was Hitler's imposition of a German protectorate over a Czech rump state that had belonged to the Austro-Hungarian Empire for the first thirty years of his life really part of a grand strategy for "world mastery," "world dominion," or "domination of the world by force"?

Among British elites of the twentieth century, there was always a streak of Germanophobia, an inordinate fear that Germany was secretly plotting the ruin of the British Empire and the conquest of the world. We see it here in Chamberlain, Halifax, and Henderson, as we saw it in the run-up to World War I in ex–minister for war Haldane: "I thought from my study of the German General Staff that once the German war party had got into the saddle . . . it would be war not merely for the overthrow of France or Russia but for the domination of the world."[41]

On the eve of the war of 1914–1918, Churchill described the Kaiser, who was then casting about desperately for some way to avoid a war, as a "continental tyrant" whose goal was "the dominion of the world."[42]

When Haldane and Churchill claimed the Kaiser was a "continental tyrant" out for "dominion of the world," Wilhelm II was in late middle age, had been in power twenty-five years, and had yet to fight his first war.

In his 1937 *Great Contemporaries*, Churchill exonerates the Kaiser of the charge of which he had accused him before the war of 1914: "[H]istory should incline to the more charitable view and acquit William II of having planned and plotted the World War."[43]

In the same book, Churchill wrote of Hitler, "Whatever else may be thought about these exploits, they are among the most remarkable in the whole history of the world."[44] Churchill was referring not only to Hitler's political achievements, but his economic achievements. Before the end of his fourth year in power, Hitler had ended the Depression, cut unemployment from six million to one million, grown Germany's GNP by 37 percent, and increased auto production from 45,000 vehicles a year to 250,000.[45] City and provincial deficits had disappeared. This success goaded Churchill, before Hitler had ever moved on Austria or Czechoslovakia, to confide to American Gen. Robert Wood, at his flat in London in November 1936, "Germany is getting too strong and we must smash her."[46]

If Hitler was out to conquer the world, the proof cannot be found in the armed forces with which he began the war. As U.S. Maj. Gen. C. F. Robinson wrote in a 1947 report he produced for the U.S. War Department,

> Germany was not prepared in 1939—contrary to democratic assumption—for a long war or for total war; her economic and industrial effort was by no means fully harnessed: her factories were not producing war matériel at anything like full capacity.[47]

WAS AMERICA IN MORTAL PERIL?

IN *A REPUBLIC, NOT AN EMPIRE*, this writer argued that once Göring's Luftwaffe had lost the Battle of Britain, Germany presented no mortal threat to the United States:

If there had been a point of maximum peril for America in the war in Europe it was in the summer of 1940, after France had been overrun and England seemed about to be invaded, with the possible scuttling or loss of the British fleet. But after the Royal Air Force won the Battle of Britain, the invasion threat was history. If Göring's Luftwaffe could not achieve air supremacy over the Channel, how was it going to achieve it over the Atlantic? If Hitler could not put a soldier into England in the fall of 1940, the notion that he could invade the Western Hemisphere—with no surface ships to engage the United States and British fleets, and U.S. air power dominant in the Western Atlantic—was preposterous.[48]

In refutation, *The New Republic* enlisted history professor Jeffrey Herf, who wrote that, even with the victory of the Royal Air Force, America was still in mortal peril. Herf cited as his authority Gerhard Weinberg, the "great historian of Hitler's foreign policy."

In his important essay "Hitler's Image of the United States," Weinberg shows how, after overrunning France in 1940, Hitler's inner circle began planning a Third World War— against the United States. In 1943, Hitler launched a huge battleship-construction program, the "Z Plan," to confront the American Navy. At the same time he set up naval bases on the coasts of France and Africa. In *Tomorrow the World: Hitler, Northwest Africa and the Path Toward America*, Norman Goda further documents Germany's plans to build a massive surface fleet, develop a trans-atlantic bomber, and procure naval bases in French Africa, the Canary Islands, the Azores, and the Cape Verde Islands.[49]

This is comic-book history.
Hitler did order up plans to seize the Canaries, Cape Verdes, and

Azores, but these were to secure a German hold on Gibraltar, which Hitler never took, as General Franco never gave his army permission to cross Spain.

If Hitler's "inner circle" was planning to "confront the American Navy," why did Hitler not demand that the French turn over their fleet to Admiral Raeder at France's surrender in June 1940? The Germans had been forced to turn over the High Seas Fleet after the armistice of 1918. Yet when Churchill ordered "Catapult," to secure or sink the French fleet lest it fall into Nazi hands, the French warships were at anchor at Toulon, Alexandria, Dakar—and Mers el-Kebir, where they were sunk by the Royal Navy. Throughout the war, the U.S. Navy did not encounter a single German surface warship. Yet Herf claims the Nazis came close to having "open season . . . on the harbors and cities of the East Coast."[50]

And if Hitler was contemplating building battleships in 1943, he was contemplating a fleet for Jutland, not World War II. As of 1943, Germany had sent two battleships to sea, *Bismarck*, sunk on her maiden voyage, and *Tirpitz*, then hiding in Norwegian fjords. By 1943, the battleship era was over and the carrier era had begun. At Midway, in June 1942, in one of the decisive sea battles of history, the U.S. Navy sank *Hiryu*, *Soryu*, *Akagi*, and *Kaga*, the four carriers that were the heart of the Imperial Japanese Fleet's strike force, without seeing them, except from the cockpits of U.S. torpedo- and dive-bombers. By war's end, the United States had scores of aircraft carriers with combat experience at Leyte Gulf and the Battle of the Philippine Sea. Of Hitler's Z Plan, Roger Chesneau writes in his authoritative *Aircraft Carriers*:

> The celebrated "Z-Plan" envisaged a fleet of four carriers in service by the late 1940s, but a lack of enthusiasm by the Luftwaffe (who would operate the aircraft) and, as time passed, the decision to divert production and resources to more immediate needs meant that none was commissioned.[51]

Denman dates the launching of the Z Plan to the end of 1938 and its scrapping, due to the demands of the other services, to September 1939, when the war began.[52]

The Germans did attempt to construct two aircraft carriers, the *Graf Zeppelin* and the *Peter Strasser.* However, the German "pilots had no experience of shipboard operating procedure and, of course, there were no specialized carrier aircraft."[53]

> Work on both carriers was suspended in mid-1940 because of the demands of the submarine programme; the second ship, apparently to have been named *Peter Strasser,* was still on the slip at the Germaniawerft yard at Kiel and was immediately scrapped, but *Graf Zeppelin* was resumed in 1942. . . . [B]y early 1943 she was languishing again. She was scuttled at Stettin by the Germans a few months before the end of the war and although taken over and raised by the Russians, she was lost under tow to Leningrad in August or September 1947.[54]

Thus concludes Chesneau's two-page history of the Hitler carrier force that was to threaten the American homeland. Had Hitler pursued the plan, by the mid-1940s four carriers manned by inexperienced German sailors would have been child's play for a U.S. Navy of more than a thousand warships.

In 1942, the year Herf says Germany "set up naval bases" in Africa, U.S. troops invaded North Africa and, by spring 1943, occupied it from Morocco to Tunisia. And as the Azores and Cape Verde Islands belonged to Portugal and the Canary Islands to Spain, whose dictator Franco had denied Hitler passage to Gibraltar in 1940, how was Germany to seize these islands, build these bases, and construct those huge ships under the gunsights of the U.S. Navy and the British battle fleets that had dominated the Atlantic since Trafalgar?

THE NEW YORK BOMBER

WHAT OF HISTORIAN GODA'S transatlantic bomber, also mentioned by *Washington Post* columnist Michael Kelly, who wrote, "[I]n 1939 and 1940 [Hitler] ordered up . . . the Messerschmitt 264 the Nazis called the 'Amerika-bomber'—intended for that war"?[55] This super-bomber also appears in Weinberg:

> [S]pecifications were issued in 1937 and 1938 for what became the ME-264 and was soon referred to inside the government as the "America-Bomber" or the "New York Bomber." Capable of carrying a five-ton load of bombs to New York, a smaller load to the Middle West, or reconnaissance missions over the West Coast and then returning to Germany without intermediate bases, such long-range planes would bring Germany's new air force directly into the skies over America.[56]

Now, this is a remarkable plane. But, intending no disrespect to the professor, even today the U.S. Air Force does not have a bomber that can fly from Germany to our Midwest and West Coast, loiter about, and return to Germany without refueling. And air-to-air refueling had not been invented in the 1940s. German bombers flew at less than three hundred miles per hour. A trip over the Atlantic and back would require twenty hours of flying to drop a five-ton load on New York. A trip from Germany to the West Coast and back is twelve thousand miles—a forty-hour flight. How this flying fuel tank, without a fighter escort, was to survive its encounters with British and U.S. fighters on a daylong voyage across the Atlantic to the U.S. mainland and back was unexplained.

Throughout the war, writes military historian Bernard Nalty, "the Luftwaffe . . . lacked a four-engine heavy bomber. . . . Germany had not yet developed aerial engines efficient enough for a heavy bomber."[57]

The Dorniers and Heinkels that bombed London and Coventry were two-engine planes built for close air support. The Americans and British, not the Germans, studied the lessons of the Italian evangelist of airpower, Giulio Douhet, who had argued that future fleets of heavy bombers would fight their way through to enemy cities and destroy the people's will to resist. U.S. B-29s killed more civilians in one raid over Tokyo than the Luftwaffe killed in Britain in the entire war. Throughout the war, not one German bomb fell on North or South America.

"The world greatly overestimated Germany's [air] strength," the United States Bombing Survey concluded in 1946.[58] When the war began, German bombers lacked the range even to reach London. Writes one historian of airpower:

The Luftwaffe was a failure. Despite its early victories, the German air force proved unable to retain control of the air over Europe and after five years of war it lay broken. The importance of this failure is too often overlooked. It was, however, immense. . . .

[The] Luftwaffe was regarded primarily as an offensive, tactical weapon. This was the fatal error. Strategic bombing and fighter defence were developed too little, too late and with too much muddle. More than any other single factor, the failure of the Luftwaffe contributed to the eventual defeat of the Third Reich.[59]

British air marshal Arthur Harris of Bomber Command concurred in this assessment of the Luftwaffe:

The Germans had allowed their soldiers to dictate the whole policy of the Luftwaffe, which was designed expressly to assist the army in rapid advances. . . . Much too late in the day they saw the advantage of a strategic bombing force. . . . In

September, 1940, the Germans found themselves with almost unarmed bombers, so that in the Battle of Britain, the destruction of the German bomber squadrons was very similar to shooting cows in a field.[60]

Famed American geostrategist Robert Strausz-Hupé is dismissive of those who claim Hitler represented a grave military threat to the United States:

> Hitler could . . . count upon at least 1,000 aircraft assigned to tactical units. But this air force was too weak to blast Britain into submission, and the German Navy was not strong enough to insure a landing of sufficient German troops to conquer the poorly prepared British isles. Without a chance of defeating Britain, "let alone the British Empire, Germany could not win the war."[61]

When the Battle of Britain began in early August 1940, writes Niall Ferguson, the British had a narrow edge in fighter planes over the Luftwaffe, but many more trained pilots. As the battle raged, the Brits shot down German planes at a rate of two-to-one, while British factories churned out 1,900 new Hurricanes and Spitfires to 775 produced by the factories of Marshal Göring.[62]

In *The Luftwaffe*, James Corum chides Professor Weinberg for his failure to understand the purposes and capabilities of the Luftwaffe:

> Even as distinguished a historian as Gerhard Weinberg refers to the bombing of Guernica and Rotterdam as Nazi "terror bombing." In fact, the Luftwaffe did not have a policy of terror bombing civilians as part of its doctrine prior to World War II. . . . Guernica in 1937 and Rotterdam in 1940 were bombed for tactical military reasons in support of military operations. Civilians were certainly killed in both inci-

dents, but in neither case was that the goal or intent of the bombing. Indeed, the Luftwaffe specifically rejected the concept of terror bombing in the interwar period.[63]

Early in the war, the Luftwaffe did manage to convert the Focke Wulf Condor, a four-engine Lufthansa airliner, into a naval bomber, and thirty of these converted planes did succeed in sinking eighty-five Allied vessels.[64]

Was Germany ever a direct military threat to the United States?

Consider: In early spring 1917, the United States had the seventeenth-largest army on earth. By late 1918, America had two million men in France and two million more ready to go. As John Eisenhower writes in *Yanks: The Epic Story of the American Army in World War I*, "From a force of only 200,000 officers and men of the Regular Army and National Guard in April 1917, America had raised an army of over four million of whom about half had crossed the Atlantic."[65] No other nation on earth could have done that.

Even before Pearl Harbor, as Ike's grandson David wrote in his highly acclaimed *Eisenhower at War: 1943–1945*, U.S. Navy admirals and Army generals had formulated a Victory Program that would brush the British aside and "practically go it alone in Europe by mobilizing a massive force of 210 divisions backed by huge fleets of ships and aircraft."[66]

Historians search Nazi archives in vain for plans to dispatch armies to Canada or Latin America to attack the United States. There are no known German plans to acquire the thousand ships needed to convey and convoy such an army and its artillery, tanks, planes, guns, munitions, equipment, fuel, and food across the Atlantic. Or to resupply such an army. During the war, the Nazis managed to get eight spies ashore on Long Island and Florida by submarine. They were rounded up and secretly tried, and six of them executed within a month.

When FDR warned of a Hitler master plan to conquer South and

Central America and divide it into five Nazi-controlled regions, he was spouting British propaganda cooked up in the skunk works of William Stephenson, *The Man Called Intrepid*, sent by Churchill to do whatever was necessary to bring America into the war. "Even after Nazi archives were sacked," writes W. H. Chamberlin, "no concrete evidence of any plan to invade the Western Hemisphere was discovered, although loose assertions of such plans were repeated so often before and during the war that some Americans were probably led to believe in the reality of this nonexistent design."[67]

NAZISM AND COMMUNISM

BUT WHAT OF NAZI IDEOLOGY? In its rejection of the dignity of man and the evil of its deeds, it is comparable to Stalinism. And John Lukacs argues that Nazism and Hitler were not only as evil, but a far greater threat to the West. Citing Churchill's speech of June 18, 1940, that should England fall as France had, "the whole world, including the United States . . . will sink into the abyss of a New Dark Age," Lukacs writes:

> Churchill understood something that not many people understand even now. The greatest threat to western civilization was not Communism. It was National Socialism. The greatest and most dynamic power in the world was not Soviet Russia. It was the Third Reich of Germany. The greatest revolutionary leader of the twentieth century was not Lenin or Stalin. It was Hitler.[68]

This, surely, is debatable. For Hitler never remotely represented the strategic threat to the U.S. homeland that a nuclear-armed Russia did during forty years of Cold War. Lukacs seems to concede the point in *Five Days*. "Against America," he wrote, Hitler "could do nothing."[69]

In U.S. cultural and intellectual circles, communism had immense appeal. The Roosevelt administration was honeycombed with Soviet spies, Communists, and collaborators. Had Henry Wallace been retained as vice president in 1944 and become president on FDR's death, his treasury secretary might have been Harry Dexter White and his secretary of state Lawrence Duggan, both closet Communists and Soviet agents.

As an ideology, Nazism was handicapped by the narrowness of its appeal. It was not even an ideology of white supremacy—Hitler was prepared to turn Slavs into serfs—but of "Aryan" supremacy. Communism appealed to peoples of all colors and continents who wished to throw off the yoke of colonialism and bring an end to European domination. It offered all mankind a vision of a paradise on earth. Outside of Great Britain, Hitler was among the last unabashed admirers of the British Empire.

In Hollywood, communism made such inroads by the late-1930s that anti-Communist films could not be made and pro-Soviet films were routinely turned out. Hitler's rabid anti-Semitism meant Nazism was dead on arrival. Compared to the Communist Party and its fellow travelers the German-American Bund and Silver Shirts were an insignificant force—regularly thrown out of America First rallies. To Americans, Hitler and Mussolini were figures of Chaplinesque ridicule. Lenin, Stalin, and Trotsky all had acolytes and admirers in government, in the press, and on the faculties and within the student bodies of America's elite colleges and universities.

As Yale scholar and historian Bruce Russett wrote, "Nazism as an ideology was almost certainly less dangerous to the United States than is Communism. Marxism-Leninism has a worldwide appeal; Nazism lacks much palatability to non-Aryan tastes."[70]

Moreover, while Hitler believed in the superiority and salvific power of Nazi ideology for Germany, he did not believe in imposing it or exporting it to the West. In May 1942, he admonished his comrades:

I am firmly opposed to any attempt to export National Socialism. If other countries are determined to preserve their democratic systems and thus rush to their ruin, so much the better for us. And all the more so, because during this same period, thanks to National Socialism, we shall be transforming ourselves, slowly but surely, into the most solid popular community that it is possible to imagine.[71]

Stalin believed in ruthlessly imposing communism on all subject lands and peoples. "This war is not as in the past," Stalin explained to Yugoslav Communist leader Milovan Djilas in 1945, "whoever occupies a territory also imposes his own social system. . . . It cannot be otherwise."[72]

From Béla Kun in Budapest in 1919 to Fidel Castro in Cuba in 1959, Communists followed Stalin's rule. But by its nature, nationalism, especially a virulent strain like Nazism, is difficult to export. When Britain went to war, Oswald Mosley, the head of the British Union of Fascists, volunteered at once to fight for Britain.

Lukacs is right that Hitler, like Lenin, was both revolutionary and ruler, architect and dictator of the state he created. But no one in Hitler's entourage could sustain his ideology. Like Fascism, Nazism could not long survive the death of the messiah. But the Soviet state was built to last. It was a far more formidable regime, for it was rooted in something more enduring than the charisma of a fanatic but mortal man.

This is not to minimize the magnetic appeal of Hitler and his "New Germany" to millions of disoriented souls disillusioned with democracy after the Great War, Versailles, and the Great Depression. As Taylor writes:

Though the National Socialists did not win a majority of votes at any free general election, they won more votes than any other German party had ever done. A few months after coming to power they received practically all the votes recorded. . . . No dictatorship has been so ardently desired or so firmly supported by so many people as Hitler's was in Germany. . . . [T]he most evil system of modern times was also the most popular.[73]

Hitler also had imitators in Europe, Latin America, and among Arab leaders who shared his hatred of the Jews. But as Arnold Beichman of the Hoover Institution writes, "[F]ascism, as a concept, has no intellectual basis at all nor did its founders even pretend to have any. Hitler's ravings in *Mein Kampf*. . . Mussolini's boastful balcony speeches, all of these can be described in the words of Roger Scruton, as an 'amalgam of disparate conceptions.' "[74]

Historian Richard Pipes believes that Stalinism and Hitlerism were siblings of the same birth mother: "Bolshevism and Fascism were heresies of socialism."[75]

On which was the greater danger, Nazism or communism, Robert Taft, speaking after Hitler's invasion of Russia, seems close to the mark:

It Hitler wins, it is a victory for Fascism. If Stalin wins, it is a victory for communism. From the point of view of ideology there is no choice.

But the victory of communism would be far more dangerous for the United States than the victory of Fascism. There has never been the slightest danger that the people in this country would ever embrace bundism or nazism. . . . But communism masquerades, often successfully, under the guise of democracy, though it is just as alien to our principles as nazism itself. It is a greater danger to the United States because it is a false philosophy which appeals to many. Fascism is a false philosophy which appeals to very few.[76]

British historian Hugh Trevor-Roper, writing of the ideological threat of Hitler, seems to agree with Taft:

Even the war with the West was secondary [to Hitler]. Long ago he had formulated his attitude toward the West. The West, in spite of its victory in 1918—achieved only through the famous "Stab in the Back"—and though still powerful at this crucial moment, was, when seen in the long perspective of history, clearly in decline. It could be left to decline. Fundamentally, Hitler had no interest in it.[77]

The Taft and Trevor-Roper position raises a central question. If Hitler's ambitions were in the east, and he was prepared to respect Britain's vital interests by leaving the Low Countries and France alone, was it wise to declare war on Germany—over a Poland that Britain could not save?

As we learned after Hitler's death, Nazism's roots were shallow and easily pulled up. But Marxist beliefs and ideology—even after the failure and collapse of the Soviet state—retain a hold on the minds of men and reappear constantly in new mutations.

None of this is to minimize the evil of Nazi ideology, or the capabilities of the Nazi war machine, or the despicable crimes of Hitler's regime, or the potential threat of Nazi Germany to Great Britain once war was declared. Had Hitler invested in submarines and magnetic mines instead of *Bismarck* and *Tirpitz*, had he built fleets of four-engine bombers that could have attacked British ports and the docks and ships on which Britain depended for survival, Hitler could have forced the British to sue for peace. But Germany could not defeat the Royal Navy, the Dominions, or the United States. Nazi Germany was a land power, not a sea power, a continental power, not a world power. In the end, the Germans defeated but a single major power, France. Unlike Napoleon, Hitler would never take Egypt, never sleep in Moscow, never occupy Spain.

Though he spoke of world domination, Germany, the size of Oregon and Washington, was too small to swallow Russia, the British Empire, the United States, Latin America, Africa, the Middle East, and Asia. German soldiers, artillery, and tanks were among the best in the world, but the British Spitfires proved a match for Göring's Messerschmitts, and the Luftwaffe bomber force never rivaled Bomber Command, let alone the monster air fleets of "Hap" Arnold and Curtis LeMay. By December 1939, Britain was producing more planes and America, with many times the productive power of Germany, had not begun to move its weight into the balance. When it did, Hitler was finished.

As for Hitler's vast military buildup, which could only mean a war for the world, this, too, writes A.J.P. Taylor, is a myth:

> In 1938–39, the last peacetime year, Germany spent on armaments about 15% of her gross national product. The British proportion was almost exactly the same. German expenditure on armaments was actually cut down after Munich and remained at this lower level, so that British production of aeroplanes, for example, was way ahead of German by 1940. When war broke out in 1939, Germany had 1450 modern fighter planes and 800 bombers, Great Britain and France had 950 fighters and 1300 bombers. The Germans had 3500 tanks; Great Britain and France had 3850. In each case Allied intelligence estimated German strength at more than twice the true figure. As usual, Hitler was thought to have planned and prepared for a great war. In fact, he had not.[78]

David Calleo agrees with Taylor. Before the war began, Hitler had never put the economy on a war footing. While he did rearm,

> [Hitler] greatly exaggerated the extent of rearmament to his contemporaries and was careful not to curtail civilian consumption. As a result, Germany was surprisingly unready for a long war. Indeed, not until 1943 was the economy fully mobilized. Hitler . . . apparently gambled on blitzkrieg.[79]

On May 16, 1940, as the Germans were breaking through in the Ardennes, FDR delivered a radio address calling on America to produce fifty thousand planes a year. In 1939, U.S. capacity, due to foreign orders, had expanded from nearly six thousand planes a year to more than double that. As a potential military power, the United States was of a different order of magnitude from Britain or Germany. Only Stalin's immense and populous Soviet Union possessed anything like America's latent power.

In the summer of 1941, as his Panzers sliced through the Red Army on the road to Leningrad, Moscow, and the Caucasus, Hitler did muse over eliminating Russia, driving into the Middle East, linking up with Japan on the trans-Siberian railway or in India, even a final assault on the United States. But, four weeks after Pearl Harbor, Hitler had awakened from his reveries and confided to the Japanese ambassador that he did "not yet" know "how America could be defeated."[80]

On January 10, 1942, with Britain isolated, his armies deep inside Russia, Hitler confided, "Confronted with America, the best we can do is hold out against her to the end."[81] General Alfred Jodl would testify shortly after the Nazi surrender that from "the high point of the start of 1942," Hitler realized "victory was no longer attainable."[82]

On January 27, 1942, with the Americans holed up on Bataan, Hitler was absorbed in self-pity: "Here, too, I am ice cold. If the German people are not prepared to stand up for their own preservation, fine. Then they should perish."[83] Seven weeks after Pearl Harbor, Hitler had begun to contemplate the annihilation of the Third Reich.

CHAPTER 14

Man of the Century

I DO NOT CARE so much for the principles I advocate as for the impression which my words produce and the reputation they give me.[1]

— WINSTON CHURCHILL, 1898

Winston has no principles.[2]

— JOHN MORLEY, 1908
Cabinet Colleague

Churchill will write his name in history; take care that he does not write it in blood.[3]

— A. G. GARDINER, 1913
Pillars of Society

As THE TWENTIETH CENTURY ended, a debate ensued over who had been its greatest man. The *Weekly Standard* nominee was Churchill. Not only was he Man of the Century, said scholar Harry Jaffa, he was the Man of Many Centuries.[4] To Kissinger he was "the quintessential hero." A BBC poll of a million people in 2002 found that Britons considered Churchill the "greatest Briton of all time."

His life was surely among the most extraordinary, his youth full of those "crowded hours" of which Theodore Roosevelt spoke after San Juan Hill. He came under fire as a correspondent attached to the

Spanish army in Cuba, fought with the Malakind Field Force in India, rode in the last cavalry charge of the Empire at Omdurman, was taken prisoner in the Boer War, escaped to march to the relief of Ladysmith and capture of Pretoria, wrote bestselling books about his war experiences, became an international celebrity, and entered Parliament at twenty-six. At thirty-six, he was First Lord of the Admiralty, where his was the most powerful voice in the Cabinet for war. "Winston, who has got on all his war paint, is longing for a sea fight in the early hours of tomorrow morning," wrote Asquith on August 4, 1914, for Britain the first day of the Great War, "the whole thing fills me with sadness."[5]

Cashiered after the Dardanelles disaster, Churchill went to France to fight and returned as Minister for War and Air in Lloyd George's Cabinet. He would participate in all the great decisions, become the dominant British leader of the twentieth century, the most famous of all prime ministers. His six-volume history of World War II would win him the Nobel Prize for Literature, besting Hemingway. Few statesmen have approached his mastery of the language. His conversation and speeches sparkle with wit, insight, and brilliance. One biographer titled his book on Churchill simply *The Great Man*. But what was the legacy of the most famous of all British statesmen?

THE ARMORED TRAIN

IT WAS THE BOER WAR that made Churchill famous and revealed the qualities that would make him both admired and distrusted all his life.

Sailing to South Africa as a correspondent for the *Morning Post*, Churchill was anxious to see a battle up close. With 150 soldiers in three trucks, attached in front of and behind the engine, Churchill rode an armored train north to scout out Boer-infested territory south of the besieged town of Ladysmith in Natal. Historian Thomas Pakenham relates:

> The patrols were made by armored train, unaccompanied by mounted troops. It was a parody of modern mobile war: an innovation that was already obsolete. Imprisoned on its vulnerable railway line, the armored train was as helpless against field-guns in the veld as a naval dreadnought sent into battle with its rudder jammed.[6]

As the train chugged north, Churchill observed Boers on horseback, observing him. The Boers let the train pass, then piled rocks onto the tracks. Farther north, the train drew fire from a Boer field gun. Immediately, it went into reverse and roared back down the tracks, slamming into the rocks. The trucks were derailed and Boer sharpshooters with Mausers and a field piece began to pour fire into the British. Churchill helped clear the tracks to enable the engine to flee south with fifty survivors, mostly wounded. He, along with fifty-eight other British, were forced to surrender—a debacle and a humiliation for the British army. The Boers had suffered only four wounded.

Churchill was imprisoned in Pretoria, escaped, and returned to South Africa. Few incidents in his young life are more instructive in understanding the future leader Churchill would become.

Gen. Redvers Buller, the commander in South Africa, described the operation as one of "inconceivable stupidity."[7] And Churchill, more than any other, had apparently been responsible. Writes Pakenham:

> [I]t was Churchill's burning desire to see a battle, it appears, that helped persuade the officer commanding the armoured train, Churchill's unfortunate friend, Captain Aylmer Haldane, not to turn back when they first saw the signs of Botha's trap on their journey northwards.[8]

Churchill would embellish the story, contending he had been taken prisoner by the Boer general and future prime minister Louis Botha himself. But when he returned to South Africa, Churchill gave Major General Hildyard "a damning account," admitting they had run "confidently on to within range of the Boers, being unaware they had guns with them and hoping to give them a lesson." To John Atkins of the *Manchester Guardian*, Churchill blurted that the Boers had rounded them all up "like cattle. The greatest indignity of my life."[9]

Of the British colonial army it was said that it exhibited a courage that was matched only by stupidity. In the armored train incident, Churchill had shown both reckless daring and dismal judgment. Both would mark his long career. Yet when his own depiction of the incident and his escape ran in the British press, he became an international figure and returned home one of the most famous young men in the world. Before his twenty-sixth birthday, Churchill was elected to Parliament, where he would remain, with two brief interludes, for sixty-four years.

As we have seen, Churchill defected to the Liberal Party in 1904, on the eve of its ascendancy, and was rewarded with the Cabinet posts of Home Secretary and First Lord of the Admiralty. In *The Strange Death of Liberal England*, George Dangerfield described the young Cabinet minister Winston Churchill thus:

> By nature flamboyant, insolent in his bearing, impatient in his mind, and Tory in his deepest convictions, he was a curious person to be found holding a responsible position in the Liberal Party, and few men could have been more distrusted, or have taken a more curious pleasure in being distrusted.[10]

Even his devoted friend, Asquith's daughter, Lady Violet Bonham Carter, said of him, "Winston was very unpopular. . . . The Liberals regarded him as an arriviste and a thruster—and the Conservatives as a deserter, a rat and a traitor to his class."[11]

A parliamentary colleague once rose to complain that Churchill "walks in, makes his speech, walks out, and leaves the whole place as if God almighty had spoken . . . He never listens to any man's speech but his own."[12] "The comment," writes Lynne Olson, a chronicler of Churchill's rise to prime minister, "received loud cheers from both sides of the chamber."[13]

Few denied his brilliance, many questioned his judgment.

In 1916, Churchill, out of the admiralty, challenged the adequacy of the naval building program in the House of Commons, then suggested that Admiral Sir John Fisher, gone since the Dardanelles disaster, and watching from the balcony, be recalled. "[T]he following day," writes one biographer, "Balfour tore Churchill apart by contrasting his previous statements about Fisher's failure to support him with his current praise for his gifts."[14]

Then it was that Lloyd George said of him, "Poor Winston. . . . A brilliant fellow without judgment which is adequate to his fiery impulse. His steering gear is too weak for his horse-power."[15]

When Baldwin began his third premiership, in 1935, Churchill, though he had served in Baldwin's second cabinet as Chancellor of the Exchequer from 1924 to 1929, was not recalled. Why was he excluded by Baldwin? Though all conceded his extraordinary gifts, Churchill was seen as a man of erratic judgment.

His decision as Chancellor to return Britain to the gold standard had proved a disaster. It overvalued British exports, pricing them out of foreign markets. This helped to bring on the General Strike of 1926, advancing the Depression and bringing down the Baldwin government in 1929. The gold decision won for Winston the title role in Keynes's sequel to *The Economic Consequences of the Peace*. Keynes titled it *The Economic Consequences of Mr. Churchill.*

In January 1931, Churchill resigned from the shadow cabinet in furious opposition to his party's support for self-government for India. "Churchill's resignation and his invective-filled campaign against the government over India were major factors in his future exclusion from any high posts in the Baldwin and Chamberlain administrations."[16]

In the debate over India Churchill seemed at times "almost demented with fury," noted one government supporter. He launched bitter personal attacks against Baldwin . . . and his rhetorical assaults on India and those seeking its independence were extreme, even poisonous. Hindus, he declared were a "foul race protected by their pollution from the doom that is their due."[17]

When Gandhi, after release from prison, met the viceroy at his palace in Delhi, Churchill exploded on the floor of the Commons:

It is alarming and almost nauseating to see Mr. Gandhi, a seditious Middle Temple lawyer, now posing as a fakir of the type well-known in the East, striding half-naked up the steps of the Vice-regal palace, while he is still organizing and conducting a defiant campaign of civil disobedience, to parlay on equal terms with the representative of the King-Emperor.[18]

"Such a spectacle," said Churchill, "can only increase the unrest in India and the danger to which white people have been exposed."[19] To grant independence to India, Churchill went on, would constitute a "crime against civilisation" and a "catastrophe which will shake the world."[20] Invective of a high order, but unworthy of a statesman.

His last-ditch defense of Edward VIII in the abdication crisis over the king's determination to marry the twice-divorced Mrs. Simpson reinforced the impression of wretched judgment. Churchill urged Edward to hold on to his throne, and, on December 7, 1936, "filled with emotion and brandy," he implored the Commons not to rush to judgment, only to be shouted down by a hostile House.[21]

Robert Boothby, the personal assistant to Churchill as Chancellor, who looked to him to lead the Conservatives who wished to stand up to the dictators, wrote Churchill, after his five-minute disaster, "What happened this afternoon makes me feel that it is almost impossible for those who are most devoted to you personally to follow you blindly . . . in politics. Because they cannot be sure where the hell they are going to be landed next."[22]

Another acolyte agreed. This abdication crisis, wrote Harold Macmillan, "undermined the reputation and political stature of the greatest and most prescient statesman then living."[23]

Baldwin merrily confided to friends that he would like to say of Churchill on the floor of the House:

When Winston was born, lots of fairies swooped down on his cradle with gifts—imagination, eloquence, industry, ability—and then a fairy came who said, "No one person has a right to so many gifts," picked him up and gave him such a shake and twist that with all his gifts he was denied judgment and wisdom. And that is why while we delight to listen to him in this House we do not take his advice.[24]

Churchill would never forgive Baldwin for leaving him out of his last Cabinet. Asked to pen a tribute on Baldwin's eightieth birthday in 1947, the world-famous Churchill came up with the line "It would have been better for our country if he had never lived."[25] It was not used at the Baldwin tribute.

Chamberlain, who succeeded Baldwin in 1937, "had a similar view and, moreover, feared that Churchill would demand excessive spending for defense and make jingoistic speeches offending foreign governments."[26]

In November 1938, when Churchill asked for a vote on setting up a Ministry of Supply, only to be humiliated when almost no one supported him, Chamberlain jabbed the needle in. Echoing Baldwin, the prime minister observed to laughter from the House:

I have the greatest admiration for my right hon. Friend's many brilliant qualities. He shines in every direction . . .

[but] if I were asked whether judgment is the first of my right hon. Friend's many admirable qualities, I should have to ask the House of Commons not to press me too far.[27]

"The shaft went home because it corresponded so closely with the view many Conservatives had of Churchill," writes biographer John Charmley.[28]

Yet to call these the "wilderness years" of Winston Churchill is hyperbole. Churchill remained in Parliament throughout and was, the prime minister excepted, the most famous political figure in Britain, with an entourage and following not unlike that of an opposition leader.

FINEST HOUR

WHAT MAKES CHURCHILL the Man of the Century?

Comes the reply: He was the indispensable man who saved Western civilization. Without Churchill, Britain might have accepted an armistice or sued for peace in 1940. The war in the west would have been over. Hitler, victorious, would have turned on Russia and crushed her, and the world would have been at his feet. By standing alone from June 1940 to June 1941, the British bulldog held on until Hitler committed his fatal blunders—invading the Soviet Union and declaring war on the United States. These decisions sealed his doom. But without Churchill's heroic refusal to accept any peace or armistice, Hitler would have won the war and the world.

Churchill's claim to be Man of the Century rests on a single year: 1940. Assuming power as the German invasion of France began on May 10, he presided over the miraculous evacuation of Dunkirk and the Battle of Britain, as Fighter Command defended the island in one of the more stirring battles of the century. Magnificent it was, and, in that hour, it was the good fortune of Churchill to have been chosen by destiny to give the British lion its roar. Asked what year he would like to live over again, Churchill replied, "1940 every time, every time."²⁹ He was the man of destiny who inspired Britain to keep fighting until the New World came to the rescue of the Old.

In *Five Days in London: May 1940*, John Lukacs reveals that Churchill did entertain the idea of a negotiated peace in the last hours before Dunkirk. Lukacs describes the situation in the War Cabinet meeting on May 26, when Foreign Secretary Halifax "no longer wished merely to state his views; now he wanted to extract a commitment from Churchill."³⁰

Halifax recounted how he put the proposition to Churchill:

> We had to face the fact that it was not so much now a question of imposing a complete defeat on Germany but of safeguarding the independence of our Empire. . . . We should naturally be prepared to consider any proposals which might lead to this, provided our liberty and independence were assured. . . . If he [Churchill] was satisfied that matters vital to the independence of this country were unaffected, (would he be) prepared to discuss such terms?³¹

Here, Lukacs writes, is how Churchill answered Halifax:

> At this juncture Churchill knew that he could not answer with a categorical no. He said that he "would be thankful to get out of our present difficulties on such terms, provided we retained the essentials and the elements of our vital strength, even at the cost of some territory"—an extraordinary admission.³²

Churchill thus considered a negotiated peace with Nazi Germany. He considered ceding some imperial territory if Britain's independence could be assured and the essentials of the empire preserved. These would include the Royal Navy. Chamberlain, who sat between Halifax and Churchill at the Cabinet meeting, recalled in his diary Churchill's response to Halifax's suggestion that they negotiate with Hitler through Mussolini, who had not yet entered the war:

The P.M. [Churchill] disliked any move toward Musso. It was incredible that Hitler would consent to any terms that we could accept—though if we could get out of this jam by giving up Malta & Gibraltar & some African colonies he would jump at it. But the only safe way was to convince Hitler that he couldn't beat us. . . . I [Chamberlain] supported this view.[33]

In the War Cabinet meeting of May 28, 1940, Churchill gave his final rebuke to those who held out hope for a negotiated peace with Germany: "The Germans would demand our Fleet . . . our naval bases and much else. We should become a slave state."[34]

"This was surely right," Niall Ferguson wrote in 2006.[35] But was it?

Where is the evidence that Hitler intended to demand the British fleet, when he did not demand the French fleet? Where is the evidence he sought to make Britain a "slave state"? As we saw in the last chapter, in June 1940, at the apex of his power after France's surrender and the British evacuation, Hitler wanted the British Empire to survive and endure. He wanted to end the war.

Lukacs contends that even had Churchill entertained the idea of a negotiated peace, he resisted the temptation and became the indispensable man who made the decision to fight on. Lukacs's point seems indisputable. Churchill held on until the Soviet Union was invaded and Hitler declared war on the United States, the decisions that would bring Hitler and his regime down in fiery ruin.

INDISPENSABLE MAN

WAS CHURCHILL TRULY THE indispensable man in Hitler's defeat?

F. H. Hinsley, whose 1951 *Hitler's Strategy* relies heavily on Hitler's war directives and conversations with Adm. Erich Raeder, documents the case convincingly.

As we have seen, after the British guarantee to Poland, Hitler came to believe that he would have to fight for Danzig. But he did not want war with Britain. Among the reasons Hitler struck his pact with Stalin was to convince the British that the fate of Poland was sealed. But when Chamberlain reaffirmed his war guarantee to Poland on August 24, a stunned Hitler, his diplomatic coup having failed, called off the invasion scheduled for the twenty-fifth.

In the days before September 1, Hitler sought to give Britain a way out of its guarantee by offering a negotiated solution to the Danzig crisis if Warsaw would send a plenipotentiary in twenty-four hours to Berlin. Henderson believed the offer was sincere. Whether it was or not, it showed that Hitler desperately wanted to avoid war with Great Britain.

In his directive of August 31 ordering the invasion of Poland, Hitler instructed his army not to cross any western frontier, his navy not to attack any Allied ships, and his Luftwaffe not to fire on any Allied plane, except in defense of the Fatherland.

After Warsaw fell, "Hitler made peace overtures to London and Paris on 6 October. These overtures were rejected on 12 October."[36] After the fall of France in June 1940, Hitler again took the initiative to end the war:

> On 19 July, he delivered, at last, a direct appeal; he had previously hoped that Great Britain would need no prompting. "In this hour," he declared in a speech to the Reichstag, "I feel it to be my duty before my own conscience to appeal once more to reason and common sense in Great Britain. . . . I can see no reason why this war need go on. . . ." The speech was followed by diplomatic approaches to [Britain] through Sweden, the United States and the Vatican.[37]

"There is no doubt that Hitler was anxious for the result and serious in the attempt," writes Hinsley. " 'A speedy termination of the War,' he told Raeder on July 21, 'is in the interests of the German people.' "[38]

Alan Clark, defense aide to Margaret Thatcher, believes that only Churchill's "single-minded determination to keep the war going," his "obsession" with Hitler, prevented his accepting Germany's offer to end the war in 1940.

> There were several occasions when a rational leader could have got, first reasonable, then excellent terms from Germany. Hitler actually offered peace in July 1940 before the Battle of Britain started. After the RAF victory, the German terms were still available, now weighted more in Britain's favor.[39]

But Hitler's offer was "at once rejected by the British Government and Press, its rejection being officially confirmed on 22 July by the British foreign secretary."[40]

From May 1940 to June 1941, Hitler would cast about for a way to end the war he had never wanted. Lukacs and Hinsley document Hitler's search for some path to peace with the British Empire.

On May 20, 1940, after the Ardennes breakthrough, Alfred Jodl wrote in his diary, "The Fuhrer is beside himself with joy. . . . The British can get a separate peace any time, after restoration of the colonies."[41]

After Dunkirk, Ribbentrop wrote that he had wondered if Hitler could make a quick peace with England. "The Fuhrer was enthused with the idea himself," and proceeded to lay out to Ribbentrop the peace terms he was prepared to offer the British:

> It will only be a few points, and the first point is that nothing must be done between England and Germany which would in any way violate the prestige of Great Britain. Secondly, Great Britain must give us back one or two of our old colonies. That is the only thing we want.[42]

As Churchill rejected peace with Germany, Hitler, fearing defeat if the war were not concluded soon, explored military options. He ordered up various plans—for an invasion of England; of Iceland; of Ireland; seizure of the Azores, the Cape Verdes, the Canary Islands, and Gibraltar; a sweep through Turkey and Syria to Suez. By mid-1940, writes Hinsley, Hitler was coming to the conclusion that crushing Russia was "the only solution for the problems created by the British refusal to collapse."[43]

Lukacs agrees. Hitler's ultimate purpose in invading Russia in 1941, Lukacs writes, was not Lebensraum, or eradicating "Jewish-Bolshevism," or preempting a Soviet attack. The June 1941 invasion of Russia was a preemptive strike to remove Britain's last hope of winning the war. Lukacs quotes Hitler in the summer of 1940, as the Battle of Britain was getting under way:

> If results of the air war are not satisfactory, [invasion] preparations will be halted. . . . England's hope is Russia and America. If hope on Russia is eliminated, America is also eliminated. . . . Russia [is] the factor on which England is mainly betting. Should Russia, however, be smashed, then England's last hope is extinguished. . . . Decision: in the course of this context, Russia must be disposed of. Spring '41.[44]

Lukacs and Hinsley, in their contention that Hitler invaded Russia to remove Britain's last hope of winning the war, are supported by Kershaw, biographer of Hitler, and Michael Bloch, biographer of Ribbentrop.

According to Kershaw, on July 13, 1940, Franz Halder, chief of the German army General Staff, wrote in his diary:

> The Fuhrer is greatly puzzled by Britain's persisting unwillingness to make peace. He sees the answer (as we do) in Britain's hope in Russia, and therefore counts on having to compel her by main force to agree to peace.[45]

On July 22, 1940, when Foreign Secretary Lord Halifax spurned his peace offer, Hitler, anticipating British rejection, had already, on

July 21, "raised with his commanders-in-chief the prospect of invading the Soviet Union that very autumn."[46] Realizing the impracticality of an invasion so soon and in the fall, Hitler, on July 29, told General Jodl the attack would come in May.[47] Bloch says Hitler informed Jodl three days earlier:

> On the 26th [of July 1940] he [Hitler] told Jodl that he had decided to launch such an invasion [of Russia] the following spring; and on the 31st, in a military conference at the Berghof, he confided to his service chiefs the extraordinary thinking which lay behind this decision. England, he said, continued to resist only because secretly encouraged to do so by the Russians, and to expect eventual Russian aid. Thus if Germany could knock out Russia, England would immediately come to terms.[48]

Thus, six weeks after France's surrender, before the Battle of Britain had begun, Hitler had made and revealed the decision that would seal the fate of tens of millions. Meeting at his Alpine retreat, the Berghof, Hitler announced to his generals:

> With Russia smashed, Britain's last hope would be shattered. Germany then will be master of Europe and the Balkans. Decision: Russia's destruction must therefore be made part of this struggle. Spring 1941 . . . If we start in May 1941, we would have five months to finish the job.[49]

On December 7, Hitler informed Admiral Raeder it was "necessary to eliminate at all costs the last remaining enemy on the continent before she can collaborate with Great Britain."[50]

On December 18, Hitler issued the directive for Operation Barbarossa. Thus, writes Kershaw, "by the late autumn it was clear that [Hitler] had returned to the chosen path from which he had never seriously wandered: attacking the Soviet Union at the earliest opportunity with the strategic aim of attaining final victory in the war by conquering London via Moscow."[51]

On January 8, 1941, Hitler clarified and expanded upon his reasoning for attacking Russia:

> Britain is sustained in this struggle by hopes placed in U.S.A. and Russia. . . . Britain's aim for some time to come will be to set Russia's strength in motion against us. If the U.S.A. and Russia should enter the war against Germany the situation would become very complicated. Hence any possibility for such a threat to develop must be eliminated at the very outset.[52]

In November, Roosevelt had been reelected and had begun swiftly to maneuver the United States toward a collision with Germany.

On May 29, 1941, Hitler told his confidant Walter Hewel, who would take his life twenty-four hours after Hitler, that once Russia was defeated "this will force England to make peace. Hope this year."[53]

In early June, Hitler spoke to General Fritz Halder, who wrote in a diary entry of June 14: Hitler "calculates 'that the collapse of Russia will induce England to give up the struggle. The main enemy is still Britain.' "[54]

On June 21, Hitler spoke again with Hewel, who wrote, "The Fuhrer expects a lot from the Russian campaign. . . . He thinks that England will have to give in."[55] Hitler then wrote to Mussolini: "[T]he situation in England itself is bad. . . . [They have only] hopes. These hopes are based solely on one assumption: Russia and America. We have no chance of eliminating America. But it does lie in our power to eliminate Russia."[56]

On July 25, as the eastern campaign appeared certain to end in swift victory, Hitler predicted: "Great Britain will not continue to fight if she sees there is no longer a chance of winning."[57]

On August 18, he told Field Marshal Keitel, "The ultimate objective of the Reich is the defeat of Great Britain."[58]

On August 22, Hitler told Halder his aim was "to finally eliminate Russia as England's allied power on the continent and thereby deprive England of any hope of change in her fortunes."[59]

On October 28, Hitler told Admiral Kurt Fricke, "The fall of Moscow might even force England to make peace at once."[60]

To deprive England of its last hope for victory, Hitler invaded the one nation that more than any other would bring the Reich down. Hitler's invasion of Russia truly met Bismarck's definition of preventive war: "Committing suicide—out of fear of death."

In his June 18, 1940, speech, as France was falling, Churchill made a prophetic remark: "Hitler knows that he will have to break us in this island or lose the war." Churchill was right. If Hitler could not break the British or achieve an armistice or peace with Britain, the war would go on, with a rising probability that the Soviet Union or the United States, or both, would become involved. And if they did, given their size and latent power, Hitler would "lose the war."

Thus, by his refusal even to consider a negotiated peace, or armistice, Churchill caused Hitler to commit his fatal blunder: invading Russia. This would add four more years to the war and bring death to tens of millions and indescribable ruin to the continent of Europe, but also the downfall of Hitler.

Churchill was thus the indispensable man, both in the destruction of Hitler's Reich and in the continuation of the war from 1940 to 1945.

Was it worth it? A few British historians say Britain and the world would be a better place had England ended the war in 1940 after victory in the Battle of Britain, or in 1941 after the invasion of Russia. Most yet believe that if the cost of exterminating the Nazi regime of Hitler, Himmler, and Goebbels was forty or fifty million more dead, the price had to be paid.

THE COSTS OF VICTORY

ASKED HOW HE COULD ally with Stalin, whose crimes he knew so well, Churchill answered "that he had only one single purpose—the destruction of Hitler—and his life was much simplified thereby. If Hitler invaded Hell, he would at least have made a favourable reference to the Devil."[61]

Yet in his Ahab-like pursuit of Hitler "at all cost," did Churchill ever reckon the cost of a war to the death—for Britain, the empire, and Europe? For as the war went on for five years after Dunkirk, those costs—financial, strategic, moral—mounted astronomically. Let us begin with the moral cost of Churchill's appeasement of the greatest mass murderer of the century.

When Hitler turned on Stalin, his accomplice in the rape of Poland, Churchill welcomed Stalin into the camp of the saints, writes conservative scholar Robert Nisbet, "in words that might have been addressed to a Pericles or George Washington":

> Before the whole world Churchill greeted the Soviets as fellow freedom fighters protecting their own liberties and democracy. Reading it today, one becomes slightly nauseated by Churchill's words. . . . It was one thing to make the best of things, to accept and even help Stalin in the war against the Nazis. . . . It was something else and hardly necessary, given Stalin's then desperate straits, to lavish gratitude upon the cruel, terror-minded despot, who, after all, had helped ignite World War II against the West.[62]

George Kennan, then in Moscow, wrote back to the State Department that, while "material aid" might be extended to Russia, "I feel strongly" that

> we should do nothing at home to make it appear that we are following the course Churchill seems to have entered upon

in extending moral support to the Russian cause in the present Russian-German conflict. . . . It is . . . no exaggeration
to say that in every border country concerned, from Scandinavia—including Norway and Sweden—to the Black Sea,
Russia is generally more feared than Germany. . . .[63]

Indeed, there was no reason to repose any trust in Moscow, for
Stalin was now fighting on the side of the Allies only because he had
been betrayed by his partner Hitler.

But Churchill embraced Britain's new and gallant ally: "The
Russian danger . . . is our danger, and the danger of the United
States, just as the cause of any Russian fighting for his hearth and
home is the cause of the free men and free people in every quarter of
the globe."[64]

Eighteen months earlier, however, in a January 20, 1940, broadcast, Churchill had hailed the heroism of Finland in resisting Russia's
onslaught in the Winter War and poured out his contempt of Soviet
ideology:

> The service rendered by Finland to mankind is magnifi-
> cent. . . . Many illusions about Soviet Russia have been dis-
> pelled by these fierce weeks of fighting above the Arctic
> Circle. Everyone can see how Communism rots the soul of a
> nation; how it makes it abject and hungry in peace and
> proves it base and abominable in war.[65]

Now, in his first great act of appeasement, Churchill let Eden persuade him to declare war on Finland, the heroic little country
Churchill had praised in January of 1940 for resisting Stalin's aggression as "superb, nay sublime—in the jaws of peril."[66]

When Churchill first met Stalin in Moscow in 1942, he tried to
explain to the Man of Steel how the terrible toll on British ships and
sailors had forced a pause in convoys to Murmansk. Stalin responded
by insulting Churchill to his face:

This is the first time in history that the British navy has ever turned tail and fled from the battle. You British are afraid of fighting. You should not think that the Germans are supermen. You will have to fight sooner or later. You cannot win a war without fighting.[67]

This abuse exceeded anything Chamberlain had taken from Hitler and came out of the mouth of a Bolshevik butcher who had been Hitler's willing partner in the rape of Poland and Hitler's enabler in his attack on the West. When Britain had been fighting alone, Stalin was aiding Nazi Germany and accusing Britain and France of having started the war.

When Stalin brought up Churchill's role in 1919 as the champion of Allied intervention in Russia, Churchill asked, "Have you forgiven me?"[68]

The ex-seminarian replied, "All that is in the past. It is not for me to forgive. It is for God to forgive."[69] This scene is almost unimaginable.

On his return from that September 1942 trip to Moscow, Churchill appeared captivated, rising in Parliament to tell his countrymen they were truly fortunate to be allied to so great a man:

This great rugged war chief. . . . He is a man of massive outstanding personality, suited to the sombre and stormy times in which his life has been cast; a man of inexhaustible courage and will-power, and a man of direct and even blunt speech. . . . Above all, he is a man with that saving sense of humour which is of high importance to all men and all nations, but particularly to great men and great nations. Stalin left upon me the impression of a deep, cool wisdom, and a complete absence of illusions of any kind.[70]

To appease his great ally, Churchill would agree to Stalin's annexation of the Baltic republics, his plunder from the devil's pact with

Hitler, and turn a blind eye to the Katyn massacre. When the Polish government-in-exile asked him to look into the 1940 mass murder of the Polish officer corps in Soviet captivity, fifteen thousand Poles executed in all, Churchill was dismissive: "There is no use prowling round the three year old graves of Smolensk."[71]

Churchill's answer suggests he suspected or knew the truth, that Stalin had perpetrated the Katyn massacre. If he thought an investigation would implicate the Nazis in the mass murder of Poland's officer corps, Churchill would have pursued it.

At Teheran in 1943, Churchill presented Stalin with a Crusader's sword.[72] In early 1944, "Churchill put pressure on the Poles to accept border changes that made Munich look like a simple frontier adjustment."[73]

In September 1944, Churchill crossed the Atlantic for a summit with FDR at Quebec's Citadel. At the banquet on September 13, U.S. Treasury Secretary Morgenthau and his deputy, Harry Dexter White, a Soviet spy, were seated at Churchill's table, where the secretary laid out his Morgenthau Plan. Devised by White to ensure Stalin's domination of Europe, the plan "envisaged turning the Ruhr into a 'ghostland.' The industrial region of the Saar was to be destroyed. . . . All machinery and factory materials were to be turned over to the Russians."[74] Germany was to be converted into an agricultural nation.

"It is no exaggeration to say that the Morgenthau Plan . . . if applied in its full rigor, would have been an undiscriminating sentence of death for millions of Germans," wrote U.S. historian W. H. Chamberlin.[75] When one U.S. official pointed out to Morgenthau that Germany's population could not survive on farming, that millions would starve, Morgenthau suggested the Allies ship the surplus Germans to North Africa. Historian Gregor Dallas describes the initial reaction of Churchill:

> Morgenthau had only got through a few sentences when
> Churchill began fidgeting and muttering. When he got to

the end, the Treasury Secretary received a "verbal lashing" such as he had never received in his life. Churchill said the plan—the "Morgenthau Plan" as it has gone down in history—was "unnatural, un-Christian and unnecessary." "I'm all for disarming Germany, but we ought not to prevent her from living decently," said Churchill. . . . "I agree with Burke. You cannot indict a whole nation."[76]

Churchill, however, was informed by aides that "Stage II" of Lend-Lease, upon which the economic survival of Britain depended, might hinge on his support of the Morgenthau Plan. By Friday the fifteenth, he had broken. "The future of my people is at stake," Churchill told a protesting Eden, who said the plan would never be approved by the Cabinet, "and when I have to choose between my people and the German people, I am going to choose my people."[77] Churchill initialed the plan, inserting the words that the destruction of the warmaking capacity of the Ruhr and Saar would be but "one step in the direction of converting Germany into a country primarily agricultural and pastoral in character."[78]

In Washington, a storm broke over the savage peace to be imposed. Secretary of War Stimson memoed FDR that the Morgenthau Plan was a flagrant violation of the principles of the Atlantic Charter and his own words about "freedom from want and freedom from fear." In his diary, Stimson wrote that Morgenthau's "Carthaginian views" amounted to "Semitism gone wild with vengeance."[79] In a week, the U.S. press was ablaze over the plan and FDR was backpedaling. Churchill, however, would carry the plan to Stalin and Molotov.

Seven days after the Wehrmacht had crushed the Polish Home Army, which had risen in Warsaw on a signal from the Red Army, which then sat idle on the east bank of the Vistula to observe the slaughter, Churchill slipped into Moscow "to divide the spoils of Eastern Europe."[80] There, he revealed to Stalin what he called his "naughty document":

"Americans including the President would be shocked by the division of Europe into spheres." On Rumania, Russia had 90%, Britain 10%; in Greece Britain had 90%, Russia 10%. Stalin ticked it.

"Might it not be thought cynical if it seemed we'd disposed of these issues, so fateful to millions of people, in such an offhand manner?" said Churchill, half guilty at, half revelling in, the arrogance of the Great Powers.[81]

As Stalin's armies were already in Rumania and Bulgaria and had joined hands with Tito's Partisans in Yugoslavia, Churchill was discussing where the Iron Curtain would fall across Europe, and secretly and cynically ceding Eastern Europe and the Balkans to Stalin, save Greece. The couplet of Kipling, who lost his son in the Great War, comes to mind: "If any question why we died, / Tell them, because our fathers lied."

Churchill's concessions at Moscow were far worse than Chamberlain's at Munich. For the Poles were terrified of Stalin's Russia, while the Sudeten Germans clamored to join Hitler's Germany. What did Churchill think the fate of the Poles, who had defeated the Red Army in 1920, would be under Stalin? How could he not have known what Stalin had in store for the Poles when Stalin in 1944 had refused U.S. and British planes permission to fly supplies to the dying Home Army?

At Yalta in February 1945, Churchill gave moral legitimacy to Stalin's control of half of Europe by signing a "Declaration on Liberated Europe." Writes Nisbet, the one hundred million Europeans east of the Oder

had to watch what democracy and freedom they had known before the war disappear, and then suffer the added humiliation of seeing such words as "free elections," "sovereignty," "democracy," "independence," and "liberation" deliberately corrupted, debased, made duplicitous, in the Declaration on Liberated Europe, the very title of which, given the ugly reality underneath, was a piece of calculated Soviet effrontery—one, however, that both Churchill and FDR acquiesced in.[82]

Yet Churchill "was so pleased with Yalta, noted a British diplomat, he was 'drinking buckets of Caucasian champagne which would undermine the health of any ordinary man.' "[83] Within days of his return from the Crimea, Churchill got word on how Stalin interpreted the Declaration on Liberated Europe:

> On March 6, messages reached Churchill about the mass arrests taking place in Cracow, with whole trainloads of Polish intellectuals, priests, professors, and labor union leaders being taken to a huge work-prison camp in Voroshilovgrad. As many as 6,000 Home Army officers were put in a camp near Lublin, overseen and directed by Soviet officials indifferent to the publicity.[84]

To Churchill, the independence and freedom of one hundred million Christian peoples of Eastern Europe were not worth a war with Russia in 1945. Why, then, had they been worth a war with Germany in 1939?

To this day, a question remains unanswered. Did Churchill ever give a damn about Poland? His ambivalence toward and his often-expressed contempt for, Polish leaders and the Polish people with whom Britain was allied, was on public display in his history of the world war. In 1948, long after Poland had been consigned to Stalin's custody, Churchill wrote that the Nazis were "not the only vultures upon the carcass" of Czechoslovakia:[85]

> The heroic characteristics of the Polish race must not blind us to their record of folly and ingratitude which over

centuries has led them through measureless suffering. . . .
We see them hurrying, while the might of Germany glow-
ered against them, to grasp their share of the pillage and
ruin of Czechoslovakia. . . . Glorious in revolt and ruin;
squalid and shameful in triumph. The bravest of the brave,
too often led by the vilest of the vile! And yet there were always two Polands; one struggling to proclaim the truth and
the other grovelling in villainy.[86]

Churchill wrote these savage words after Polish pilots helped win
the Battle of Britain and Polish patriots had endured nine years of
Nazi and Stalinist hell. From these words one begins to understand
why Churchill seemed so unconcerned with the fate of the Poles for
whom his nation had gone to war. The moral issue cannot be ignored. Was it moral to issue a war guarantee to Poland that Britain's
leaders knew they had neither the power nor the intent to honor? Ask
the Poles, the ones who survived.

In his 2005 work on Churchill subtitled *A Study in Character*,
Robert Holmes may have come closest to the truth when he wrote
that Churchill "had no objection to throwing other peoples to the
wolves if it genuinely helped the British sledge to reach safety."[87]

In defense of Churchill, Andrew Roberts wrote in 2007: "Once it
dawned on Churchill that Russia wanted to swallow up and partition
Poland once again—just as she had done so often in previous centuries—it was simply beyond his power to prevent it."[88]

The Roberts defense raises the question: Did it take until 1945
for it to dawn "on Churchill that Russia wanted to swallow up and
partition Poland," when Russia had already partitioned Poland with
Hitler's Germany in 1939? To suggest it did not dawn on Churchill
until Yalta that Stalin would hold any land and people he conquered
is to suggest Churchill was childishly naive. But how can this be,
when Churchill had been among the most farsighted statesmen in as-
sessing the character of the Bolshevik regime and in urging its extermination in 1919?

Churchill had to know in 1939, when he was pounding the war drums and calling for partnership with Stalin, that any victory in alliance with Stalin would bring Communism into the heart of Europe and replace Nazi tyranny with Bolshevik tyranny. Was it worth bankrupting and bleeding his country and bringing down the empire for this? Was it worth declaring war to keep 350,000 Danzigers separate from a Germany they wished to rejoin, if the cost was to consign one hundred million people to the mercy of Stalin's butchers?

In 1919, like no other Western leader, Churchill had excoriated the "foul baboonery of Bolshevism."[89] By 1919, writes Martin Gilbert,

> Churchill had no doubt that of "all the tyrannies in history," he told an audience in London that April, "the Bolshevik tyranny is the worst, the most destructive, the most degrading." The atrocities committed under Lenin and Trotsky were "incomparably more hideous, on a larger scale, and more numerous than any for which the Kaiser is responsible."[90]

To Churchill, the Soviet regime consisted of a "foul combination of criminality and animalism."[91] So savage were his denunciations that Lloyd George began to describe Churchill as a "dangerous man" with "Bolshevism on the brain."[92]

Churchill knew of the mass murders on Lenin's orders, the massacre of the Czar's family, Stalin's slave-labor camps, the forced starvation in Ukraine, the Great Purge of the old comrades and Russian officer corps, the show trials, the pact with Hitler, the rape of Finland and the Baltic republics, Katyn. As historian John Lewis Gaddis writes, "[T]he number of deaths resulting from Stalin's policies before World War II . . . was between 17 and 22 million," a thousand times the number of deaths attributed to Hitler as of 1939, the year Churchill was clamoring for war on Hitler and an alliance with Stalin.[93]

Among the most knowledgeable statesmen in the West, Churchill had to know this. Yet in January 1944, twenty-five years after he had urged the Allies to invade Russia and kill the Bolshevik snake in its crib, twenty years after he had castigated the Labour Party for entering trade negotiations with the "foul filth butchers of Moscow," Churchill was writing Foreign Secretary Eden of the "deep-seated changes which have taken place in the character of the Russian state and government, the new confidence which has grown in our hearts toward Stalin."[94]

Addressing the House of Commons on May 24, 1944, Churchill declared, "Profound changes have taken place in Soviet Russia. The Trotzkyite form of communism has been completely wiped out. . . . The religious side of Russian life has had a wonderful rebirth."[95]

In October 1944, after meeting with Stalin to discuss the secret deal to divide the Balkans and leave Stalin in control of all but Greece, Churchill wrote Clementine: "I have had very nice talks with the Old Bear. I like him the more I see him. Now they respect us & I am sure they wish to work with us."[96]

This is the very echo of Chamberlain at Munich.

At Yalta, Churchill raised a glass to Stalin:

> It is no exaggeration or compliment of a florid kind when I say that we regard Marshal Stalin's life as most precious to the hopes and hearts of all of us. . . . I walk through this world with greater courage and hope when I find myself in a relation of friendship and intimacy with this great man, whose fame has gone out not only over all Russia, but the world.[97]

Allowances may be made for toasts between heads of state on foreign soil, but they do not extend to remarks made when Churchill returned from the summit that will live in infamy alongside Munich.

"Poor Neville Chamberlain believed he could trust Hitler. He was wrong. But I don't think I'm wrong about Stalin," Churchill said on his return from Yalta.[98] He declared to the House, "I know of no Government which stands to its obligations, even in its own despite, more solidly than the Russian Soviet Government."[99] "This must surely rank as one of the most serious political misjudgments in history," wrote Royal Navy captain and historian Russell Grenfell.[100]

If Chamberlain was naive about Hitler, how defend Churchill's naive trust in Stalin, twenty-five years after Lenin's Revolution and Red Terror?

In 1943, General Franco had written the British ambassador in Madrid to express his fear that Stalinism and the Soviet Union would emerge from the war deep inside Germany and dominate Europe. General Franco asked the ambassador to send his memo on to London. Churchill himself wrote back to reassure the Spanish ruler:

> Do you really believe that a single nation is strong enough to dominate Europe after this war? And that it will be actually Russia. . . . I venture to prophesy that, after the war, England will be the greatest military Power in Europe. I am sure that England's influence will be stronger in Europe than it has ever been before since the days of the fall of Napoleon.[101]

Three years later, on March 5, 1946, Churchill would be in Fulton, Missouri, declaring, "From Stettin in the Baltic to Trieste in the Adriatic, an iron curtain has descended across the continent." Churchill was describing the line he and the Old Bear had drawn up together at Teheran, Moscow, and Yalta.

In defense of his decision to approve Stalin's annexation of that half of Poland he had gotten out of the Hitler-Stalin pact, Churchill wrote in 1953:

> I wanted the Poles to be able to live freely and live their own lives in their own way. That was the object which I had

always heard Stalin proclaim with the utmost firmness, and it was because I trusted his declarations about the sovereignty, independence, and freedom of Poland that I rated the frontier question as less important.[102]

But how could a statesman of Churchill's rank—twenty-five years after he had described Bolshevism as the bloodiest tyranny in history—place his "trust" in a despot who had massacred, starved, and murdered millions of his own countrymen? Upon what ground could Churchill stand to condemn his dead rival Chamberlain for having briefly trusted Hitler, when he, Churchill, admits to having trusted Stalin to respect "the sovereignty, independence and freedom of Poland"?

ETHNIC CLEANSING AND SLAVE LABOR

AT MUNICH, CHAMBERLAIN HAD agreed to the transfer of 3.25 million Sudeten Germans to Berlin, rather than fight a futile war to keep them under a Czech rule they wished to be rid of. At Teheran and Yalta, Churchill signed away one hundred million Christians to Stalin's terror and agreed to let him annex the Baltic states and 40 percent of Poland, the nation for whose "integrity" Britain had gone to war. At his wartime summits with Stalin, Churchill also agreed to the ethnic cleansing of thirteen to fifteen million Germans from their ancestral homes, two million of whom would die in the exodus. He agreed to Stalin's use of Germans as slave laborers, and to the forced repatriation of millions of Russians, Ukrainians, and Cossacks to a barbaric Asiatic regime he had called the foulest murderers in all of history.

After Normandy, thousands of German prisoners who were ethnic Russians fell into British hands and were transferred to England. As they had been captured fighting in German uniforms, they were entitled under the 1929 Geneva Convention to treatment as POWs.

But when their disposition was debated in London, an exasperated Churchill memoed Sir Alexander Cadogan of the Foreign Office: "I thought we had arranged to send all the Russians back to Russia. . . . We ought to get rid of them all as soon as possible. This was your promise to Molotov as I understood it."[103]

As British historian A. N. Wilson writes, "The tragedy of the twentieth century is that in order to defeat Hitler, Churchill believed it was not merely necessary but desirable to ally himself to Stalin."[104]

More than "ally himself to Stalin," Churchill colluded with Stalin in such historic crimes as the forcible return of millions of resisting POWs and Russians, whether "Soviet citizens" or not, from Allied-occupied territory to the NKVD. Stalin was especially interested in the Cossacks who had fought Soviet rule in the civil war of 1919–1920 and fled with their families to the West. Though they had never been "Soviet citizens," the Cossacks were sent back. As Solzhenitsyn writes in *The Gulag Archipelago*,

> In Austria that May [1945], Churchill . . . turned over to the Soviet command the Cossack corps of 90,000 men. Along with them, he also handed over many wagonloads of old people, women, and children who did not want to return to their native Cossack rivers. This great hero, monuments to whom will in time cover all England, ordered that they, too, be surrendered to their deaths.[105]

Britain's betrayal of the Cossacks was "an act of double-dealing consistent with the spirit of traditional English diplomacy," Solzhenitsyn wrote of Churchill and others who betrayed them. "In their own countries FDR and Churchill are honored as embodiments of statesmanlike wisdom. To us, in our Russian prison conversations, their consistent shortsightedness and stupidity stood out as astonishingly obvious."[106]

In the winter of 1940, Churchill had made an explicit pledge to the German people: "We are opposed to any attempt . . . to break up Germany. We do not seek the humiliation or dismemberment of your country." But, as the tide began to turn against Germany, Churchill began to weasel out of his pledge to the German people and the Atlantic Charter commitments he had made at Placentia Bay in August 1941.[107] Article 2 of the Charter's program for peace, agreed to by FDR and Churchill, read: "The Alliance desires to see no territorial changes that do not accord with the freely expressed wishes of the peoples concerned."

But at Teheran in 1943, Churchill agreed to Stalin's annexation of half of Poland. To compensate the Poles, Churchill would agree to transfer to Warsaw the eastern provinces of Germany. As he related in his memoirs, Churchill used three matchsticks to show a "pleased" Stalin how this might be done.[108]

On October 14, 1944, at the British embassy in Moscow, Churchill and Eden bullied the Poles into ceding half their country to Stalin. They applied

> massive pressure on [the Polish leader] Mikolajczyk to in-
> duce him to give his consent to the Curzon Line without
> Lvov or Galicia. The encounter is so revealing of the reali-
> ties of power politics, that one can hardly help thinking back
> to the infamous Berlin meeting in March 1939 between
> President Hacha of Czechoslovakia and the German dicta-
> tor, who, after receiving Hacha with the honours due a Head
> of State, proceeded to instruct him to sign away the inde-
> pendence of his people.[109]

At the meeting, Churchill acted as Stalin's enforcer, brutalizing his Polish ally to yield or face the consequences. Unless you accept the new borders demanded by Moscow, Churchill told Stanislaw Mikolajczyk, "you are out of business for ever. The Russians will sweep through your country and your people will be liquidated. You are on the verge of annihilation."[110]

Stalin was pleased. As Churchill's plane took off from Moscow, the Soviet dictator was seen standing in the rain, waving a white handkerchief.[111]

On May 24, 1944, Churchill declared that the principles of the Atlantic Charter did not apply to a defeated Germany: "There is no question of Germany enjoying any guarantee that she will not undergo territorial changes if it should seem that the making of such changes renders more secure and more lasting the peace in Europe."[112] On December 15, Churchill rose in the House of Commons and formally repudiated the Atlantic Charter:

> Expulsion is the method which, so far as we have been able to see, will be the most satisfactory and lasting. There will be no mixture of populations to cause endless trouble. . . . A clean sweep will be made. I am not alarmed by these large transferences which are more possible in modern conditions than they ever were before.[113]

At Yalta in February 1945, Churchill and FDR sought to limit the German lands ceded to Poland, but capitulated to Stalin's demand that the new provisional Polish-German border be set at the Oder and western Neisse rivers. This meant "11 million people—9 million inhabitants of the eastern German provinces and 2 million from Old Poland and the Warta District" would be driven out of their homes.[114]

Two million Germans would die in this largest forced transfer of populations in history, a crime against humanity of historic dimensions in which twenty times as many Germans were driven from their homes between 1944 and 1948 as the 600,000 Palestinians of the war of 1948, and more Germans died than all the Armenians who perished in the Turkish massacres of World War I. The territories of East Prussia, Pomerania, Eastern Brandenburg, Silesia, Danzig, Memel, and the Sudetenland were relentlessly and ruthlessly "cleansed" of Germans, whose families had inhabited them for centuries. While this crime against humanity was being perpetrated, the Allies at Nuremberg, including Stalin's USSR, were prosecuting the Germans for crimes against humanity. Alfred M. de Zayas, an American historian of the horror, says Churchill "knew what was going on."[115]

> The responsibility for the decision to uproot and resettle millions of human beings, to evict them from their homes and spoliate them—and this as a quasi-peacetime measure—is . . . a war crime for which individuals bear responsibility, even if many would still hesitate to put the correct label on the crime and its perpetrators.[116]

To Anne O'Hare McCormick of the *New York Times*, Churchill and FDR acquiesced in "the most inhuman decision ever made by governments dedicated to the defense of human rights."[117]

In his Iron Curtain speech at Fulton, Churchill would invoke the same defense as the Germans prosecuted at Nuremberg—ignorance: "The Russian-dominated Polish Government has been encouraged to make enormous and wrongful inroads upon Germany, and mass expulsions of millions of Germans on a scale grievous and undreamed-of are now taking place."[118] Nor was this the last of the human rights atrocities to which Churchill gave assent:

> A fateful decision was made . . . on February 11, 1945. The discussion revolved around reparations for the Soviet Union, which demanded the use of German work forces. This was nothing more or less than trade in human beings, slavery. But the statesmen had coined a euphemistic phrase for it: "Reparations in kind." Churchill and Roosevelt agreed to the Soviet demand. The Yalta agreement on "reparations in kind" . . . clearly demonstrates the

complicity of Roosevelt and Churchill in this slave labor program.[119]

After Churchill returned from Yalta to celebrate his agreement with Stalin, a disgusted Labour MP, John Rhys Davies, rose in the House of Commons on March 1, 1945, to declare, "We started this war with great motives and high ideals. We published the Atlantic Charter and then spat on it, stomped on it and burnt it, as it were, at the stake, and now nothing is left of it."[120]

Churchill's last meeting with Stalin came at Potsdam in July 1945. According to Eden, his performance was "very bad."[121] Not only had he not read his briefs, Churchill seemed captivated by Stalin: "I like that man."[122]

By August 1945, Churchill had become alarmed at the consequences of what he had done at Teheran, Yalta, and Potsdam. Now out of power, he told Parliament, "Sparse and guarded accounts of what has happened and is happening [in the new Poland] have filtered through, but it is not impossible that tragedy at a prodigious scale is unfolding itself behind the iron curtain which at the moment divides Europe in twain."[123] Added *Time*, "Europe had emerged from history's most terrible war into history's most terrifying peace."[124]

Yet as late as November 1945, Churchill, though out of power, was again praising Stalin so effusively—"this truly great man, the father of his nation"—that Molotov ordered Churchill's speech published in *Pravda*.[125]

At war's end, Hitler and his evil and odious regime had been buried, and Churchill had played a historic role in its demise. But all three of the great causes of his life—keeping socialism from Britain's door, preserving his beloved empire, and preventing any single hostile power from dominating Europe—had been lost. And he had been dismissed by the people he had led to victory, and had himself been a collaborator in the betrayal of the peoples for whom Britain had gone to war.

Churchill had been right when the others had been wrong—about the character of the Bolsheviks, the amorality of Hitler, the imperative to rearm. But he had been horribly wrong when others had been right.

AS MILITARY STRATEGIST

NOR DOES CHURCHILL'S REPUTATION as a legendary military strategist survive scrutiny. From August 1914 to May 25, 1915, when he was replaced by Balfour as First Lord, Churchill was involved in two of the greatest blunders of the Great War. First came the Antwerp fiasco of 1914, where he sent his untested naval brigade to help defend Antwerp and went over to command the resistance, only to see Antwerp seized by the Germans in weeks and his naval unit decimated and interned for the duration.

In 1915 came the Dardanelles disaster and resignation as First Lord. The campaign was MacArthurian in concept: to breach the Dardanelles with battleships, slice Turkey in two, seize Constantinople, convince the Balkan neutrals to join the Allies, and open a new supply route to Russia. But the execution was appalling. Churchill had violated Nelson's dictum: Ships do not fight forts. The Royal Navy's attempt to force the Dardanelles without landing ground troops to assault the Turkish forts from the rear resulted in the loss of three battleships and the crippling of three more by mines on the first day. There followed weeks of delay as the Turks fortified Gallipoli peninsula. Then came the British-French-Anzac invasion that resulted in months of battle, two hundred thousand casualties, and the worst Allied rout of the war.

In September 1939, Churchill returned to the Admiralty and began to urge an invasion of neutral Norway to cut Germany off from Swedish iron ore, which, during the winter when Sweden's closest port was iced over, was transported across Norway to Narvik, then to Germany. Attlee and Labour had balked at any violation of Scandinavian neutrality, and the Cabinet went back and forth on the wisdom of mining neutral waters and seizing Narvik.

Churchill, however, tipped Britain's hand to Berlin. On February 17, the destroyer *Cossack* intercepted the *Altmark* in Norway's coastal waters, rescuing British prisoners being taken to Germany for internment. Most were seamen from merchant ships sunk by the *Graf Spee*. An infuriated Hitler now feared the British would invade Norway and turn his northern flank. He ordered plans prepared to preempt the British with an invasion of his own. Appointing von Falkenhorst to head it, Hitler told him, "The success which we have gained in the East and which we are going to win in the West would be annihilated by a British occupation of Norway."[126] As Andrew Roberts writes:

> The captured records of Hitler's conferences reveal that in early 1940 he still considered "the maintenance of Norway's neutrality to be the best course for Germany," but that in February he came to the conclusion that: "The English plan to land there and I want to be there before them." His definite decision to order an attack on Norway was taken a few days after Churchill had ordered the British destroyer HMS *Cossack* to sail into Norwegian waters and board the German ship *Altmark* in order to liberate British prisoners. Churchill capitalised on this success and much was made of the event. The Norwegian Government protested against the violation of their neutrality, but their passive acceptance served to convince Hitler that Norway was actually Britain's accomplice, and it became the detonating spark of the pre-emptive action that he now ordered: the invasion of Norway.[127]

On April 9, despite Churchill's assurances that the Royal Navy had absolute command of the North Sea, German troops, many concealed in the holds of merchant ships, seized Oslo and five other

Norwegian ports, including Narvik, within hours of the anticipated arrival of British marines. On April 11, the First Lord rose to reassure Parliament, "Herr Hitler has committed a grave strategic error in spreading the war so far to the north and in forcing Scandinavia out of neutrality. . . ."[128]

> [I]t is the considered view of the Admiralty that we have greatly gained by what has occurred in Scandinavia and in northern waters in a strategic and military sense. For myself, I consider that Hitler's action in invading is as great a strategic and political error as that which was committed by Napoleon in 1807 or 1808, when he invaded Spain.[129]

Churchill's assurances could not long cover up the debacle the British had suffered in Norway. For "the disastrous British campaign in Norway," writes Ian Kershaw, "the main responsibility rested with Churchill, but it was Chamberlain who paid the political price."[130] And for having succeeded where Churchill failed, in the preemptive occupation of neutral Norway, Admiral Raeder was sentenced at Nuremberg to life imprisonment.

According to Roberts, Churchill had blabbed his Norwegian plans at a secret meeting of neutral press attachés and German intelligence had picked up vital information on the British attack.

Lloyd George was apoplectic:

> We are not suffering from one blunder. The Norwegian fiasco is one of a series of incredible botcheries. . . .
>
> When we decided that it was essential for our own protection that we should invade the territorial waters of Norway despite Norwegian protests, we ought to have anticipated a swift counter-stroke from Germany.[131]

George Kennan reached the same conclusion: The British, by violating Norwegian neutrality, had drawn Hitler into Scandinavia.

The British themselves, toying as they did with the idea of an expeditionary force across northern Norway to Finland, and finally deciding to encroach on Norwegian neutrality themselves by mining the leads along the Norwegian coast, had a heavy responsibility for Hitler's decision to move on Scandinavia. . . .[132]

Churchill had blundered disastrously. During April and May, Britain suffered repeated defeats in Norway until the force was withdrawn. While the debacle was Churchill's doing, it was Chamberlain who fell. Churchill's greatest fiasco since Gallipoli vaulted him to national power.

Two years later, under pressure from Stalin to open a second front, Churchill, now prime minister, launched a cross-Channel raid on the French port of Dieppe. A bloodbath ensued, with two-thirds of the six thousand commandos, mostly Canadians, killed, wounded, or captured, and RAF losses of three-to-one against the Luftwaffe. Canadians have never forgotten what one officer called the bloodiest nine hours in Canadian military history. Many blame Churchill for the loss of their bravest sons in an assault even German defenders regarded as a suicidal sacrifice of brave soldiers.

In his fortnightly letters on strategy and security, published in 1939 as *Step by Step*, Churchill repeatedly denigrated the submarine as an obsolete weapon of war and contended the airplane was vastly overrated as a threat to battleships. On March 22, 1937, Churchill wrote:

The technical discoveries since the war have placed the submarine in a position of far less strength and far greater danger than was apparent even at the moment when the U-boat warfare was decisively mastered. So far as any lessons can yet be drawn from the Spanish war, it would seem that the claims of air experts to destroy warships at their pleasure and discretion have, to put it mildly, not so far been made good.[133]

On May 17, 1937, Churchill again wrote:

> I do not myself believe that well-built modern warships properly defended by armour and antiaircraft guns, especially when steaming in company, are likely to fall prey to hostile aircraft. . . . [T]he submarine also is not nowadays regarded as the menace it used to be. . . . [T]he new methods which have been discovered and perfected make the submarine liable almost certainly to be found and thereafter hunted to death far more easily than was possible even in the days when the British Navy strangled the U-boats.[134]

On September 1, 1938, Churchill again disparaged airpower as against battle fleets, and dismissed the submarine:

> [A]ircraft will not be a mortal danger to properly-equipped modern war fleets, whether at sea or lying in harbour under the protection of their own very powerful anti-aircraft batteries reinforced by those on shore. . . .
>
> This, added to the undoubted obsolescence of the submarine as a decisive war weapon, should give a feeling of confidence and security, so far as the seas and oceans are concerned, to the Western democracies.[135]

Churchill could not have been more wrong. During his eight months as First Lord,

> the carrier HMS *Courageous* was torpedoed in Bristol Channel in September 1939. In the next month, a German submarine penetrated the defences of Scapa Flow and sank the battleship HMS *Royal Oak*. In the first nine months of the war, Britain lost 800,000 tons of shipping to a relatively small number of enemy submarines and magnetic mines.[136]

In the first year of Churchill's premiership, antiquated British Sword-fish biplanes torpedoed, crippled, and sank Italian battleships in Taranto harbor, and a Swordfish from the *Ark Royal* crippled the rudder and steering gear of *Bismarck*, enabling British warships to close in for the kill.

On December 10, 1941, three days after Pearl Harbor, where Japanese aircraft had crippled or sunk eight U.S. battleships, the battleship *Prince of Wales*, on which Churchill had crossed to Placentia Bay for his Atlantic Charter summit with FDR, was sunk, along with the battle cruiser *Repulse*, within an hour of each other, by Japanese fighter-bombers and torpedo planes. Six months later at Midway, four Japanese carriers were sent to the bottom by U.S. aircraft. Churchill had rarely been more wrong.

THE MORAL PROGRESS OF CHURCHILL

FROM MOST BIOGRAPHIES, the young Churchill appears to have been the model of a Christian warrior. As a young officer who rode in the cavalry charge at Omdurman, he came home to tell the story in *The River War*. In the book Churchill expressed his moral outrage that Lord Kitchener had left fifteen thousand wounded Dervishes to die on a field of battle and profaned the tomb and desecrated the body of the Mahdi. In a passage deeply offensive to Kitchener, Churchill called this a "wicked act, of which the true Christian . . . must express his abhorrence."[137]

The young author, however, gave himself cover from retribution by friends of the Sirdar by dedicating his 250,000-word, two-volume history—to the prime minister. The dedication read:

> The Marquess Of Salisbury, K.G., Under Whose Wise Direction The Conservative Party Have Long Enjoyed Power And The Nation Prosperity, During Whose Administrations

The Reorganization Of Egypt Has Been Mainly Accomplished, And Upon Whose Advice Her Majesty Determined To Order The Reconquest Of The Soudan.[138]

"Everyone likes flattery," said Disraeli, "and when you come to Royalty you should lay it on with a trowel."

Nevertheless, Churchill's conduct as a twenty-three-year-old cavalryman seems in the most admirable and honorable tradition of a soldier. But something happened to Churchill at the Admiralty, and with the coming of the Great War for which he had so ardently lusted.

Churchill had no more respect for the rights of neutral nations than von Moltke, who had said, "Success alone justifies war."[139] Had the German army not first violated Belgian neutrality in 1914, Churchill planned to do so himself—with a blockade of Antwerp. As First Lord, he urged the Cabinet to seize Dutch and Danish islands, though both nations were neutral. He pressed for a blockade of the Dardanelles when Turkey was still neutral.

Churchill's starvation blockade was without modern precedent. To deny food to women and children was a violation of international law and a transgression against human rights. During the Boer War, Lord Salisbury had declared:

Foodstuffs, with a hostile destination, can be considered contraband of war only if they are supplies for the enemy's forces. It is not sufficient that they are capable of being so used; it must be shown that this was in fact their destination at the time of the seizure.[140]

The starvation blockade of the First Lord Winston Churchill, writes historian Ralph Raico, "was probably the most effective weapon employed on either side in the conflict. . . . About 750,000 German civilians succumbed to hunger and diseases caused by malnutrition."[141] That is almost a hundred times the number of civilian dead attributed to German atrocities in Belgium.

As to the purpose of the hunger blockade, Churchill was direct: "to starve the whole population—men, women, and children, old and young, wounded and sound—into submission."[142]

Churchill would claim that, on the evening of Armistice Day, 1918, he had urged Lloyd George to send shiploads of food to Germany.[143] In a September 17, 1937, column, answering a charge in the German press that he was an enemy of Germany, Churchill wrote in self-defense:

> At the moment of the Armistice, as is well known, I proposed filling a dozen great liners with food, and rushing them into Hamburg as a gesture of humanity. As Secretary of State for War in 1919, I pressed upon the Supreme Council the need of lifting the blockade, and laid before them the reports from the generals on the Rhine which eventually produced that step.[144]

There is, however, no supporting evidence that Churchill ever made any sustained effort to end the starvation blockade he imposed as First Lord in August 1914.

While Germany introduced poison gas to the battlefield, Churchill became an enthusiast of its use against enemies of the empire. When the Iraqis resisted British rule in 1920, Churchill, as Secretary for War and Air, wrote Sir Henry Trenchard, a pioneer of air warfare: "I do not understand this squeamishness about the use of gas. . . . I am strongly in favor of using poisoned gas against uncivilised tribes [to] spread a lively terror."[145]

Churchill's defenders contend he was referring to nonlethal gas and believed it more humane than high-explosive bombs and shells. But the gas the British used did kill Kurds and Iraqis, and during World War II, Churchill would drop the distinction between nonlethal and deadly gas. The same day he took office as prime minister, he ordered the bombing of civilians. After the fall of France, Churchill wrote a somber letter to Lord Beaverbrook, Minister of Air Production:

When I look round to see how we can win the war I see that there is only one sure path. We have no Continental army which can defeat the German military power. The blockade is broken and Hitler has Asia and probably Africa to draw from. Should he be repulsed here or not try invasion, he will recoil eastward, and we have nothing to stop him. But there is one thing that will bring him down and that is an absolutely devastating, exterminating attack by very heavy bombers from this country upon the Nazi homeland.[146]

This letter "is of great historical significance," writes Paul Johnson, "marking the point at which the moral relativism of the totalitarian societies invaded the decision-making process of a major legitimate power."[147]

Churchill led the West into adopting the methods of barbarism of their totalitarian enemies. By late 1940, writes Johnson, "British bombers were being used on a great and increasing scale to kill and frighten the German civilian population in their homes."[148]

The policy, initiated by Churchill, approved in cabinet, endorsed by parliament and, so far as can be judged, enthusiastically backed by the bulk of the British people—thus fulfilling all the conditions of the process of consent in a democracy under law—marked a critical stage in the moral declension of humanity in our times.[149]

"The adoption of terror bombing was a measure of Britain's desperation," writes Johnson, and, one might add, of the moral decline of Winston Churchill.[150] "So far as air strategy was concerned," writes A.J.P. Taylor, "the British outdid German frightfulness first in theory, later in practice, and a nation which claimed to be fighting for a moral cause gloried in the extent of its immoral acts."[151]

"WOLVES WITH THE MINDS OF MEN"

In *ADVANCE TO BARBARISM*, to which the dean of St. Paul's Cathedral wrote the foreword, historian F.J.P. Veale traces Britain's abandonment of the rules of civilized warfare to May 11, 1940. Just twenty-four hours after the German army invaded France, Bomber Command sent eighteen Whitley bombers on a night run far from the front, on Westphalia. Writes Veale, italicizing his words: "This raid on the night of May 11, 1940, although in itself trivial, *was an epoch-making event since it was the first deliberate breach of the fundamental rule of civilized warfare that hostilities must only be waged against the enemy combatant forces.*"[152]

It had taken Churchill only twenty-four hours as prime minister to remove the keystone upholding "the whole structure of civilized warfare as it had been gradually built up in Europe during the preceding two centuries."[153] From there, that "structure of civilized warfare . . . collapsed in ruins."[154]

B. H. Liddell Hart confirms it: "[W]hen Mr. Churchill came into power, one of the first decisions of his Government was to extend bombing to the non-combatant area."[155] While the Luftwaffe had bombed cities, Liddell Hart noted the critical strategic and moral difference with what Britain was doing: "Bombing [of Warsaw and Rotterdam] did not take place until German troops were fighting their way into these cities and thus conformed to the old rules of siege bombardment."[156]

In his first meeting with Stalin in 1942, Churchill brought up the Royal Air Force bombing of German cities to ingratiate himself with the tyrant by impressing upon him how ruthless Britain intended to be.

Churchill now spoke of the bombing of Germany. This was already considerable, he said, and would increase. Britain looked upon the morale of the German civilian population "as a military target. We sought no mercy and we would show no mercy." Britain hoped to "shatter" twenty German cities, as several had already been shattered. "If need be, as the war went on, we hoped to shatter almost every dwelling in almost every German city."[157]

At this point in the conversation, writes Martin Gilbert, the "record of the meeting noted, 'Stalin smiled and said that would not be bad' . . . and thence forward the atmosphere became progressively more cordial."[158]

What Churchill had been describing to Stalin was a British policy to "de-house" the civilian population of Germany.[159] Who was instigator and architect of the policy to carpet-bomb German cities? Frederick Lindemann, "the Prof," an intimate of Churchill's whom he had brought into his war Cabinet as science adviser. Lindemann had "an almost pathological hatred for Nazi Germany, and an almost medieval desire for revenge."[160]

C. P. Snow, a science adviser to the war government, wrote that Lindemann had a zealot's faith in the efficacy of bombing. Early in 1942, when Britain had failed to achieve a single major victory, Lindemann presented his great paper to the Cabinet.

The paper laid down a strategic policy. The bombing must be directed especially against German working-class houses. Middle-class houses have too much space round them, and so are bound to waste bombs. . . . The paper claimed that— given a total concentration of effort on the production and use of bombing aircraft—it would be possible, in all the larger towns of Germany (that is, those with more than 50,000 inhabitants), to destroy fifty percent of all houses.[161]

This was to be accomplished in just eighteen months, from March 1942 to September 1943. Snow, in his 1960 Godkin lectures at Harvard, asked—about himself and his colleagues in wartime—"What will people of the future think of us? Will they say, as Roger Williams said of some of the Massachusetts Indians, that we were wolves with the minds of men? Will they think we resigned our humanity? They will have the right."[162]

In his 1944 *Bombing Vindicated*, J. M. Spaight, Principal Secretary for the Air Ministry, claims full credit for Churchill's Britain for having been first to initiate the bombing of civilians:

> Because we were doubtful about the psychological effect of propagandist distortion of the truth that it was we who started the strategic bombing offensive, we have shrunk from giving our great decision of May 11th, 1940, the publicity which it deserved. . . . It was a splendid decision. It was as heroic, as self-sacrificing, as Russia's decision to adopt her policy of "scorched earth."[163]

Our "splendid . . . heroic and self-sacrificing" decision to bomb cities, insists Spaight, gave Britons the right to stand as equals alongside the Red Army. For these preemptive strikes on German cities brought Luftwaffe retaliation on British cities, giving "Coventry and Birmingham, Sheffield and Southampton, the right to look Kiev and Kharkov, Stalingrad and Sebastopol in the face. Our Soviet Allies would have been less critical of our inactivity in 1942 if they had understood what we have done."[164]

Though British propaganda broadcasts charged that the Luftwaffe had begun the bombing of cities by brutally targeting London, Spaight believed that British cities might have been spared had Churchill not first resorted to city bombing: "There was no certainty, but there was a reasonable probability that our capital and our industrial centres would not have been attacked if we had continued to refrain from attacking those of Germany."[165]

"To achieve the extirpation of Nazi tyranny there are no lengths

PATRICK J. BUCHANAN

of violence to which we will not go," Churchill told Parliament on September 21, 1943.[166] By 1944, he had come back around to the idea of using chemical and biological warfare on civilians. In one secret project, he commissioned the preparation of five million anthrax cakes to be dropped onto the pastures of north Germany to poison the cattle and through them the people. As the Glasgow *Sunday Herald* reported in 2001,

> The aim of Operation Vegetarian was to wipe out the German beef and dairy herds and then see the bacterium spread to the human population. With people then having no access to antibiotics, this would have caused many thousands—perhaps even millions—of German men, women and children to suffer awful deaths.[167]

The anthrax cakes were tested on Gruinard Island, off Wester Ross in Scotland, which was not cleared of contamination until 1990.

In July of 1944, as the Allies were still attempting a breakout from Normandy, Churchill minuted General "Pug" Ismay of the Chief of Staffs committee,

> I want you to think very seriously over this question of poison gas. . . . We could drench the cities of the Ruhr and many other cities in Germany in such a way that most of the population would be requiring constant medical attention. . . . [I]f we do it, let us do it one hundred percent. In the meantime, I want the matter studied in cold blood by sensible people and not by that particular set of psalm-singing uniformed defeatists. . . . I shall of course have to square Uncle Joe and the President.[168]

"It is absurd to consider morality on this topic," Churchill told his RAF planners.[169]

On the fiftieth anniversary of the destruction of Dresden, the *Washington Post*'s Ken Ringle wrote, "[I]f any one person can be blamed for the tragedy at Dresden, it appears to have been Churchill."[170]

Before leaving for Yalta, Churchill ordered Operation Thunderclap, massive air strikes to de-house German civilians to turn them into refugees to clog the roads over which German soldiers had to move to stop a Red Army offensive. Air Marshal Arthur "Bomber" Harris put Dresden on the target list. On the first night of the raid, 770 Lancasters arrived over Dresden around 10 P.M.:

> In two waves three hours apart, 650,000 incendiary bombs rained down on Dresden's narrow streets and baroque buildings, together with another 1,474 tons of high explosives. . . . The fires burned for seven days.
>
> More than 1,600 acres of the city were devastated (compared to 100 acres burned in the German raid on Coventry) and melting streets burned the shoes off those attempting to flee. Cars untouched by fire burst into flames just from the heat. Thousands sought refuge in cellars where they died, robbed of oxygen by the flames, before the buildings above them collapsed.
>
> Novelist Kurt Vonnegut, who as one of twenty-six thousand Allied prisoners of war in Dresden helped clean up after the attack, remembers tunneling into the ruins to find the dead sitting upright in what he would describe in "Slaughterhouse Five" as "corpse mines." Floating in the static water tanks were the boiled bodies of hundreds more.[171]

The morning after the Lancasters struck, five hundred B-17s arrived over Dresden in two waves with three hundred fighter escorts to strafe fleeing survivors. Estimates of the dead in the firestorm range from 35,000 to 250,000. The Associated Press reported, "Allied war chiefs have made the long-awaited decision to adopt deliberate terror bombing of German populated centers as a ruthless expedient to hasten Hitler's doom."[172]

In a memo to his air chiefs, Churchill acknowledged what Dresden had been about: "It seems to me that the moment has come when the question of bombing of German cities simply for the sake of increasing the terror, though under other pretexts, should be reviewed."[173] Sensing they were about to be scapegoated for actions Churchill himself ordered, the air chiefs returned the memo. In his 1947 memoir, *Bomber Offensive*, Air Marshal Harris implies that Churchill gave the order to incinerate Dresden: "I will only say that the attack on Dresden was at the time considered a military necessity by much more important people than myself."[174]

Writes A.J.P. Taylor of his countrymen at war:

> What mattered was the outlook: the readiness by the British, of all people, to stop at nothing when waging war. Civilized restraints, all considerations of morality, were abandoned. By the end of the war, men were . . . ready to kill countless women and children. . . . This was the legacy of the bombing strategy which the British adopted with such high-minded motives.[175]

Concludes F.J.P. Veale: "The indiscriminate bombing of civilians, enemy cities, and civilian property brought about a terrifying and unprecedentedly destructive reversion to primary and total warfare" as once practiced "by Sennacherib, Genghis Khan, and Tamerlane."[176]

The old Churchill had made young Churchill a prophet. As he had written in his novel *Savrola*, long before the war in which he led his nation, "Chivalrous gallantry is not among the peculiar characteristics of excited democracy."[177]

Americans, too, played a role in adopting methods of barbarism from which earlier generations would have recoiled in horror and disgust. During World War I, we condemned the British starvation blockade before we went in, but supported it with our warships after we went in. If Churchill initiated terror bombing, America perfected it. Boasted Curtis LeMay of his famous raid on Tokyo, "We scorched and boiled and baked to death more people in Tokyo that night of March 9–10 than went up in vapor in Hiroshima and Nagasaki combined."[178] We and the British fought for moral ends. We did not always use moral means by any Christian definition, and Churchill played the lead role in Western man's reversion to barbarism.

CHURCHILL'S CONVICTIONS

THE FEROCITY WITH WHICH Churchill pursued war against civilians can be traced to his convictions. He was less a Christian than a pagan in the Roman tradition. Though he might sing "Onward Christian Soldiers" at Placentia Bay and sign an Atlantic Charter on the rights of peoples, these had nothing to do with how he prosecuted war. His views on some issues were not that far removed from the man in Berlin for whom he had expressed grudging admiration in *Great Contemporaries.*

Indeed, Churchill might justly be called a post-Christian man. After reading the exuberantly anti-Christian *Martyrdom of Man* by Winwood Reade in Bangalore as a twenty-one-year-old subaltern, Churchill wrote his mother:

> One of these days the cold bright light of science & reason will shine through the cathedral windows & we shall go out into the fields to seek God for ourselves. The great laws of Nature will be understood—our destiny and our past will be clear. We shall then be able to dispense with the religious toys that have agreeably fostered the development of mankind.[179]

After his capture in the armored train disaster by the fiercely Christian Boers, who fought for God and country, Churchill confessed to having been profoundly shaken when he heard a sound,

> which was worse even than the sound of shells: the sound of Boers singing psalms. "It struck the fear of God into me. What sort of men are we fighting? They have the better cause—and the cause is everything—at least I mean to them it is the better cause."[180]

In truth, the Boers had the "better cause." And Churchill could count himself fortunate that his captors were pious Christians and not Afghan or Sioux.

Nor did Churchill in his last days hold out hope for the world to come. He approached his end a despairing atheist, telling his lifelong friend Violet Bonham Carter that "death meant extinction" and "eternity was a nightmare possibility."[181]

Writing in *The Spectator* in scorn of "the cult of Churchill," Michael Lind put on the record views of the Great Man that might shock Americans. Churchill was no egalitarian humanist. In 1910, he informed Prime Minister Asquith of his gnawing social concern:

> The unnatural and increasingly rapid rise of the feeble-minded and insane classes, coupled as it is with a steady restriction among the thrifty, energetic and superior stocks, constitutes a national and race danger which it is impossible to exaggerate. I feel that the source from which the stream of madness is fed should be cut off and sealed up before another year has passed.[182]

When the Mental Deficiency Act was advanced to sterilize the feeble-minded and "other degenerate types," Asquith's government agreed to consider the measure. Writes Edwin Black, author of *War Against the Weak,*

Home Secretary Winston Churchill, an enthusiastic supporter of eugenics, reassured one group of eugenicists that
Britain's 120,000 feeble-minded persons "should, if possible,
be segregated under proper conditions so that their curse
died with them and was not transmitted to future generations." The plan called for the creation of vast colonies.
Thousands of Britain's unfit would be moved into these
colonies to live out their days.[183]

"Hitler's ultimately genocidal programme of 'racial hygiene' began
with the kind of compulsory sterilization of the 'feeble-minded and
insane classes' that Churchill urged on the British government,"
writes Lind.[184]

Though a philo-Semite and supporter of Zionism, Churchill's
views on the roots of Bolshevism seem not markedly different from
those of Hitler. In the *Illustrated Sunday Herald* of February 8, 1920,
after the failed Allied intervention in Russia, Churchill wrote that in
the "creation of Bolshevism" the role of "atheistical Jews . . . probably outweighs all others."[185] Contrasting the patriotism of "National
Russian Jews" with the "schemes of the International Jews,"
Churchill describes the latter:

[A] sinister confederacy . . . [of] men reared up among the
unhappy populations of countries where Jews are persecuted
on account of their race. Most, if not all, of them have for-
saken the faith of their forefathers, and divorced from their
minds all spiritual hopes of the next world. This movement
among the Jews is not new. From the days of Spartacus-
Weishaupt to those of Karl Marx, and down to Trotsky
(Russia), Bela Kun (Hungary), Rosa Luxembourg (Germany),
and Emma Goldman (the United States), this world-wide
conspiracy for the overthrow of civilisation and for the re-
constitution of society on the basis of the arrested development, of envious malevolence, and impossible equality, has

been steadily growing. . . . [T]his band of extraordinary personalities from the underworld of the great cities of Europe
and America have gripped the Russian people by the hair of
their heads and have become practically the undisputed
masters of that enormous empire.[186]

Had Churchill not been a dedicated Zionist, he might have suffered the fate of Father Coughlin, though it needs to be emphasized:
Churchill was no anti-Semite. He admired Jews, respected their abil-
ities and accomplishments, befriended Zionists and national Jews,
and loathed only those apostates to their faith who had cast their lot
with Lenin and Trotsky.

"All is race," wrote Disraeli in *Tancred*, "there is nothing else."
Churchill would have agreed. In *Eminent Churchillians*, Andrew
Roberts writes that his views were not only "more profoundly racist
than most," they influenced his conduct as a statesman.[187]

> Churchill's racial assumptions occupied a prime place both
> in his political philosophy and in his views on international
> relations. He was a convinced white . . . supremacist and
> thought in terms of race to a degree that was remarkable
> even by the standards of his own time. He spoke of certain
> races with a virulent Anglo-Saxon triumphalism which was
> wholly lacking in other twentieth-century prime ministers,
> and in a way which even as early as the 1920s shocked some
> Cabinet colleagues.[188]

To Churchill, blood and race were determinant in the history of
nations and civilizations. Introducing the peoples of the Sudan in *The
River War*, his memoir of the campaign in which he had served under
Kitchener, Churchill wrote:

> The qualities of mongrels are rarely admirable, and the mix-
> ture of the Arab and negro types has produced a debased and

cruel breed, more shocking because they are more intelligent than the primitive savages. The stronger race soon began to prey upon the simple aboriginals. . . . All, without exception, were hunters of men.[189]

To Churchill, Negroes were "niggers" or "blackamoors," Arabs "worthless," Chinese "chinks" or "pigtails," Indians "baboos," and South African blacks "Hottentots."[190]

Churchill's physician Lord Moran wrote in his diary that, while FDR was thinking of the importance of a China of four hundred million, Churchill "thinks only of the color of their skin; it is when he talks of India and China that you remember he is a Victorian."[191] Years after the war, Moran wrote, "It would seem that he has scarcely moved an inch from his attitude toward China since the day of the Boxer Rebellion [of 1899–1901]."[192]

Writing to the Palestine Commission in 1936, Churchill made his convictions clear: "I do not admit . . . that a great wrong has been done to the Red Indians of America or the black people of Australia . . . by the fact that a stronger race, a higher grade race . . . has come and taken their place."[193]

Churchill, writes Andrew Roberts, "found Indians 'the beastliest people in the world, next to the Germans.' "[194]

> During the 1943 Bengal famine, in which over a million Indians died, [Churchill] reassured the Secretary of State for India, Leo Amery, that they would nevertheless continue to breed "like rabbits." After such an outburst in 1944, Amery was prompted to tell the Prime Minister that he "didn't see much difference between his outlook and Hitler's."[195]

During the war, Churchill ranted against Indian demands for independence. "I hate Indians," he said. "They are a beastly people with a beastly religion."[196] Beseeched by Amery and the Indian viceroy to release food stocks in the wartime famine, "Churchill responded with a telegram asking why Gandhi hadn't died yet."[197]

One may find like comments in other leaders of the nineteenth and early twentieth centuries. But Churchill, as First Lord of the Admiralty in two wars and prime minister for five years of the bloodiest war in history, was in a position to act on his beliefs. And he did.

"KEEP ENGLAND WHITE"

THOSE RACIAL BELIEFS were behind the uncompromising stand Churchill took on "what was then called coloured immigration from the British Commonwealth" in his last days as prime minister in the mid-1950s.[198] Churchill was a restrictionist. His thinking paralleled that of Lord Salisbury, who had declared: "It is not for me merely a question of whether criminal negroes should be allowed in or not . . . it is a question whether great quantities of negroes, criminal or not, should be allowed to come."[199]

"Churchill's feelings were strongly in [Salisbury's] direction," writes historian Peter Hennessey.[200] To the governor of Jamaica, Sir Hugh Foot, Churchill said in 1954 that were immigration from the Caribbean not halted, "we would have a magpie society: that would never do."[201]

Colored immigration weighed heavily on his mind. Churchill told one interviewer, "I think it is the most important subject facing this country, but I cannot get any of my ministers to take notice."[202] Writes Hennessey, "Just as [Churchill] was distressed by the break-up of the British Empire, he was, for all his imperial romance, deeply disturbed about its black or brown members coming to the mother country."[203]

Future prime minister Harold Macmillan, in his diary entry on the Cabinet meeting of January 20, 1955, wrote: "More discussion about the West Indian immigrants. A Bill is being drafted—but it's not an easy problem. P.M. [Churchill] thinks 'Keep England White' a good slogan!"[204]

Had Churchill endured in office, there might have been legislation, says Hennessey. London would look entirely different today. But by April, against his will, Churchill was out as prime minister, no longer able to lead a campaign to "Keep England White"—an astonishing slogan in a day when Dr. Martin Luther King, a disciple of Gandhi whom Churchill had detested, was starting out in Montgomery. In 1968, Enoch Powell, Tory shadow minister of defense, would take up the banner of Salisbury and Churchill and deliver his "Rivers of Blood" speech. By then, time had passed the restrictionists by, and England was on its way to becoming the multiracial, multicultural nation of today, no longer Churchill's England.

STATESMAN—OR WAR CHIEF?

THAT CHURCHILL WAS A GREAT war leader who inspired as he led his people is undeniable. But was he a great statesman?

"You ask: What is our policy?" he had roared to the House of Commons on May 13, 1940.

> I will say, "It is to wage war, by sea, land and air, with all our might and with all the strength that God can give us: to wage war against a monstrous tyranny, never surpassed in the dark lamentable catalogue of human crime. That is our policy."
>
> You ask, What is our aim? I can answer with one word: Victory—victory at all costs, victory in spite of all terror, victory however long and hard the road may be; for without victory there is no survival.[205]

This is the rhetoric of a war chief.

When Hitler invaded Russia, Churchill welcomed Stalin into the camp of the saints. On September 21, 1943, after the tide had turned at Stalingrad and the vast Red Army was moving inexorably westward toward Europe, Churchill was still monomaniacal on the evil of Germany:

> The twin roots of all our evils, Nazi tyranny and Prussian militarism, must be extirpated. Until this is achieved, there are no sacrifices we will not make and no lengths in violence to which we will not go.[206]

It was this mind-set that led Churchill to accept the Soviet annexation of eastern Poland and Eastern Europe, to endorse FDR's call at Casablanca for "unconditional surrender," to agree to Morgenthau's plan to turn Germany into a pasture, to test anthrax cakes to poison German civilians, to unleash waves of bombers on the defenseless cities of a defeated country.

This single-minded determination of Churchill to pulverize and punish Germany played directly into the hands of Goebbels and Stalin. The Nazi propaganda minister used the Allied demand for unconditional surrender and the vindictive Morgenthau Plan to convince Germans they must go on fighting to the death, as defeat meant no survival for the nation. Eisenhower believed the demand for an unconditional surrender at Casablanca extended the war by years and cost countless lives. And the destruction of Germany to which Churchill had dedicated himself left a power vacuum in Europe Stalin inevitably filled. Britain fought Nazi tyranny for six years, only to pave the path to power for a greater tyranny.

Within months of the war's end, Churchill was bewailing the "Iron Curtain" that had fallen across Europe and the horrors taking place on the far side. Within a few years, he was to call for the rearmament of those same Germans he had called "Huns," to help defend Christian civilization. Evil as they were, "Nazi tyranny and Prussian militarism" had not been "the twin roots of all our evils." When the Nazi tyranny fell, others—Stalin's, Tito's, Mao's, Kim Il Sung's, some mightier and even more murderous—arose.

"War," said the soldier-scholar Clausewitz, "is a continuation of policy by other means."[207] The warrior's goal is victory. The statesman's goal is a peace that leaves the nation more secure. Churchill succeeded magnificently as a war leader. He failed as a statesman.

As time went by, Churchill seemed to realize it. "As the blinkers of war were removed," writes John Charmley, "Churchill began to perceive the magnitude of the mistake that had been made."[208] After the war, he told Robert Boothby, "Historians are apt to judge war ministers less by the victories achieved under their direction than by the political results which flowed from them. Judged by that standard, I am not sure that I shall be held to have done very well."[209]

Stalin kept in mind always what Europe would look like after the war. Churchill seemed not to have thought long or deeply over the fate of the continent if Germany, Europe's ancient barrier to Oriental despotism and barbarism, were annihilated. Blindly, he helped bring it about.

Full of honors, late in life Churchill must have realized the depth of his failure. For had not he himself written, "Those who can win a war well can rarely make a good peace and those who could make a good peace would never have won the war." Yet statesmen have done both: Washington, Wellington, Bismarck, and MacArthur come to mind.

"MILKING THE BRITISH COW"

WHAT WAS THE LEGACY of Winston Churchill?

If one traces his career from his entry into the inner Cabinet as First Lord in 1911 to his final departure from 10 Downing Street in 1955, that half century encompasses the collapse of British power. In 1911, the sun never set on the British Empire. In 1955, all was lost save honor. India was gone. Egypt and the Suez Canal were gone. Palestine was gone. All the colonies in Asia and Africa were going. Russians and Americans were the hegemons of Europe and the

Dominions were looking to Washington, not London, for protection and leadership. Britain was no longer great. The long and brilliant career of the Man of the Century coincided precisely with the decline and fall of Britain as a world power and a great power.

When Churchill at last yielded office to Eden in 1955, the ex–Labour minister Anuerin Bevan said satirically: "Sir Winston Churchill's superlative personal gifts have eased the passage of Britain to the status of a second-rate power."[210]

The twentieth century was not the British Century. It was the American Century. Churchill believed the two English-speaking peoples would be eternal partners, with British statesmen playing Greeks to America's Romans. But when Britain was in her darkest hour, FDR shook her down for every dime. Poring over a list of British assets in the Western Hemisphere that Morgenthau had requested, Roosevelt "reacted with the coolness of a WASP patrician: 'Well, they aren't bust—there's lots of money there.' "[211]

Looking back, Alan Clark was appalled by Churchill's groveling to the Americans:

> Churchill's abasement of Britain before the United States has its origins in the same obsession [with Hitler]. The West Indian bases were handed over; the closed markets for British exports were to be dismantled; the entire portfolio of (largely private) holdings in America was liquidated. "A very nice little list," was Roosevelt's comment when the British ambassador offered it. "You guys aren't broken yet."[212]

Before Lend-Lease aid could begin, Britain was forced to sell all her commercial assets in the United States and turn over all her gold. FDR sent his own ship, the *Quincy*, to Simonstown near Cape Town to pick up the last $50 million in British gold reserves.[213]

"[W]e are not only to be skinned but flayed to the bone," Churchill wailed to his colleagues.[214] He was not far off. Churchill drafted a letter to FDR saying that if America continued along this line, she would "wear the aspect of a sheriff collecting the last assets of a helpless debtor."[215] It was, said the prime minister, "not fitting that any nation should put itself wholly in the hands of another."[216] Desperately dependent as Britain was on America, Churchill reconsidered, and rewrote his note in more conciliatory tones.

And FDR knew exactly what he was doing. "We have been milking the British financial cow, which had plenty of milk at one time, but which has now about become dry," Roosevelt confided to one Cabinet member.[217]

Writes A.J.P. Taylor of how Roosevelt humbled Churchill:

> Great Britain became a poor, though deserving cousin—not to Roosevelt's regret. So far as it is possible to read his devious mind, it appears that he expected the British to wear down both Germany and themselves. When all independent powers had ceased to exist, the United States would step in and run the world.[218]

At Teheran and Yalta, where FDR should have supported his British ally, he mocked Churchill to amuse Stalin. FDR thought the British Empire an anachronism that ought to be abolished. "We are therefore presented," writes Captain Grenfell, "with the extraordinary paradox that Britain's principal enemy was anxious for the British empire to remain in being, while her principal ally, the United States, was determined to destroy it."[219]

When Churchill's successor Eden invaded Suez in 1956 to retake the Canal from the Egyptian dictator who had nationalized it, Harold Macmillan assured the Cabinet, "I know Ike. He will lie doggo."[220]

Like many Brits, Macmillan misread Ike and the Americans. Ike ordered Britain out of Egypt. Faced with a U.S. threat to sink the pound, the humiliated Brits submitted and departed. Eden fell. The new Romans would not be needing any Greeks. Correlli Barnett is savage on Churchill's naiveté in believing in a "special relationship" with the Americans:

> The Second World War saw the disastrous culmination of the long-standing but unreciprocated British belief in the existence of a "special relationship" between England and America. For the Americans—like the Russians, like the Germans, like the English themselves—were motivated by a desire to promote their own interests rather than by sentiment, which was a commodity they reserved for Pilgrim's Dinners, where it could do no harm. Churchill's policy therefore provided the Americans with the opportunity first, of prospering on British orders, and secondly, of humbling British world power, a long-cherished American ambition. From 1940 to the end of the Second World War and after, it was America, not Russia, which was to constitute that lurking menace to British interests which Churchill, in his passionate obsession with defeating Germany, failed to perceive.[221]

Canadian historian Edward Ingram seconds Barnett, calling Britain's "alignment with the United States . . . a strangling alliance in which one party uses the alliance to destroy the other."[222]

> The relationship between the United Kingdom and Britain is shown in the U.S. offer during World War II to defend the United Kingdom but not the British Empire. As the destruction of Britain as a world power was the price to be paid for the safety of the United Kingdom, Englishmen and Scots were asked to buy safety for themselves by throwing [other subjects] and Indians to the wolves.[223]

"We must never get out of step with the Americans—never," Churchill told Violet Bonham Carter.[224] Charmley considers this maxim to reflect one of Churchill's greatest failures of vision, how he "imperfectly understood the dynamics of American power and its hostility to the Empire to which he had devoted so much of his life."[225]

In *Eminent Churchillians*, Andrew Roberts writes of how one British writer had wittily graded George VI as king and sovereign:

> Considering that King George VI's sixteen-year reign spanned Anschluss, Munich, the Second World War, the communist domination of Eastern Europe, the loss of India and the twilight of empire, post-war Austerity and Britain's eclipse as a global superpower, one might sympathize with Evelyn Waugh's valediction, "George VI's reign will go down in history as the most disastrous my country has known since Matilda and Stephen."[226]

"Of course," writes Roberts charitably, "the King was in no way personally to blame for any of this."[227] No, the King was not. But, then, who was? What did Churchill recommend at Anschluss? Did he not applaud Chamberlain's war guarantee to Poland that led to the Second World War, Stalin's domination of Eastern Europe, Britain's bankruptcy, the postwar Austerity, the early and humiliating end of the British Empire, and Britain's eclipse as a world power? Who sacrificed everything to stand atop the rubble of Hitler's Reich? If the reign of George VI was, as Waugh said, the "most disastrous my country has known since Matilda and Stephen," but the king was not to blame, who was? Who made British history in the reign of the late and unlamented George VI?

The title of the last book of his six-volume history of World War II, *Triumph and Tragedy*, was apposite. Churchill's words are immortal, but the deeds with which he brought triumph to himself produced tragedy for his nation and the world. He inherited a great empire, but left an island-nation off the coast of Europe with three centuries of its wealth, power, and prestige sunk. After Potsdam and his dismissal, when the lasting ruin the war had visited on his nation had sunk in, Churchill seemed often to be melancholy. Returning by train to Washington following his Iron Curtain speech in Fulton, Missouri, Churchill was talking with Clark Clifford and Truman's spokesman Charlie Ross of the events that had shaped his life; suddenly he blurted, "If I were to be born again, I would wish to be born in the United States. Your country is the future of the world. . . . Great Britain has passed its zenith."[228]

In Cairo in 1943, Churchill was entertaining Macmillan. The war had passed its crisis point and Churchill seemed briefly to realize that, after all the spilled blood and lost treasure, Stalin might emerge as the master of Europe—"one monstrous regime . . . about to replace another that was slowly being strangled to death."[229] He turned suddenly to Macmillan.

" 'Cromwell was a great man, wasn't he?' Churchill asked.

" 'Yes, sir, a very great man,' Macmillan replied.

" 'Ah, but he made one terrible mistake,' Churchill went on. 'Obsessed in his youth by fear of the power of Spain, he failed to observe the rise of France. Will that be said of me?' "[230]

Yes, it will be said of him.

He had been a great man—at the cost of his country's greatness.

CHAPTER 15

America Inherits the Empire

ONE MAY PICK UP something useful from among the
most fatal errors.[1]

—JAMES WOLFE, 1757
Hero of Quebec

IN THE TWIN CATASTROPHES of Western civilization, World
Wars I and II, Britain was the indispensable nation and Churchill an
indispensable man.

It was Britain's secret commitment to fight for France, of which
the Germans were left unaware, that led to the world war with a
Kaiser who never wanted to fight his mother's country. It was Britain's
declaration of war on August 4, 1914, that led Canada, Australia, New
Zealand, South Africa, and India to declare war in solidarity with the
Mother Country and drew Britain's ally Japan into the conflict. It was
Britain's bribery of Italy with promises of Habsburg and Ottoman
lands in the secret Treaty of London in 1915 that brought Italy in.
Had Britain not gone in, America would have stayed out.

It was Britain that converted a Franco-German-Russian war into
a world war of four years that brought down the German, Russian,
Ottoman, and Austro-Hungarian empires and gave the world Lenin,
Stalin, Mussolini, and Hitler.

It was Britain whose capitulation to U.S. pressure and dissolution
of her twenty-year pact with Japan in 1922 insulted, isolated, and enraged that faithful ally, leading directly to Japanese militarism, aggression, and World War II in the Pacific.

It was Britain's lead in imposing the League of Nations sanctions on Italy over Abyssinia that destroyed the Stresa Front, isolated Italy, and drove Mussolini into the arms of Hitler.

Had the British stood firm and backed Paris, the French army could have chased Hitler's battalions out of the Rhineland in 1936 and reoccupied it.

Had the British not gone to Munich, Hitler would have had to fight for the Sudetenland and Europe might have united against him.

Had Britain not issued the war guarantee to Poland and declared war over Poland, there might have been no war in Western Europe and no World War II.

Britain was thus the indispensable nation in turning two European wars into world wars. And as is written in the opening pages of this book, their role in both world wars was heroic. But was it wise?

INDISPENSABLE MAN

CHURCHILL HAD PLAYED A crucial role in plunging his nation into the war of 1914. Britain then brought in the Dominions, Italy, Japan, and the United States. Asquith, Grey, Churchill, and Haldane had planned to make any war with Germany a world war. They succeeded, and Britain emerged triumphant. Her greatest rival since Napoleon saw its High Seas Fleet scuttled, its overseas trade ravaged, its colonies confiscated. Germany had been defeated, disgraced, divided, dismembered, disarmed, and driven into unpayable debt. But the cost had been seven hundred thousand British dead, a national debt fourteen times what it had been in 1914, rebellions across the empire, and Britain's inevitable eclipse as first nation on earth.

The British Century was over. The American Century had begun.

The cost to Western civilization was perhaps ten million dead soldiers, and millions of civilians dead from starvation and disease. The Great War begat Versailles and Versailles begat the Second World War.

To "stop Hitler," Britain gave a war guarantee to Poland. To honor it, Britain declared war. Both decisions were victories for Churchill. This war lasted six years and ended in the ruin of Europe, Stalinization of eleven nations, and collapse of the British and French empires.

In the two phases of the Great Civil War of the West, a hundred million Europeans perished as victims of war or the monsters bred by war. Nor did the killing stop with Hitler's suicide in his bunker. From the Baltic to the Balkans, Stalin's murders went on and on, and a triumphant Communism conquered China and North Korea, leading to the mass murder of tens of millions of Asian friends of the West. Looking back at the fruits of these two world wars in 1950, George Kennan wrote:

> [T]oday, if one were offered the chance of having back again the Germany of 1913—a Germany run by conservative but relatively moderate people, no Nazis and no Communists, a vigorous Germany, united and unoccupied, full of energy and confidence, able to play a part again in the balancing-off of Russian power in Europe—well, there would be objections to it from many quarters, and it wouldn't make everybody happy, but in many ways it wouldn't sound so bad, in comparison with our problems of today. Now, think what this means. When you total up the score of two [world] wars, in terms of their ostensible objective, you find that if there has been any gain at all, it is pretty hard to discern.[2]

The price of Britain's victory in 1945 was four hundred thousand more dead, the fall of the empire, an end to the days of hope and glory, and bankruptcy of the nation. Britain faced socialism at home, a near-absolute dependency on the United States, and the displacement of Nazi Germany as dominant power in Europe by a Stalinist Russia with a revolutionary agenda that posed a far greater menace to

British interests and Western civilization. All the British Dominions and colonies now turned to America for their defense and leadership. For coming belatedly to the rescue of the Mother Country, America had demanded and taken title to her estate. Britannia was allotted a cottage by the sea—to live out her declining years. But the Great Man was given his own statue in Parliament Square.

HOW AMERICA TRIUMPHED

IN NEGOTIATING WITH Stalin, Churchill, as we have seen, made far greater blunders than had Chamberlain in dealing with Hitler. He had put his trust in Stalin, believing that if Britain gave him all he demanded, Stalin would cooperate in building a lasting peace. By March 1946, when Churchill gave his Iron Curtain speech, it was apparent to all but the incurably gullible that Churchill had been had, that the Soviet Union was—and had always been—a mortal enemy of the West.

The Americans had watched the initial crisis from afar. On September 3, 1939, the same day Britain and France declared war, FDR had assured the nation in a Fireside Chat, "There will be no blackout on peace in the United States."

This war was not America's war, FDR told his countrymen. In 1940, the year of Churchill's Norwegian debacle, Dunkirk, and the fall of France, FDR won reelection on a pledge: "While I am talking to you mothers and fathers, I give you one more assurance. I have said this before but I shall say it again and again and again. Your boys are not going to be sent into any foreign wars."

FDR was lying. But in the election of 1940, he had to echo America First. For even after Hitler had occupied Europe from the Atlantic to the Vistula, America was saying, "This is not our war."

Though derided as isolationists, the America First patriots kept the United States out of the war until six months after Hitler had invaded Russia. Thus the Red Army bore the brunt of bloody combat to bring Hitler down, as would seem only right. For Stalin had colluded with Hitler in the rape of Poland and had launched wars of aggression against as many nations as his partners in Berlin.

Not until four years after France had fallen and three years after the Soviet Union had been invaded did U.S. troops land on the Normandy beaches to open the Second Front. There the Americans and British faced a German army one-fourth the size of the German armies on the Eastern Front. Because we stayed out of the war until after the Soviet Union had been invaded, America lost four hundred thousand men, while Soviet combat losses are estimated at ten times that. How many more U.S. military cemeteries would there be in Europe had we had to face a German army of three million instead of the seven hundred thousand troops under Rommel and von Rundstedt on D-Day?

America is the last superpower because she stayed out of the world wars until their final acts. And because she stayed out of the alliances and the world wars longer than any other great power, America avoided the fate of the seven other nations that entered the twentieth century as great powers. The British, French, German, Austro-Hungarian, Russian, Ottoman, and Japanese empires are all gone. We alone remain, because we had men who recalled the wisdom of Washington, Jefferson, and John Quincy Adams about avoiding entangling alliances, staying out of European wars, and not going "abroad in search of monsters to destroy."

THE ROAD LESS TRAVELED BY

After America emerged as the undisputed leader of the West in 1945, however, the shocks, reversals, and humiliations at the hands of Stalin were greater than those that had caused Britain to declare war in 1939. America, however, chose a different course. Embracing the wisdom of George Kennan, America pursued a policy of containment and conscious avoidance of a Third World War.

When Stalin trashed the Yalta agreement, terrorizing the peoples of Poland and Eastern Europe for whom Britain had gone to war, America was stunned and sickened but issued no ultimata. When Moscow blockaded Berlin in violation of Allied rights, Truman responded with an airlift, not armored divisions or atom bombs. When Stalin's agents carried out the Prague coup in 1948, Truman did not see in Czechoslovakia an issue that justified war, as Churchill had when the Czechs were forced to give up the Sudetenland. America's answer was NATO, drawing a red line across Europe that the West could defend, as Britain should have done in that March of 1939, instead of handing out the insane war guarantee to Poland. And where the British had failed to line up a Russian alliance before giving its war guarantee, America enlisted ten European allies before committing herself to defend West Germany.

Unlike Churchill in the 1930s, American leaders of the late 1940s and 1950s believed that, while the fate of Poland and Czechoslovakia was tragic, both were beyond any U.S. vital interest. From 1949 to 1989, the American army never crossed the Yalta line. When East Germans rose in 1953 and Hungarians in 1956, Eisenhower declined to act. In 1959, Ike welcomed the "Butcher of Budapest" to Camp David. When Khrushchev built the Berlin Wall, Kennedy called up the reserves, then sent them home after a year. In the missile crisis of 1962, Kennedy cut a secret deal to take U.S. missiles out of Turkey for Khrushchev's taking Russian missiles out of Cuba. When the Prague Spring was crushed in 1968, LBJ did nothing.

U.S. inaction was not due to cowardice but cold calculation as to what was worth risking war with a nuclear-armed Soviet Union and what was not worth risking war. When the Polish workers' movement, Solidarity, was crushed in 1981, Ronald Reagan denounced the repression but he neither broke diplomatic relations with Warsaw nor imposed economic sanctions.

Eisenhower and Reagan were not Chamberlains, but neither were they Churchills. Who ruled in the capitals east of the Elbe was not to them a vital U.S. interest worth a war. They believed in defending what we had, not risking war to retake what Roosevelt and Churchill had given up at Teheran and Yalta. Reagan believed America and freedom were the future, that Communism was headed for the ash heap of history, that we need not, indeed, must not blunder into a war to hasten its inevitable end. Patience and perseverance were required, the use of proxies to bedevil the Soviet Empire at its outposts in Afghanistan, Angola, and Nicaragua, and carrying a bigger stick—that was the Reagan way.

For half a century, the United States confronted Stalinist enemies as evil as Hitler, but more powerful and more dedicated to our destruction. Yet America never went to war with the Soviet Union. We won the Cold War—by avoiding the blunders Britain made that plunged her into two world wars.

Unlike the Brits of 1914 and 1939, Americans did not feel the need to "pull the bully down" if it meant war with a great power such as the Soviet Union of Stalin, Khrushchev, and Brezhnev. Our way was not as glorious as Churchill's way, but Reagan won the Cold War and world leadership without firing a shot, while Churchill, who had inherited a world empire, left behind a small dependency. To win a war without fighting is the greatest victory, said Sun Tzu. That was Reagan's achievement.

REPLICATING CHURCHILLIAN FOLLY

WITH THE END OF THE Cold War in 1989 and the collapse of the Soviet Union in 1991, America was at her apogee. All the great European nations—Britain, France, Germany, Italy—were U.S. allies, as were Turkey, Israel, Saudi Arabia, and Egypt in the Middle East, and Australia, South Korea, and Japan in the Far East. In the Reagan era, Russia was converted from the "evil empire" of the early 1980s into a nation where he could walk Red Square arm in arm with Gorbachev, with Russians straining to pat him on the back.

Four hundred million people in Europe and the USSR had been set free. The Red Army had begun to pack and go home. The captive nations looked on Reagan's America as their liberator. With all the territory and security any country could ask for, the first economic, political, cultural, and military power on earth, America ought to have adopted a policy to protect and preserve what she had. For she had everything. Instead we started out on the familiar road. We were now going to create our own New World Order.

After 9/11, the project took on urgency when George W. Bush, a president disinterested and untutored in foreign policy, was converted to a Wilsonian ideology of democratic fundamentalism: Only by making the whole world democratic can we make America secure. "Marxism is a religion," Joseph Schumpeter said in 1942; and, as James A. Montanye, an economist and student of Schumpeter, has written:

> To the believer, [Democratic Fundamentalism, like Marxism], presents, first, a system of ultimate ends that embody the meaning of life and are absolute standards by which to judge events and actions; and, secondly, a guide to those ends which implies a plan of salvation and the indication of the evil from which mankind, or a chosen section of mankind, is to be saved. . . . [It] belongs to that subgroup [of "isms"] which promises paradise this side of the grave.[3]

Democratic Fundamentalism, added Montanye, is akin to "the religious fervors of old."[4]

Bush professes his faith in the ideology of democratic fundamentalism in his neobiblical rhetoric: As Christ said, "He who is not with me is against me," Bush declared, "Either you are with us or you are with the terrorists." "This war is a struggle between good and evil." "The evil ones . . . have no country, no ideology; they're motivated by hate." America's "ultimate goal" is "ending tyranny in our world."

After seven years of a foreign policy rooted in such "moral clarity," the world of 1989 has disappeared and America has begun to resemble the Britain of Salisbury and Balfour, a superpower past her prime, with enemies rising everywhere.

In Latin America, Castro has found a successor in Hugo Chávez. Across the Middle East, Islamic peoples seek to expel us. We are mired in wars in Iraq and Afghanistan and defied by that surviving partner of the "Axis of Evil," Iran. China may be about to become for us what Wilhelmine Germany became for Britain. Notwithstanding all the neoconservative blather about our being an "omnipower" in "a unipolar world," we are bedeviled on every continent.

What happened?

Rather than follow the wisdom of conservative men like Kennan, Eisenhower, and Reagan, we began to emulate every folly of imperial Britain in her plunge from power. With all our braying about being the "indispensable nation" and "Bring 'em on!" braggadocio, we exhibited an imperial hubris the whole world came to detest.

There is hardly a blunder of the British Empire we have not replicated. As Grey and Churchill seized on von Kluck's violation of Belgian neutrality to put their precooked plans for war into effect, the neoconservatives seized on 9/11 to persuade our untutored president that he had a historic mission to bring down Saddam Hussein, liberate Iraq, establish a strategic position flanking Iran and Syria, democratize the Middle East and the Islamic world, and make himself the Churchill of his generation.

As Chamberlain gave a war guarantee to Poland he could not honor, the United States began to hand out NATO war guarantees to six Warsaw Pact nations, the three Baltic republics, and, soon, Ukraine and Georgia. Should a hostile regime come to power in Moscow and reoccupy these nations, we would have to declare war. Yet no matter how much we treasure the newly free Lithuania, Latvia, and Estonia, their independence is not a vital U.S. interest, and never has been. And the threatened loss of their independence cannot justify war with a nuclear-armed Russia.

As Britain had a "balance-of-power" policy not to permit any nation to become dominant in Europe, the 2002 National Security Strategy of the United States declares our intention not to permit any nation to rise to a position to challenge U.S. dominance on any continent—an attempt to freeze in place America's transient moment of global supremacy. But time does not stand still. New powers arise. Old powers fade. And no power can for long dominate the whole world. Look again at that graveyard of empires, the twentieth century. Even we Americans cannot stop the march of history.

As Britain threw over Japan and drove Italy into the arms of Hitler, Bush pushes Russia's Putin into the arms of China by meddling in the politics of Georgia, Ukraine, and Belarus, planting U.S. bases in Central Asia, and hectoring him for running an autocratic state that does not pass muster with the National Endowment for Democracy.

Ours is a peculiarly American blindness. Under the Monroe Doctrine, foreign powers are to stay out of our hemisphere. Yet no other great power is permitted to have its own sphere of influence. We bellow self-righteously when foreigners funnel cash into our elections, yet intrude massively with tax dollars in the elections of other nations—to promote our religion of democracy.

As the British launched an imperial war in Iraq after their victory over the Ottoman Empire, we launched a war in Iraq after our victory over the Soviet Empire. Never before have our commitments been so numerous or extensive. Yet our active-duty forces have been reduced to one-half of 1 percent of our population, one-ninth the number under arms in May 1945.

We are approaching what Walter Lippmann called "foreign policy bankruptcy." Our strategic assets, armaments, and allies cannot cover our strategic liabilities, our commitments to go to war on behalf of scores of nations from Central and South America to the Baltic and the Balkans, to the Middle East, the Gulf, Japan, South Korea, the Philippines, Australia, and Taiwan. Like the British before us, America has reached imperial overstretch. Either we double or treble our air, sea, and land forces, or we start shedding commitments, or we are headed inexorably for an American Dienbienphu. For if the U.S. Army and Marine Corps are stretched to the limit by the insurgencies in Mesopotamia and Afghanistan, how can we police the rest of the planet?

We cannot. If two or three of the IOUs we have handed out are called in, the bankruptcy of U.S. foreign policy will be exposed to the world.

America is as overextended as the British Empire of 1939. We have commitments to fight on behalf of scores of nations that have nothing to do with our vital interests, commitments we could not honor were several to be called in at once. We have declared it to be U.S. policy to democratize the planet, to hold every nation to our standards of social justice and human rights, and to "end tyranny in the world."

And to show the world he meant business, President Bush had placed in his Oval Office a bust of Winston Churchill.

NOTES

EPIGRAPH

1. Andrew Roberts, *Salisbury: Victorian Titan* (London: Weidenfeld & Nicolson, 1999), p. 687.
2. Emrys Hughes, *Winston Churchill: British Bulldog* (New York: Exposition Press, 1955), p. 30.

PREFACE: WHAT HAPPENED TO US?

1. Charles L. Mee, Jr., *The End of Order: Versailles 1919* (New York: E. P. Dutton, 1980), pp. xvi–xvii.
2. Ibid., p. xvii.
3. Ibid., p. 259.
4. G. J. Meyer, *A World Undone: The Story of the Great War 1914–1918* (New York: E. P. Dutton, 2006), pp. 123, 141.

INTRODUCTION: THE GREAT CIVIL WAR OF THE WEST

1. Captain Russell Grenfell, R.N., *Unconditional Hatred: German War Guilt and the Future of Europe* (New York: Devin-Adair, 1953), p. 68.
2. Russell Kirk, *America's British Culture* (New Brunswick, N.J.: Transaction, 1993), p. 7.
3. Thomas A. Bailey, *Woodrow Wilson and the Lost Peace* (New York: Macmillan, 1944), p. 18; Thomas Fleming, *The Illusion of Victory: America in World War I* (New York: Basic, 2003), p. 319.
4. Walter Lippmann, *U.S. War Aims* (Boston: Little, Brown, 1944), p. 174.
5. *Everyone's Mark Twain*, Compiled by Caroline Thomas Harnsberger (New York: A. S. Barnes, 1972), p. 150.

6. Percy Bysshe Shelley, *Selected Poetry and Prose*, Introduction by Kenneth Neill Cameron (New York: Rinehart, 1958), p. 32.

7. Roy Denman, *Missed Chances: Britain and Europe in the Twentieth Century* (London: Indigo, 1997), p. 1.

8. Erik von Kuehnelt-Leddihn, *Leftism Revisited: From De Sade and Marx to Hitler and Pol Pot* (Washington: Regnery Gateway, 1990), p. 206.

9. Michael Riccards, "Two Years, 10 Major Decisions," *Washington Times*, Aug. 5, 2007, p. B7; Patrick J. Buchanan, *The Death of the West: How Dying Populations and Immigrant Invasions Imperil Our Country and Civilization* (New York: St. Martin's Press, 2002), p. 73.

10. Charles L. Mee, Jr., *The End of Order: Versailles 1919* (New York: E. P. Dutton, 1980), p. xvii.

11. A.J.P. Taylor, *English History: 1914–1945* (New York: Oxford University Press, 1965), p. 274; Alistair Horne, *To Lose a Battle: France 1940* (Boston: Little, Brown, 1969), p. 22.

12. Winston S. Churchill, *The Gathering Storm* (Boston: Houghton Mifflin, 1948), p. iv.

13. John Meacham, "Bush, Yalta and the Blur of Hindsight," *Washington Post*, Sunday, May 15, 2005, p. B1; Patrick J. Buchanan, "Was World War II Worth It?" Creators.com, May 11, 2005.

CHAPTER 1: THE END OF "SPLENDID ISOLATION"

1. Robert K. Massie, *Dreadnought: Britain, Germany and the Coming of the Great War* (New York: Ballantine, 1991), p. 241; Andrew Roberts, *Salisbury: Victorian Titan* (London: Weidenfeld & Nicolson, 1999), p. 628.

2. Massie, p. 241.

3. Roy Denman, *Missed Chances: Britain and Europe in the Twentieth Century* (London: Indigo, 1997), p. 8.

4. Henry A. Kissinger, *Diplomacy* (New York: Simon & Schuster, 1994), p. 178.

5. Bradford Perkins, *The Great Rapprochement: England and the United States, 1895–1914* (New York: Atheneum, 1968), p. 9.
6. Roberts, p. 617.
7. Philip Magnus, *King Edward the Seventh* (New York: E. P. Dutton, 1964), p. 255.
8. Roberts, p. 687.
9. Roberts, p. 688.
10. Roberts, p. 688; Massie, p. 247.
11. Roberts, p. 710.
12. Peter Clarke, *Hope and Glory: Britain 1900–1990* (New York: Penguin Press, 1996), p. 35.
13. Kenton J. Clymer, *John Hay, The Gentleman as Diplomat* (Ann Arbor: University of Michigan Press, 1975), p. 158.
14. Ibid.
15. Ibid.
16. Correlli Barnett, *The Collapse of British Power* (New York: William Morrow, 1972), p. 255.
17. Hajo Holborn, *The Political Collapse of Europe* (New York: Alfred A. Knopf, 1969), p. 72.
18. Denman, p. 8.
19. Massie, pp. 589–90.
20. Winston S. Churchill, *Great Contemporaries* (Chicago: University of Chicago Press, 1973), p. 27.
21. Ibid.
22. Kissinger, p. 134.
23. Carl L. Becker, *Modern History: The Rise of a Democratic, Scientific and Industrialized Civilization* (New York: Silver Burdett, 1946), p. 641.
24. Henrik Bering, "Prussian Maneuvers," *Policy Review*, April–May 2007, p. 94.
25. Michael Sturmer, *The German Empire: 1870–1918* (New York: Modern Library, 2000), p. 83.
26. Holborn, p. 53.

27. George F. Kennan, *The Fateful Alliance: France, Russia and the Coming of the First World War* (New York: Pantheon, 1984), p. 253.
28. Ibid., p. 250.
29. Ibid., p. 251.
30. Giles MacDonogh, *The Last Kaiser: The Life of Wilhelm II* (New York: St. Martin's Press, 2000), p. 251.
31. Magnus, p. 272.
32. MacDonogh, p. 252.
33. Ibid., p. 2.
34. Ibid., p. 461.
35. Ibid., p. 2.
36. Ibid., pp. 306–7.
37. Magnus, p. 338.
38. Barbara W. Tuchman, *The Guns of August* (New York: Macmillan, 1962), p. 2.
39. Massie, p. 185.
40. Arthur Herman, *To Rule the Waves: How the British Navy Shaped the Modern World* (New York: HarperCollins, 2004), p. 471.
41. Ibid., p. 473.
42. Ibid.
43. Ibid., p. 476.
44. MacDonogh, p. 224.
45. Lawrence James, *The Rise and Fall of the British Empire* (New York: St. Martin's Griffin, 1994), p. 335.
46. G. J. Meyer, *A World Undone: The Story of the Great War 1914–1918* (New York: Delacorte Press, 2006), p. 527.
47. Thomas Pakenham, *The Boer War* (New York: Random House, 1979), p. 264.
48. Ibid.
49. Francis Neilson, *The Churchill Legend* (Brooklyn, N.Y.: 29 Books, 2004), p. 113.
50. Ibid.

51. Denman, p. 24.
52. Neilson, p. 115.
53. Magnus, p. 340.
54. Neilson, p. 106; Barbara Tuchman, *The Proud Tower: A Portrait of the World Before the War 1890–1914* (New York: Ballantine, 1994), p. 275; MacDonogh, p. 306; Ralph Raico, "World War I— The Turning Point," *The Costs of War: America's Pyrrhic Victories.* Edited with an Introduction by John Denson (New Brunswick, N.J.: Transaction, 1999), p. 215.
55. Tuchman, *Proud Tower,* p. 275; Roy Hattersley, *The Edwardians* (New York: St. Martin's Press, 2004), p. 58.
56. Magnus, p. 358.
57. MacDonogh, p. 281.
58. Holborn, p. 76.
59. Ibid., p. 78.
60. Ibid., p. 81.
61. Massie, p. 820; Emrys Hughes, *Winston Churchill: British Bulldog* (New York: Exposition Press, 1955), p. 57.
62. Robert Holmes, *In the Footsteps of Churchill: A Study in Character* (New York: Basic, 2005), p. 101.
63. James, p. 337.
64. Andreas Hillgruber, *Germany and the Two World Wars,* Translated by William C. Kirby (Cambridge, Mass.: Harvard University Press, 1981), p. 16.
65. Ibid.
66. Niall Ferguson, *The Pity of War* (New York: Basic, 1999), p. 71.
67. John Laughland, *The Tainted Source: The Undemocratic Origins of the European Idea* (London: Warner, 1998), p. 111.
68. Ibid.
69. Ibid.
70. Ibid.
71. Martin Gilbert, *Churchill: A Life* (New York: Henry Holt, 1991), p. 555.

72. Ibid.
73. David Steele, *Lord Salisbury: A Political Biography* (New York: Routledge, 1999), p. 121; Steven Mayer, "Carcass of Dead Policies: The Irrelevance of NATO," *Parameters*, Winter 2003–4, p. 83.
74. Ferguson, p. 64.
75. Tuchman, *Guns of August*, p. 52; Ferguson, p. 66.
76. Raico, p. 219.
77. Ferguson, p. 153; MacDonogh, p. 360; Raico, p. 208; Meyer, p. 9.
78. Massie, p. 852.
79. Herman, pp. 490–91; Massie, pp. 852–53.

CHAPTER 2: LAST SUMMER OF YESTERDAY

1. Niall Ferguson, *The Pity of War* (New York: Basic, 1999), p. xxxv.
2. Giles MacDonogh, *The Last Kaiser, The Life of Wilhelm II* (New York: St. Martin's Press, 2000), p. 371.
3. A.J.A. Morris, *The Scaremongers: The Advocacy of War and Rearmament 1896–1914* (London: Routledge & Kegan Paul, 1984), p. 355.
4. Ferguson, p. 70.
5. Winston Churchill, *The World Crisis: 1911–1918* (New York: Free Press, 2005), pp. 94–95; Robert K. Massie, *Dreadnought: Britain, Germany and the Coming of the Great War* (New York: Random House, 1991), p. 879; Roy Denman, *Missed Chances: Britain and Europe in the Twentieth Century* (London: Indigo, Cassell, 1997), p. 21; Martin Gilbert, *Churchill: A Life* (New York: Henry Holt, 1991), p. 264.
6. Massie, p. 879.
7. Ibid.; John Charmley, *Churchill: The End of Glory: A Political Biography* (New York: Harcourt Brace & Company, 1993), p. 96; Violet Bonham Carter, *Winston Churchill: An Intimate Portrait* (New York: Harcourt, Brace & World, 1965), p. 246; William

Manchester, *The Last Lion, Winston Spencer Churchill: Visions of Glory 1874–1932* (Boston: Little, Brown, 1983), p. 465.

8. MacDonogh, p. 355; Gilbert, p. 265.
9. Massie, p. 889.
10. Churchill, p. 99.
11. Barbara W. Tuchman, *The Guns of August* (New York: Macmillan, 1962), p. 91.
12. Manchester, p. 472.
13. Morris, p. 358.
14. Manchester, p. 472.
15. Gilbert, p. 266.
16. Charmley, pp. 95–96.
17. Ibid., p. 96.
18. Simon Schama, *A History of Britain: The Fate of Empire: 1776–2000* (New York: Hyperion, 2002), p. 436; Gilbert, p. 268; Charmley, p. 96.
19. MacDonogh, p. 355.
20. Andreas Hillgruber, *Germany and the Two World Wars*, Translated by William C. Kirby (Cambridge, Mass.: Harvard University Press, 1981), p. 37.
21. Charmley, p. 33.
22. Massie, p. 893.
23. Tuchman, p. 130.
24. Hillgruber, p. 9.
25. Ibid., p. 32.
26. G. J. Meyer, *A World Undone: The Story of the Great War 1914–1918* (New York: Delacorte Press, 2006), p. 94.
27. Ibid.
28. John Keegan, *The First World War* (New York: Vintage, 2000), p. 31.
29. Massie, p. 895.
30. A.J.P. Taylor, *A History of the First World War* (New York: Berkley, 1966), p. 14.
31. Ibid.

32. Tuchman, p. 25.

33. Ibid.

34. Massie, p. 895; Tuchman, p. 26.

35. Massie, p. 896; Denman, p. 25.

36. MacDonogh, p. 352.

37. Winston Churchill, *Great Contemporaries* (Chicago: University of Chicago Press, 1973), p. 137.

38. Roy Jenkins, *Churchill: A Biography* (New York: Plume, 2002), p. 239; Gilbert, p. 271; Massie, p. 898.

39. Bonham Carter, p. 251.

40. Charmley, p. 97.

41. Peter Rowland, *David Lloyd George: A Biography* (New York: Macmillan, 1975), p. 280; Denman, p. 21.

42. Rowland, p. 283.

43. Ferguson, pp. 443–44.

44. Rowland, p. 282.

45. Meyer, p. 133.

46. Charmley, p. 97; Gilbert, p. 271; Jenkins, p. 239; Rowland, p. 282.

47. Manchester, p. 464.

48. Niall Ferguson, *Empire: The Rise and Demise of the British World Power Order and the Lessons for Global Power* (New York: Basic, 2003), p. 294.

49. Manchester, p. 464.

50. Ferguson, *Pity*, p. 67.

51. Gilbert, p. 236.

52. C. Paul Vincent, *The Politics of Hunger: The Allied Blockade of Germany 1915–1919* (Athens, Ohio: Ohio University Press, 1985), p. 4.

53. Churchill, *World Crisis*, p. 102.

54. Ralph Raico, "World War I: The Turning Point," in *The Costs of War: America's Pyrrhic Victories*, Second Expanded Edition, John Denson, ed. (New Brunswick, N.J.: Transaction, 1999), p. 215.

55. Tuchman, p. 117.
56. Massie, p. 907.
57. Ibid.; Manchester, p. 474.
58. Massie, p. 908.
59. Rowland, pp. 283–84.
60. Ibid., p. 284.
61. Meyer, p. 134.
62. Roy Hattersley, *The Edwardians* (New York: St. Martin's Press, 2003), p. 480.
63. Meyer, p. 134.
64. Emrys Hughes, *Winston Churchill: British Bulldog* (New York: Exposition Press, 1955), p. 62.
65. Gilbert, p. 275; Hattersley, p. 480. Hattersley attributes the description of Churchill to Margot Asquith rather than Lloyd George.
66. Bonham Carter, p. 295; Ferguson, p. 178.
67. Manchester, p. 471.
68. Robert Payne, *The Great Man: A Portrait of Winston Churchill* (New York: Coward, McCann & Geoghegan, 1974), p. 150.
69. Keegan, p. 3.
70. Meyer, p. 67.
71. Keegan, p. 3.
72. Ferguson, *Pity*, p. 163; Denman, p. 22.
73. Ferguson, ibid.
74. Ibid., p. 173; A.J.P. Taylor, *English History: 1914–1945* (Oxford: Oxford University Press, 1965), p. 4.
75. Taylor, p. 161.
76. Ferguson, *Pity*, p. xxxvii.
77. Ibid., p. 168; Captain Russell Grenfell, R.N., *Unconditional Hatred: German War Guilt and the Future of Europe* (New York: Devin-Adair, 1953), p. 18.
78. Morris, p. 359.
79. Ferguson, *Empire*, p. 298.
80. Ferguson, *Pity*, p. 163.

81. Francis Neilson, *The Churchill Legend* (Brooklyn, N.Y.: 29 Books, 2004), p. 117.

82. Ibid.

83. Francis Neilson, *The Makers of War* (Appleton, Wisc.: C. C. Nelson, 1950), p. 19.

84. Bonham Carter, p. 266.

85. Peter Clarke, *Hope and Glory: Britain 1900–1990* (London: Penguin Press, 1996), p. 72.

86. Correlli Barnett, *The Collapse of British Power* (Great Britain: Sutton, 1997), p. 57; Vincent, p. 4.

87. Barnett, p. 57.

88. Ibid.

89. Ibid.

90. Hajo Holborn, *The Political Collapse of Europe* (New York: Alfred A. Knopf, 1969), p. 96.

91. Taylor, *English History*, pp. 2–3.

92. David Fromkin, *Europe's Last Summer: Who Started the Great War?* (New York: Alfred A. Knopf, 2004), p. 250.

93. Patrick J. Buchanan, *Death of the West* (New York: St. Martin's Press, 2002), p. 73.

94. Keegan, p. 66.

95. Massie, p. 869; MacDonogh, p. 356.

96. Ferguson, *Pity*, p. 149.

97. Ibid., p. 156; Meyer, pp. 52–53.

98. MacDonogh, p. 355.

99. Massie, p. 875; Tuchman, p. 79.

100. Massie, ibid.; MacDonogh, p. 361; Tuchman, p. 80.

101. Massie, ibid.; MacDonogh, p. 361.

102. MacDonogh, p. 294.

103. Ferguson, *Pity*, p. 168.

104. Ibid., p. 169.

105. Ibid.

106. Tuchman, p. 75.

107. MacDonogh, p. 360.

108. Massie, p. 901; Tuchman, p. 53.

109. Ferguson, *Pity*, p. xxxvii.

110. Churchill, *Great Contemporaries*, p. 38.

111. Tuchman, p. 76.

112. Fromkin, p. 250.

113. Andrew Roberts, *A History of the English-Speaking Peoples Since 1900* (New York: HarperCollins, 2007), pp. 53, 81.

114. Ibid., p. 79.

115. Grenfell, pp. 54–55.

116. Henrik Bering, "Prussian Maneuvers," *Policy Review*, April–May 2007, p. 90.

117. Denman, p. 24.

118. Ferguson, *Pity*, pp. 170–71.

119. Gilbert, p. 270; Meyer, p. 71.

120. John Laughland, *The Tainted Source: The Undemocratic Origins of the European Idea* (London: Warner, 1998), p. 114.

121. MacDonogh, pp. 259–60.

122. David Calleo, *The German Problem Reconsidered: Germany and the World Order, 1870 to the Present* (New York: Cambridge University Press, 1988), p. 44.

123. Ferguson, *Pity*, p. 172.

124. Ibid., pp. 172–73.

125. Ibid., p. 444.

126. Lawrence James, *The Rise and Fall of the British Empire* (New York: St. Martin's Griffin, 1994), p. 367.

127. Jim Powell, *Wilson's War: How Woodrow Wilson's Great Blunder Led to Hitler, Lenin, Stalin and World War II* (New York: Crown Forum, 2005), p. 43.

128. Ibid.

129. Ibid.

130. Neilson, *Makers of War*, p. 113.

131. Hughes, p. 60.

132. Neilson, *The Churchill Legend*, p. 169.

133. Ibid., p. 159.

134. Grenfell, pp. 3–4; Hughes, p. 63.

135. Jenkins, p. 239.

136. Tuchman, pp. 91, 94; Manchester, p. 474.

137. Manchester, p. 470.

138. Ibid.

139. Ibid.

140. Ibid., p. 471.

141. Ibid., p. 473; Gilbert, p. 272; Churchill, *Great Contemporaries*, p. 148.

142. Gilbert, p. 274; Jenkins, p. 240; Ralph Raico, "Rethinking Churchill," *The Costs of War: America's Pyrrhic Victories*, Second Expanded Edition, John Denson, ed. (New Brunswick, N.J.: Transaction, 1999), p. 330.

143. Charmley, p. 99.

144. Gilbert, p. 281.

145. Ibid., p. 285.

146. Ibid., pp. 294–95.

147. Richard Holmes, *In the Footsteps of Churchill: A Study in Character* (New York: Basic, 2005), p. 72.

148. Gilbert, pp. 277–78.

149. Walter Millis, *Road to War: America 1914–1917* (Boston: Houghton Mifflin, 1935), p. 48; Raico, "Turning Point," p. 220.

CHAPTER 3: "A POISONOUS SPIRIT OF REVENGE"

1. Peter Rowland, *David Lloyd George: A Biography* (New York: Macmillan, 1975), p. 476.

2. Richard A. Odorfer, *The Soul of Germany: A Unique History of the Germans from the Earliest Times to Present* (New Braunfels, Tex.: Richard A. Odorfer, 1995), p. 290.

3. John Keegan, *The First World War* (New York: Vintage, 2000), p. 405; G. J. Meyer, *World Undone: The Story of the*

Great War 1914–1918 (New York: Delacorte Press, 2006), pp. 563–64.

4. Charles Callan Tansill, *Back Door to War: The Roosevelt Foreign Policy 1933–1941* (Chicago: Henry Regnery, 1952), p. 10.

5. Ibid., p. 11.

6. Roy Denman, *Missed Chances: Britain and Europe in the Twentieth Century* (London: Indigo, 1997), p. 32.

7. Jim Powell, *Wilson's War: How Woodrow Wilson's Great Blunder Led to Hitler, Lenin, Stalin and World War II* (New York: Crown Forum, 2005), pp. 2–3; C. Paul Vincent, *The Politics of Hunger: The Allied Blockade of Germany, 1915–1919* (Athens, Ohio: Ohio University Press, 1985), p. 70.

8. Roy Hattersley, *The Edwardians* (New York: St. Martin's Press, 2004), p. 95.

9. Rowland, p. 463.

10. Ibid., p. 470.

11. Denman, p. 38; Peter Clarke, *Hope and Glory: Britain 1900–1990* (London: Allen Lane, Penguin Press, 1996), p. 102; Margaret MacMillan, *Paris 1919: Six Months That Changed the World* (New York: Random House, 2002), p. 189.

12. Francis Neilson, *The Churchill Legend* (Brooklyn, N.Y.: 29 Books, 2004), pp. 254, 256.

13. George Kennan, *American Diplomacy 1900–1950* (New York: A Mentor Book, 1951), pp. 55–56.

14. Thomas A. Bailey, *Woodrow Wilson and the Lost Peace* (New York: Macmillan, 1944), p. 153.

15. Vincent, p. 85; Thomas Fleming, *The Illusion of Victory: America in World War I* (New York: Basic, 2003), p. 324.

16. Richard Holmes, *In the Footsteps of Churchill* (New York; Basic, 2005), p. 72; Martin Gilbert, *Churchill: A Life* (New York: Henry Holt, 1991), p. 143.

17. A.J.P. Taylor, *A History of the First World War* (New York: Berkley, 1966), p. 171.

18. Bailey, p. 34.
19. Ibid., p. 37.
20. Norman Davies, *God's Playground: A History of Poland in Two Volumes*, Volume II: *1795 to the Present* (New York: Columbia University Press, 1982), p. 393.
21. Tansill, p. 21.
22. Denman, p. 43.
23. Taylor, p. 169.
24. Bailey, p. 242; MacMillan, p. 187; Fleming, p. 366.
25. Fleming, p. 382.
26. Erik von Kuehnelt-Leddihn, *Leftism Revisited: From De Sade and Marx to Hitler and Pol Pot* (Washington: Regnery Gateway, 1990), p. 218.
27. Captain Russell Grenfell, R.N., *Unconditional Hatred: German War Guilt and the Future of Europe* (New York: Devin-Adair, 1953), p. 241.
28. Denman, p. 49.
29. Taylor, p. 158.
30. Bailey, p. 309; William Henry Chamberlin, *America's Second Crusade* (Chicago: Henry Regnery, 1950), p. 5.
31. Ralph Raico, "World War I: The Turning Point," in *The Costs of War: America's Pyrrhic Victories*, Second Expanded Edition, John Denson, ed. (New Brunswick, N.J.: Transaction, 1999), p. 222.
32. Neilson, p. 250.
33. Ibid., p. 251.
34. Fleming, p. 323.
35. Odorfer, p. 289.
36. Bailey, p. 305.
37. Charles L. Mee, Jr., *The End of Order: Versailles 1919* (New York: E. P. Dutton, 1980), p. 129; Vincent, p. 112; Odorfer, p. 289.
38. Raico, p. 240; Fleming, p. 355.
39. Denman, p. 34.
40. Ibid., p. 35.
41. Herbert Hoover and Hugh Gibson, *The Problems of Lasting*

Peace (New York: Doubleday, Doran, 1943), reprinted in *Prefaces to Peace: A Symposium* (New York: Simon & Schuster, 1943), pp. 227–28.

42. Tansill, p. 24.
43. Odorfer, p. 292; Fleming, p. 376.
44. Denman, p. 48; Mee, pp. 215–16.
45. Fleming, p. 377.
46. Bailey, p. 290; Fleming, p. 377.
47. Paul Johnson, *Modern Times: The World from the Twenties to the Eighties* (New York: Harper & Row, 1983), p. 26.
48. Fleming, p. 377; Mee, p. 218.
49. Odorfer, p. 292.
50. Otto Friedrich, *Before the Deluge: A Portrait of Berlin in the 1920s* (New York: Harper & Row, 1972), pp. 49–50; Patrick J. Buchanan, *A Republic, Not an Empire* (Washington, D.C.: Regnery, 1999), p. 214.
51. A. David Andelman, *A Shattered Peace: Versailles 1919 and the Price We Pay Today* (Hoboken, N.J.: John T. Wiley & Sons, 2007), p. 290.
52. Ibid.
53. Kuehnelt-Leddihn, p. 218.
54. William Manchester, *The Last Lion, Winston Spencer Churchill: Visions of Glory 1874–1932* (Boston: Little, Brown, 1983), p. 660.
55. Odorfer, p. 294; Mee, p. 249.
56. Bailey, p. 303.
57. Ibid., p. 292.
58. Francis Neilson, *The Makers of War* (Appleton, Wisc.: C. C. Nelson, 1950), p. 151.
59. Fleming, p. 387.
60. Alistair Horne, *To Lose a Battle: France 1940* (Boston: Little, Brown, 1969), p. 19.
61. Henry Kissinger, *Diplomacy* (New York: Simon & Schuster, 1994), p. 233.
62. Ibid., p. 234.

63. Andrew Roberts, *A History of the English-Speaking Peoples Since 1900* (New York: HarperCollins, 2007), p. 147.

64. Kissinger, p. 240; Luigi Villari, *Italian Foreign Policy Under Mussolini* (New York: Devin-Adair, 1956), p. 205.

65. Wenzel Jaksch, *Europe's Road to Potsdam* (New York: Frederick A. Praeger, 1963), p. 210.

66. Ibid., pp. 210–11.

67. Ibid., pp. 276–77.

68. Stephen Sisa, *The Spirit of Hungary: A Panorama of Hungarian History and Culture, 2nd Edition* (USA: A Wintario Project, 1990), p. 235.

69. Ibid., p. 233.

70. Andelman, p. 155.

71. Ibid., p. 161.

72. Ibid., pp. 164–65.

73. Ibid., p. 162.

74. Ibid., p. 191.

75. Ibid.

76. Raico, p. 240; Denman, p. 30.

77. Jozsef Cardinal Mindszenty, *Memoirs* (New York: Macmillan, 1974), pp. 305–6.

78. George Kennan, *Memoirs: 1925–1950* (Boston: Little, Brown, 1967), p. 94.

79. Davies, p. 404.

80. Andelman, p. 215.

81. Winston S. Churchill, *The World Crisis: 1911–1918, With a New Introduction by Martin Gilbert* (New York: Free Press, 2005), p. 692.

82. Denman, p. 41; Kissinger, p. 241; MacMillan, p. 197.

83. Rowland, p. 485; Raico, p. 245.

84. John Laughland, *The Tainted Source: The Undemocratic Origins of the European Idea* (London: Warner, 1998), p. 119.

85. Kuehnelt-Leddihn, p. 206.

86. Denman, p. 49; Horne, p. 20.
87. Villari, p. 5.
88. Ibid.
89. Kissinger, p. 272.
90. Lawrence James, *The Rise and Fall of the British Empire* (New York: St. Martin's Griffin, 1997), p. 366.
91. Correlli Barnett, *The Collapse of British Power* (Great Britain: Sutton, 1997), p. 71.
92. Winston S. Churchill, *Great Contemporaries* (New York: W. W. Norton, 1991), p. 208.
93. Niall Ferguson, *The Pity of War* (New York: Basic, 1999), p. 436.
94. Mee, p. xviii.
95. Ibid., p. 259.
96. Bailey, p. 134.
97. MacMillan, p. 12.
98. Niall Ferguson, *Empire: The Rise and Demise of the British World Order and the Lessons for Global Power* (New York: Basic, 2003), p. 310.
99. Jaksch, p. 218.
100. Ibid.
101. Ibid.; Emrys Hughes, *Winston Churchill: British Bulldog* (New York: Exposition Press, 1955), p. 94.
102. Hughes, p. 94.
103. Mee, p. 75.
104. Richard Toye, *Lloyd George and Churchill: Rivals for Greatness* (London: Macmillan, 2007), p. 200.
105. Ibid., p. 223.
106. Odorfer, p. 290.
107. Kissinger, p. 241.
108. Barnett, p. 392; Meyer, p. 536.
109. Andreas Hillgruber, *Germany and the Two World Wars* (Cambridge, Mass.: Harvard University Press, 1981), p. 47.
110. Daniel Patrick Moynihan, *Pandaemonium: Ethnicity in Interna-

tional Politics (New York: Oxford University Press, 1994), pp. 78–79.

111. Ibid., p. 102.
112. Rowland, pp. 494–95.
113. Ibid., p. 495.
114. Bailey, p. 323.
115. Villari, p. 92.
116. Mee, p. 267.
117. Kuehnelt-Leddihn, p. 221.

CHAPTER 4: "A LOT OF SILLY LITTLE CRUISERS"

1. Rudyard Kipling, "Recessional," *The Oxford Book of English Verse: 1250–1918*, Chosen and Edited by Sir Arthur Quiller-Couch (New York: Oxford University Press, 1955), p. 1076.
2. Correlli Barnett, *The Collapse of British Power* (New York: William Morrow, 1977), p. 252; Paul Johnson, *Modern Times: The World from the Twenties to the Eighties* (New York: Harper & Row, 1983), p. 173.
3. Barnett, pp. 250–51; Johnson, p. 173.
4. Barnett, p. 251; Johnson, p. 173.
5. Barnett, p. 254.
6. Ibid., p. 262.
7. Alfred Leroy Burt, *The Evolution of the British Empire and Commonwealth from the American Revolution* (Boston: D.C. Heath, 1956), p. 745.
8. Barnett, p. 253.
9. Barnett, p. 265.
10. A.J.P. Taylor, *A History of the First World War* (New York: Berkley, 1966), p. 169.
11. Barnett, p. 264.
12. Ibid., p. 265.
13. Ibid., p. 263.
14. Ibid., p. 267; Johnson, p. 174.

15. Burt, p. 747.
16. Thomas A. Bailey, *A Diplomatic History of the American People*, Seventh Edition (New York: Meredith, 1964), p. 644.
17. Johnson, p. 188.
18. Arthur Herman, *To Rule the Waves: How the British Navy Shaped the Modern World* (New York: HarperCollins, 2004), p. 522.
19. Ibid.
20. Ibid.
21. Barnett, p. 249.
22. John T. Flynn, *Country Squire in the White House* (New York: Doubleday, Duran, 1940), pp. 20–23.
23. James Morris, *Farewell the Trumpets: An Imperial Retreat* (New York: Harcourt, Brace & Company, 1978), pp. 216–17.
24. Ibid., p. 217.
25. Robert H. Ferrell, *American Diplomacy: A History* (New York: W. W. Norton, 1959), p. 335; Johnson, p. 174.
26. Ferrell, p. 335.
27. Herman, p. 520.
28. Barnett, p. 272.
29. Ibid., p. 273.
30. Bradford Perkins, *The Great Rapprochement: England and the United States, 1895–1914* (New York: Atheneum, 1968), p. 4.
31. Barnett, p. 262.
32. Robert Debs Heinl, Jr., *Dictionary of Military and Naval Quotations* (Annapolis, Md.: United States Naval Institute, 1967), pp. 8–9.
33. Barnett, p. 275; Johnson, p. 175; Ian Kershaw, *Fateful Choices: The Decisions That Changed the World, 1940–1941* (New York: Penguin Press, 2007), p. 15.
34. Johnson, p. 174.
35. Ibid.; Herman, p. 520.
36. Niall Ferguson, *Empire: The Rise and Demise of the British World Power Order and the Lessons for Global Power* (New York: Basic, 2003), p. 322.

37. Johnson, p. 175.
38. Roy Jenkins, *Churchill: A Biography* (New York: Penguin Putnam, 2001), p. 395.
39. Ibid.
40. Ibid., p. 396.
41. Ibid., p. 415.
42. Ibid., p. 397.
43. Barnett, p. 276.
44. Johnson, p. 175.
45. Barnett, p. 278.
46. Herman, p. 520.
47. Charles Callan Tansill, *Back Door to War: The Roosevelt Foreign Policy 1933–1941* (Chicago: Henry Regnery, 1952), p. 100.
48. Ibid.
49. Ibid., p. 101.
50. Barnett, p. 349.
51. Tansill, p. 521.
52. Ibid.
53. Ibid., p. 522.
54. Winston S. Churchill, *Step by Step: 1936–1939* (London: Odhams Press, 1939), pp. 19–20.
55. Winston S. Churchill, *The Gathering Storm* (Boston: Houghton Mifflin, 1948), p. 13.
56. Ibid., p. 14.

CHAPTER 5: 1935: COLLAPSE OF THE STRESA FRONT

1. Ivone Kirkpatrick, *Mussolini: A Study in Power* (London: Discus, 1964), p. 285.
2. Richard Collier, *Duce!: A Biography of Benito Mussolini* (New York: Viking Press, 1971), p. 134.
3. Charles L. Mee, Jr., *The End of Order: Versailles 1919* (New York: E. P. Dutton, 1980), pp. 58–59.

4. Ibid., p. 59.
5. Peter Rowland, *David Lloyd George: A Biography* (New York: Macmillan, 1975), p. 491.
6. Luigi Villari, *Italian Foreign Policy Under Mussolini* (New York: Devin-Adair, 1956), p. vi.
7. Collier, p. 94.
8. Villari, p. vii.
9. Emrys Hughes, *Winston Churchill: British Bulldog* (New York: Exposition Press, 1955), p. 143.
10. Ian Kershaw, *Hitler 1889–1936: Hubris* (New York: W. W. Norton, 1998), p. 246.
11. R.J.B. Bosworth, *Mussolini* (London: Arnold, 2002), p. 267.
12. Ibid.
13. Kirkpatrick, p. 282.
14. Ibid.
15. Ibid., p. 283.
16. Bosworth, p. 281.
17. Kirkpatrick, p. 284.
18. Richard Lamb, *Mussolini as Diplomat: Il Duce's Italy on the World Stage* (New York: Fromm International, 1999), p. 105.
19. Collier, p. 117.
20. Kershaw, p. 522.
21. Richard Evans, *The Third Reich in Power: 1933–1939* (New York: Penguin Press, 2005), p. 620.
22. Bosworth, p. 275.
23. Kirkpatrick, p. 284.
24. Ibid., p. 285.
25. John Toland, *Adolf Hitler* (Garden City: N.Y.: Doubleday, 1976), pp. 353–54.
26. Toland, p. 354; Kershaw, p. 524.
27. Kirkpatrick, p. 287.
28. Toland, p. 354.
29. J. Kenneth Brody, *The Avoidable War: Lord Cecil & The Politics of*

Principle, vol. I (New Brunswick, N.J.: Transaction, 1999), p. 122; Toland, pp. 354–55.

30. Brody, p. 123; Toland, p. 355.
31. Toland, p. 355.
32. Ibid.; Brody, p. 123; Kirkpatrick, p. 288; Collier, p. 124.
33. Kirkpatrick, p. 287.
34. Ernest May, *Strange Victory: Hitler's Conquest of France* (New York: Hill and Wang, 2000), p. 35.
35. Ibid.
36. Norman Cameron and R. H. Stevens, translators, *Hitler's Table Talk 1941–1944: His Private Conversations* (New York: Enigma, 2000), p. 417.
37. A.J.P. Taylor, *The Origins of the Second World War* (New York: Atheneum, 1961), p. 86.
38. Evans, p. 626.
39. Lamb, p. 112.
40. Correlli Barnett, *The Collapse of British Power* (Great Britain: Sutton, 1997), p. 331.
41. A.J.P. Taylor, *The Origins of the Second World War*, Second Edition with a Reply to Critics (New York: Fawcett, 1969), p. 57.
42. Barnett, p. 331.
43. William L. Shirer, *The Collapse of the Third Republic: An Inquiry into the Fall of France in 1940* (New York: Simon & Schuster, 1969), p. 240.
44. Ibid., p. 241.
45. Jasper Ridley, *Mussolini* (New York: St. Martin's Press, 1997), p. 250.
46. Brody, pp. 269–70.
47. Ibid., p. 276.
48. Ibid., pp. 278–79.
49. Lamb, p. 111.
50. Kershaw, p. 555.
51. Ibid.

52. Roy Denman, *Missed Chances: Britain and Europe in the Twenti-eth Century* (London: Indigo, 1997), p. 78.

53. Ibid., p. 79.

54. Toland, p. 371.

55. Evans, p. 629.

56. Lamb, p. 114.

57. Barnett, p. 407.

58. Ibid.

59. Alan Bullock, *Hitler: A Study in Tyranny* (New York: Harper & Row, 1962), p. 338.

60. Kershaw, p. 558.

61. Roy Jenkins, *Churchill: A Biography* (London: Plume, 2001), p. 482.

62. William Manchester, *The Last Lion, Winston Spencer Churchill: Alone: 1932–1940* (Boston: Little, Brown, 1988), p. 412; Brody, p. 207.

63. Villari, pp. 127–28.

64. Collier, p. 124.

65. Brody, p. 285.

66. Kirkpatrick, p. 292; Brody, p. 280; Ridley, p. 250; Collier, p. 124.

67. Kirkpatrick, pp. 292–93; Ridley, p. 250.

68. Kirkpatrick, p. 310.

69. Charles Callan Tansill, *Back Door to War: The Roosevelt Foreign Policy 1933–41* (Chicago: Henry Regnery, 1952), p. 116.

70. Martin Gilbert, *Churchill: A Life* (London: Pimlico, 2000), p. 545; Manchester, pp. 163–64.

71. Paul Johnson, *Modern Times: The World from the Twenties to the Eighties* (New York: Harper & Row, 1983), p. 320.

72. Bosworth, p. 302.

73. Ibid., p. 303.

74. Ibid.

75. Collier, p. 130.

76. Toland, p. 379.

77. Barnett, p. 353.

78. Ibid., p. 356.

79. Denman, p. 91.

80. Lamb, p. 149.

81. Johnson, p. 321.

82. A.J.P. Taylor, *From Sarajevo to Potsdam* (New York: Harcourt, Brace & World, 1967), p. 140.

83. Bullock, p. 340.

84. Henry A. Kissinger, *Diplomacy* (New York: Simon & Schuster, 1994), p. 300.

85. Barnett, p. 380; Johnson, p. 321; Peter Clarke, *Hope and Glory: Britain 1900–1990* (London: Allen Lane, Penguin Press, 1996), p. 185.

86. Villari, p. 195.

87. Lynne Olson, *Troublesome Young Men: The Rebels Who Brought Churchill to Power and Helped Save England* (New York: Farrar, Straus and Giroux, 2007), p. 87.

88. Denman, p. 91.

89. Taylor, pp. 95–96.

90. Lamb, p. 126.

91. Manchester, p. 160; Gilbert, p. 546.

92. Jenkins, p. 484.

93. Manchester, p. 161.

94. Ibid., p. 160.

95. Ibid.

96. Jenkins, p. 485.

97. Robert Payne, *The Great Man: A Portrait of Winston Churchill* (New York: Coward, McCann & Geoghegan, 1974), p. 190; Collier, p. 93; Gilbert, p. 480; Emrys Hughes, *Winston Churchill: British Bulldog* (New York: Exposition Press, 1955), p. 120.

98. Payne, p. 190; Hughes, p. 120.

99. Payne, p. 208; Hughes, p. 122.

100. Villari, p. 43.

101. Payne, p. 208.
102. Ibid., p. 190.
103. Taylor, pp. 56–57.
104. Villari, p. 101.
105. Kissinger, p. 299.
106. Barnett, p. 381.

CHAPTER 6: 1936: THE RHINELAND

1. A.J.P. Taylor, *A History of the First World War* (New York: Berkley, 1963), p. 163; C. P. Vincent, *The Politics of Hunger: The Allied Blockade of Germany 1915–1919* (Athens, Ohio: Ohio University Press, 1985), p. 70.
2. David Carlton, *Anthony Eden: A Biography* (London: Allen Lane, Penguin Press, 1981), p. 82.
3. Correlli Barnett, *The Collapse of British Power* (New York: William Morrow, 1972), p. 335.
4. Ibid., pp. 335–36.
5. Ian Kershaw, *Hitler 1889–1936: Hubris* (New York: W. W. Norton, 2000), p. 587.
6. A.J.P. Taylor, *The Origins of the Second World War*, Second Edition with a Reply to Critics (Greenwich, Conn.: Fawcett, 1969), p. 98.
7. Kershaw, p. 587.
8. Ibid.; William L. Shirer, *The Rise and Fall of the Third Reich: A History of Nazi Germany* (New York: Simon & Schuster, 1960), p. 292.
9. Kershaw, p. 587.
10. Shirer, p. 291; William L. Shirer, *The Collapse of the Third Republic: An Inquiry into the Fall of France in 1940* (New York: Simon & Schuster, 1969), p. 261.
11. Kershaw, p. 585.
12. Ibid.
13. Shirer, *Third Reich*, p. 292; Alistair Horne, *To Lose a Battle:*

France 1940 (Boston: Little, Brown, 1969), p. 37; Roy Denman, *Missed Chances: Britain and Europe in the Twentieth Century* (London: Indigo, 1997), p. 83.

14. Ernest May, *Strange Victory: Hitler's Conquest of France* (New York: Hill and Wang, 2000), p. 38.

15. Wayne Cole, *Roosevelt & The Isolationists: 1932–45* (Lincoln, Neb.: University of Nebraska Press, 1983), p. 201; Patrick J. Buchanan, *A Republic, Not an Empire: Reclaiming America's Destiny* (Washington, D.C.: Regnery, 1999), p. 254.

16. William Henry Chamberlin, *America's Second Crusade* (Chicago: Henry Regnery, 1962), p. 7.

17. William Manchester, *The Last Lion: Winston Spencer Churchill: Alone, 1932–1940* (Boston: Little, Brown, 1988), p. 188; Shirer, *Third Republic*, p. 277.

18. Taylor, *Origins*, p. 99.

19. John Charmley, *Churchill: The End of Glory: A Political Biography* (New York: Harcourt Brace & Company, 1993), p. 309.

20. Andrew Roberts, *Eminent Churchillians* (New York: Simon & Schuster, 1994), p. 6.

21. Ibid.

22. Ibid., p. 12.

23. Ibid.

24. Barnett, pp. 382–83.

25. Peter Rowland, *David Lloyd George: A Biography* (New York: Macmillan, 1975), p. 728.

26. Ibid., p. 733.

27. Ibid.; Andrew Roberts, *The Holy Fox: A Life of Lord Halifax* (London: Orion, 1997), p. 69.

28. Rowland, p. 735.

29. Ibid., p. 736.

30. Lynne Olson, *Troublesome Young Men: The Rebels Who Brought Churchill to Power and Helped Save England* (New York: Farrar, Straus and Giroux, 2007), p. 87.

31. Manchester, p. 83; Olson, p. 68.

32. Winston Churchill, *Great Contemporaries* (Chicago: University of Chicago Press, 1973), p. 265.

33. Ibid., p. 268.

34. Ibid., p. 265.

35. Ibid., p. 261; Charmley, p. 271.

36. Churchill, p. 268.

37. Winston S. Churchill, *Step by Step: 1936–1939* (London: Odhams Press, 1947), p. 158; Robert Holmes, *In the Footsteps of Churchill: A Study in Character* (New York: Basic, 2005), p. 187; Emrys Hughes, *Winston Churchill: British Bulldog* (New York: Exposition Press, 1955), p. 144.

38. Roy Jenkins, *Churchill: A Biography* (New York: Penguin Putnam, 2002), pp. 490–91.

39. Churchill, *Step by Step*, p. 2.

40. Ibid., p. 3.

41. Horne, p. 37; Manchester, p. 181; Alfred Leroy Burt, *The British Empire and Its Commonwealth* (Boston: D. C. Heath, 1956), p. 821; Shirer, *Third Reich*, p. 293.

42. Barnett, p. 384; Paul Johnson, *Modern Times: The World From the Twenties to the Eighties* (New York: Harper & Row, 1983), p. 349.

43. Manchester, p. 182; Shirer, *Third Reich*, p. 294; Shirer, *Third Republic*, p. 275.

44. Roberts, *Holy Fox*, p. 59.

45. Shirer, *Third Republic*, p. 263.

46. Alan Bullock, *Hitler: A Study in Tyranny* (New York: Harper & Row, 1962), p. 345; Shirer, *Third Reich*, p. 293; Shirer, *Third Republic*, p. 281; Denman, p. 83; Manchester, p. 177.

47. Shirer, *Third Reich*, p. 293; Shirer, *Third Republic*, p. 281; Denman, p. 83; Manchester, p. 177.

48. Shirer, *Third Reich*, p. 293.

49. Winston Churchill, *The Gathering Storm* (Boston: Houghton Mifflin, 1948), p. 194; May, p. 37.

50. May, Ibid.

51. Ibid., p. 38.

52. Shirer, *Third Republic*, p. 281.

53. Horne, p. 38.

54. Ibid.; Manchester, p. 191.

55. Horne, p. 38; Shirer, *Third Republic*, p. 280.

56. Manchester, p. 189.

57. Horne, p. 39; Manchester, p. 191.

58. Shirer, *Third Reich*, p. 295.

59. Ibid.; Manchester, p. 192.

60. Barnett, p. 336.

61. Shirer, *Third Republic*, p. 282.

62. Horne, p. 39.

63. Manchester, p. 189.

64. Ian Kershaw, *Hitler 1936–1945: Nemesis* (New York: W. W. Norton, 2000), p. 4.

CHAPTER 7: 1938: ANSCHLUSS

1. Adolf Hitler, *Mein Kampf*, Complete and Unabridged, Fully Annotated (New York: Reynal & Hitchcock, 1939), p. 3.

2. William L. Shirer, *The Rise and Fall of the Third Reich: A History of Nazi Germany* (New York: Simon & Schuster, 1960), p. 353.

3. Francis Neilson, *The Makers of War* (Appleton, Wisc.: C. C. Nelson, 1950), p. 171.

4. Richard Lamb, *Mussolini as Diplomat: Il Duce's Italy on the World Stage* (New York: Fromm International, 1999), p. 91.

5. Alan Bullock, *Hitler: A Study in Tyranny* (New York: Harper & Row, 1962), p. 178.

6. Ralph Raico, "Rethinking Churchill," in *The Costs of War: America's Pyrrhic Victories*, Second Expanded Edition, John Denson, ed. (New Brunswick, N.J.: Transaction, 1999), p. 246.

7. Roy Denman, *Missed Chances: Britain and Europe in the Twentieth Century* (London: Indigo, 1997), p. 59.

8. Ibid., pp. 3, 59.
9. Edmund Burke, "Second Speech on Conciliation with America: The Thirteen Resolutions," John Bartlett, *Familiar Quotations,* Thirteenth and Centennial Edition (Boston: Little Brown, 1955), p. 360.
10. Sir Nevile Henderson, *Failure of a Mission* (New York: G. P. Putnam's Sons, 1940), p. 204.
11. Ian Kershaw, *Hitler 1936–1945: Nemesis* (New York: W. W. Norton, 2000), p. 91.
12. Ibid.
13. Gene Smith, *The Dark Summer: An Intimate History of the Events That Led to World War II* (New York: Macmillan, 1987), p. 69.
14. Ibid., pp. 69–70; Correlli Barnett, *The Collapse of British Power* (New York: William Morrow, 1972), p. 467; Andrew Roberts, *The Holy Fox: A Life of Lord Halifax* (London: Orion, 1997), p. 7.
15. Roberts, p. 72.
16. Ibid.; Smith, p. 70.
17. Roberts, p. 72.
18. Ibid.
19. A.J.P. Taylor, *The Origins of the Second World War,* Second Edition with a Reply to Critics (Greenwich, Conn.: Fawcett Premier, 1969), p. 134; Roberts, p. 71.
20. Taylor, p. 134.
21. Henderson, p. 96; Barnett, p. 467.
22. B. H. Liddell Hart, *History of the Second World War* (New York: G. P. Putnam's Sons, 1970), p. 8.
23. Roberts, p. 73.
24. Ibid.
25. Niall Ferguson, *The War of the World: Twentieth Century Conflict and the Descent of the West* (New York: Penguin Press, 2006), p. 338.

26. John Toland, *Adolf Hitler* (Garden City, N.Y.: Doubleday, 1976), p. 433.
27. William Manchester, *The Last Lion, Winston Spencer Churchill: Alone, 1932–1940* (Boston: Little, Brown, 1988), p. 249.
28. Ibid.
29. Taylor, p. 137.
30. Richard J. Evans, *The Third Reich in Power 1933–1939* (New York: Penguin Press, 2005), p. 643.
31. Kershaw, p. 53.
32. Ibid.
33. Ibid.
34. Evans, p. 649.
35. Toland, pp. 434–35.
36. Taylor, p. 140.
37. Toland, p. 436.
38. Taylor, p. 134.
39. Manchester, p. 250.
40. Taylor, pp. 137, 140.
41. Shirer, p. 334; Manchester, p. 276.
42. Toland, p. 442.
43. Kershaw, p. 74.
44. Gottfried-Karl Kindermann, *Austria—First Target and Adversary of National Socialism 1933–1939* (Vienna: Austrian Cultural Association, 2002), p. 32.
45. Toland, p. 442; Kindermann, pp. 32–33.
46. Shirer, p. 337; Taylor, p. 143; Bullock, p. 428.
47. Taylor, p. 144.
48. Toland, p. 446.
49. Ibid.
50. Ibid.
51. Ibid., p. 449.
52. Shirer, p. 343; Toland, p. 449; Taylor, p. 145; Manchester, p. 276; Denman, p. 97.

53. Toland, p. 451.

54. Ibid., p. 455.

55. Shirer, p. 348; Denman, p. 97.

56. Toland, p. 452.

57. Ibid., p. 453.

58. Ibid.

59. Bullock, p. 437.

60. Kershaw, p. 81.

61. Ibid., p. 13; Manchester, pp. 282–83.

62. Taylor, p. 146.

63. Lynne Olson, *Troublesome Young Men: The Rebels Who Brought Churchill to Power and Helped Save England* (New York: Farrar, Straus and Giroux, 2007), p. 100.

64. Taylor, p. 128.

65. Graham Stewart, *Burying Caesar: The Churchill-Chamberlain Rivalry* (Woodstock, N.Y.: Overlook Press, 2001), p. 290.

66. Ibid.

67. Ibid.

68. Robert Payne, *The Great Man: A Portrait of Winston Churchill* (New York: Coward, McCann & Geoghegan, 1974), p. 218.

CHAPTER 8: MUNICH

1. William Shirer, *The Collapse of the Third Republic: An Inquiry into the Fall of France in 1940* (New York: Simon & Schuster, 1969), p. 340; John Charmley, *Churchill: The End of Glory* (New York: Harcourt, Brace & Company, 1993), p. 331; John Toland, *Adolf Hitler* (Garden City: N.Y.: Doubleday, 1976), p. 462; Graham Stewart, *Burying Caesar: The Churchill-Chamberlain Rivalry* (Woodstock, N.Y.: Overlook Press, 2001), p. 293.

2. Hanson Baldwin, *The Crucial Years 1939–1941: The World at War* (New York: Harper & Row, 1976), p. 58; Gene Smith, *The Dark Summer: An Intimate History of the Events That Led to World War II* (New York: Macmillan, 1987), pp. 103–4.

3. Toland, p. 493.

4. Smith, p. 105.

5. William L. Shirer, *The Rise and Fall of the Third Reich: A History of Nazi Germany* (New York: Simon & Schuster, 1960), p. 419; A.J.P. Taylor, *The Origins of the Second World War*, Second Edition, With a Preface for the American Reader and a New Introduction, "Second Thoughts" (New York: Atheneum, 1961), p. 186; Stewart, pp. 308–9.

6. Roy Denman, *Missed Chances: Britain and Europe in the Twentieth Century* (London: Indigo, 1997), p. 118; Toland, p. 493.

7. David Dutton, *Neville Chamberlain* (London: Arnold, 2001), p. 52.

8. Stewart, p. 309.

9. Dutton, p. 53.

10. Lynne Olson, *Troublesome Young Men: The Rebels Who Brought Churchill to Power and Helped Save England* (New York: Farrar, Straus and Giroux, 2007), p. 144.

11. Dutton, p. 53.

12. Shirer, *Third Reich*, p. 420; Taylor, p. 186; Smith, p. 106; Toland, p. 493; Stewart, p. 310.

13. Stewart, p. 310.

14. Dutton, p. 52; Denman, p. 118; Smith, p. 93.

15. William Henry Chamberlin, *America's Second Crusade* (Chicago: Henry Regnery, 1950), p. 99.

16. Ibid.

17. Charles Callan Tansill, *Back Door to War: The Roosevelt Foreign Policy 1933–41* (Chicago: Henry Regnery, 1952), p. 428.

18. Ibid.

19. Ibid., p. 429.

20. Ibid., p. 430.

21. Correlli Barnett, *The Collapse of British Power* (New York: William Morrow, 1972), p. 547; Toland, p. 493; Shirer, *Third Reich*, p. 420.

22. Dutton, p. 52.

23. Ibid., p. 55.

24. Smith, p. 107.

25. A. N. Wilson, *After the Victorians: The Decline of Britain in the World* (Farrar, Straus and Giroux, 2005), p. 366.

26. Barnett, p. 551; Ernest May, *Strange Victory: Hitler's Conquest of France* (New York: Hill and Wang, 2000), p. 192.

27. Stewart, p. 299.

28. Dutton, p. 54.

29. Martin Gilbert, *Churchill: A Life* (New York: Henry Holt, 1991), p. 596; Charmley, p. 346; Robert Payne, *The Great Man: A Portrait of Winston Churchill* (New York: Coward, McCann & Geoghegan, 1974), p. 220; Roy Jenkins, *Churchill: A Biography* (London: Plume, 2001), p. 526.

30. Smith, p. 108.

31. Jenkins, p. 527; Barnett, p. 550; Payne, p. 220; Shirer, *Third Reich*, p. 420.

32. Jenkins, p. 527.

33. Jenkins, pp. 527–28; Toland, p. 495; Payne, p. 220.

34. Winston S. Churchill, *Step by Step: 1936–1939* (London: Odhams Press, 1947), p. 275; Emrys Hughes, *Winston Churchill: British Bulldog* (New York: Exposition Press, 1955), p. 167.

35. Taylor, p. 186.

36. Donald Cameron Watt, *How War Came: The Immediate Origins of the Second World War, 1938–1939* (New York: Pantheon, 1989), p. 30; Barnett, p. 550; Smith, p. 104; Denman, p. 102.

37. Shirer, *Third Reich*, p. 424; Shirer, *Third Republic*, p. 406.

38. Paul Johnson, *Modern Times: The World from the Twenties to the Eighties* (New York: Harper & Row, 1983), p. 355.

39. May, p. 215.

40. Tansill, p. 409.

41. Shirer, *Third Republic*, p. 407.

42. Taylor, p. 192.

43. A.J.P. Taylor, *English History:* 1914–1945 (New York: Oxford University Press, 1965), p. 430.

44. Patrick J. Buchanan, *A Republic, Not an Empire* (Washington, D.C.: Regnery, 1999), p. 211; letter from historian Robert Ferrell to author, author's *Republic* files.

45. Taylor, *Origins,* p. 189.

46. Erik von Kuehnelt-Leddihn, *Leftism Revisited: From de Sade and Marx to Hitler and Pol Pot* (Washington, D.C.: Regnery Gateway, 1990), p. 220.

47. Francis Neilson, "The Making of a Tyrant," *American Journal of Economics and Sociology,* 1958, p. 397.

48. Ibid., p. 390.

49. Wenzel Jaksch, *Europe's Road to Potsdam* (New York: Frederick A. Praeger, 1963), p. 274.

50. David Carlton, *Anthony Eden, A Biography* (London: Allen Lane, Penguin Press, 1981), p. 137.

51. Tansill, p. 397.

52. Shirer, *Third Republic,* p. 343.

53. Shirer, *Third Reich,* p. 365.

54. Shirer, *Third Republic,* p. 347.

55. Shirer, *Third Reich,* p. 365.

56. Ibid., p. 366.

57. Sir Nevile Henderson, *Failure of a Mission* (New York: G. P. Putnam's Sons, 1940), p. 142.

58. Alan Bullock, *Hitler: A Study in Tyranny* (New York: Harper & Row, 1962), p. 447.

59. Ibid.

60. Taylor, *English History,* p. 430; Stewart, p. 300; Maurice Cowling, *The Impact of Hitler: British Politics and British Policy 1933–1940* (Cambridge, U.K.: Cambridge University Press, 2005), pp. 189–90.

61. Smith, pp. 91–92.

62. Stewart, p. 295.

63. Walter Lippmann, *U.S. War Aims* (Boston: Little, Brown, 1944), p. 173.

64. Smith, p. 207.

65. Shirer, p. 403; Toland, pp. 485–86; Smith, p. 100; Stewart, p. 306.

66. Taylor, *Origins*, p. 189.

67. Denman, p. 111.

68. Olson, p. 128.

69. Stewart, p. 311; Niall Ferguson, *The War of the World: Twentieth Century Conflict and the Descent of the West* (New York: Penguin Press, 2006), p. 366.

70. Olson, p. 127.

71. John Lukacs, *Five Days in London: May 1940* (New Haven, Conn.: Yale University Press, 1999), p. 10.

72. Churchill, p. 269; Francis Neilson, *The Churchill Legend* (Brooklyn, N.Y.: 29 Books, 2004), p. 311.

73. Shirer, *Third Republic*, p. 356.

74. Ibid., p. 344.

75. Charmley, p. 331.

76. Henderson, p. 227.

77. Taylor, *Origins*, p. xxvi.

78. Andrew Roberts, *The Holy Fox: A Life of Lord Halifax* (London: Orion, 1997), p. 49; Lukacs, p. 50.

79. Roberts, p. 49.

80. Peter Clarke, *Hope and Glory: Britain 1900–1990* (London: Allen Lane, Penguin Press, 1996), p. 185.

81. Ibid.

82. Barnett, p. 328.

83. May, p. 175.

84. Alistair Horne, *To Lose a Battle: France 1940* (Boston: Little, Brown, 1969), p. 21.

85. A.J.P. Taylor, *English History*, p. 422.

86. Charmley, p. 152.

87. Taylor, *Origins*, p. xxvii.

88. Henderson, p. 157.
89. Shirer, *Third Reich*, p. 398; Shirer, *Third Republic*, p. 377; Toland, p. 485; Taylor, *Origins*, p. 182.
90. Smith, p. 98.
91. Ibid.
92. Ibid, p. 99.
93. Bullock, p. 461; Tansill, p. 422; Toland, p. 484.
94. Bullock, p. 461.
95. Ibid.
96. Ibid., p. 463.
97. Charmley, p. 351.
98. Shirer, *Third Reich*, p. 401.
99. Henderson, pp. 165–66.
100. Toland, p. 485.
101. Wilson, p. 365.
102. Ibid.
103. Smith, p. 104.
104. Stewart, p. 300; Shirer, *Third Republic*, p. 362.
105. Barnett, p. 535; Toland, p. 482; Stewart, p. 303.
106. Smith, p. 110.
107. Ibid., p. 109.
108. Stewart, p. 350.
109. Ibid.
110. Ibid.; Smith, p. 123; Tansill, p. 445.
111. Henderson, p. 179.

CHAPTER 9: FATAL BLUNDER

1. Graham Stewart, *Burying Caesar: The Churchill-Chamberlain Rivalry* (Woodstock, N.Y.: Overlook Press, 2001), p. 346; Martin Gilbert, *Churchill: A Life* (New York: Henry Holt, 1991), p. 609.
2. Gene Smith, *The Dark Summer: An Intimate History of the Events That Led to World War II* (New York: Macmillan, 1987), p. 122.

3. David Dutton, *Neville Chamberlain* (London: Arnold, 2001), p. 57.

4. A.J.P. Taylor, *English History 1914–1945* (New York: Oxford University Press, 1965), p. 420.

5. Paul Johnson, *Modern Times: The World from the Twenties to the Eighties* (New York: Harper & Row, 1983), p. 356.

6. Charles Callan Tansill, *Back Door to War: The Roosevelt Foreign Policy 1933–41* (Chicago: Henry Regnery, 1952), p. 509.

7. A.J.P. Taylor, *The Origins of the Second World War*, Second Edition with a Preface for the American Reader and a New Introduction, "Second Thoughts" (New York: Atheneum, 1961), p. 195.

8. Smith, p. 18.

9. Andreas Hillgruber, *Germany and the Two World Wars*, Translated by William C. Kirby (Cambridge, Mass.: Harvard University Press, 1981), pp. 58–59; Smith, p. 18.

10. Norman Davies, *God's Playground: A History of Poland*, Volume II: *1795 to the Present* (New York: Columbia University Press, 1982), pp. 420–21; William Henry Chamberlin, *America's Second Crusade* (Chicago: Henry Regnery, 1950), p. 44.

11. Hillgruber, p. 59.

12. Tansill, p. 510.

13. William Manchester, *The Last Lion, Winston Spencer Churchill: Alone, 1932–1940* (Boston: Little, Brown, 1988), p. 403.

14. Taylor, *Origins*, p. 196.

15. Ibid., p. 213.

16. Maurice Cowling, *The Impact of Hitler: British Politics and British Policy 1933–1940* (Cambridge, U.K.: Cambridge University Press, 2005), p. 276.

17. Tansill, p. 510.

18. Donald Cameron Watt, *How War Came: The Immediate Origins of the Second World War* (New York: Pantheon, 1989), p. 143.

19. B. H. Liddell Hart, *History of the Second World War* (New York: G. P. Putnam's Sons, 1970), p. 10.

20. Cowling, p. 188.
21. Simon Newman, *March 1939: The British Guarantee to Poland* (Oxford: Clarendon Press, 1976), p. 89.
22. Tansill, p. 453.
23. Watt, p. 155.
24. George Kennan, *Memoirs: 1925–1950* (Boston: Little, Brown, 1967), p. 96.
25. John Lukacs, *George Kennan: A Study of Character* (New Haven: Yale University Press, 2007), p. 43.
26. Newman, p. 91.
27. Ibid.; Watt, p. 154.
28. Watt, p. 145.
29. John Toland, *Adolf Hitler* (Garden City, N.Y.: Doubleday, 1976), p. 517.
30. Ibid.
31. Ibid.
32. Ibid.; Richard Evans, *The Third Reich in Power: 1933–1939* (New York: Penguin Press, 2005), p. 683.
33. Sir Nevile Henderson, *Failure of a Mission* (New York: G. P. Putnam's Sons, 1940), p. 214; Smith, p. 131.
34. Henderson, p. 219.
35. Henry A. Kissinger, *Diplomacy* (New York: Simon & Schuster, 1994), p. 316.
36. Taylor, *Origins*, pp. 202–3.
37. Michael Bloch, *Ribbentrop*, Foreword by Hugh Trevor-Roper (London: Abacus, 2003), p. 233.
38. Alan Bullock, *Hitler: A Study in Tyranny* (New York: Harper & Row, 1962), p. 479.
39. Ian Kershaw, *Hitler 1936–1945: Nemesis* (New York: W. W. Norton, 2000), p. 84.
40. Ibid., p. 92.
41. Tansill, p. 454; William Shirer, *The Rise and Fall of the Third Reich: A History of Nazi Germany* (New York: Simon & Schuster, 1960), p. 451.

42. Smith, p. 132.
43. Newman, p. 103, Dutton, p. 58; Watt, p. 167.
44. Manchester, p. 401.
45. Ibid.
46. Watt, p. 170.
47. Ibid., p. 402.
48. Stewart, p. 355; Smith, p. 133; Taylor, *Origins*, p. 205; Dutton, p. 58; Cowling, p. 295.
49. Taylor, *Origins*, p. 207.
50. Alexander De Conde, *A History of American Foreign Policy* (New York: Charles Scribner's Sons, 1963), p. 576; Smith, p. 185.
51. Smith, p. 164.
52. Andrew Roberts, *The Holy Fox: The Life of Lord Halifax* (London: Orion, 1997), p. 147; Roy Denman, *Missed Chances: Britain and Europe in the Twentieth Century* (London: Indigo, 1997), pp. 120–21.
53. Newman, p. 184.
54. Bullock, p. 497; Taylor, *Origins*, p. 210; Newman, p. 162.
55. Correlli Barnett, *The Collapse of British Power* (New York: William Morrow, 1972), p. 560; Denman, p. 121; Taylor, *Origins*, p. 211; Bullock, p. 498; Chamberlin, p. 58.
56. Taylor, *English History*, p. 441.
57. Ernest May, *Strange Victory: Hitler's Conquest of France* (New York: Hill and Wang, 2000), p. 193.
58. Manchester, p. 406.
59. Ibid.
60. Emrys Hughes, *Winston Churchill: British Bulldog* (New York: Exposition Press, 1955), p. 175.
61. Denman, p. 122.
62. Peter Rowland, *David Lloyd George: A Biography* (New York: Macmillan, 1975), p. 757.
63. Hart, pp. 7, 11; Manchester, p. 406; Telford Taylor, *Munich: The Price of Peace* (Garden City, N.Y.: Doubleday, 1979), p. 971.
64. Hart, pp. 7, 11–12.

65. Manchester, p. 406.

66. Ibid., p. 407.

67. Roberts, *Holy Fox*, p. 148.

68. May, p. 193.

69. Denman, p. 121.

70. Henderson, p. 236.

71. Johnson, p. 363.

72. Ibid., p. 358.

73. Francis Neilson, *The Churchill Legend* (Brooklyn, N.Y.: 29 Books, 2004), p. 328.

74. Winston S. Churchill, *Step by Step: 1936–1939* (London: Odhams Press, 1947), p. 344; Manchester, p. 407.

75. Manchester, p. 407.

76. Ibid.

77. Ibid.

78. Churchill, *Step by Step*, p. 343.

79. Winston S. Churchill, *The Gathering Storm* (Boston: Houghton Mifflin, 1948), p. 347.

80. Ibid., p. 348.

81. Hart, p. 704.

82. Ibid., p. 15; Neilson, p. 318; Hughes, p. 177.

83. Smith, p. 145.

84. Niall Ferguson, *The War of the World: Twentieth Century Conflict and the Descent of the West* (New York: Penguin Press, 2006), p. 377.

85. Luigi Villari, *Italian Foreign Policy Under Mussolini* (New York: Devin-Adair, 1956), p. 216.

86. Ibid.

87. Johnson, pp. 356–57.

88. Watt, pp. 185–86.

89. Stewart, pp. 356–57.

90. Capt. Russell Grenfell, R.N., *Unconditional Hatred: German War Guilt and the Future of Europe* (New York: Devin-Adair, 1953), p. 22.

91. Tansill, p. 513.
92. Ibid.
93. Kissinger, pp. 316–17.
94. Peter Clarke, *Hope and Glory: Britain 1900–1990* (London: Allen Lane, Penguin Press, 1996), p. 190.
95. Henderson, pp. 225–26.
96. Denman, p. 121.
97. Shirer, *Third Reich*, p. 466.
98. Taylor, *Origins*, p. 211.
99. Barnett, p. 560.
100. Ibid.
101. Ibid., p. 562.
102. Denman, p. 3.
103. Hart, p. 11.
104. Hughes, p. 175.
105. Newman, p. 136.
106. Richard M. Nixon, *Six Crises* (Garden City, N.Y.: Doubleday, 1962), p. xv.
107. Newman, pp. 218–19.
108. Roberts, p. 144.
109. Ibid.
110. Ibid, p. 147.
111. Graham Stewart, *Burying Caesar: The Churchill-Chamberlain Rivalry* (Woodstock, N.Y.: Overlook Press, 2001), p. 358.
112. Gilbert, p. 612; Manchester, p. 413; Stewart, p. 358.
113. Gilbert, p. 612; Manchester, p. 412.
114. Gilbert, p. 612; Manchester, pp. 412–13.
115. Watt, p. 190.
116. Chamberlin, p. 51.
117. Neilson, p. 409; Patrick J. Buchanan, *A Republic, Not an Empire* (Washington, D.C.: Regnery, 1999), p. 277; Hanson W. Baldwin, *Great Mistakes of the War* (New York: Harper, 1949), p. 10.
118. Denman, p. 151.

119. George Kennan letter to Pat Buchanan, November 5, 1999, PJB Files.

120. Ibid.

CHAPTER 10: APRIL FOOLS

1. A.J.P. Taylor, *The Origins of the Second World War*, Second Edition with a Preface for the American Reader and a New Introduction, "Second Thoughts" (New York: Atheneum, 1961), p. 54; Correlli Barnett, *The Collapse of British Power* (New York: William Morrow, 1972), p. 331; Henry A. Kissinger, *Diplomacy* (New York: Simon & Schuster, 1994), p. 273.

2. F. H. Hinsley, *Hitler's Strategy* (Cambridge, U.K.: Cambridge University Press, 1951), p. 16.

3. William Henry Chamberlin, *America's Second Crusade* (Chicago: Henry Regnery, 1950), p. 61.

4. Ibid., p. 45.

5. Charles Callan Tansill, *Back Door to War: The Roosevelt Foreign Policy 1933–41* (Chicago: Henry Regnery, 1952), p. 510.

6. Chamberlin, p. 61.

7. Tansill, p. 514.

8. Chamberlin, p. 52.

9. Taylor, p. 203.

10. Ernest May, *Strange Victory: Hitler's Conquest of France* (New York: Hill and Wang, 2000), p. 193.

11. Martin Gilbert, *Churchill: A Life* (New York: Henry Holt, 1991), p. 612.

12. May, pp. 193–94.

13. Ibid., p. 194.

14. William Manchester, *The Last Lion, Winston Spencer Churchill: Alone, 1932–1940* (Boston: Little, Brown, 1988), p. 412.

15. William Shirer, *The Collapse of the Third Republic: An Inquiry into the Fall of France in 1940* (New York: Simon & Schuster, 1969), pp. 422–23.

16. Ibid.

17. Peter Rowland, *David Lloyd George: A Biography* (New York: Macmillan, 1975), p. 757; Gene Smith, *The Dark Summer: An Intimate History of the Events That Led to World War II* (New York: Macmillan, 1987), p. 163.

18. Andrew Roberts, *The Holy Fox: A Life of Lord Halifax* (London: Orion, 1997), p. 151.

19. Simon Newman, *March 1939: The British Guarantee to Poland* (Oxford: Clarendon Press, 1976), p. 221.

20. Tansill, p. 519.

21. Ibid.

22. Manchester, pp. 407–8.

23. Ibid., p. 408.

24. Newman, p. 212.

25. Taylor, p. xxvii.

26. George Kennan, *Memoirs: 1925–1950* (Boston, Little Brown, 1967), p. 88.

27. Taylor, p. 185.

28. Norman Davies, *God's Playground: A History of Poland in Two Volumes*; vol. II: *1795 to the Present* (New York: Columbia University Press, 1982), p. 431.

29. Newman, p. 213.

30. Alan Bullock, *Hitler: A Study in Tyranny*, Completely Revised Edition (New York: Harper & Row, 1962), p. 501.

31. Ibid.

32. Ibid., pp. 504–5.

33. Ibid., p. 505.

34. Ibid.

35. Newman, p. 214.

CHAPTER 11: "AN UNNECESSARY WAR"

1. Keith Feiling, *The Life of Neville Chamberlain* (London: Macmillan, 1946), p. 320; Correlli Barnett, *The Collapse of British Power* (New York: William Morrow, 1972), p. 458.

2. Nicholas Bethell, *The War Hitler Won: The Fall of Poland, September 1939* (New York: Holt, Rinehart and Winston, 1973), pp. 97, 141.

3. Martin Gilbert, *Churchill: A Life* (New York: Henry Holt, 1991), p. 410; John Charmley, *Churchill: The End of Glory* (New York: Harcourt, Brace & Company, 1993), p. 152; Historical Papers: Documents from the British Archives, www.fco.gov.uk.

4. Henry A. Kissinger, *Diplomacy* (New York: Simon & Schuster, 1994), p. 252; Hajo Holborn, *The Political Collapse of Europe* (New York: Alfred A. Knopf, 1969), p. 128.

5. Francis Neilson, *The Makers of War* (Appleton, Wisc.: C. C. Nelson, 1950), p. 71; Emrys Hughes, *Winston Churchill: British Bulldog* (New York: Exposition Press, 1955), p. 169.

6. Winston S. Churchill, *The Gathering Storm* (Boston: Houghton Mifflin, 1948), p. 349; A.J.P. Taylor, *English History 1914–1945* (New York: Oxford University Press, 1965), p. 446; Gene Smith, *The Dark Summer: An Intimate History of the Events That Led to World War II* (New York: Macmillan, 1987), p. 164; William Henry Chamberlin, *America's Second Crusade* (Chicago: Henry Regnery, 1950), p. 59.

7. Smith, pp. 159–60.

8. Chamberlin, p. 65.

9. Winston S. Churchill, *Step by Step: 1936–1939* (London: Odhams Press, 1947), p. 47.

10. Ibid., p. 48.

11. Ibid., pp. 60–61.

12. Ibid., p. 330.

13. Humphrey Carpenter, *W. H. Auden: A Biography* (Boston: Houghton Mifflin, 1981), pp. 218–19.

14. Smith, p. 197.

15. Niall Ferguson, *The War of the World: The Twentieth Century Conflict and the Descent of the West* (New York: Penguin Press, 2006), p. 379.

16. Bethell, p. 5.
17. Richard J. Evans, *The Third Reich in Power 1933–1939* (New York: Penguin Press, 2005), p. 699.
18. Charles Callan Tansill, *Back Door to War: The Roosevelt Foreign Policy 1933–41* (Chicago: Henry Regnery, 1952), p. 549.
19. Barnett, p. 333.
20. Kissinger, p. 317.
21. Roy Denman, *Missed Chances: Britain and Europe in the Twentieth Century* (London: Indigo, 1997), p. 3.
22. Barnett, pp. 572–73.
23. Tansill, p. 550.
24. Ibid., p. 553.
25. Ibid.
26. Albert Speer, *Inside the Third Reich* (New York: Macmillan, 1970), p. 165.
27. F. H. Hinsley, *Hitler's Strategy* (Cambridge: Cambridge University Press, 1951), pp. 28–29.
28. Andreas Hillgruber, *Germany and the Two World Wars*, Translated by William C. Kirby (Cambridge, Mass.: Harvard University Press, 1981), p. 77.
29. Bethell, p. 84.
30. Ernest May, *Strange Victory: Hitler's Conquest of France* (New York: Hill and Wang, 2000), p. 203.
31. Ibid.; Chamberlin, p. 70; David Dutton, *Neville Chamberlain* (London: Arnold, 2001), p. 59; Smith, p. 277.
32. Bethell, pp. 80–81.
33. Chamberlin, p. 70.
34. Dutton, p. 59.
35. Bethell, p. 165.
36. Ibid., p. 90.
37. Niall Ferguson, *Empire: The Rise and Demise of the British World Power Order and the Lessons for Global Power* (New York: Basic, 2003), p. 287.

38. Norman Davies, *God's Playground: A History of Poland in Two Volumes;* vol. II: *1795 to the Present* (New York: Columbia University Press, 1982), p. 432.

39. Hillgruber, p. 72; Norman Davies, *Europe: A History* (New York: Oxford University Press, 1996), p. 995; Davies, *God's Playground*, p. 432; Bethell, p. 92.

40. Hillgruber, p. 72.

41. Taylor, *History*, p. 450; Lukacs, p. 55.

42. John Lukacs, *Five Days in London: May 1940* (New Haven, Conn.: Yale University Press, 1999), p. 12.

43. Taylor, *Origins*, p. xxvii.

44. Taylor, *History*, p. 467.

45. Davies, *God's Playground*, p. 430.

46. Davies, *Europe*, p. 993.

47. Sir Nevile Henderson, *Failure of a Mission* (New York: G. P. Putnam's Sons, 1940), p. 251.

48. Hillgruber, p. 74.

CHAPTER 12: GRUESOME HARVEST

1. Ralph Franklin Keeling, *Gruesome Harvest* (Chicago: Institute of American Economics, 1947), p. 130.

2. Correlli Barnett, *The Collapse of British Power* (New York: William Morrow, 1972), p. 15.

3. Alistair Horne, *To Lose a Battle: France 1940* (Boston: Little, Brown, 1969), p. 559.

4. Ibid.

5. Ibid.

6. Emrys Hughes, *Winston Churchill: British Bulldog* (New York: Exposition Press, 1955), p. 196.

7. John Charmley, *Churchill: The End of Glory* (New York: Harcourt, Brace & Company, 1993), p. 514.

8. Luigi Villari, *Italian Foreign Policy Under Mussolini* (New York: Devin-Adair, 1956), p. 162.

9. "The Madness of Myths," *The Economist*, November 9, 2006, a review of Norman Davies, *Europe at War 1939–1945: No Simple Victory*. Economist.com

10. Norman Davies, *Rising '44: The Battle for Warsaw* (New York: Viking Penguin, 2004), p. 158.

11. Ibid.

12. B. H. Liddell Hart, *History of the Second World War* (New York: G. P. Putnam's Sons, 1970), p. 3.

13. Ibid.

14. Norman Davies, "How We Didn't Win the War . . . But the Russians Did," *Sunday Times*, November 5, 2006. http://www .timesonline.co.uk.

15. Villari, p. 96.

16. John Toland, *Adolf Hitler* (Garden City, N.Y.: Doubleday, 1976), p. 511.

17. Ibid.

18. Ian Kershaw, *Fateful Choices: The Decisions That Changed the World, 1940–1941* (New York: Penguin Press, 2007), p. xv.

19. *The Goebbels Diaries: 1942–1943*, Edited, Translated, and with an Introduction by Louis P. Lochner (Garden City, N.Y.: Doubleday, 1948), p. 86.

20. Ibid., p. 115.

21. Ibid., p. 148.

22. Ibid.

23. Niall Ferguson, *Empire: The Rise and Demise of the British World Order and the Lessons for Global Power* (New York: Basic, 2003), p. 296.

24. Ibid., p. 354.

25. Davies, "How We Didn't Win the War.

26. Winston S. Churchill, *The Gathering Storm* (Boston: Houghton Mifflin, 1948), pp. iv–v.

27. Martin Gilbert, *Churchill: A Life* (New York: Henry Holt, 1991), p. 646.

28. Churchill, p. 223; William Manchester, *The Last Lion, Winston Spencer Churchill: Alone, 1932–1940* (Boston: Little, Brown, 1988), p. 266.

29. Alan Clark, "A Reputation Ripe for Revision," *London Times*, January 2, 1993.

30. Sir Nevile Henderson, *Failure of a Mission* (New York: G. P. Putnam's Sons, 1940), p. 240.

CHAPTER 13: HITLER'S AMBITIONS

1. B. H. Liddell Hart, *History of the Second World War* (New York: G. P. Putnam's Sons, 1970), p. 6.

2. A.J.P. Taylor, *The Origins of the Second World War*, Second Edition with a Preface for the American Reader and a New Introduction, "Second Thoughts" (New York: Atheneum, 1961), p. xx.

3. Correlli Barnett, *The Collapse of British Power* (New York: William Morrow, 1972), p. 386.

4. Ibid.

5. Andreas Hillgruber, *Germany and the Two World Wars*, Translated by William C. Kirby (Cambridge, Mass.: Harvard University Press, 1981), p. 51.

6. Ibid., pp. 51–52.

7. Ibid., p. 53.

8. Ian Kershaw, *Hitler 1889–1936: Hubris* (New York: W. W. Norton, 2000), p. 249; William Henry Chamberlin, *America's Second Crusade* (Chicago: Henry Regnery, 1950), p. 49; Hillgruber, pp. 48, 50.

9. Kershaw, p. 247.

10. David Calleo, *The German Problem Reconsidered: Germany and the World Order* (New York: Cambridge University Press, 1988), p. 103.

11. A.J.P. Taylor, *From Sarajevo to Potsdam* (New York: Harcourt, Brace & World, 1967), p. 134.

12. Kershaw, p. 247.

13. Ibid.
14. Ibid., p. 246.
15. Alan Bullock, *Hitler: A Study in Tyranny* (New York: Harper & Row, 1962), p. 337.
16. Ibid.
17. Roy Denman, *Missed Chances: Britain and Europe in the Twentieth Century* (London: Indigo, 1997), p. 129.
18. John Toland, *Adolf Hitler* (New York: Doubleday, 1976), p. 611.
19. Ibid.
20. Niall Ferguson, *Empire: The Rise and Demise of the British World Power Order and the Lessons for Global Power* (New York: Basic, 2003), pp. 330–31.
21. B. H. Liddell Hart, *The Other Side of the Hill* (London: Papermac, 1970), pp. 200–201; Captain Russell Grenfell, R.N., *Unconditional Hatred: German War Guilt and the Future of Europe* (New York: Devin-Adair, 1953), pp. 165–66; Francis Neilson, *The Churchill Legend* (Brooklyn, N.Y.: 29 Books, 2004), p. 397; Hughes, pp. 187–88.
22. Denman, p. 130.
23. Ibid.
24. Paul Kennedy, "Die Kriegsmarine—The Neglected Service," *Hitler's War Machine*, Robert Cecil, ed. cons. (London: Salamander, 1996), p. 160.
25. F. H. Hinsley, *Hitler's Strategy* (Cambridge: Cambridge University Press, 1951), pp. 1, 3.
26. Hart, *History*, p. 7.
27. A.J.P. Taylor, *English History 1914–1945* (New York: Oxford University Press, 1965), p. 504.
28. Winston S. Churchill, *The Gathering Storm* (Boston: Houghton Mifflin, 1948), pp. 413, 425.
29. Albert Speer, *Inside the Third Reich* (New York: Macmillan, 1970), p. 165.
30. Ian Kershaw, *Fateful Choices: The Decisions That Changed the World, 1940–1941* (New York: Penguin Press, 2007), p. 22.

31. Ibid.; Nicholas Bethell, *The War Hitler Won: The Fall of Poland, September, 1939* (New York: Holt Rinehart Winston, 1973), p. 291.

32. Ian Kershaw, *Hitler 1936–45: Nemesis* (New York: W. W. Norton, 2000), p. 202.

33. Hillgruber, p. 69; Paul Johnson, *Modern Times: The World from the Twenties to the Eighties* (New York: Harper & Row, 1983), pp. 361–62; Kershaw, *Fateful Choices*, p. 63.

34. John Lukacs, *June 1941: Hitler and Stalin* (New Haven: Yale University Press, 2006), pp. 22–23 (fn).

35. Henry A. Kissinger, *Diplomacy* (New York: Simon & Schuster, 1994), p. 346.

36. Chamberlin, pp. 51, 49.

37. Taylor, *English History*, pp. 94–95, 108.

38. David Dutton, *Neville Chamberlain* (New York: Oxford University Press, 2001), p. 58; Taylor, *Origins*, p. 205; Graham Stewart, *Burying Caesar: The Churchill-Chamberlain Rivalry* (New York: Overlook Press, 2001), p. 355; Gene Smith, *The Dark Summer: An Intimate History of the Events That Led to World War II* (New York: Macmillan, 1987), p. 133.

39. Telford Taylor, *Munich: The Price of Peace* (Garden City, N.Y.: Doubleday, 1979), p. 970.

40. Sir Nevile Henderson, *Failure of a Mission* (New York: G. P. Putnam's Sons, 1940), p. 226.

41. Robert K. Massie, *Dreadnought: Britain, Germany and the Coming of the Great War* (New York: Ballantine, 1991), p. 901; Barbara W. Tuchman, *The Guns of August* (New York: Macmillan, 1962), p. 53.

42. Niall Ferguson, *The Pity of War* (New York: Basic, 1999), p. xxxvii.

43. Winston Churchill, *Great Contemporaries* (Chicago: University of Chicago Press, 1973), p. 38.

44. Ibid., p. 262; Francis Neilson, *The Makers of War* (Appleton, Wisc.: C. C. Nelson, 1950), p. 100; Hughes, p. 141.

45. Neilson, *Makers of War,* p. 109.

46. Ibid.; Hughes, p. 145.

47. Neilson, *The Churchill Legend,* p. 284.

48. Patrick J. Buchanan, *A Republic, Not an Empire* (Washington, D.C.: Regnery, 1999), pp. 277–78.

49. Jeffrey Herf, "Fact Free: Buchanan's Hitler Problem, Part II," *The New Republic,* October 18, 1999, p. 16.

50. Ibid., p. 17.

51. Roger Chesneau, *Aircraft Carriers of the World: 1914 to the Present: An Illustrated Encyclopedia* (London: Arms & Armor Press, 1992), p. 76.

52. Denman, p. 129.

53. Chesneau, p. 76.

54. Ibid., p. 77.

55. Michael Kelly, "Republican Stunts," *Washington Post,* October 6, 1999, p. A33.

56. Gerhard L. Weinberg, *Germany, Hitler & World War II* (Cambridge: Cambridge University Press, 1996), pp. 196–97.

57. Bernard C. Nalty, *The Air War* (New York: MetroBooks, 1999), pp. 24–27.

58. Taylor, *English History,* p. 410.

59. Matthew Cooper, "Die Luftwaffe—Strategically a Failure," in *Hitler's War Machine,* p. 110.

60. Hughes, p. 189.

61. Charles Callan Tansill, *Back Door to War: The Roosevelt Foreign Policy 1933–41* (Chicago: Henry Regnery, 1952), p. 551.

62. Niall Ferguson, *The War for the World: Twentieth Century Conflict and the Descent of the West* (New York: Penguin Press, 2006), pp. 393–95.

63. James S. Corum, *The Luftwaffe: Creating the Operational Air War, 1918–1940* (Lawrence, Kan.: University Press of Kansas, 1997), p. 7.

64. Ibid., p. 281.

65. Richard Bernstein, "We're Coming Over, and We Won't Come Back Till It's Over, Over There," *New York Times*, July 4, 2001, p. B12.

66. David Eisenhower, *Eisenhower at War 1943–1945* (New York: Random House, 1986), p. 72.

67. Chamberlin, p. 50.

68. John Lukacs, *Five Days in London: May 1940* (New Haven, Conn.: Yale University Press, 1999), p. 217.

69. Ibid., p. 206.

70. Bruce M. Russett, *No Clear and Present Danger: A Skeptical View of the United States Entry into World War II* (Boulder, Col.: Westview Press [HarperCollins], 1997), pp. 42–43.

71. Norman Cameron and R. H. Stevens, Translators, *Hitler's Table Talk: 1941–1944: His Private Conversations*, Introduced and with a New Preface by H. R. Trevor-Roper (New York: Enigma, 2000), p. 490.

72. John Lewis Gaddis, *We Now Know: Rethinking Cold War History* (New York: Oxford University Press, 1997), p. 14; John Meacham, "Bush, Yalta and the Blur of Hindsight," *Washington Post*, Sunday, May 15, 2005, p. B1.

73. Taylor, *Sarajevo to Potsdam*, pp. 136–38.

74. Arnold Beichman, "The Surprising Roots of Fascism," *Policy Review*, Hoover Institution. http://www.policyreview.org/aug00/beichman.

75. Ibid.

76. Robert Nisbet, *Roosevelt and Stalin: The Failed Courtship* (Washington, D.C.: Regnery Gateway, 1988), p. 24.

77. Cameron and Stevens, p. xxx.

78. Taylor, *Origins*, p. xxi.

79. David Calleo, *The German Problem Reconsidered: Germany and the World Order, 1870 to the Present* (New York: Cambridge University Press, 1988), p. 103.

80. Hillgruber, p. 95.

81. Cameron and Stevens, p. 199.

82. Hillgruber, p. 96.

83. Ibid.

CHAPTER 14: MAN OF THE CENTURY

1. Ralph Raico, "Rethinking Churchill," in *The Costs of War: America's Pyrrhic Victories*, Second Expanded Edition, John Denson, ed. (New Brunswick, N.J.: Transaction, 1999), p. 321 (fn).

2. Emrys Hughes, *Winston Churchill: British Bulldog* (New York: Exposition Press, 1955), p. 35.

3. Robert Payne, *The Great Man: A Portrait of Winston Churchill* (New York: Coward, McCann & Geoghegan, 1974), p. 216.

4. Raico, p. 321.

5. Martin Gilbert, *Churchill: A Life* (New York: Henry Holt, 1991), p. 274; Roy Jenkins, *Churchill: A Biography* (London: Plume, 2001), p. 240.

6. Thomas Pakenham, *The Boer War* (New York: Random House, 1979), p. 177.

7. Ibid., pp. 177, 222.

8. Ibid., p. 178.

9. Ibid., pp. 290–91.

10. George Dangerfield, *The Strange Death of Liberal England* (New York: Capricorn, 1961), p. 89.

11. Lynne Olson, *Troublesome Young Men: The Rebels Who Brought Churchill to Power and Helped Save England* (New York: Farrar, Straus and Giroux, 2007), p. 45.

12. Ibid., p. 46.

13. Ibid.

14. Richard Toye, *Lloyd George and Churchill: Rivals for Greatness* (London: Macmillan, 2007), p. 162.

15. Ibid., p. 163.

16. Olson, p. 75.

17. Ibid., p. 76.

18. Toye, p. 282.

19. Ibid.

20. Olson, p. 76.

21. Ibid., p. 81.

22. Ibid., p. 82.

23. Ibid.

24. Ernest R. May, *Strange Victory: Hitler's Conquest of France* (New York: Farrar, Straus and Giroux, 2000), p. 173.

25. Andrew Roberts, "Blood, Toil, Tears, etc.: Is There Anything New to Be Said About Winston Churchill?" *Weekly Standard*, September 26, 2005. http//www.weeklystandard.com.

26. May, p. 173.

27. Gilbert, p. 604; Graham Stewart, *Burying Caesar: The Churchill-Chamberlain Rivalry* (New York: Overlook Press, 2001), p. 341.

28. John Charmley, *Churchill: The End of Glory* (New York: Harcourt, Brace & Company, 1993), p. 356.

29. Lord Blake, "Winston Churchill, the Historian," Speech to the Winston S. Churchill Societies of Edmonton, Calgary and Vancouver, May 1988, p. 6. Published by the Churchill Centre, Washington, D.C., info@winstonchurchill.org.

30. John Lukacs, *Five Days in London: May 1940* (New Haven, Conn.: Yale University Press, 1999), p. 113.

31. Ibid.

32. Ibid.

33. Ibid., p. 120; Ian Kershaw, *Fateful Choices: Ten Decisions That Changed the World, 1940–1941* (New York: Penguin Press, 2007), pp. 11, 35.

34. Niall Ferguson, *The War of the World: Twentieth Century Conflict and the Descent of the West* (New York: Penguin Press, 2006), p. 381.

35. Ibid.

36. F. H. Hinsley, *Hitler's Strategy* (Cambridge: Cambridge University Press, 1951), pp. 34–35.

37. Ibid., p. 79.

38. Ibid.

39. Alan Clark, "A Reputation Ripe for Revision," *London Times,* January 2, 1993.

40. Hinsley, p. 82.

41. Ibid., p. 81.

42. Ibid.

43. Ibid., p. 130.

44. John Lukacs, *June 1941: Hitler and Stalin* (New Haven and London: Yale University Press, 2006), p. 27.

45. Kershaw, p. 54.

46. Ibid., p. 66.

47. Ibid., p. 68.

48. Michael Bloch, *Ribbentrop,* Foreword by Hugh Trevor-Roper (London: Abacus, 2003), pp. 311–12.

49. Kershaw, p. 54.

50. Hinsley, p. 131.

51. Kershaw, p. 70.

52. Hinsley, p. 131.

53. Lukacs, *June 1941*, p. 92.

54. Ibid.

55. Ibid.

56. Ibid.

57. Hinsley, p. 131.

58. Lukacs, *June 1941*, p. 137.

59. Ibid.

60. Ibid.

61. Charmley, p. 453; Lukacs, *June 1941*, p. 104.

62. Robert Nisbet, *Roosevelt and Stalin: The Failed Courtship* (Washington, D.C.: Regnery Gateway, 1988), p. 9.

63. George Kennan, *Memoirs: 1925–1950* (Boston: Little, Brown, 1967), p. 133.

64. Nisbet, p. 19.

65. Hughes, p. 178.

66. Gilbert, p. 632; Charmley, p. 472.
67. Nisbet, p. 30; Gilbert, p. 728.
68. Simon Sebag Montefiore, *Stalin: The Court of the Red Tsar* (New York: Vintage, 2003), p. 420.
69. Charmley, p. 508.
70. Hughes, pp. 217–18.
71. Raico, p. 324.
72. Ibid.
73. Charmley, p. 560.
74. Gregor Dallas, *1945: The War That Never Ended* (New Haven, Conn: Yale University Press, 2005), p. 274.
75. William Henry Chamberlin, *America's Second Crusade* (Chicago: Henry Regnery, 1950), p. 306; F.J.P. Veale, *Advance to Barbarism: How the Reversion to Barbarism in Warfare and War-Trials Menaces Our Future*, Foreword by the The Very Rev. William Ralph Inge, Dean of St. Paul's (Appleton, Wisc.: C. C. Nelson, 1953), p. 153.
76. Dallas, p. 272.
77. Ibid., p. 273.
78. Ibid., p. 274.
79. Ibid., p. 275.
80. Montefiore, p. 476.
81. Ibid.
82. Nisbet, p. 71.
83. Charmley, p. 617; John Meacham, "Bush, Yalta and the Blur of Hindsight," *Washington Post*, May 15, 2005, p. B1; Gilbert, p. 821.
84. Nisbet, p. 78.
85. Winston S. Churchill, *The Gathering Storm* (Boston: Houghton Mifflin, 1948), p. 322.
86. Ibid., p. 323.
87. Robert Holmes, *In the Footsteps of Churchill: A Study in Character* (New York: Basic, 2005), p. 188.
88. Andrew Roberts, *A History of the English-Speaking Peoples Since 1900* (New York: HarperCollins, 2007), p. 360.

89. Hughes, p. 94.

90. Gilbert, pp. 411–12; Hughes, p. 92.

91. Toye, p. 200.

92. Ibid.

93. John Lewis Gaddis, *Now We Know: Rethinking Cold War History* (New York: Oxford University Press, 1997), p. 8.

94. Hughes, p. 109; Charmley, p. 556; Raico, "Rethinking Churchill," p. 345.

95. Hughes, p. 240.

96. Raico, p. 345.

97. Winston S. Churchill, *The Second World War: Triumph and Tragedy* (Boston: Houghton Mifflin, 1953), p. 361; Jenkins, p. 781.

98. Charmley, p. 619; Meacham, op. cit.

99. Ibidem; Churchill, *Triumph and Tragedy*, p. 401.

100. Captain Russell Grenfell, R.N., *Unconditional Hatred: German War Guilt and the Future of Europe* (New York: Devin-Adair, 1953), pp. 152–53.

101. Luigi Villari, *Italian Foreign Policy Under Mussolini* (New York: Devin-Adair, 1956), p. 377; Hughes, p. 202.

102. Churchill, *Triumph and Tragedy*, p. 368.

103. Nikolai Tolstoy, *Victims of Yalta* (London: Corgi, 1986), p. 128.

104. A. N. Wilson, *After the Victorians: The Decline of Britain in the World* (New York: Farrar, Straus and Giroux, 2005), p. 350.

105. Aleksandr Solzhenitsyn, *The Gulag Archipelago 1918–1956: An Experiment in Literary Investigation II*, Translated from the Russian by Thomas P. Whitney (New York: Harper & Row, 1974), pp. 259–60.

106. Ibid., p. 259.

107. Alfred M. de Zayas, *Nemesis at Potsdam: The Expulsion of the Germans from the East*, Third Edition Revised (Lincoln, Neb.: University of Nebraska Press, 1989), p. 38.

108. Winston Churchill, *Closing the Ring* (Boston: Houghton Mifflin, 1953), p. 362; de Zayas, p. 38.

109. de Zayas, pp. 46–47.

110. Dallas, p. 292.

111. Ibid., p. 294.

112. Alfred-Maurice de Zayas, *The German Expellees: Victims in War and Peace* (New York: St. Martin's Press, 1993), p. 84.

113. de Zayas, *The Expellees*, pp. 79–80.

114. Ibid., p. 80.

115. Ibid.

116. Ibid., p. 77.

117. de Zayas, *Nemesis*, p. 89.

118. Ibid.

119. de Zayas, *Expellees*, p. 81.

120. Ibid., p. 84.

121. Charmley, p. 645.

122. Ibid.

123. de Zayas, *Nemesis*, p. 108.

124. Ibid., p. 59.

125. Montefiore, p. 534.

126. Hinsley, p. 51.

127. Andrew Roberts, *Hitler and Churchill: Secrets of Leadership* (London: Weidenfeld & Nicolson, 2003), pp. 71–72.

128. Winston S. Churchill, "House of Commons Speech, April 11, 1940," *Blood, Sweat and Tears* (New York: Putnam, 1941), pp. 295–312.

129. Ibid.

130. Kershaw, p. 23.

131. Francis Neilson, *The Churchill Legend* (Brooklyn, N.Y.: 29 Books, 2004), p. 323.

132. Kennan, p. 123.

133. Winston S. Churchill, *Step by Step: 1936–1939* (London: Odhams Press, 1947), p. 104.

134. Ibid., pp. 120–21.

135. Ibid., pp. 264, 265.

136. Roberts, *Hitler and Churchill*, p. 71.

137. Gilbert, pp. 99–100.

138. Jenkins, p. 35.

139. Robert K. Massie, *Dreadnought: Britain, Germany and the Coming of the Great War* (New York: Ballantine, 1991), p. 895; Barbara W. Tuchman, *The Guns of August* (New York: Macmillan, 1962), p. 26.

140. Charles Callan Tansill, *America Goes to War* (Gloucester, Mass.: Peter Smith, 1965), p. 148.

141. Raico, p. 331.

142. Ralph Raico, "World War I: The Turning Point," in *The Costs of War: America's Pyrrhic Victories*, Second Expanded Edition, John Denson, ed. (New Brunswick, N.J.: Transaction, 1999), p. 222.

143. Toye, p. 193.

144. Churchill, *Step by Step*, p. 155.

145. Geoff Simons, *Iraq: From Sumer to Saddam* (New York: St. Martin's Press, 1994), pp. 147, 179–181; Jonathan Glancy, "Gas, Chemical Bombs: Britain Has Used Them All Before in Iraq," *Guardian*, April 9, 2003; Michael Lind, "Churchill for Dummies," *The Spectator*, April 24, 2004; Ben Fenton, "Churchill Wanted to Use Gas on Enemies," *Daily Telegraph*, January 3, 1997.

146. Paul Johnson, *Modern Times: The World from the Twenties to the Eighties* (New York: Harper & Row, 1983), p. 370; Gilbert, p. 668; A.J.P. Taylor, *English History 1914–1945* (New York: Oxford University Press, 1965), p. 518; Davis, p. 69.

147. Johnson, *Modern Times*, p. 370.

148. Ibid.

149. Ibid.

150. Ibid.

151. Taylor, *English History*, p. 518.

152. Veale, p. 122.

153. Ibid., p. 128.

154. Ibid.

155. Ibid., p. 130.
156. George N. Crocker, *Roosevelt's Road to Russia* (Washington, D.C.: Regnery, 1986), p. 167.
157. Gilbert, p. 727.
158. Ibid., pp. 727–28.
159. Mike Davis, *Dead Cities* (New York: New Press, 2002), p. 68.
160. John W. Wheeler-Bennett & Anthony Nicholls, *The Semblance of Peace: The Political Settlement After the Second World War* (London: Macmillan, 1972), p. 179.
161. C. P. Snow, *Science and Government: The Godkin Lectures at Harvard University* (London: Oxford University Press, 1961), p. 48.
162. Ibid., p. 49.
163. Veale, p. 121; Grenfell, p. 126.
164. Ibid.
165. Grenfell, p. 127.
166. Hughes, p. 146.
167. George Rosie, "UK Planned to Wipe Out Germany with Anthrax," *Glasgow Herald*, September 14, 2001; Davis, p. 76.
168. Prime Minister's Personal Minute to General Ismay for COS Committee, "Winston Churchill's Secret Poison Gas Memo." http://globalresearch.ca/articles/CHU407A.html.
169. Davis, p. 76.
170. Patrick J. Buchanan, *Where the Right Went Wrong* (New York: St. Martin's Press, 2004), p. 119.
171. Ibid., pp. 119–20.
172. Davis, p. 78; Veale, p. 135.
173. Raico, "Rethinking Churchill," p. 353.
174. Veale, p. 130.
175. A.J.P. Taylor, *From Sarajevo to Potsdam* (New York: Harcourt, Brace & World, 1967), p. 178.
176. Veale, p. 138.
177. Roberts, *Hitler and Churchill*, p. xxv.

178. Jonathan Yardley, "A Distinguished Philosopher Asks If Killing Innocents Is Ever Justifiable," *Washington Post*, Book World, April 9, 2006, p. 2.

179. Edward Short, "Winston Churchill and the Old Cause," *Crisis*, December 2005, p. 27.

180. Pakenham, p. 291.

181. Short, p. 31.

182. Roberts, *Eminent Churchillians* (New York: Simon & Schuster, 1994), pp. 211–12; Michael Lind, op. cit.

183. Edwin Black, *War Against the Weak: Eugenics and America's Campaign to Create a Master Race* (New York: Thunder's Mouth Press, 2003), p. 215.

184. Lind, op. cit.

185. Ibid.; Winston S. Churchill, "A Struggle for the Soul of the Jewish People," *Illustrated Sunday Herald*, February 8, 1920.

186. Churchill, "A Struggle" Lind, op. cit.

187. Roberts, *Eminent Churchillians*, p. 211.

188. Ibid.

189. Winston Churchill, *The River War: An Account of the Reconquest of the Sudan* (Mineola, N.Y.: Dover, 2006), p. 8.

190. Roberts, *Eminent Churchillians*, p. 213.

191. Gerhard L. Weinberg, *Visions of Victory: The Hopes of Eight World War II Leaders* (New York: Cambridge University Press, 2005), pp. 144–45.

192. Ibid., p. 145.

193. Lind, op. cit.

194. Roberts, *Eminent Churchillians*, p. 213.

195. Ibid.

196. Pankaj Mishra, "Exit Wounds: The Legacy of Indian Partition," *The New Yorker*, August 13, 2007, p. 82.

197. Ibid.

198. Peter Hennessey, *Having It So Good: Britain in the Fifties* (London: Allen Lane, 2006), p. 221.

199. Roberts, *Churchillians*, p. 226.

200. Hennessey, p. 224.

201. Ibid.; Roberts, *Churchillians*, p. 225.

202. Roberts, *Churchillians*, p. 230.

203. Hennessey, p. 224.

204. Ibid.; Peter Catterall, ed., *The Macmillan Diaries: The Cabinet Years, 1950–1957* (London: MacMillan, 2004), p. 382.

205. William Manchester, *The Last Lion, Winston Spencer Churchill: Alone 1932–1940* (Boston: Little, Brown, 1988), pp. 682–83.

206. Grenfell, p. 92.

207. Ibid., p. 106.

208. Raico, "Rethinking Churchill," p. 357.

209. Ibid.

210. Villari, p. 378.

211. Charmley, p. 438.

212. Clark, op. cit.

213. Gilbert, p. 687.

214. Ibid., p. 692; Charmley, p. 443.

215. Gilbert, p. 687.

216. Ibid.

217. Charmley, p. 443.

218. Taylor, *Sarajevo to Potsdam*, pp. 178–79.

219. Grenfell, pp. 233–34.

220. Peter Clarke, *Hope and Glory: Britain 1900–1990* (London: Allen Lane, Penguin Press, 1996), p. 260.

221. Correlli Barnett, *The Collapse of British Power* (New York: William Morrow, 1972), p. 589.

222. Edward Ingram, "Hegemony, Global Reach, and World Power: Great Britain's Long Cycle," in *Bridges and Boundaries: Historians, Political Scientists and the Study of International Relations*, Colman Elman and Miriam Fendius Elman, eds. (Cambridge, Mass.: MIT Press, 2001), p. 229.

223. Ibid.

224. Gideon Rachman, "How Conflict in Iraq Has Put a Special Relationship Under Strain," *Financial Times*, October 31, 2006, p. 15.

225. Charmley, p. 467.

226. Roberts, *Eminent Churchillians*, p. 52.

227. Ibid.

228. Bob Withers, *The President Travels by Train: Politics and Pullmans* (Lynchburg, Va.: TLC, 2000), p. 106.

229. Payne, p. 140.

230. Ibid., pp. 140–41; Charmley, p. 467.

CHAPTER 15: AMERICA INHERITS THE EMPIRE

1. Robert Debs Heinl, Jr., *Dictionary of Military and Naval Quotations* (Annapolis, Md.: United States Naval Institute, 1967), p. 148.

2. George F. Kennan, *American Diplomacy 1900–1950* (New York: New American Library, 1951), p. 51.

3. James A. Montanye, "The Apotheosis of American Democracy," *The Independent Review*, Summer 2006, p. 5.

4. Ibid.

BIBLIOGRAPHY

Books

Andelman, David A. *A Shattered Peace: Versailles 1919 and the Price We Pay Today*. Hoboken, N.J.: John T. Wiley & Sons, 2008.

Bailey, Thomas A. *A Diplomatic History of the American People* (Seventh Edition). New York: Meredith, 1964.

Bailey, Thomas A. *Woodrow Wilson and the Lost Peace*. New York: Macmillan, 1944.

Baldwin, Hanson W. *The Crucial Years 1939–1941: The World at War*. New York: Harper & Row, 1976.

Barnett, Correlli. *The Collapse of British Power*. New York: William Morrow, 1972.

Bethell, Nicholas. *The War Hitler Won: The Fall of Poland, September, 1939*. New York: Holt Rinehart Winston, 1973.

Black, Edwin. *War Against the Weak: Eugenics and America's Campaign to Create a Master Race*. New York: Thunder's Mouth Press, 2003.

Bloch, Michael. *Ribbentrop*. Foreword by Hugh Trevor-Roper. London: Abacus, 2003.

Bonham Carter, Violet. *Winston Churchill: An Intimate Portrait*. New York: Harcourt, Brace & World, 1965.

Bosworth, R.J.B. *Mussolini*. London: Arnold, 2002.

Brody, J. Kenneth. *The Avoidable War: Lord Cecil & the Policy of Principle: 1933–35*. New Brunswick, N.J.: Transaction, 1999.

Buchanan, Patrick J. *A Republic, Not an Empire: Reclaiming America's Destiny*. Washington, D.C.: Regnery, 1998.

Bullock, Alan. *Hitler: A Study in Tyranny* (Completely Revised Edition). New York: Harper & Row, 1962.

Burt, Alfred Leroy. *The Evolution of the British Empire and Commonwealth from the American Revolution.* Boston: D.C. Heath, 1956.

Calleo, David. *The German Problem Reconsidered: Germany and the World Order, 1870 to the Present.* New York: Cambridge University Press, 1988.

Cameron, Norman and R. H. Stevens, *Hitler's Table Talk: 1941–1944: His Private Conversations* (Introduced with a New Preface by H. R. Trevor-Roper). New York: Enigma, 2000.

Carlton, David. *Anthony Eden: A Biography.* London: Allen Lane, Penguin, 1981.

Cecil, Robert, editorial consultant. *Hitler's War Machine.* London: Salamander, 1996.

Chamberlin, William Henry. *America's Second Crusade.* Chicago: Henry Regnery, 1962.

Charmley, John. *Churchill: The End of Glory: A Political Biography.* New York: Harcourt Brace & Company, 1993.

Chesneau, Roger. *Aircraft Carriers of the World: 1914 to the Present: An Illustrated Encyclopedia.* London: Arms & Armor Press, 1992.

Churchill, Winston. *Closing the Ring.* Boston: Houghton Mifflin, 1953.

Churchill, Winston S. *The Gathering Storm.* Boston: Houghton Mifflin, 1948.

Churchill, Winston S. *Great Contemporaries.* Chicago: University of Chicago Press, 1973.

Churchill, Winston S. *Great Contemporaries* (First American Edition). New York: W. W. Norton, 1990.

Churchill, Winston S. *The River War.* Mineola, N.Y.: Dover Publications, 2006.

Churchill, Winston S. *Step by Step: 1936–1939.* London: Odhams Press, 1947.

Churchill, Winston S. *Triumph and Tragedy.* Boston: Houghton Mifflin, 1953.

Churchill, Winston S. *The World Crisis: 1911–1918* (With an Introduction by Martin Gilbert). New York: Free Press, 2005.

Clark, Christopher. *Iron Kingdom: The Rise and Downfall of Prussia 1600–1947.* Cambridge, Mass.: Belnap Press of Harvard University Press, 2006.

Clarke, Peter. *Hope and Glory: Britain 1900–1990.* London: Allen Lane, Penguin Press, 1996.

Clymer, Kenton J. *John Hay, The Gentleman as Diplomat.* Ann Arbor: University of Michigan Press, 1975.

Cole, Wayne. *Roosevelt & The Isolationists: 1932–45.* Lincoln, Neb.: University of Nebraska Press, 1983.

Collier, Richard. *Duce!: A Biography of Benito Mussolini.* New York: Viking Press, 1971.

Corum, James S. *The Luftwaffe: Creating the Operational Air War, 1918–1940.* Lawrence, Kan.: University Press of Kansas, 1997.

Cowling, Maurice. *The Impact of Hitler: British Politics and British Policy 1933–1940.* Cambridge: Cambridge University Press, 1975.

Crocker, George N. *Roosevelt's Road to Russia.* Washington, D.C.: Regnery, 1986.

Dallas, Gregor. *1945: The War That Never Ended.* New Haven and London: Yale University Press, 2005.

Dangerfield, George. *The Strange Death of Liberal England.* New York: Capricorn, 1961.

Davies, Norman. *Europe: A History.* New York: Oxford University Press, 1996.

Davies, Norman. *Europe at War 1939–1945: No Simple Victory.* London: MacMillan, 2006.

Davies, Norman. *God's Playground: A History of Poland in Two Volumes, Volume II: 1795 to the Present.* New York: Columbia University Press, 1982.

Davies, Norman. *Rising '44: The Battle for Warsaw.* New York: Viking Penguin, 2004.

Davis, Mike. *Dead Cities.* New York: The New Press, 2002.

DeConde, Alexander. *A History of American Foreign Policy*. New York: Charles Scribner's Sons, 1963.

Denman, Roy. *Missed Chances: Britain and Europe in the Twentieth Century*. London: Indigo, Cassell Group, 1997.

de Zayas, Alfred-Maurice. *The German Expellees: Victims in War and Peace*. New York: St. Martin's Press, 1993.

de Zayas, Alfred M. *Nemesis at Potsdam: The Expulsion of the Germans from the East* (Third Edition Revised). Lincoln, Neb.: University of Nebraska Press, 1989.

Dutton, David. *Neville Chamberlain*. New York: Oxford University Press, 2001.

Eisenhower, David. *Eisenhower at War: 1943 to 1945*. New York: Random House, 1986.

Epstein, Julius. *Operation Keelhaul: The Story of Forced Repatriation from 1944 to the Present*. Old Greenwich, Conn.: Devin-Adair, 1973.

Evans, Richard J. *The Third Reich in Power*. New York: Penguin Press, 2005.

Ferguson, Niall. *Empire: The Rise and Demise of the British World Power Order and the Lessons for Global Power*. New York: Basic, 2003.

Ferguson, Niall. *The Pity of War*. New York: Basic, 1999.

Ferguson, Niall. *The War of the World: Twentieth Century Conflict and the Descent of the West*. New York: Penguin Press, 2006.

Ferrell, Robert H. *American Diplomacy: A History*. New York: W. W. Norton, 1959.

Fleming, Thomas. *The Illusion of Victory: America in World War I*. New York: Basic, 2003.

Friedrich, Otto. *Before the Deluge: A Portrait of Berlin in the 1920s*. New York: Harper & Row, 1972.

Fromkin, David. *Europe's Last Summer: Who Started the Great War?* New York: Alfred A. Knopf, 2004.

Gaddis, John Lewis. *Now We Know: Rethinking Cold War History*. New York: Oxford University Press, 2002.

Gilbert, Martin. *Churchill: A Life*. New York: Henry Holt, 1991.

Gilbert, Martin. *The Routledge Atlas of the First World War.* (Second Edition). London and New York: Routledge, 2002.

Grenfell, Captain Russell, R.N. *Unconditional Hatred: German War Guilt and the Future of Europe.* New York: Devin-Adair, 1953.

Hattersley, Roy. *The Edwardians.* New York: St. Martin's Press, 2004.

Hayes, Carlton J. H.; Marshall Whited Baldwin; and Charles Woolsey Cole. *History of Europe* (Revised Edition). New York: Macmillan, 1956

Henderson, Sir Nevile. *Failure of a Mission.* New York: G. P. Putnam's Sons, 1940.

Hennessey, Peter. *Having It So Good: Britain in the Fifties.* London, Allen Lane, Penguin Press, 2006.

Herman, Arthur. *To Rule the Waves: How the British Navy Shaped the Modern World.* New York: HarperCollins, 2004.

Hillgruber, Andreas. *Germany and the Two World Wars* (Translated by William C. Kirby). Cambridge, Mass.: Harvard University Press, 1981.

Hinsley, F. H. *Hitler's Strategy.* Cambridge: At the University Press, 1951.

Holborn, Hajo. *The Political Collapse of Europe.* New York: Alfred A. Knopf, 1963.

Holmes, Richard. *In the Footsteps of Churchill: A Study in Character.* New York: Basic, 2005.

Horne, Alistair. *To Lose a Battle: France 1940.* Boston: Little, Brown, 1969.

Hughes, Emrys. *Winston Churchill, British Bulldog: His Career in War and Peace.* New York: Exposition Press, 1955.

Ingram, Edward. "Hegemony, Global Reach, and World Power: Great Britain's Long Cycle," in Colman Elman and Miriam Fendius Elman, eds., *Bridges and Boundaries: Historians, Political Scientists and the Study of International Relations.* Cambridge, Mass.: MIT Press, 2001.

Jaksch, Wenzel. *Europe's Road to Potsdam.* New York: Frederick A. Praeger, 1963.

James, Lawrence. *The Rise and Fall of the British Empire*. New York: St. Martin's Griffin, 1994.

Jenkins, Roy. *Churchill: A Biography*. New York: Penguin Putnam, 2002.

Johnson, Paul. *Modern Times: The World from the Twenties to the Eighties*. New York: Harper & Row, 1983.

Judd, Denis. *Empire: The British Imperial Experience from 1765 to the Present*. New York: Basic, 1996.

Keegan, John. *The First World War*. New York: Vintage, 2000.

Keeling, Ralph Franklin. *Gruesome Harvest*. Chicago: Institute of American Economics, 1947.

Kennan, George F. *American Diplomacy 1900–1950*. New York: A Mentor Book, New American Library, 1951.

Kennan, George F. *Memoirs: 1925–1950*. Boston: Little, Brown, 1967.

Kershaw, Ian. *Fateful Choices: The Decisions That Changed the World, 1940–1941*. New York: Penguin Press, 2007.

Kershaw, Ian. *Hitler 1889–1936: Hubris*. New York: W. W. Norton, 2000.

Kershaw, Ian. *Hitler 1936–1945: Nemesis*. New York: W. W. Norton, 2000.

Kindermann, Gottfried-Karl. *Austria—First Target and Adversary of National Socialism: 1933–1938*. Vienna: Austrian Cultural Association, 2002.

Kirkpatrick, Ivone. *Mussolini: A Study in Power*. New York: Avon, 1964.

Kissinger, Henry. *Diplomacy*. New York: Simon & Schuster, 1994.

Kuehnelt-Leddihn, Eric von. *Leftism Revisited: From De Sade and Marx to Hitler and Pol Pot*. Washington, D.C.: Regnery Gateway, 1990.

Lamb, Richard. *Mussolini as Diplomat: Il Duce's Italy on the World Stage*. New York: Fromm International, 1999.

Laughland, John. *The Tainted Source: The Undemocratic Origins of the European Idea*. London: Warner, 1998.

Liddell Hart, B. H. *History of the Second World War.* New York: G. P. Putnam's Sons, 1970.

Liddell Hart, B. H. *The Other Side of the Hill.* London: Papermac, 1970.

Lippmann, Walter. *U.S. War Aims.* Boston: Little, Brown, 1944.

Lochner, Louis, ed., trans. *The Goebbels Diaries: 1942–1943.* Garden City, N.Y.: Doubleday & Company, 1948.

Lukacs, John. *Five Days in London: May 1940.* New Haven and London: Yale University Press, 1999.

Lukacs, John. *George Kennan: A Study of Character.* New Haven and London: Yale University Press, 2007.

Lukacs, John. *June 1941: Hitler and Stalin.* New Haven and London: Yale University Press, 2006.

MacDonogh, Giles. *The Last Kaiser: The Life of Wilhelm II.* New York: St. Martin's Press, 2000.

MacMillan, Margaret. *Paris 1919: Six Months That Changed the World.* New York: Random House, 2002.

Magnus, Philip. *King Edward the Seventh.* New York: E. P. Dutton, 1964.

Manchester, William. *The Last Lion, Winston Spencer Churchill: Alone, 1932–1940.* Boston: Little, Brown, 1988.

Manchester, William. *The Last Lion, Winston Spencer Churchill: Visions of Glory, 1874–1932.* Boston: Little, Brown, 1983.

Massie, Robert K. *Dreadnought: Britain, Germany and the Coming of the Great War.* New York: Random House, 1991; New York: Ballantine, 1992 (paperback ed.).

May, Ernest. *Strange Victory: Hitler's Conquest of France.* New York: Hill and Wang, 2000.

Mee, Charles L., Jr. *The End of Order: Versailles 1919.* New York: E. P. Dutton, 1980.

Meyer, G. J. *A World Undone: The Story of the Great War 1914–1918.* New York: Delacorte Press, 2006.

Millis, Walter. *Road to War: America 1914–1917.* Boston and New York: Houghton Mifflin, 1935.

Montefiore, Simon Sebag. *Stalin: The Court of the Red Tsar.* New York: Vintage, 2003.

Morris, A.J.A. *The Scaremongers: The Advocacy of War and Rearmament 1896–1914.* London and Boston: Routledge & Kegan Paul, 1984.

Morris, James. *Farewell the Trumpets: An Imperial Retreat.* New York: Harcourt, Brace & Company, 1978.

Moynihan, Daniel Patrick. *Pandaemonium: Ethnicity in International Politics.* New York: Oxford University Press, 1994.

Nalty, Bernard C. *The Air War.* New York: MetroBooks, 1999.

Neilson, Francis. *The Churchill Legend.* Brooklyn, N.Y.: 29 Books, 2004.

Neilson, Francis. *The Makers of War.* Appleton, Wisc.: C. C. Nelson, 1950.

Newman, Simon. *March 1939: The British Guarantee to Poland.* Oxford: Clarendon Press, 1976.

Nisbet, Robert. *Roosevelt and Stalin: The Failed Courtship.* Washington, D.C.: Regnery Gateway, 1988.

Odorfer, Richard A. *The Soul of Germany: A Unique History of the Germans from the Earliest Times to Present.* New Braunfels, Tex.: Richard A. Odorfer, 1995.

Olson, Lynne. *Troublesome Young Men: The Rebels Who Brought Churchill to Power and Helped Save England.* New York: Farrar, Straus and Giroux, 2007.

Pakenham, Thomas. *The Boer War.* New York: Random House, 1979.

Payne, Robert. *The Great Man: A Portrait of Winston Churchill.* New York: Coward, McCann & Geoghegan, 1974.

Perkins, Bradford. *The Great Rapprochement: England and the United States 1895–1914.* New York: Atheneum, 1968.

Powell, Jim. *Wilson's War: How Woodrow Wilson's Great Blunder Led to Hitler, Lenin, Stalin & World War II.* New York: Crown Forum, 2005.

Raico, Ralph. "Rethinking Churchill" and "World War I: The Turning Point," *The Costs of War: America's Pyrrhic Victories* (Second Expanded Edition; John Denson, ed.) New Brunswick, N.J.: Transaction, 1999.

Ridley, Jasper. *Mussolini: A Biography.* New York: St. Martin's Press, 1997.

Roberts, Andrew. *Eminent Churchillians.* New York: Simon & Schuster, 1994.

Roberts, Andrew. *A History of the English-Speaking Peoples Since 1900.* New York: HarperCollins, 2007.

Roberts, Andrew. *Hitler and Churchill: Secrets of Leadership.* London: Weidenfeld & Nicolson, 2003.

Roberts, Andrew. *The Holy Fox: A Life of Lord Halifax.* London: Orion, 1997.

Roberts, Andrew. *Salisbury: Victorian Titan.* London: Weidenfeld & Nicolson, 1999.

Rowland, Peter. *David Lloyd George: A Biography.* New York: Macmillan, 1975.

Russert, Bruce M. *No Clear and Present Danger: A Skeptical View of the United States Entry into World War II.* Boulder, Col.: Westview-Press, 1997.

Schama, Simon. *A History of Britain: The Fate of Empire, 1776–2000.* New York: Hyperion, 2002.

Shirer, William L. *The Collapse of the Third Republic: An Inquiry into the Fall of France in 1940.* New York: Simon & Schuster, 1969.

Shirer, William L. *The Rise and Fall of the Third Reich: A History of Nazi Germany.* New York: Simon & Schuster, 1960.

Simons, Geoff. *Iraq: From Sumer to Saddam.* New York: St. Martin's Press, 1994.

Sisa, Stephen. *The Spirit of Hungary: A Panorama of Hungarian Culture and History* (Second Edition). A Wintanio Project, 1990.

Smith, Gene. *The Dark Summer: An Intimate History of the Events That Led to World War II.* New York: Macmillan, 1987.

Snow, C. P. *Science and Government: The Godkin Lectures at Harvard University.* London: Oxford University Press, 1961.

Solzhenitsyn, Aleksandr. *The Gulag Archipelago 1918–1956: An Experiment in Literary Investigation II* (Translated from the Russian by Thomas P. Whitney). New York: Harper & Row, 1974.

Speer, Albert. *Inside the Third Reich.* New York: Macmillan, 1970.

Steele, David. *Lord Salisbury: A Political Biography.* New York: Routledge, 1999.

Steininger, Rolf. *South Tyrol: A Minority Conflict of the Twentieth Century.* New Brunswick, N.J.: Transaction, 2003.

Stewart, Graham. *Burying Caesar: The Churchill-Chamberlain Rivalry.* Woodstock, N.Y.: Overlook Press, 2001.

Sturmer, Michael. *The German Empire: 1870–1918.* New York: Modern Library, 2000.

Tansill, Charles Callan. *America Goes to War.* Gloucester, Mass.: Peter Smith, 1963.

Tansill, Charles Callan. *Back Door to War: The Roosevelt Foreign Policy 1933–41.* Chicago: Henry Regnery, 1952.

Taylor, A.J.P. *English History: 1914–1945.* New York and Oxford: Oxford University Press, 1965.

Taylor, A.J.P. *From Sarajevo to Potsdam.* New York: Harcourt, Brace & World, 1967.

Taylor, A.J.P. *A History of the First World War.* New York: Berkley, 1966.

Taylor, A.J.P. *The Origins of the Second World War,* Second Edition with a Reply to Critics. Greenwich, Conn.: Fawcett, 1961.

Taylor, A.J.P. *The Origins of the Second World War,* With a Preface for the American Reader and a New Introduction, "Second Thoughts." New York: Atheneum, 1961.

Taylor, Telford. *Munich: The Price of Peace.* Garden City, N.Y.: Doubleday, 1979.

Toland, John. *Adolf Hitler.* Garden City, N.Y.: Doubleday, 1976.

Tolstoy, Nikolai. *The Minister and the Massacres*. London: Century Hutchinson, 1986.

Tolstoy, Nikolai. *Victims of Yalta*. London: Corgi, 1986.

Tooley, Hunt. *The Western Front: Battle Ground and Home Front in the First World War*. New York: Palgrave Macmillan, 2003.

Toye, Richard. *Lloyd George and Churchill: Rivals for Greatness*. London: Macmillan, 2007.

Tuchman, Barbara W. *The Guns of August*. New York: Macmillan, 1962.

Tuchman, Barbara W. *The Proud Tower: A Portrait of the World Before the War: 1890–1914*. New York: Ballantine, 1994.

Veale, F.J.P. *Advance to Barbarism: How the Reversion to Barbarism in Warfare and War-Trials Menaces Our Future*. Appleton, Wisc.: C. C. Nelson, 1953.

Villari, Luigi. *Italian Foreign Policy Under Mussolini*. New York: Devin-Adair, 1956.

Vincent, C. Paul. *The Politics of Hunger: The Allied Blockade of Germany, 1915–1919*. Athens, Ohio: Ohio University Press, 1985.

Watt, Donald Cameron. *How War Came: The Immediate Origins of the Second World War, 1938–1939*. New York: Pantheon, 1989.

Weinberg, Gerhard L. *Germany, Hitler & World War II*. Cambridge,: Cambridge University Press, 1996.

Weinberg, Gerhard L. *Visions of Victory: The Hopes of Eight World War II Leaders*. Cambridge, New York et al.: Cambridge University Press, 2005.

Wheeler-Bennett, John W. *Munich: A Prologue to Tragedy*. New York: Duell, Sloan and Pearce, 1948.

Wheeler-Bennett, John W., Anthony Nicholls. *The Semblance of Peace: The Political Settlement After the Second World War*. London: MacMillan, 1972.

Wilson, A. N. *After the Victorians: The Decline of Britain in the World*. New York: Farrar, Straus and Giroux, 2005.

ARTICLES, SPEECHES

Bering, Henrik. "Prussian Maneuvers." *Policy Review*, April–May, 2007, pp. 86–95.

Bernstein, Richard. "We're Coming Over, and We Won't Come Back Till It's Over, Over There." *New York Times*, July 4, 2001, p. B12.

Blake [Lord]. "Winston Churchill the Historian." Speech to the Winston S. Churchill Societies of Edmonton, Calgary and Vancouver, Winston Churchill Centre, Washington, D.C., May 1988.

(Rt. Hon.) Churchill, Winston S. "Zionism versus Bolshevism: A Struggle for the Soul of the Jewish People." *Illustrated Sunday Herald*, Feb. 8, 1920.

Fenton, Ben. "Churchill Wanted to Use Gas on Enemies." *Daily Telegraph*, January 3, 1997.

Glancy, Jonathan. "Gas, Chemicals, Bombs: Britain Has Used Them All Before in Iraq." *Guardian*, April 9, 2003.

Herf, Jeffrey. "Fact Free: Buchanan's Hitler Problem, Pt II." *The New Republic*, October 18, 1999.

Kelly, Michael. "Republican Stunts." *Washington Post*, Oct. 6, 1999, p. A33.

Lind, Michael. "Churchill for Dummies." *The Spectator*, April 24, 2004.

Mayer, Steven. "Carcass of Dead Policies: The Irrelevance of NATO." *Parameters*, Winter 2003–2004, pp. 83–97.

Meacham, John. "Bush, Yalta and the Blur of Hindsight." *Washington Post*, May 15, 2005, p. B1.

Mishra, Punkaj. "Exit Wounds: The Legacy of Indian Partition." *The New Yorker*, August 13, 2007, pp. 80–84.

Montanye, James A. "The Apotheosis of American Democracy." *The Independent Review*, Summer 2006, pp. 5–17.

Neilson, Francis. "The Making of a Tyrant." *American Journal of Economics and Sociology*, July, 1958, pp. 383–98.

Rachman, Gideon. "How Conflict in Iraq Has Put a Special Relationship Under Strain." *The Financial Times*, October 31, 2006, p. 15.

Rosie, George. "UK Planned to Wipe Out Germany with Anthrax." *Glasgow Herald*, Sept. 14, 2001.

Short, Edward. "Winston Churchill and the Old Cause." *Crisis*, December 2005, pp. 27–31.

Weinberg, Gerhard L. "Hitler's Image of the United States." *American Historical Review*, vol. lxix, October 1963 to July 1964, pp. 1006–21.

Internet Articles, Historical Documents, News Releases

"President Discusses Freedom and Democracy in Latvia." May 7, 2005, http://www.whitehouse.gov/news/releases/2005/05.

"Prime Minister's Personal Minute to General Ismay for COS Committee." "Winston Churchill's Secret Poison Gas Memo." Center for Research on Globalisation, www.globalresearch.ca.

Beichman, Arnold. "The Surprising Roots of Fascism." *Policy Review*, Hoover Institution. http://www.policyreview.org/aug00/beichman.

Buchanan, Patrick J. "Was World War II Worth It?" Creators.com, May 11, 2005.

Davies, Norman. "How We Didn't Win the War . . . But the Russians Did." http://www.timesonline.co.uk November 11, 2006.

Additional

Letter, George Kennan to Pat Buchanan, re: *A Republic, Not an Empire: Reclaiming America's Destiny*, Nov. 5, 1999.

ACKNOWLEDGMENTS

I was probably the only first-grader at my parish school in 1943 who knew the *Lusitania* had been carrying contraband when torpedoed off the Irish coast in 1915, and that Americans had been warned not to sail upon her by the German consul in an ad in the *New York Times*.

For awakening a lifetime love of history, I owe a debt to my father. His dinner table at which eventually sat nine children was a nightly tutorial in the heroes and villains of the great dramas of the bloodiest century in human history.

My thanks also to British historian Andrew Roberts for his having hosted a luncheon in London at the time of the funeral of my friend Sir James Goldsmith. Andrew, Paul Johnson, Alan Clark, and I argued late into a bibulous afternoon about the war guarantee to Poland in March 1939. Out of that lunch came the idea for this book.

My gratitude also goes to the late George F. Kennan. In 1999, when *A Republic, Not an Empire* was published and under attack, I sent Dr. Kennan a copy, as I had cited his views. Weeks later, a gracious letter came back informing me he had taken time to read the book and agreed with the thesis. The war guarantee had been a tragic mistake. It was then that I decided I would one day write a book on the war guarantee that guaranteed the war in which scores of millions of the best and bravest of our world perished and a mortal wound was inflicted upon our civilization.

Among others who must be thanked are Fredi Friedman, editor, agent, and friend since she came to visit me in the Reagan White House to suggest I write my memoirs. While those memoirs have yet to be begun, Fredi and I have sinced worked together on seven books. Her steadfast support for this one is especially appreciated.

My thanks also to Sean Desmond, who has edited previous books of mine and rolled the dice with *Churchill, Hitler and "The Unnecessary War."*

My gratitude goes also to two scholars who volunteered to read and critique the manuscript, both of whom recommended further reading into the history of the era, including many of the titles now in the bibliography. They are the independent historian Joseph R. Stromberg of Auburn, Alabama, and David Gordon, the editor of *The Mises Review.*

And, again, my thanks to Dr. Frank Mintz of Martinsburg, West Virginia, my friend of a decade, for his monthly runs to McLean, carrying corrected copies of the manuscript and endnotes, and with whom I have spent dozens of hours conversing about these chapters and the historic events and figures whose roles are herein presented.

Finally, eternal gratitude to Shelley, who has indulged my addiction to this book and tolerated my nightly trips to the basement in predawn hours to insert anecdotes and arguments, ideas and quotations mined from the stack of histories and biographies on the bed table.

INDEX

Page numbers in *italics* refer to maps.

Patrick J. Buchanan, America's leading populist conservative, was a senior adviser to three American presidents, ran twice for the Republican presidential nomination, in 1992 and 1996, and was the Reform Party candidate in 2000. The author of nine other books, including the bestsellers *Right from the Beginning; A Republic, Not an Empire; The Death of the West; State of Emergency,* and *Day of Reckoning,* Buchanan is a syndicated columnist and a founding member of three of America's foremost public affairs shows, NBC's *The McLaughlin Group,* and CNN's *The Capital Gang* and *Crossfire.* He is now a senior political analyst for MSNBC.